WELSH SOCIETY AND NATIONHOOD

GLANMOR WILLIAMS

WELSH SOCIETY
AND NATIONHOOD

HISTORICAL ESSAYS PRESENTED TO
GLANMOR WILLIAMS

Edited by

R. R. Davies, Ralph A. Griffiths,
Ieuan Gwynedd Jones and Kenneth O. Morgan

CARDIFF

UNIVERSITY OF WALES PRESS

1984

© University of Wales, 1984

British Library Cataloguing in Publication Data

Welsh society and nationhood.
  Wales—History
  I. Davies, R.R.   II. Williams, Glanmor, *1920-*
  942.9   DA714

ISBN 0-7083-0860-0

Printed in Wales by Qualitex Printing Limited, Cardiff

Contents

Figures

Hall, Tower and Church: Some Themes and Sites Reconsidered, pp.134-52.

Plates

Foreword

In September 1982 Glanmor Williams retired from the Chair of History at the University College of Swansea which he had held for a quarter of a century. It was widely felt by his colleagues and friends that this was an appropriate occasion to salute his remarkable services to scholarly and other activities in Wales. We therefore present this volume to him as a token of our admiration and affection and as a tribute to an outstanding historian who has greatly enriched the intellectual and public life of his country. The themes that we have chosen for the volume are ones which have long preoccupied Glanmor Williams in his writings —religion, social change and the idea of nationhood in Wales. All fourteen contributors have been associated with Professor Williams, either as academic colleagues at Swansea or elsewhere in the University of Wales, or as fellow-scholars in his wide-ranging fields of historical interest. We are well aware that only a small fraction of Glanmor Williams's wide circle of friends and academic associates figure, of necessity, in the list of contributors to this volume. But we trust that it may serve as a fitting tribute to him not only from the contributors but also from all those who have been associated with his career, or who have been inspired by his teaching and writings, or who are in other ways personally indebted to him.

We thank our fellow-contributors for their encouragement and enthusiasm and the Director and Board of the University of Wales Press for their co-operation and advice.

R.R.D.
R.A.G.
I.G.J.
K.O.M.

St. David's Day, 1983

The Contributors

F. G. COWLEY, Sub-Librarian, University College of Swansea.

R. R. DAVIES, Professor of History, University College of Wales, Aberystwyth.

G. R. ELTON, Regius Professor of Modern History, University of Cambridge.

RALPH A. GRIFFITHS, Professor of Medieval History, University College of Swansea.

SIR JOHN HABAKKUK, Principal of Jesus College, Oxford.

GERAINT H. JENKINS, Senior Lecturer in Welsh History, University College of Wales, Aberystwyth.

IEUAN GWYNEDD JONES, Sir John Williams Professor of Welsh History, University College of Wales, Aberystwyth.

H. R. LOYN, Professor of Medieval History, Westfield College, University of London.

KENNETH O. MORGAN, Fellow and Praelector in Modern History and Politics, The Queen's College, Oxford.

PRYS MORGAN, Senior Lecturer in History, University College of Swansea.

DAVID B. QUINN, Emeritus Professor of Modern History, University of Liverpool.

PETER SMITH, Secretary, Royal Commission on Ancient and Historical Monuments in Wales, Aberystwyth.

DAVID WALKER, formerly Senior Lecturer in History, University College of Swansea.

J. E. CAERWYN WILLIAMS, Emeritus Professor of Irish, University College of Wales, Aberystwyth.

Glanmor Williams

IEUAN GWYNEDD JONES

IT is as 'Glan' that he is universally known, and it is to Glan, friend and colleague, most generous and wise of scholars, the *doyen* of Welsh history, that these essays are presented. For more than a quarter of a century and with undiminished strength his influence on the course of Welsh historical studies has been paramount, and happily and to our great profit it continues to be so still.

Seldom can one scholar have exerted so beneficent and profound an influence on his subject as has Glanmor Williams on his. A multitude of students remember courses of lectures memorable for their clarity of exposition and elegance of style, and many others the probing, questing and enlightening nature of his teaching in seminar and tutorial. Nor are these recollections confined to university people alone, for Glan has never begrudged the time to prepare with equal care for extra-mural classes, and he has always responded readily to the frequent requests of local groups and societies, however small and however distant, for his services as a lecturer. He has that rare ability to communicate effectively at the academic level appropriate to the occasion and always the subject has been elevated above the speaker.

His influence on historical studies is exerted in ways more diverse than is normally the case. Professor of History in the University College of Swansea from 1957 until his retirement in 1982, and for much of that time Head of the Department of History, this influence has been exerted not so much by precept as by good example. During the years of rapid expansion he provided the Department with decisive leadership and represented its interests and those of his colleagues with unfailing loyalty in the councils of the College. He served as Vice-Principal (1975-8) and was the foundation Dean of the Faculty of Economic and Social Studies. The close involvement of History with Russian and American Studies was consistently advocated and carefully nourished by him and the teaching of History at Swansea was consequently greatly enriched. Hence, appointments to the lecturing staff, especially in his first decade or so as professor, were critical in the development of the subject and in the establishment of a large, varied and reputable department. His voice has frequently been the decisive one in securing the necessary funds for research. With his predecessor at Swansea, D. B. Quinn (a contributor to this volume), he encouraged the College to create research fellowships in Welsh Social History in 1954, and it was he who supervised the team of researchers funded by the Social Science Research Council who, between 1969 and 1976, set out to locate, collect and preserve manuscript, printed and aural sources relating to the history of the South Wales coalfield, and which are now preserved at Swansea. But none of this prevented him from playing a full part in the social life of the College—in the drama society, on the cricket field, and ever in demand as an after-dinner speaker where his wit and a seemingly endless supply of anecdotes were exercised to splendid advantage.

His contribution to historical studies in the University of Wales has been unique. For almost forty years he has served the Board of Celtic Studies, since 1970 as its chairman. It was during his chairmanship of the Board's History and Law Committee that the *Welsh History Review* was launched in 1960 under his editorship, and the decision taken in 1970 to inaugurate a series of monographs, *Studies in Welsh History,* of which he is co-editor. These two developments have made possible that steady accumulation and publication of scholarly work—not least by scores of young historians—which is the outstanding feature of the recent renaissance in Welsh history.

Beyond his College and University, Glan's efforts on behalf of Welsh History have been as important as they are diverse. In his native county he was prominent in establishing the Glamorgan History Society in 1957 and was its chairman for many years. He was one of the first co-editors of *Morgannwg* (the Transactions of the Glamorgan History Society), and to the Gower Society he has given very considerable assistance both as a regular contributor to its journal, *Gower,* and as a lecturer and guide in its field excursions. Of massive and enduring importance has been the appearance under his General Editorship of three large volumes of the Glamorgan County History, one of which was also edited by him and another jointly edited with the late A. H. John. But over and above these large and time-consuming projects has been the ungrudging advice and practical help he has so readily given to local history societies, to authors and publishers throughout the country. This activity has gone largely unsung, but it reflects the high value he places upon local history, the role of the untutored amateur, and the importance of nurturing the links between professional historians and the intelligent layman. His membership of the Historic Buildings Council (Wales) and of the Royal Commission on Ancient and Historical Monuments (Wales)—he is vice-chairman of the former and chairman of the latter—and of the Advisory Committee on Public Records and of the British Library Board, have provided him with a unique opportunity to relate the work of all these bodies to the academic world and to bring to them all a rare breadth of experience. Elected a Fellow of the Royal Historical Society in 1953, he is currently one of its vice-chairmen.

But it is as the pre-eminent historian of Wales that we salute him on this occasion. It is his example and inspiration that have been at the heart of the remarkable renaissance in Welsh History since the Second World War. Although the range and extent of his writings is very great, his prime allegiance has been to the sixteenth century, notably to the story of the impact of the Protestant Reformation on church and society. His *magnum opus* on *The Welsh Church from Conquest to Reformation* is assuredly one of the most satisfying and rounded studies of the medieval church anywhere in Europe, deeply impressive in its sensitivity and truly pioneering in its use of literary and homiletic sources to penetrate the religiosity of the period. Significantly, Glan's initial honours degrees at the University College of Wales, Aberystwyth, were in History and Welsh, and it is on these solid foundations, combining the technical skill of the historian with the trained sensitivities of the literary scholar, that his rich and elegant studies of the life of the church and of the great Reformation scholars and divines have been based. Equally he has set on foot new ways of understanding eighteenth-century religious movements, and he was largely instrumental in proposing lines of investigation which have transformed our view of Victorian Wales. His is indeed a fertile mind, always concerned with large questions and major themes, far-seeing, the master of soundly-based generalization.

For Glan, literature, especially poetry and the novel, is not merely or mainly a key to understanding the past: like music, it is a source of delight and of renewal. Along with his deeply-felt religious convictions, it is expressive of his profound respect for the culture of the working-class community from which he sprang, and is the richest part of his inheritance from his parents. A collier by occupation, his father was a cultured and gentle man, and highly respected in the religious communities gathered in the chapels of Dowlais and Merthyr Tydfil. Glan has never forgotten his roots nor lost the common touch which was so characteristically the style of the uncommon people among whom he lived and with whom he was educated, and much of his writing is an exploration of the historical forces which produced those communities. Hence those seminal essays, in both Welsh and English, on language and nationality. To these themes he brings not only a deep love of his country and an intimate knowledge of its literature, but also the detachment and calm of the historian. His love of the Welsh language is reflected in his mastery of it and in his use of it as the appropriate medium for some of his best published work. Year in and year out, he has contributed at least one essay or substantial review to a Welsh-language journal: his first book was in Welsh.

Nid anghofiodd yr Athro Glanmor Williams erioed 'y graig y'i naddwyd ohoni'. Mae'r agosatrwydd a'r cyfeillgarwch sydd mor nodweddiadol o bobl ei gynefin wedi aros yn rhan annatod o'i gymeriad yntau. Defnyddiodd y Gymraeg a'r Saesneg yn feistrolgar er mwyn cyfleu ei ddehongliad o'r gorffennol i'w gydwladwyr. Trwy drafod problemau hanesyddol yn Gymraeg fe roddodd rym a rhychwant i'r iaith gyfoes. Ar yr un pryd datguddiodd i'r Cymry di-Gymraeg yn ein plith, ac yn wir i'r byd yn gyffredinol, hanes ein cenedl a'i werthfawrogiad o'r diwylliant Cymreig. Ni fu gennym erioed ladmerydd mwy effeithiol nag ef, a mawr yw ein diolch iddo. Gellir dweud am Glanmor Williams, fel y dywedwyd am Gymro mawr arall, yr ysgolhaig Edward Lhuyd, 'What he does is purely out of love to the good of learning and his country'. Dyna, yn y bôn, pam y mae'n gymwynaswr mawr i'r genedl, a dyna pam y mae'n haeddu'r anrhydedd hwn.

No cloistered scholar, Glanmor Williams has always been deeply involved in the affairs of his immediate community and of the country at large. As with his father before him, the Baptist chapel where he is a deacon plays an important part in his life. In 1975 he was president of the Baptist Union of Wales, and for many years he has served the small and the ailing churches of the area. His almost prodigal readiness to assist others and to give unstintingly of his time and talents, have brought upon him heavy public responsibilities. His membership of the Hughes-Parry Commission on the Welsh Language occupied much of his time between 1963 and 1965 when the Report was published, and later, in 1973, he succeeded his friend Sir David Hughes-Parry as chairman of the Pantyfedwen Foundations, remaining in that demanding and sensitive office for nearly ten years. His administrative gifts and his ability to bring people of diverse and necessarily conflicting interests into fruitful co-operation, and himself to distill much enjoyment out of the experience, were given full scope during the years 1965 to 1971 when he served as National Governor of the BBC and Chairman of the Broadcasting Council for Wales. It was appropriate that the citation for his CBE in 1982 should be 'for public service to Wales'.

So, though it is the scholar and the public servant whom we primarily honour with this volume, it is the warm and ebullient personality, the wise counsellor and loyal friend whom we celebrate. Above all, we rejoice in the fact that his intellectual pursuits have never deadened his sense of fun, or blunted his appreciation of a joke, or stopped the flow of his wit. From his scholarship we have learned much, from his public services we have all benefited, and by his friendship and that of his wife, Fay, we are all enriched. It is in gratitude for these things and as a mark of the high esteem in which he is held that we offer these essays to Glan.

The Conversion of the English to Christianity: Some Comments on the Celtic Contribution

H. R. LOYN

THERE was a time when to write or talk about the conversion of the English to Christianity was a delight because of its very simplicity. The pattern was neatly shaped and the chronology straightforward and precise. Two themes interwove to provide the pattern: the Roman and the Celtic. Three generations provided the chronological framework, the dominant Roman from 597 to 632, the predominant Celtic from 633 to 663, from the accession of King Oswald to the Synod of Whitby, and the third triumphant generation from 663 to 690 when, under the principal direction of a Greek and a North African, Theodore of Tarsus and Abbot Adrian, the Christian Church in England was welded into familiar diocesan shape. Shadows now darken the clarity of the picture from many different directions. It is recognised increasingly that the neatness of the pattern owes as much to art as to nature, to the shaping hand of the master historian, Bede, and to the permanent influence of his *Ecclesiastical History of the English People,* completed in its final approved form in 731. The apparently straightforward narration can prove deceptive if the chronological sequence is held to lead inevitably to the stable order of the Theodoran Church and Northumbrian monasticism. Certainty over both the contributors to the conversion and the totality of the achievement diminishes the closer the record is examined. Even so, ancient pedagogic instincts were not without sense. There is enough general truth to the picture to make it at least a working basis for deeper investigation.

In no field of activity on these conversion questions has there been more constructive interest than in the matter of direct Celtic contribution. The main thrust has been along two paths: to acknowledge that the concept of a single Celtic Church is highly misleading and to recognise further that the differences between Roman and Celtic were by no means as simple as was once thought. Within the Celtic world itself the North is recognised to have held the chief though not the exclusive political focal point for the story of the conversion, Iona first and then Lindisfarne; but it is recognised firmly also that the British contribution, in spite of an adverse press, was not negligible. Among the practising Christians in the Celtic communities the monastic and eremitic elements were strong and the abbots tended to be more influential than the bishops, but the old pasteboard picture of Celtic monk-preacher and Latin organising bishop will not stand close scrutiny as a convincing analysis of the nature of the participants in the process of the conversion. The Romans themselves were monks. The Celts did not neglect the importance of episcopal office. Yet differences of course existed and not only in the matters which received full attention in seventh-century England: the nature of the calendar, the method of tonsure, the ritual of baptism. In inner life, too, as reflected in attitudes towards the priesthood, learning, language and the importance of penance and confession, group-differences of the first importance existed and the most sensitive of modern interpretations places principal emphasis on these matters concerning the inner life of the individual churches. [1]

To take first the contribution from the British Church, the church that survived in unbroken descent from the Christianity that existed in these islands in Roman days. In AD 400 Roman Britain was as Christian as any other part of the Roman world, with the institutional apparatus of bishops and priests and dioceses common to the post-Constantine Empire. Attempts to suggest that survival of other religions, imperial, military, or Celtic, were stronger in Roman Britain than elsewhere in the western provinces have not been successful. [2] Roman Britain suffered barbarian invasion in common with the rest of the West, but its suffering was unique in one important respect. The predominant barbarian groups on the continent were almost exclusively Christian at the moment of their onslaught and where they were not (as with the Salian Franks) they were quickly Christianised. The Germanic peoples who invaded and settled Britain were heathen and a substantial part of them remained so until well into the second half of the seventh century. The full implications of this uniquely long sustained heathen domination of Roman territory are only slowly coming back into historical synthesis, supporting those who have long advocated a break in continuity between the British and Anglo-Saxon worlds rather than continuity, and helping too those who, blind to the glamour of the historic Arthur, have held the fifth and sixth centuries to be the most miserable and unhappy in the recorded history of Britain.

Heathen dominance is one thing. Complete disappearance of all knowledge and vestige of an accepted religion is quite another. Exceptionally interesting work by archaeologists and place-name experts is serving to enrich our knowledge of this unhappy phase in British history. At St. Albans, a key site if ever there were one, an intelligible picture is emerging of sustained knowledge of the sanctity of the site through the darkest of the heathen years. [3] Analogies with

---

[1] H. Mayr-Harting, *The Coming of Christianity to Anglo-Saxon England* (London, 1972); P. Hunter Blair, *The World of Bede* (London, 1970); and the work of Kathleen Hughes, notably *The Church in Early Irish Society* (London, 1966).

[2] J. N. L. Myers suggested some time ago that it was not the persistence of paganism, but the emergence of the Pelagian heresy which seems to have been the 'most significant feature of the religious life of early sub-Roman Britain', a judgement that would still meet with general acceptance: M. W. Barley and R. P. C. Hanson (eds.), *Christianity in Britain, 300-700* (Leicester, 1968), p. 6.

[3] Martin Biddle, 'Alban and the Anglo-Saxon Church', in R. Runcie (ed.), *Cathedral and City: St. Albans Ancient and Modern* (1977), pp. 23-62, provides the best modern guide. Accounts of recent excavations also appear in the work of Martin and Birthe Biddle, notably in *The Chapter House Excavations* (Fraternity of the Friends of St. Albans Abbey, Occ. Publ. 1, St. Albans).

events on the continent, at Xanten and at Bonn, suggest the setting up of a *martyrium* on the site of the third-century execution of St. Alban proto-martyr. Bede was deeply interested in St. Alban and St. Albans and makes a special point of telling us how St. Germanus, on his first visit to Britain in AD 429, reinforced the special sanctity of the shrine by adding relics of all the apostles and of various martyrs to it; the prestige of St. Alban contributed heavily to a great military victory against the Saxons and the Picts. In Bede's own day St. Albans was still known under two names, either *Verlamacæstir* or *Wæclingacæstir*.[4] The persistence of the former name, direct from Roman *Verulamium,* is not remarkable in itself in the light of the known importance of the settlement deep into the fifth century, but it makes a point when the strength of the alternative form is taken into account. *Wæclingacæstir* preserves the name of the settlers, the *Wæclingas,* who occupied the Roman fortified place at Verulamium, and it is from their name that Watling Street, arguably the most famous highway in Britain, came to be called. St. Albans, the one-day staging post on a journey north from London, remained a significant point through which travellers passed and there is no reason to believe that travellers were exclusively heathen. Continued knowledge of the site does not imply continued existence as a Christian place of worship, but when Offa came to found his great abbey at St. Albans there were strong traditions, fully in accord with the topographical details preserved in the early *Passiones* and Bede, that the abbey was set up on the very place occupied by the *martyrium* of the fourth century and by the church set up in the early years of the Conversion age in the seventh.

No case for continuous awareness of specific Christian sites in heathen England is quite as strong as at St. Albans, but there are enough pointers, even in areas of early and heavy Anglo-Saxon settlement such as East Anglia, Essex, and Kent, to imply elements of continuity in folk-memory of sacred Christian sites stronger than might be inferred from orthodox historical records. Canterbury, as we shall see, is a special case, relatively strong for once in evidence from the written word. Recent investigations of place-names have helped carry the argument a stage further. The very existence of a variety of 'Celtic' place-names (such as Dover or Wendover)—some in forms that suggest bilingualism on the part of the Anglo-Saxons who adopted them, others showing the typical English monoglot at work—demonstrates quite clearly that throughout nearly all of England some remnants of the Romano-British population survived long enough to transmit at least the names of natural features (mountains, big rivers and Roman towns) to the new Germanic conquerors and settlers. More attention is now being given to the transmission of elements such as *castrum* or *funta,* signifying recognisable physical features, fortifications or a formal fountain construction that would distinguish *funta* from a simple spring or well.[5] The most important of these elements for our purposes is undoubtedly *eccles* which, either in simple form or in

---

[4] B. Colgrave and R. A. B. Mynors (eds.), *Bede's Ecclesiastical History of the English People* (Oxford, 1969: referred to below as Bede, *HE*), i. 7, 34-5. We are told that after the martyrdom of St. Alban, when peaceful Christian times returned, a church of wonderful workmanship was built there as a memorial to his martyrdom, and that to this day (that is to say, to Bede's day) sick people were healed and miracles performed at the site.

[5] Margaret Gelling, 'Latin loan-words in Old English place-names', in P. Clemoes (ed.), *Anglo-Saxon England* 6 (Cambridge, 1977), pp. 1-13.

compounds such as Ecclesfield or Eccleston, represents early borrowing from Primitive Welsh *Egles,* in itself of course a straight adaptation of Latin *ecclesia.* [6] We know that in the fourth century, the last *complete* century of Roman Britain, it was quite common for Christian worship to be conducted in private houses, but this was no longer true, to judge from continental parallels, in the fifth and sixth, certainly not in the towns and probably not in the countryside as the *pagani* were drawn into the Christian fold. A Christian community expected to have an identifiable building set apart for the celebration of the sacraments. Professor Cameron has pointed out to us features of outstanding interest in the distribution of the element *eccles* in English place-names. Only three occur in the areas of earliest settlement (Jackson 1). [7] The other seventeen certain forms are widely distributed, although with a heavy concentration in the north-west midlands. All compound names occur in districts of Britain not settled by the English at an early date, for the most part post-AD 600. Topographically, they all lie significantly close to rivers and streams and many of them very close to Roman roads or other Roman sites. Mrs Margaret Gelling has suggested that the three apparent anomalies, two in Kent and one in East Anglia, may well represent a different chronological stage in the acceptance of the form into the English toponymic word-bank, a comment that certainly makes good historical sense. [8] *Eccles* at its most typical appears in territory still uneasily in political balance between Welsh and English at the time of the initiation of the Conversion of the English (Jackson 3).

The full significance of the existence and distribution of these *eccles*-names, with their pointer to the physical presence of British Christian churches, has perhaps been too long neglected as evidence for the unspectacular but long-lasting elements in conversion, when conversion came not so much by dramatic missionary effort as by gradual absorption with Christian communities as peace was established and rural communities drawn together under the discipline of new kingdoms and aristocracies. A similar pattern of heathen Dane and native English Christian may well have occurred in the area we know as the Danelaw in the tenth century, three hundred years after the events signalled in our place-name Eccles and its variants.

Such conclusions perhaps do little more than emphasize points already implied by Bede. In his carefully constructed account of the Augustinian mission to the court of Ethelbert at Canterbury, Bede builds up an intelligible sequence of

[6] The basic and seminal work for the understanding of this element is presented by Kenneth Cameron in 'Eccles in English Place-Names', *Christianity in Britain 300-700,* pp. 87-92.

[7] K. Jackson, *Language and History in Early Britain* (Edinburgh, 1953). His map of British river names remains essential for modern investigation. See also my *Anglo-Saxon England and the Norman Conquest* (London, 1962), pp. 8 ff. Area I runs roughly east of a line drawn from the Yorkshire Wolds to the east of Salisbury Plain and so to the Hampshire coast near Southampton; essentially it consists of the river valleys, save in their highest reaches, that drain from the highland spine of England into the sea between Flamborough Head and the Solent. Area III covers the north-west (Cumbria and the greater part of Lancashire), the Welsh Marches and much of the south-west (Dorset, Somerset and Devon to the line of the Tamar).

[8] Op. cit., p. 11, where the suggestion is made that the names in question could be 'the result of an early borrowing from Latin which was used in a few place-names in the south-east, but which dropped out of the language after a short period of use'.

events: reception by the king, preaching at a great council attended by the most powerful men in the kingdom, permission to preach and then, finally, a foothold at St. Martin's.[9] The mission's success is attributed quite as much to example as to doctrine or political force. Ethelbert compelled no one to accept Christianity. He himself was already well placed to receive the new faith. His queen, Bertha, daughter of Charibert, Merovingian king of Paris, was a Christian and had been allowed to come to Kent only on condition that she should be allowed to practice her faith and religion unhindered. She had been accompanied by a bishop, Liudhard, and she used to pray at St. Martin's. Bede's physical description of St. Martin's has its interest. He describes it as nearby, to the east of the city, a church (*ecclesia*) built in honour of St. Martin in ancient times, while the Romans still inhabited Britain (*dum adhuc Romani Brittaniam incolerent*).[10] It is probable that the western part of the chancel of the existing church of St. Martin's was itself part of the nave of the church referred to by Bede, presumably reconstructed of Roman material on a known site after a period of disuse for Bertha and her bishop/chaplain Liudhard.[11] The Augustinian mission was given permission, after Ethelbert himself had been converted to the faith, to preach everywhere and to build or restore churches (*ecclesias fabricandi vel restaurandi licentiam acciperent*). With the help of the king, Augustine restored a church said to have been built in ancient times by the work of Roman believers, dedicated it to the Saviour, and established his principal base there (Christchurch, the modern cathedral). Ethelbert also built and endowed, with Augustine's encouragement, a monastery dedicated to St. Peter and St. Paul (later St. Augustine's Abbey) as a mausoleum for the bodies of St. Augustine and his successor-bishops of Canterbury and of the kings of Kent.[12] Britain may indeed have lost its Christianity in the new heathen Germanic kingdoms, but the physical remains of churches took long to decay and in some parts deserted British churches remained a familiar feature well into Conversion times. Reference to one such area, connected with the monastery at Ripon, deserves special attention.

Eddius Stephanus in his life of Bishop Wilfrid, written in the early-eighth century, was primarily anxious to record the gifts made to the abbey of Ripon when he referred to the deserted British churches.[13] He tells how St. Wilfrid, the bishop, at a great assembly stood in the presence of Kings Ecgfrith and Ælfwine and read out clearly a list of the lands, the *regiones,* which had previously (and then on that very day) been made to him with the agreement and subscription of the bishops and all the chief men. He read out also (*lucide enuntiavit necnon et*) a list of the consecrated places (*loca sancta*) in diverse parts which the British clergy (*clerus Bryttanus*) had deserted when fleeing from the hostile sword wielded by the warriors of his own Northumbrian nation. Eddius says further that it was truly a gift well pleasing to God that the kings had assigned so many lands for the service of God and he names the *regiones* (a term used earlier in his paragraphs of the

[9] Bede, *HE,* i. 25-33.
[10] Ibid., i. 26, pp. 76-7.
[11] H. M. and J. Taylor, *Anglo-Saxon Architecture,* I (Cambridge, 1965), 143-5.
[12] Bede, *HE,* i. 33, pp. 76-7 and 114-15.
[13] B. Colgrave (ed), *The Life of Bishop Wilfrid by Eddius Stephanus* (Cambridge, 1926), c. xvii, pp. 36-7.

specific royal donation): around Ribble and Yeadon and the region of the
dwellers around Dent (*Dunutinga*) and Catlow and other places. Wilfrid was no
political innocent and it may well be that the distinction made between the
specific grants, including Dent (a likely candidate in its remote vale for British
survival), and the vague reference to areas deserted by British clergy represents
no more than the staking of a public claim to future grants on the part of an
ambitious prelate. Wilfrid certainly paid little attention to existing political
divisions when it suited his purpose not to do so, and his ambitions may well have
ranged extensively in the north-west from Cheshire to Cumbria. He was prepared
to be shocked at the schismatic British and Irish for failing to observe the proper
Easter, but his followers in exile in the 680s were scattered under alien lords in
diverse places throughout all Britain (*per diversa loca totius Britanniae*).[14] Later in his
life, at Rome in 704, he was quite willing to make his true confession of faith, and
to corroborate it with his subscription on behalf of all the northern part of Britain
and Ireland and the islands, inhabited by the races of Angles and Britons as well
as by Scots and Picts.[15]

Yet though awareness of the activities of the British Church persisted and, in
some instances the physical remains, contact at the highest level was uneasy
throughout the Conversion period. St. Augustine found this on his arrival. There
were clearly no organised Christian communities to whom he could turn within
direct English rule, but part of his brief was to re-establish contact with the British
Church.[16] Bede in a very famous passage described a synod at Aust and the
subsequent disastrous meeting between Augustine and seven British bishops who
were accompanied by many learned men, chiefly from the great monastery of
Bangor Iscoed in north-east Wales. With typical economy and precision, Bede
analysed the three principal reasons for the failure to reach agreement: the British
refused to conform to the dating of Easter, to accept the rites of baptism according
to the custom of the holy Roman and apostolic Church, and to preach the word of
God to the English people in fellowship with the Roman mission.[17] His incidental
allusions to the healing of a blind Englishman, the test of humility imposed on
Augustine by the advice of a British hermit, the divine retribution visited upon
Bangor Iscoed by the heathen Ethelfrith enrich the narrative, but do not obscure
Bede's main clear line of disapproval. The British Church is seen to suffer for its
tenacity in clinging to custom and also for failure to join in the great enterprise of
conversion. The monks slaughtered by Ethelfrith are dismissed as *perfidi*.[18]
Bede's uncharacteristic lack of sympathy and understanding is a clear pointer to
the continuing animosity between the Roman and the British Church that existed
during his own lifetime. They were regarded as men, rigidly conservative,

---

[14] Ibid., c. xliv, pp. 90-1: *monachis suis per diversa loca totius Britanniae exterminatis et sub alienis dominis moerentes . . .*

[15] Ibid., c. liii, pp. 114-15: *pro omni aquilonali parte Brittanniae et Hiberniae insulisque quae ab Anglorum et Brittonum necnon Scottorum et Pictorum gentibus colebantur.*

[16] Bede, *HE,* ii. 2.

[17] Ibid., pp. 134-6.

[18] Ibid., pp. 142-3: *ut etiam temporalis interitus ultione sentirent perfidi.*

refusing to recognise self-evident truth.[19]

The same negative attitude towards the British Christians is characteristic of much of the written record of the seventh and early-eighth centuries. There was a tendency to regard them as somewhat long-winded bores, stubborn in their own old-fashioned customs and beliefs, speaking a tongue which jarred on English and Latin susceptibilities. When Saint Guthlac in his fen fastness in eastern England was haunted by devils, it clearly came as no surprise to him to hear them speaking a British tongue which fortunately he was able to recognise because of his own period of exile among Welsh speakers.[20] Bede is consistent in his hostility towards Celtic observance, more opposed to Welsh Christians than to those from Iona whose achievements of course lay obvious and potent all around him in Northumbria and who had had the good sense to subscribe to the Roman custom on Easter in 716. Bede's deep knowledge of the historical sources enabled him time after time to draw on his storehouse of examples to make his point. He does not consider that Augustine may have been tactless—even arrogant—in his approach to the British bishops, but rather recognises the subsequent slaughter of the British monks at the hands of Ethelfrith to be well merited and to serve as an illustration of Augustine's gift of prophecy.[21] On this matter at least Bede lets his Englishness get the better of his Christianity. Again in his account of the infamous year 632-33, when he describes the slaughter both of the Church and the people of Northumbria after the death of Edwin, he is more savage in his strictures on Cadwallon of Gwynedd, Christian as he was by name and profession, than he was towards Penda who (with the whole Mercian race) was still an idolator and ignorant of the name of Christ. Cadwallon is said to have paid no respect to the Christian religion which had sprung up among the Northumbrians and, in a telling aside, Bede added:

> Quippe cum usque hodie moris sit Brettonum fidem religionemque Anglorum pro nihili habere, neque in aliquo eis magis communicare quam paganis. (Indeed to this very day it is the habit of the Britons to despise the faith and the religion of the English and not to co-operate with them in anything any more than with the heathen.)[22]

Bede was consistently aware, with his own ecclesiastical problems in mind, that the social differences between the Celtic people and the English ran deep. At an early stage in his discussion of the Conversion he quoted a letter from Augustine's immediate successor, Archbishop Laurentius, that extended the differences to Ireland.[23] Laurentius intended to exercise his pastoral care not only on the British (*veterum Brittaniae incolarum*), but also on the Irish. He quickly discovered that the Irish also observed different customs from the Romans, much to his

---

[19] A point made shrewdly and convincingly by Kenneth Harrison, 'Easter cycles and the equinox in the British Isles', in P. Clemoes (ed.), *Anglo-Saxon England 7*, p. 1, where he suggests that the Britons were felt to be wrong-headed 'because, among other things, they were ignoring an observable fact'.

[20] B. Colgrave (ed.), *Felix's Life of St. Guthlac* (Cambridge, 1956), c. xxxiv.

[21] Bede, *HE*, ii. 2, pp. 140-1: *quod ita per omnia, ut praedixerat, divino agente iudicio paratum est.*

[22] Ibid., ii. 20, pp. 204-5.

[23] Ibid., ii. 4, pp. 144-7

disappointment (*cognoscentes Brittones, Scottos meliores putavimus!*). He learned from an Irish bishop, Dagan, as well as from his knowledge of Abbot Columban, that the Irish did not differ from the Britons in their way of life. His illustration of difference was telling: 'for when Bishop Dagan came to us he refused to take food not only with us but even in the very house (*hospitio*) in which we took our meals'. [24] Nearly a century later, in the first decade of the eighth century when Bishop Aldhelm wrote a letter of exhortation to Geraint, British king of the 'West Welsh' in Devon and Cornwall, he made the same plaint:

> . . . quod ultra Sabrinae fluminis fretum Demetarum sacerdotes, de privata propria conversationis munditia gloriantes, nostram communionem magnopere abhominantur, in tantum, ut nec in ecclesia nobiscum orationum officia celebrare nec ad mensam ciborum fercula pro caritatis gratia pariter percipere dignentur. (. . . because beyond the bounds of the river Severn the priests of Dumnonia, taking excessive pride in the elegance of their own observance, hold our communion in such contempt that they will not deign to celebrate the sacred offices of prayer with us in church, nor in like measure will they share the dishes of the festive board with us at table.)

Worse, the British priests are said to have thrown away any food they had touched to the dogs and the pigs; and forty days' penance was insisted on before an English catholic was acceptable to their community. [25] Emphasis on the need for catholic unity and acceptance of the primacy of Peter and of Rome runs through the work of Bede and of Aldhelm, but even so their common insistence on social difference and reluctance to communicate, in the general as well as the ecclesiastical sense, also runs through their testimony.

Communication can indeed not have been easy. Delicate and intricate work on linguistic problems has shown that the language of Roman Britain in the fifth century was overwhelmingly 'Celtic'. [26] The Latin of inscriptions was school Latin, ceremonial Latin: men in their ordinary run of business in the field, the camp, and the court spoke primitive Welsh. In such a world, with German speakers and Welsh speakers living their separate lives, only political force could compel long-lasting and deep communication. In a sense in the south-west this situation was not reached until the end of the seventh century, when first Caedwalla and then Ine forced political accord on the reluctant peoples. Ine's laws show clearly that large sections of British people were drawn into the kingdom of Wessex, men of 600 shillings wergeld, men of specific office, Welsh horse-thegns and the like, and it can be assumed that at two levels this had great

[24] Ibid., p. 146-7

[25] A. W. Haddan and W. Stubbs (eds.), *Councils and Ecclesiastical Documents,* iii (Oxford, 1871): AD 705. Letter of Abbot Aldhelm to Geruntius, p. 271: 'Ast vero, si quilibet de nostris, id est catholicis, ad eos habitandi gratia perrexerint, non prius ad consortium solidatatis suae adsciscere dignantur, quam quadraginta dierum spatia in penitendo peragere conpellantur.'

[26] K. Jackson, *Language and History,* remains the fundamental guide and the implication of his firm thesis that Old English showed no evidence of contact with spoken Latin points clearly to the existence of a dominant vernacular in Brythonic Celtic or British throughout Roman Britain.

influence on ecclesiastical life.[27] At the top level the minsters of the English resembled the *clas* churches of the Welsh communities, churches where a group of priests and deacons would live and from where they would serve a wide area. Of equal importance are the small territorial churches set up on the estates of the great men of the neighbourhood. With improved training in Latin and a common liturgy, some of the major problems of communication at least were eased.

Indications of this easing in contact came from the work of Aldhelm who, apart from Bede, was the most distinguished scholar of the period. He was an active man, born *c.* 639, abbot of Malmesbury (*c.* 675-705) and for the last four years of his life the first bishop of Sherborne (705-9). His training and education took place under the abbacy of Maeldwbh in the 650s and 660s. Many of the peculiarities of Aldhelm's style and vocabulary have been laid in the past at the door of his Irish instructors, but the ablest of modern critics has shown that Aldhelm's astounding skill at handling complex rhythmic Latin prose is more akin to the Mediterranean world (and so to the school at Canterbury) than to the Irish.[28] Aldhelm's own attitude to Irish learning was ambivalent. He protested about those heading for Ireland (with dire warnings about prostitutes and brothels) when so much sound learning in Greek and Latin was available in Britain. At the time he wrote, the vigorous school of Canterbury under Abbot Adrian must have been predominantly in his mind, but we may have been unwise to ignore completely native British traditions. Mayr-Harting, for example, has drawn attention to Aldhelm's use of a version of Isidore's *Etymologies* which can well be attributed to south-west Britain and which bears a direct relation to the Spanish exemplar from which it was derived.[29] Mayr-Harting is rightly sceptical of over-emphasis on a possible maintenance of permanent and meaningful cultural links along the traditional sea-routes from Spain to Brittany and Cornwall, but this does not mean to say that contacts with fellow-christians at the scholarly level in south Wales and in Devon and Cornwall were as weak as they sometimes appear to be at the political level.

In similar fashion, contacts must on occasion have been strong in the Conversion Age further north along what was to become the Mercian border and the valley of the Severn. After 573 the communities dependent on the *civitates* of Bath, Cirencester and Gloucester fell into English hands.[30] Half a century later the Mercians led by Penda (at that stage quite probably a landless prince making his way, possibly with Northumbrian help) won political mastery of the Severn valley, establishing there the subordinate people of the Hwicce who set up a bishopric at Worcester after their conversion to Christianity. Another subordinate people, the Magonsaetan, moved further west to Hereford. In both areas British

---

[27] D. Whitelock (ed.), *English Historical Documents,* I (London, 1955; 2nd ed., 1979), no. 32: the Laws of Ine, pp. 398-406, Ine 23. 3 (a Welsh rent-payer, *gafolgelda*), 24. 2 (Welsh 600-man), 32 (Welsh wergelds), 33 (Welsh horseman, carrying messages), 46. 1 (Welshman's accusation), 54. 2 (penally enslaved Welshman), and 74 (a Welsh slave who kills an Englishman).

[28] M. Winterbottom, 'Aldhelm's Prose Style and its Origins', in P. Clemoes (ed.), *Anglo-Saxon England 6,* (Cambridge, 1977), pp. 39-76.

[29] H. Mayr-Harting, *The Coming of Christianity to Anglo-Saxon England,* p. 198.

[30] C. Plummer (ed.), *Two Saxon Chronicles Parallel,* I (Oxford, 1892), pp. 18-19: *genamon iii ceastra.*

survival was great, and indeed the dioceses of Hereford and Worcester constitute perfect areas for a phase of 'overlap and controlled settlement'.[31] Further north along what was to be the Welsh border, there is further direct evidence. The double house of St. Mildburg at Wenlock, founded in the third quarter of the seventh century, possessed territory deep into Wales at Llanfilo, some five miles north-east of Brecon, together with estates in the Monnow valley.[32] The Mercians in the seventh century were as often in alliance with the Welsh as in conflict with them. Penda never fought them, and his willingness to permit his son, Peada, to accept Christianity may have been occasioned by his familiarity with Welsh priests and emissaries from his allies. The rapid growth of important ecclesiastical centres across the midland belt from Wenlock to Lichfield, Repton, Breedon, and Brixworth was not due to idle chance. Dr Kirby has done well to remind us that until St. Chad became bishop at Lichfield in 669 any priests in the area would be British.[33] From the English point of view all contact across the Welsh border was not negative and bitter hostility.

Northumbria provided something of a contrast in many ways to Mercia, not least in its dealings with the British Church. The Irish mission operating from the two power-houses of Iona and Lindisfarne provided the chief native force for the conversion of the north (and indeed much of the midlands) in the middle years of the seventh century. Bishop Aidan was the leading figure in the enterprise in the critical years 635-51. Bede disapproved of his adherence to the customs of his native church, but was firm in his praise of Aidan as a man and a teacher.[34] Under King Oswald from 635 to the time of the king's death in 642 there was ceaseless activity. Preachers came to teach the new faith, churches were built, and monasteries endowed. The missionaries had special skill in instructing English children in advanced studies and in the observance of the discipline of a Rule (*inbuebantur praeceptoribus Scottis parvuli Anglorum una cum maioribus studiis et observatione disciplinae regularis*).[35] Irish monks seemed to have less difficulty than the Romans in mastering the language, perhaps a hint at a largely unrecorded mobility of people beneath the turbulence of political hostility. The two groups, Roman and Irish, co-operated freely and positively at this stage. Hunter Blair's comments are helpful to an understanding of the nature of the enterprise when he states: 'in the generations before Bede the Irish could well be ecclesiastically Roman while the English could equally be "Celtic". Bitterness grew only when tolerance yielded to dogma, and when opposition to Roman dogma was equated with heresy and sin.'[36]

[31] J. N. L. Myers, *Anglo-Saxon Pottery and the Settlement of England* (Oxford, 1969), ch. v.

[32] H. P. R. Finberg, *The Early Charters of the West Midlands* (Leicester, 1961), p. 210: the essay on St. Mildburg's Testament, pp. 197-216, contains much of permanent value.

[33] D. P. Kirby, 'Welsh Bards and the Border', in Ann Dornier (ed.), *Mercian Studies* (Leicester, 1977), pp. 31-42, especially p. 37 where the comment is made that (before 669) any clergy or monks at Lichfield could have been British.

[34] Bede *HE*, ii. 5, pp. 226-9.

[35] Ibid., iii. 3, pp. 220-1.

[36] P. Hunter-Blair, *The World of Bede* (London, 1970), p. 101.

Heavy emphasis on the Irish elements in the story of the conversion of Northumbria is inevitable, but it is not the whole story. Edwin is said to have been brought up in the company of Welsh Christians and his acceptance of the Roman mission cannot have been uncoloured by his knowledge of British Christianity. [37] His vaunted boast that men, women and children could pass unhindered and unharmed through his kingdom suggests a degree of mobility which could easily encompass traders and teachers from the neighbouring British lands. Oswald himself, for all his Irish training and sympathies, was constantly on the move in the Cumbrian lands and on the Welsh border. He was killed on campaign near Oswestry in 642. Dr Kirby has brought interesting evidence together to suggest that all movement was not military and hostile. [38] As he says, the British clergy in Elmet may well have acquiesced positively in Edwin's overlordship after his conversion. It seems reasonable to assume that there was deeper and more personal influence from existing British communities along the still fluid political borders than the written record allows.

The indirect importance of the presence of existing Christian communities along the border should certainly not be discounted in any attempt to explain the success of the Conversion. For successful it undoubtedly was. Pagan survivals continued into the eighth century and beyond. Men reverted to pagan practice in times of stress and hardship. But Bede in the early-eighth century wrote for a literate Christian public in a context which suggested that Christianity was the religion of the overwhelming majority of the population. One feature of the story continues to present a puzzle. There were no true martyrs as we would recognise the breed. Why should this be? Elsewhere when the Anglo-Saxons themselves took to the mission field martyrdoms were not uncommon. The greatest of all Anglo-Saxon missionaries, St. Boniface, Winfrith of Crediton in Devon, was martyred by the Frisians in 754. [39] Can it be that knowledge of Christianity and its practice was more widespread than Gregory and Augustine realised when the mission was being planned? The law codes of the seventh century tell of protection given to traders and travellers. Christian Britons could indeed have been well represented among their number.

Neglect of the importance of continuous personal contact, unimportant politically and therefore unrecorded, may well have been an element of weakness in our traditional picture of the Conversion. We move finally to an element of modern analysis that is strong: the better appreciation of the complexity of the

[37] The *Historia Brittonum* records the tradition that Edwin was baptised by Rhun son of Urien: *English Historical Documents*, I, no. 2 (2nd ed., 1979), with references to David Dumville's work in *Studia Celtica*. Professor Whitelock comments (p. 125) that 'it can only be a Welsh fiction that a Welsh priest baptised Edwin'.

[38] Bede is anxious consistently to stress the British dimension of Edwin's lordship: *HE*, ii. 9, pp. 162-3—*ita ut quod nemo Anglorum ante eum, omnes Brittaniae fines, qua vel ipsorum vel Brettonum provinciae habitabant, sub dicione acciperet*—and again in his summing up of Edwin's virtues (ii. 16, pp. 192-3) emphasis is put on the great peace established *in Brittania*. Pope Boniface, however, addressed Edwin simply as *rex Anglorum*. There is much of value on Northumbrian kingship and on the social texture of the kingdom in D. P. Kirby (ed.), *St. Wilfrid at Hexham*, especially in the editor's own contribution, 'Northumbria in the time of Wilfrid'.

[39] W. Levison, *England and the Continent in the Eighth Century* (Oxford, 1946); much good recent work on Boniface includes T. Reuter (ed.), *The Greatest Englishman: Essays on St. Boniface* (Exeter, 1980), and J. C. Sladden, *Boniface of Devon* (Exeter, 1980).

institutional life of the Churches within the Celtic world. 'Celtic Churches, never the Celtic Church', as we have already implied, is the modern maxim. Recent fruitful enquiries into the workings of the British and Irish Churches have enriched our basic knowledge of the Conversion process. The Irish Church as an institution—or more delicately as a federation of institutions—had developed basic ideas on organisation that were less in conflict with the episcopal territorial notions of the Romans and the Romanisers. Latent strong episcopal discipline made co-operation more difficult between the British and the Romans.

Difficulties came into the open when an obvious point of juncture occurred between jurisdictions, control, and general spheres of activity of the various institutional churches. Practical problems prompted decision and at times provoked conflict. Familiarity with early-medieval ecclesiastical legislation in any form quickly brings recognition that for many churchmen, and above all for the ecclesiastical political leaders who emerge in most formal religious situations, one central problem concerned the question of territorial integrity. Bishops grow anxious if preachers from other dioceses appear without permission in their own sphere of authority; and their anxiety, often involving appeal to secular power, reflects the general concern of their own clergy. But on the Welsh border, for example (and this would apply also to west Wales, to Devon and Cornwall), there was clearly no set pattern of ecclesiastical authority to which appeal could be made. We do not deal like with like. The latest investigator of early-medieval Welsh society summed up the situation fairly and accurately when she stated that the Llandaff charters (the focal point of her analysis) help to illuminate 'a situation which appears to have been strictly comparable neither to the Irish nor the English pattern: that is, powers of direction and control were neither vested in abbots who were the heads of monastic federations (*paruchiae*) nor in diocesan bishops of the Roman type. There were, however, species of monastic federation and of bishopric in Wales.'[40] Place names and dedications supplement charter evidence in Wales, giving trace in names such as Llandeilo or Llanilltud of properties owned by or dependent on a mother church of St. Teilo or St. Illtud. A tenacious allegiance to its native saints and monastic founders of the fifth and sixth centuries helped to preserve vestiges of original endowment and development more clearly than in the English scene, where Roman discipline, Latin names, and fondness for dedications to Christ and the apostles obscure the evidence. Welsh abbots do not, however, appear to have wielded power on the scale of the Irish. Bishops remained powerful though not in any clearly defined territorial relationship within specific diocesan bounds nor apparently always within the permanent ambit of any one kingdom. The strength of the bishop rested on the intrinsic nature of his office, but also on his territorial possessions and on his household. In south-east Wales Welsh Bicknor and Llandogo were important episcopal centres in the early centuries and so too was one of the most interesting of all Welsh ecclesiastical territories, the district of Ergyng or Archenfield, disputed land in south Herefordshire and including the fine church

---

[40] Wendy Davies, *An Early Welsh Microcosm: Studies in the Llandaff Charters* (1978). The following paragraph draws heavily on Dr Davies's work.

of Kilpeck.[41] The strong association of Ergyng with dedications of churches to St. Dyfrig indicates energetic Christian activity in the area in the sixth and seventh centuries, and the name Ergyng itself (derived from the name of a Roman settlement at Ariconium) gives a hint of continuity with the Roman past.[42] Such hints were clearly in Dr Kathleen Hughes's mind when she took us to task for not recognising sufficiently the influence of the Romano-British and sub-Roman past on the history of early-medieval Wales.[43] But even at Ergyng, one suspects, there were more points of contrast than of comparison with the position of the bishopric of Hereford, set up by Theodore of Tarsus to serve the religious needs of the people of the Magonsaetan and, *a fortiori,* to consolidate the integrity of settlement and church within permanent territorial bounds.

The Irish churches were, of course, the creation of the British Church and it is surprising at first sight that modern scholars are coming to emphasise their divergences and separateness so strongly. Some vital characteristics they continued to share in common. Professor Alcock stressed accurately the basic fact that Roman organisation depended upon the *civitas,* and that the absence of *civitates* was essential to a satisfactory explanation of the dominance of the monastic element in the Celtic world.[44] It was Kathleen Hughes, however, who put us on the central track to explore the differences between the British and Irish Churches.[45] The beauty and strength of her analysis consist in the subtle way an intelligible picture of a developing Irish society forms the basis of her thought. Building on the work of Professors Jackson and Bieler and of Father Grosjean, she showed conclusively that bishops predominated in the Irish Church as in the British up to the middle of the sixth century, that vital change occurred during the second half of the sixth century and that from the seventh century onwards the abbots rooted in their tribal reality predominated, exercising through their monastic *paruchiae* a power greater than that of the territorial bishops. Her work has thrown fresh light indeed on the conversion of the English. Iona and Lindisfarne followed closely their Irish exemplars and if the Synod of Whitby had gone the other way the Northumbrian Church would have been no more than an extension of the Irish, dominated by monastic bishops based at remote isolated spots. As it was, Colman and his followers withdrew from Northumbria after the Synod. The organising strength of Archbishop Theodore, more so than the personal drive of the turbulent Wilfrid, ensured the consolidation of the Roman case. The southern Irish had already accepted the Roman dating of Easter in the 630s, and slowly the other Celtic communities conformed. Stubborn conservatism rather than logic and reason accounted for the delay. It took a long generation

[41] The peculiar status of Ergyng is well illustrated by the fact that the Welsh bishop Cyfeiliog was captured there by the Danes in 914 (*on Ircinga felda: Two Saxon Chronicles Parallel,* I, 98-9) and redeemed by the English King Edward. The special customs of Archenfield are recorded in the Herefordshire folios of Domesday Book.

[42] *An Early Welsh Microcosm,* p. 157.

[43] 'The Celtic church: is this a valid concept?', in P. Sims-Williams (ed.), *Cambridge Medieval Celtic Studies,* I, 1-20 (especially p. 15).

[44] L. Alcock, *Arthur's Britain* (London, 1971), pp. 134-5.

[45] Especially in her first outstandingly important book, *The Church in Early Irish Society.* Of great value too is her paper mentioned above (n. 43), which is her O'Donnell lecture published posthumously.

after Whitby for the northern Irish to fall into line, by 704. Iona itself accepted the new dating in 716 and at this point the situation must indeed have appeared strange from the viewpoint of Rome. The succeeding half-century was a time of great peril for western Christendom, facing the new world force of Mohammedanism at its zenith, during which time the British Church alone stood out against the Roman ruling. Submission and acquiescence did not come until 768. It was then that the *Annales Cambriae* recorded *Pasca commutatur apud Brittones, emendante Elbodugo homine Dei.* [46] The same year, a delicate coincidence that has not often been noted, Charles, later to be known as 'the Great', succeeded his father Peppin as king of the Franks. The last of the Celtic Churches accepted the dating of Easter at the same time as the man who was to give political expression to the idea of Christian unity in the west ascended the Frankish throne. Within the whole of the settled western world, for all the divergences and contrasts in traditions, a social and religious uniformity that looked to Rome and owed much to Mediterranean precedents was coming into being.

[46] J. W. ab Ithel (ed.), *Annales Cambriae* (London, 1860), *s.a.* 768, p. 10.

Gildas, Maelgwn and the Bards

J. E. CAERWYN WILLIAMS

D R. D. P. Kirby has drawn attention to the 'nature of the oral tradition lying behind our earliest written records', and he has wisely emphasized that it was 'essentially localized, dependent for its survival on the continuing interest of a corporate community, a dynasty or an ecclesiastical body'.

> A dynasty or a church preserved only those traditions which related to its own development; if a dynasty were totally extinguished, then its traditions would die with it, and if an ecclesiastical community failed to commit its history to writing, that history would be irretrievably lost. [1]

This explains to some extent not only why the history of Dark Age Britain is shrouded in so much darkness, but also why the early traditions of Wales are so much fewer than those of Ireland. When we consider that Celtic Britain was subject to two major invasions, the Roman and the Anglo-Saxon, and that kingdoms like those of the Atrebates, the Catuvellauni and the Trinovantes (to name only three of the most important tribes in the south and south-east of the country) were submerged in the former invasion, and that kingdoms like Elfed, Rheged and Gododdin were submerged in the latter, we begin to realize how many local oral traditions were lost. We begin to understand, too, why the early literature of Ireland, a country which experienced neither of these invasions, is so much richer and more varied than that of Wales. It was in Wales that the only P-Celtic kingdoms to survive in Britain were to be found when the country suffered its final invasion, that of the Normans.

Local traditions were not the only traditions which such kingdoms as those of the Atrebates or the Gododdin cultivated. The Celts came to Britain, just as the Romans and the Anglo-Saxons came later, with basically a common culture and, as modern scholarship seems to prove, with a remarkable ability to conserve it. It is this ability which explains why the Celts, as it seems, had a common cultural heritage when the Romans arrived in Britain. This does not mean that there was no local diversity, but such diversity is not inconsistent with an overall uniformity. And that the Celts in the British Isles, like the Hindus in India, could enjoy both uniformity and diversity of traditions was due to the strong conservative nature of their cultures, which they inherited separately from their Indo-European predecessors. The resilience of those traditions is proved by the fact that, although their common culture was inevitably weakened when some of the Celts and their kingdoms were absorbed by invaders, it survived to some degree in those kingdoms in Britain where the Celts were able to preserve their

---

[1] D. P. Kirby, 'Vortigern', *Bull. Board of Celtic Studies*, XXIII (1968), 36-59, esp. p. 38.

sovereignty, and survived to a remarkable degree in Ireland to the late middle ages and even later.

To be more specific, we know that the Insular Celts of the British Isles, like the Continental Celts of Gaul, were very much under the influence and the control of the Druids. That the druidic order did not survive to the same extent in Britain as it did in Ireland was due to the Roman conquest of the former. That it eventually disappeared in both countries was due to Christianity: the order's roots were deeply planted in Celtic paganism.

A survey of the evidence provided by continental Classical authors [2] and by the early vernacular literatures of the British Isles, more especially that of Ireland, led J. A. MacCulloch to the conclusion that the druids were 'a great inclusive priesthood with different classes possessing different functions—priestly, prophetic, magical, medical, legal and poetical'. [3] Very few scholars, it may be ventured, would find reason to disagree with that conclusion, although they may not have the same approach as MacCulloch. For instance, Professor D. A. Binchy argues that originally the Celtic king was a priest-king, that his duties regarding the 'sacred law' devolved first on the druids, later—presumably after the advent of Christianity—on the *filid*, [4] and later still 'on a more specialized caste (doubtless an offshoot from the *filid*) of professional jurists, the brehons'. [5] Perhaps it is no less legitimate to assume that in the Gaulish society on the continent described by Classical authors, the *bardoi* (bards) were an offshoot of the *vātes* (prophets), the *vātes* an offshoot of the druids, and the druids an offshoot of the **rīx*, the Celtic priest-king. However that may be, it is a fact that Classical authors inform us that the Continental Celts had druids, *vātes* and bards or poets. They also tell us that there were druids in Britain when the Romans came; but by the time the latter had left, they had all but disappeared. Although their survival in Ireland to a later period is well attested, there are almost no references to druids in the earliest Welsh literature and no references to *vātes*, unless they are to be identified with Giraldus Cambrensis's *awenyddion*, but references only to bards who occasionally perform the functions of *vātes* or prophets.

It is generally assumed that the first reference we have to bards on Welsh soil [6]

---

[2] This has been published and discussed by Professor J. J. Tierney, 'The Celtic Ethnography of Posidonius', *Proc. Royal Irish Academy*, LX (1960), 189ff. Cf. D. Nash, 'Reconstructing Poseidonios' Celtic Ethnography', *Britannia*, VII (1976), 111-26.

[3] J. A. MacCulloch, *The Religion of the Ancient Celts* (1911), p. 299. On the Druids, see S. Piggott, *The Druids* (1968); Françoise Le Roux, *Les Druides* (1961). On the recrudescence of Druidism in Britain after the withdrawal of the Romans, see MacCulloch, op. cit., p. 315.

[4] A word generally translated 'poets' but best rendered by 'literati', for as a class they were, originally, historians, jurists, and poets.

[5] D. A. Binchy, *Celtic and Anglo-Saxon Kingship* (1970), p. 16.

[6] See H. Moisl, 'A Sixth-century Reference to the British *bardd*', *Bull. Board of Celtic Studies*, XXIX (1981), 269-73, for a more general reference.

is in Gildas's *De Excidio Britanniae*,[7] where he gives a rather harsh portrayal of Maelgwn, generally known as Maelgwn Gwynedd because he was king of Gwynedd until his death about 547.[8] The reason for Gildas's harshness towards Maelgwn is not far to seek. Although he had been made king, Maelgwn had vowed to become a monk and indeed studied for a while under 'the refined master of all Britain', presumably St. Illtud. Had he remained a monk he might have become a Welsh Columcille, for he had great gifts and the potentiality for immense goodness as well as for evil. Alas, he broke his vows and returned to the world and to his former life which, if we are to believe Gildas, was extremely wicked. Maelgwn had slain the king, his uncle, to attain the throne, and now, instead of returning to the wife he had put away, he resolved to kill her and to take the woman whom his nephew had married, and in order to do so killed her husband.

Although Gildas addresses Maelgwn as one of the most powerful rulers of his time in Britain, he gives very little information about the way he had achieved his power or about its extent. However, his reference to him as *draco insularis* may suggest that Maelgwn fought his way to become king of Gwynedd after being first of all the ruler of Anglesey or of a small kingdom within that island: he would not have been the last of his kind to do so. However, we can be sure that Gildas was not a person to make a distinction between political murders and those inspired by greed or lust, and behind his sombre portrait of Maelgwn we seem to see the lineaments of some greatness.

The year in which Maelgwn died, according to the *Annales Cambriae*, 547,[9] witnessed the beginning of King Ida's reign (547-59) in Northumbria, and if the *Historia Brittonum*'s synchronisation is correct, it was during his reign that Eudeyrn fought bravely against the Angles and

> Talhaern (Talhaearn) Tat Aguen (Tad Awen) gained renown in poetry; and Neirin (Aneirin) and Taliessin (Taliesin) and Bluchbard (? Blwchfardd) and Cian who is called Gweinth Guaut (? Gwenith Gwawd, 'Wheat of Song') gained renown together at the same time in British poetry.[10]

[7] For bibliographical references, see J. F. Kenney, *The Sources for the Early History of Ireland: Ecclesiastical* (repr., 1968), pp. 150-2; and T. D. O'Sullivan, *The De Excidio of Gildas: its authenticity and date* (1978), esp. p. 180, where it is concluded that the *De Excidio* was written 'ca. 515-520', 'with a real possibility remaining that it was written within a decade before the earlier, or after the later date'. See also M. Miller, 'Bede's use of Gildas,' *English Hist. Rev.,* XC (1975), 241-61. I refer to the texts and translations in H. Williams (ed.), *Gildae De Excidio Britanniae* (1899), and M. Winterbottom (ed. and tr.), *Gildas: The Ruin of Britain and other works* (1978).

[8] J. E. Lloyd, *A History of Wales from the earliest times to the Edwardian Conquest* (2 vols., 3rd ed., 1939), I, 131. N. Tolstoi, 'Early British History and Chronology', *Trans. Hon. Soc. Cymmrodorion,* 1964, part ii, pp. 237-312, esp. p. 249, argued that Maelgwn Gwynedd lived for at least a quarter of a century after AD 547. S. Lewis, 'The Tradition of Taliesin', *Trans. Hon. Soc. Cymmrodorion,* 1968, part ii, pp. 293-98, follows Tolstoi and places Gildas's *De Excidio Britanniae* in the third quarter of the sixth century.

[9] J. Williams ab Ithel (ed.), *Annales Cambriae* (Rolls Ser., 1860), p. 4.

[10] *Historia Brittonum,* c. 62. For bibliographical references, see Kenney, op. cit., pp. 152-5. See also D. N. Dumville, 'The Corpus Christi "Nennius"', *Bull. Board of Celtic Studies,* XXV (1973), 369-80. Dr Dumville is preparing a definitive edition of the *Historia Brittonum.* For an English translation, see A. W. Wade-Evans, *Nennius's 'History of the Britons'* (1938); J. Morris (ed. and tr.), *Nennius: British History and the Welsh Annals* (1980). For a discussion of this passage, see I. Williams, *The Poems of Taliesin.* English version by J. E. Caerwyn Williams (1968), pp. i-xiv.

We must allow a margin of error in this synchrony, but it seems clear that when the *Historia* was compiled early in the ninth century, there was a tradition that North British kings, who like Eudeyrn fought against the Angles, had poets to support them and to sing their praises.

It is, therefore, a reasonable assumption that Maelgwn also had poets in his court in Gwynedd. Later tradition, in naming one of them 'Heinin' or 'Henin',[11] seems to imply that he was Maelgwn's chief poet, but too much credence should not be placed on this. To later poets it was inconceivable that any major Welsh king should be without a chief poet, and so we find that Urien had two chief poets, Taliesin and Tristfardd; that Owain ab Urien had Dygynnelw; Selyf ap Cynan Garwyn, Arofan; Cadwallon, Afan Farddig; Cynddylan ap Cyndrwyn, Meigant.[12]

One of the charges Gildas brings against Maelgwn is that he turns a deaf ear to the Church but an attentive ear to his bards.

> Your excited ears hear not the praises of God, not the melodious music of the church but empty praises of yourself from the mouths of criminals who grate on the hearing like raving hucksters—mouths stuffed with lies and liable to bedew bystanders with their foaming phlegm.[13]

Even if we choose another text and another translation, Gildas's words do not sound any more flattering to the bards.

> When the attention of thy ears has been caught, it is not the praises of God, in the tuneful voice of Christ's followers, with its sweet rhythm, and the song of church melody, that are heard, but thine own praises (which are nothing); the voice of the rascally crew yelling forth, like Bacchanalian revellers, full of lies and foaming phlegm, so as to besmear everyone near them.[14]

Gildas leaves us in no doubt about his hostility to the poets in Maelgwn's court, and if we consider the situation carefully, it is not difficult to find reasons for this hostility.

The bards, who were so prominent in Maelgwn's entourage, were, as far as Gildas was concerned, illiterate. They knew no Latin and it is no less certain that they could neither read nor write their native language. Perhaps this is the reason why Gildas could not bring himself to mention them by title or profession. To call them bards or poets, thus implicitly comparing them with Latin poets (although he had no very high opinion of the Classical kind either), would be to pay them a compliment that they did not deserve.

If Gildas could think of nothing more atrocious than that a king should break his vow to become a monk and to return to his throne, the bards, on the other hand, could imagine nothing more incomprehensible than that a king should forget that he had been inaugurated to become the protector of his people, to lead them into battle and to promote their welfare in every way, or, from another

[11] *The Myvyrian Archaiology of Wales* (1870), pp. 363 *b*, 367 *b* (but cf. National Library of Wales, Peniarth MS. 53. 9).
[12] See J. Lloyd-Jones, *The Court Poets of the Welsh Princes* (1948), p. 4.
[13] Winterbottom, *Gildas: The Ruin of Britain and other works*, p. 34.
[14] Williams, *Gildae De Excidio Britanniae*, p. 81.

standpoint, that he should deny himself the opportunity to become a 'hero', to win great honour and immortal fame. Indeed, the assumption underlying the praise or celebration poetry sung by both Welsh bard and Irish *fili* is that 'praise' or 'fame' is the only thing that will never die. 'Trengid golud, ni threinc molud' ('Wealth vanishes, praise [fame] vanishes not'), says a very old Welsh proverb. And one of the constant themes of the Irish bards is expressed succinctly by Tadhg Dall Ó Huiginn: 'If the wealth of the world were to be assessed—this is the sum total of the matter—nothing in the world is other than futile except praise (*moladh*) alone'. [15] And it is only the bards who can confer praise or fame. In the words of the Gododdin, 'Beirt byt barnant wyr o gallon' [16] (the bards of the world adjudge men of valour) or, as the Irish poet tells us, 'No man can be famous without an ollav [chief poet]'. [17]

Although the bards had survived the druids with whom they had originally been intimately connected, there can be little doubt that Gildas would have regarded them as representative of the pagan religion, which in all probability was fighting a rearguard action against the Christianity which he was championing and which, to judge by the state of affairs described in his *De Excidio Britanniae,* needed to be championed. And even if some of the bards did not regard themselves as representatives of an older pre-Christian order of things, it is well nigh certain that they regarded themselves as discharging a religious or a quasi-religious function.

It is striking to note in this connection that the Welsh law books, which were compiled centuries after Gildas's time and which afterwards underwent many changes before they reached the form in which they are now extant, prescribe that the chief bard or *pencerdd* shall sing two songs, one to God and one to the king, and that they thus perpetuate the dual duty which the poet must have had in pagan times. [18]

The evidence from Celtic Gaul is also significant in this context. The Celts there had a priest called *gutuater,* whose functions were apparently an offshoot of those of the druid. The word *gutuater* has been derived from *$\hat{g}hutu\text{-}p\partial t\bar{e}r$, [19] 'father [that is, master] of the invocation [to god]'. This suggests that the *bardos,* a word which has been derived etymologically to mean 'the singer of praise [? to man]', [20] had a priestly counterpart, 'the singer of praise [to god]'. Such a differentiation in the functions of the praise-singer has its analogues in other cultures, [21] and is a development to be expected in early society, if, as it is reasonable to believe, 'praise of men' as a literary genre originated in the 'praise of gods'. Be that as it may, the *pencerdd,* when he sang one song to God and another to the king, was in

[15] E. Knott, *Tadhg Dall Ó Huiginn,* I (1922), Poem 31, § 8.

[16] I. Williams, *Canu Aneirin* (1938), 12. 285.

[17] L. McKenna, *The Book of O'Hara* (1951), Poem 14, § 3.

[18] A. R. Wiliam (ed.), *Llyfr Iorwerth* (1960), p. 21; S. J. Williams and J. E. Powell (eds.), *Llyfr Blegywryd* (1942), p. 25; H. D. Emanuel (ed.), *The Latin Texts of the Welsh Laws* (1967), pp. 118, 330, 446.

[19] J. Pokorny, *Indogermanisches etymologisches Wörterbuch,* I, 413, 829.

[20] D. M. Jones, 'Bardd', *Bull. Board of Celtic Studies,* XI (1944), 138-40.

[21] See I. Goldziher, *Abhandlungen zur arabischen Philologie* (Leiden, 1896), I. *Über die Vorgeschichte der Higâ'-Poésie,* pp. 1-105, where the distinction is drawn between the *šâᶜir* and the cultic poet, *kâhin.*

all probability performing the dual function of the Celtic *bardos* in a much earlier period, and no doubt he felt that he was performing a religious duty no less in singing to the king than in singing to God.

In this connection, it should be remembered that the primitive Celtic bard, like the king whom he praised, derived his peculiar power from the gods and that he derived it partly, if not wholly, through literal inspiration. The Welsh word *awen*, 'poetic muse', like the Old Irish word *aí*, 'poetic art', is derived from an Indo-European root meaning 'to blow, to breathe', just as the Old Welsh word *anant*, 'bards', and the Old Irish *anamain*, a technical term in metrics, are both derived from an Indo-European word, 'to breathe' (cf. Welsh *anadl*; Old Irish *anál*, 'breath').[22] The same root *ana- is hidden in Old Irish (*immus* [*imbas*]) *for-osnai*,[23] the name of a divinatory rite, which reminds us that the Celtic poet exercised magical powers just as the Indo-European poet must have done. The root word for the magical and augural language of both poets seems to be preserved in Latin *canere*, Welsh *canu*, Old Irish *canaid*, and some of their cognates. Their actual power over things is reflected in Old Irish *creth*, 'poetry'; Welsh *pryd-ydd* (cf. Welsh *pryd*, 'shape, form'; Old Irish *cruth*, 'form'); Vedic *kṛṇóti*, 'makes'; and Balto-Slavic words for 'magic, bewitching'—Old Church Slavic *čaro-ději*, 'magician', Lithuanian *keraî*, 'magic', and *keréti*, 'bewitch'.[24] The relevance of these derivations becomes clear when we realise that the Celtic poet, like his Indo-European predecessor, regarded himself as a shaman or magician, that he used words not only to praise those qualities which everyone thought to be essential in a king, but actually to call them into existence in him.

Welsh *clod*, 'fame, renown', and Old Irish *cloth*, 'fame', are both derived from the same Indo-European root as Greek *kléos*, 'glory, renown'.[25] The concept of *kléos*, Benveniste reminds us, is 'one of the most ancient and constant in the Indo-European world: Vedic *śravas*, Avestan *sravah-* are the exact correspondents of the Greek word and they have exactly the same sense. Moreover, the poetic language preserves in Greek and Vedic one and the same formulaic expression: Homeric *kléwos áphthiton*, Vedic *śravas akṣitam*, ''imperishable glory'', which was the supreme recompense of the warrior. It is this ''imperishable glory'' which the Indo-European hero desires above all else and for which he will lay down his life.'[26]

In one context in Greek we have, instead of *méga kléos*, 'great glory', *méga kûdos*, 'great kûdos'. Apparently *kûdos* came to be regarded as a synonym for *kléos*, but it had in fact a different meaning. According to Benveniste, *kûdos* was a magical power the possession of which conferred superiority especially in battle, where it was a guarantee of victory. Only the gods could bestow it, and those on whom it

---

[22] On these words, see C. Watkins, 'Indo-European Metrics and Archaic Irish Verse', *Celtica*, VI (1963), 194-249, esp. pp. 213-17; Pokorny, op. cit., pp. 81ff, 38ff. On *anant*, see J. E. C. Williams, *Bull. Board of Celtic Studies*, XXIV (1970), 44-50.

[23] For references to *immus* (*imbas*) *for-osnai* and discussion, see T. F. O'Rahilly, *Early Irish History and Mythology* (1946), pp. 323, 339ff.; N. K. Chadwick, *Scottish Gaelic Studies*, IV (1935), 97-135.

[24] C. Watkins, op. cit., pp. 214-15.

[25] Pokorny, op. cit., pp. 605-6.

[26] E. Benveniste, *Indo-European Language and Society* (tr. E. Palmer, 1973), p. 347.

was bestowed were raised to their ranks for it was a divine attribute—if one may call it that without losing sight of the fact that it was something concrete and tangible.

Probably the possession of *kûdos* among the ancient Greeks was almost synonymous with the possession of **menes* (Greek *ménos*; Sanskrit *mánas-*) among the Indo-Europeans, a word to which the meaning 'inner impulse of activity' has been given, for it appears that the gods breathed into heroes a good **menes*, an exceptional **menes* or the **menes* of men: compare the Greek personal name *Androménēs* (Ἀνδρομένης). Of course, **menes*, like *kûdos*, was the gift of the gods, but the poet in declaring that his patron had it, was in a way forcing the hands of the gods: he made it exist; or if it already existed, he made it stronger. [27]

In short, the poets in Maelgwn Gwynedd's court would have given a different meaning to Phylip Brydydd's declaration to his prince in the thirteenth century, 'Gwneuthum it glod' (I made fame for thee). [28] Whereas Phylip was thinking primarily of the effect on his present and future audience of his poems to his patron, they, like their Indo-European predecessors, would be thinking of the effect of their songs on Maelgwn personally: they were strengthening or creating in him qualities of mind and body which would produce the actions of which everyone would soon be talking.

If Gildas, as it has been suggested, spent some time as a fellow student with Maelgwn, in the days when the latter had abandoned his throne, it is no less possible that some of the bards whom Gildas so heartily despised had taken part in Maelgwn's inauguration to kingship. There is ample evidence that Irish poets played a prominent part in such ceremonies down to a much later date. We read, for example, that the poet Mac Firbis had to be present to participate in the inauguration of the Ó Dubhda, [29] and that, on the death of his father in 1432, Eoghan Ó Néill went to Tullach Óg 'and was crowned on the flag-stone of the kings there by the will of God and men, *bishops and ollavs* [that is, chief poets]'. [30]

Many Irish inauguration odes have survived, and Professor Georges Dumézil has shown us in what circumstances the earliest songs of this type may have been sung. Proceeding from the fact that among the ancient Hindus there were three modes of promotion to kingship, Dumézil analyses the one illustrated in the case of the primeval king Pṛthu into three acts: first, designation by the gods; second, recognition by the wise men; third, acceptance by the people. In the consecration of the king, the essential part was his eulogy by the bards, the *sūtas*, and it is significant that as soon as Prthu is consecrated, he proceeds to shower gifts on the bards and the people, thus giving proof that the local Earth-Goddess is once again fertile and that he, the king, is truly an *vrdidâtr*, 'a giver of the means of subsistence'. As the title of his book, *Servius et la Fortune*, suggests, Dumézil examined Roman as well as Hindu sources for this type of promotion to kingship and found traces of it in the legend of Servius who, it will be remembered, was

[27] J. E. C. Williams, *The Court Poet in Medieval Ireland* (1972), p. 23.

[28] J. Morris-Jones and T. H. Parry-Williams, *Llawysgrif Hendregadredd* (1933), p. 232. 26: Y gvneuthvm ytt glot glut rwyf gavr ygwrys.

[29] E. O'Curry, *Manuscript Materials of Ancient Irish History* (1861), pp. 126, 542.

[30] *The Annals of Ulster*, III, 119 (my italics).

made king by the acclamation of the people and was honoured as the institutor of the census. [31] Furthermore, Dumézil's exposition explains not only why the part played by the bards was important but also why they felt that they had a right to gifts from the hands of the new king and, by extension, from everyone whom they eulogized.

Perhaps the one and only constant feature of the royal inauguration ceremonies in Ireland was the symbolic marriage of the king to his land; in other words, they never lost the elements of a fertility rite. As late an inauguration as that of Feidhlimidh Ó Conchobhair in 1310 is described as the 'marriage of Feidhlimidh . . . to the province of Connacht', with the comment that 'this was the most splendid kingship-marriage ever celebrated down to that day'. [32] Giraldus Cambrensis describes an inauguration rite as it was performed in Tyrconnell. [33] To mention only one of its features, the king had to embrace a white mare, 'professing himself to be a beast also'. The pagan character of the rite is obvious and probably explains why other descriptions have not survived. [34] One may imagine Gildas's reaction to such a rite if it were practised, as it may very well have been, in the Britain of his day.

Rites like this were supposed to make the land fertile in all its produce and to keep it from barrenness, but they had to be augmented by the actions of the new king. If he ruled justly, the land would prosper; if he ruled wickedly, misfortune and calamity would befall both himself and his people.

Though Irish inauguration odes of the bardic period do not contain advice on how to be a good king, there is reason to believe that the *filid* of earlier times offered advice and instruction to their royal patrons, and collections of such precepts are extant. Indeed, 'there is some evidence to suggest that the genre of the *Speculum Principis,* which first appeared in Latin about the seventh century, may derive partly from Irish tradition'. [35] One of the oldest *Specula* of this kind in Irish is *Audacht Morainn:* indeed, its earliest redaction may be pre-Christian. Keating, [36] writing in the first half of the seventeenth century, states that the dynastic historian or ollav read aloud a *Teagasc Ríogh* at the inauguration of a king 'from the coming of Patrick . . . to the Norman Invasion', thereby drawing attention to the prosperity which would follow the pursuit of righteous truth and the misfortune which would follow the pursuit of wickedness.

The *De Excidio Britanniae* was written in part to admonish the British rulers of the time for their evil ways. It is easy to imagine how its author would have resented the presumption of the bards in arrogating to themselves the right to

---

[31] G. Dumézil, *Servius et La Fortune: essai sur la fonction sociale de louange et de blâme et sur les éléments indo-européens du cens romain* (1943).

[32] See M. Dillon, 'The Inauguration of O'Conor', in J. A. Watt, J. B. Morrall and F. X. Martin (eds.), *Medieval Studies presented to Aubrey Gwynn, S. J.* (1961), p. 186.

[33] Giraldus Cambrensis, *Topographia Hibernica,* ed. J. F. Dimock, c. xxv (Rolls Ser., 1867), p. 169.

[34] The Indo-European origin of the rite is made probable by the fact that a similar rite was practised among the Hindus. See F. R. Schröder, 'Ein altirischer Krönungsritus und das indogermanische Roßopfer', *Zeitschrift für celtische Philologie,* XVI (1927), 310-12; cf. Pokorny, ibid., p. 123.

[35] F. Kelly (ed.), *Audacht Morainn* (1976), p. xv.

[36] G. Keating, *History of Ireland,* vol. III, ed. P. S. Dinneen (1913), p. 10, and see comment by Kelly, op. cit., p. xiv.

advise these same rulers, even if their advice agreed on some points with his own.

The bards in Maelgwn's court would have resembled their Irish counterparts in many if not all of their activities, and here one should remember that there was a strong Irish element in the population of Gwynedd, especially in Anglesey, where, it may be argued, Maelgwn had his base. At the same time one has to admit that Gildas apparently refers only to their eulogizing. But if they could praise Maelgwn, they could also satirize him, and in this respect they resembled not only the *filid*[37] but also the Gaulish bards of whom Diodorus Siculus[38] said, about the middle of the first century BC, that they sang to the accompaniment of musical instruments resembling lyres sometimes praise, sometimes satire. Satire, however, was not a prerogative of Celtic bards. Archilocus, a Greek poet of the seventh century BC, is said to have satirized Lycambes for refusing to give him his daughter's hand in marriage, with the result that both Lycambes and his daughter hanged themselves.[39] Such was the power of satire in those ancient days and such it remained for many centuries after Maelgwn's death.

It may very well be that there are two other veiled references to the bards in Gildas's tirade against Maelgwn. We have already referred to his condemnation of Maelgwn's second marriage to the woman he had made a widow by murdering her husband, his own brother's son.

> The wedding was public, and, as the lying tongues of your parasites cry (but from their lips only, not from the depths of their hearts), legitimate: for she was a widow. But I call it most scandalous.[40]

> Afterwards thou didst wed her . . . in public, and (as the false tongues of thy flatterers assert, at the top of their voice, though not from the depth of their hearts) in a legitimate marriage, regarding her as a widow; but our tongues say, in desecrated wedlock.[41]

The word translated 'parasites' in the first translation and 'flatterers' in the second is *parasiti,* and this is interesting since Posidonius applied the Greek word *parasitoi* to the Celtic bards centuries before Gildas's time,[42] but the question for us is whether it refers to the sycophantic clergy or to the no less sycophantic bards. That it could refer to the latter will become apparent from the following considerations.

There is reason to believe that in Wales as in Ireland in early times a feast of some kind was an integral part of a wedding. The Welsh word *neithior* (*neithiawr*) originally meant both 'a feast' and 'a wedding',[43] just as the Irish word *banais* (from *ben* and *feis*) meant 'a wedding' and 'a wedding feast'. It has even been suggested that in Celtic pagan times the bridegroom accepted a draught of wine

---

[37] F. N. Robinson, 'Satirists and Enchanters in Early Irish Literature', in D. G. Lyon and G. F. Moore (eds.), *Studies in the History of Religions Presented to Crawford H. Toy* (1912).

[38] Diodorus Siculus, v. 31.

[39] See G. L. Hendrickson, 'Archilochus and the victims of his iambics', *American Journal of Philology*, XLVI (1925), 101-27; R. C. Elliot, *The Power of Satire: Magic, Ritual, Art* (1966).

[40] Winterbottom, *Gildas*, p. 34.

[41] Williams, *Gildae De Excidio Britanniae*, pp. 82-3.

[42] See J. E. C. Williams, 'Posidonius's Celtic Parasites', *Studia Celtica*, XIV—XV (1979-80), 313-43.

[43] I. Williams, *Canu Aneirin* (1938), p. 66.

or liquor from the bride as a token of agreement and consent to marry: in the account given in the *Historia Brittonum* of Vortigern's marriage to Hengist's daughter, the statement that she was bidden by her father to serve wine and beer should perhaps have come after Vortigern's request for her hand.[44] The Irish word *banais* was also used to denote a royal inauguration feast and it is not impossible that there was some resemblance between it and an ordinary wedding. We have seen that a royal inauguration was regarded as a marriage between the king and the local Earth-Goddess and that the poets played an important part in it. Did they have a part to play at every royal and stately wedding?

Professor Mac Cana[45] has drawn attention to the fact that the Welsh law books prescribe that the chief poet of the kingdom was entitled to a bridal gift (*cyfarws neithiawr*) from every maiden on her marriage, that is, from every maiden within the kingdom of which he was chief poet, and that furthermore this gift was to be presented during the wedding feast. Interesting as this practice is, it becomes doubly significant when it is juxtaposed with the Irish practice whereby the ollav, or chief poet, claimed the wedding dress of a newly married bride. According to Mac Cana, it is recorded in Ireland only in comparatively late sources and these do not agree with each other in all details, but that it was practised in early times seems to be indicated by the fact that there was a similar custom in ancient India. 'In several texts of the *Gṛhya-Sūtra* there are sections dealing with the marriage rite which explicitly prescribe that the bride's [wife's] shift shall be given to the brahman.'[46] Mac Cana rightly concludes: 'one can hardly doubt that we have here a congener of the Irish custom described above, and indeed the probability is that both are survivals of Indo-European tradition'.[47]

Marriage, as we know, had from the beginning a religious significance which won for it a fundamental place in the mythological thinking of primitive man. 'Marriage rites,' writes Mircea Eliade, '. . . have a divine model, and human marriage reproduces the hierogamy, more especially the union of heaven and earth. "I am Heaven", says the husband, "Thou art Earth".'[48] No doubt the coming of Christianity radically changed the character of marriage in the west, but it did so gradually and sporadically, leaving many pockets of pagan survival and not least in the Celtic lands of Ireland, Scotland, Wales and Brittany.

It is of singular interest that the *gwledd neithior*, 'the marriage feast', was so important in the calendar of the bardic order in medieval Wales that it became not only an occasion for 'grading' its members and awarding them 'licences' (*trwyddedau*), but also an occasion for a hilarious practice: one of the bards was chosen to be made the laughing-stock (*cyff clêr, cyff gwawd*) of the others, who were then invited to address mock derogatory verses to him.[49] The main source of our evidence for the second practice limits it, it is true, to 'a royal marriage feast'

[44] A. W. Wade-Evans, *Nennius's 'History of the Britons'*, p. 59.

[45] P. Mac Cana, 'An Archaism in Irish Poetic Tradition', *Celtica*, VIII (1968), 174-81; 'Elfennau Cyn-Gristnogol yn y Cyfreithiau', *Bull. Board of Celtic Studies*, XXIII (1970), 316-20.

[46] Mac Cana, *Celtica*, VIII (1968), 176.

[47] Ibid., p. 177.

[48] M. Eliade, *Cosmos and History: The Myth of the Eternal Return* (1959), p. 23.

[49] J. D. Rhys, *Cambrobrytannicæ Cymraecæve Linguae Institutiones etc.* (1592), p. 304.

(*neithior frenhinol*), but there is reason to doubt whether the distinction between a royal and a non-royal marriage feast had any significance in Wales after the Edwardian settlement. Needless to say, the entertainment thus provided by the bards was for the enjoyment of all present. It may have been meant to supersede the widespread medieval practice of directing ribald remarks at the bride and bridegroom, but it may also have been intended to replace the invective of an earlier period when it was thought that derogatory remarks were a means of averting the 'evil eye' and of expelling malign influences.

There is no reason to think that the clergy at Maelgwn's court would have had any qualms about approving his second marriage, for marriage customs in Europe did not begin to conform with the demands of the Church and its teaching until the twelfth-century reforms. [50] On the other hand, they would have had more qualms than the bards and for that reason Gildas may have been referring to the bards rather than to the clergy when using the word *parasiti*. However, we have shown reason enough to justify the belief that the bards did play an important part in the two marriages of their patron, and that they 'praised' the bride and the bridegroom at the second marriage with the same zeal as they did at the first, convinced, no doubt, that they were thereby ensuring the fertility of the union. From Gildas's point of view, they would have deserved the same censure as the clergy.

The third indirect reference to the bards is found in Gildas's charges against the clergy.

> They yawn stupidly at the precepts of holy men—if they ever do hear them: though they should constantly; while they show alert interest in sports and the foolish stories of worldly men, as though they were the means to life and not death. [51]

Dr Hugh Williams took the 'foolish stories of worldly men' (or, in his translation, the 'scandalous tales of men of the world') to refer to 'ancient', that is classical, literature. 'Gildas', he writes, 'may be understood as presenting here the views held by a fervent monk, of the men in Britain who still continued to read the ancient literature.' [52] It seems more likely that he is referring to the tales and legends told by the bards in the vernacular.

That the bards were the custodians of traditional lore and that they recited the narrative elements in it on stately and festive occasions seem certain. In *Math uab Mathonwy* we are told that Gwydion and Gilfaethwy visited the court of Pryderi 'in the guise of poets' (*yn rith beird*), Gwydion himself assuming the role of *pencerdd*. They were made welcome, and a feast was prepared in their honour:

> Gwydion was placed beside Pryderi that night. 'Why', said Pryderi, 'we should gladly have a tale (*kyuarwydyt*) from some of the young men yonder.' 'Lord,' said Gwydion, 'it is a custom with us that the first night after one comes to a great man, the chief bard (*penkerd*) shall have the say. I will tell a tale gladly.' Gwydion

---

[50] G. Duby, *Medieval Marriage: Two models from twelfth-century France* (tr. E. Forster, 1977); J. Watt, *The Church in Medieval Ireland* (1972), pp. 5-9.

[51] Winterbottom, *Gildas,* pp. 52-3.

[52] Williams, *Gildae De Excidio Britanniae,* p. 167.

was the best teller of tales (*kyuarwyd*) in the world. And that night he entertained
the court with pleasant tales and storytelling (*cyuarwydyt*) till he was praised by
everyone in the court.[53]

There is perhaps a suggestion here that the normal practice was for the young
bards to tell *cyfarwyddyd*. Furthermore, a sentence has been appended to *Breudwyt
Ronabwy* ('The Dream of Rhonabwy') purporting to explain 'why no one,
neither bard (*bard*) nor storyteller (*cyfarwyd*), knows the dream without a book'.[54]
This suggests that some distinction was drawn between the *bardd* and the
cyfarwydd, but the distinction does not imply that the *bardd* could not tell tales or
necessarily that he was less skilled than the *cyfarwydd* in that art. As an adjective,
cyfarwydd has *inter alia* the meanings 'well-informed, learned, expert, skilful,
skilled in magic', and as a noun the corresponding meanings, 'guide, well-
informed person, expert', and [legal] 'witness, spectator of crime'. Professor Mac
Cana is surely right in suggesting that the meaning 'story-teller' is secondary and
that 'there is no real evidence that the Welsh literati ever thought of it [the noun
cyfarwydd] as a class-title,'[55] that is, as the name of a professional story-teller, a
specialist in the art of story-telling. However, although there is no evidence that it
was ever so used, *cyfarwyddyd* would have been an ideal word to denote the wealth
of traditional lore which the Welsh bards, as successors to the druids, if not in
virtue of their own role in society, were expected to know and to transmit.
Originally, the material of that traditional lore would not have been very different
from that of the Irish *filid*. It comprised much more than tales in our sense of the
word.

> For the *filid* the tales were primarily part of the *coimcne*, . . . the body of inherited
> knowledge in which the authoritative view of the past depended, and as such they
> meshed closely with law, genealogy, customary ritual, and the several other
> branches of traditional learning that served to define the origins and history of the
> social order and of the tribal and ethnic elements comprised within it.[56]

In other words, the traditional lore was handed down and preserved because it
was regarded as important to the stability, continuity and general well-being of
society, and there must have been set occasions when various strands in it were
'recollected' and proclaimed in public. In Ireland the great festivals would have
provided such occasions—those celebrated at Tara, Tailtiu, Emain and
Cruachu—but there were other occasions, such as royal weddings and funerals,
royal inaugurations and 'celebrations' of various kinds.

Compared with the Irish, the Welsh evidence for public gatherings at festivals
is very sparse, but a secret report submitted to the government of the day in the
reign of Elizabeth I (1558-1603) or at the beginning of the reign of James I
(1603-25)—let us assume about 1600—gives us an intriguing but valuable

---

[53] G. Jones and T. Jones (trs.), *The Mabinogion* (1949), pp. 56-7.

[54] Ibid., p. 152.

[55] P. Mac Cana, *The Learned Tales of Mediaeval Ireland* (1980), p. 139.

[56] Ibid., pp. 18-19.

glimpse into the past:

> Upon the Sondaies and hollidaies the multitude of all sortes of men woomen and childerne of everie parishe do use to meete in sondrie places either one some hill or one the side of some mountaine where theire harpers and crowthers singe them songs of the doeings of theire auncestors, namelie, of theire warrs againste the kings of this realme and the English nacion, and then doe they ripp upp their petigres at lenght howe eche of them is discended from those theire ould princs. Here alsoe doe they spende theire time in hearinge some part of the lives of Thalaassyn, Marlin Beno Kybbye Jermon, and suche other the intended prophetts and saincts of that cuntrie. [57]

The reference to the recital of pedigrees on these occasions is particularly noteworthy.

We are told by Appian of Alexandria (Gall. xii) that when the Romans made war on the Allobroges because they would not surrender certain chiefs who had taken refuge with them, Bituitus, their king, sent an ambassador followed by attendants (and dogs!) to the Roman commander.

> A musician too was in the train who sang in barbarous fashion the praises of Bituitus, and then of the Allobroges, and then of the ambassador himself, celebrating his birth, his bravery, and his wealth; and it is for this reason chiefly that ambassadors of distinction take such persons along with them. [58]

When we recall that Diodorus Siculus refers to the Gaulish bards as poets who sang sometimes a eulogy, sometimes a satire to the accompaniment of musical instruments, we can safely deduce that Appian's musician was a bard. And we recognise in the themes of the poems which he sang the familiar recurring topics of his successors in Britain and Ireland: nobility of birth, bravery and wealth, the symbol of the success which had to be manifested in generosity.

In Ireland the ollav or chief poet of the dynasty recited the king's genealogy as part of his eulogy to him at the inauguration ceremony. It was important that he should do so for the royal genealogy was the equivalent of a charter of right, proof of the title to rule. The genealogical lore of Ireland is exceptional in its extent. Furthermore, the form in which some of it has been transmitted to us indicates that it may have been recited ceremonially, and particularly at the inauguration of a member of the dynasty to the throne.

There is an explicit reminder of the importance of royal descent in Scotland in the account of the inauguration of young Alexander III in 1249 in a traditional ceremony at Scone. The boy-king was seated on the Lia Fail, the Stone of Destiny, and after he had been consecrated by the bishop of St. Andrews and had accepted the feudal homages made to him, his royal genealogy was recited in Gaelic by a Highland shennachie. Apparently he was regarded as the latest of a line of 'upwards of a hundred kings'. [59] Centuries later, in January 1651, the last

[57] The passage is quoted by Sir I. Williams, 'Hen Chwedlau', *Trans. Hon. Soc. Cymmrodorion*, 1946, p. 28, from British Library (henceforth BL), Lansdowne MS. III, f. 110, as printed in *A Catalogue of the Manuscript Relating to Wales in the British Museum*, I, 72, but better readings are suggested in note 2 and these have been adopted here.

[58] *Appian's Roman History*, tr. H. White (Loeb Classical Library, 1928), I, 115.

[59] W. Ferguson, *Scotland's Relations with England* (1977), p. 19.

king of Scotland to be crowned at Scone, Charles II, also had his genealogy recited at the coronation ceremony.

Giraldus Cambrensis, in his *Description of Wales,* tells us that 'The Welsh value distinguished birth and noble descent more than anything else in the world. Even the common people know their family-tree by heart and can readily recite from memory the list of their grandfathers, great-grandfathers, great-great-grandfathers, back to the sixth or seventh generations' (Book I, 17). Moreover, in respect of the princes, he adds 'that the Welsh bards, singers and jongleurs kept accurate copies of the genealogies of these princes in their old manuscripts, which were, of course, written in Welsh. They would also recite them from memory, going back from Rhodri Mawr to the time of the Blessed Virgin Mary, and then farther still to Silvius, Ascanius and Aeneas.' (Book I, 3)[60]

In view of such evidence, we need have no hesitation in assuming that Maelgwn's bards were genealogists and as such were, in a sense, the historians of their time. Unfortunately, genealogies were of more than academic interest: they were politically important because dynasties ruled by virtue of their descent from ancient royal lineages. If, then, a new dynasty rose to power by overthrowing the ruling dynasty, there was overwhelming pressure on the poet-historians to make the new dynasty's *de facto* claim to the throne legitimate by adjusting the genealogies. One way to do this was by forging a link between the newcomers and their predecessors, thereby providing both continuity and legitimacy. Examples of this procedure are plentiful, especially in early Irish history. To quote an example given by Ó Corráin:

> The Dál Cais, who were historically Déisi in origin, overthrew the Eóganacht kings and seized the kingship of Munster. As a result, their genealogical traditions were altered, and the later genealogists represent them as a branch of the Eóganacht. Conversely, vassal folk and conquered peoples living within the kingdom of a dominant dynasty are often linked genealogically (and demonstrably unhistorically) to their overlords. This is not unabashed fiction or simple deception but rather the mode in which the genealogists, and, doubtless the families concerned, conceived the relationship. When the relationship changes, the genealogical affiliations of the families concerned are altered accordingly.[61]

These facts should be borne in mind when we consider Maelgwn Gwynedd's genealogy, for recent research has raised the question as to whether what purports to be his genealogy is a fabrication by a later generation of poet-historians or the tradition as transmitted by those of his own generation.

Maelgwn, according to the extant genealogies, was the son of Cadwallawn Law-hir, son of Einiawn Yrth, son of Cunedda who was the son of Edern, son of Padarn Beisrudd, son of Tegid, whose genealogy is traced back to Amalech, son of Beli Fawr and Anna *quam dicunt esse consobrina Mariae virginis, matris domini nostri Iesu Christi.*[62] This reminds us of Giraldus Cambrensis's reference to the

[60] The translations are from Gerald of Wales, *The Journey through Wales and the Description of Wales,* tr. Lewis Thorpe (1978).

[61] D. Ó Corráin, *Ireland Before the Normans* (1972), p. 76.

[62] BL, Harley MS. 3859: P. C. Bartrum, *Early Welsh Genealogical Tracts* (1966), p. 9.

genealogies which went back 'from Rhodri Mawr to the time of the Blessed Virgin Mary', and illustrates the profound influence which the introduction of ecclesiastical learning exercised on the native traditions.

Maelgwn's great-grandfather (*proavus*) in the pedigrees, Cunedda, is the subject of two traditions. One is recorded in two notes in Harleian MS. 3859. The first tells us the names of Cunedda's sons, whose number was nine. The first born was Tybiawn who died in the region of Manaw Gododdin and did not come hither (to Wales) with his father and eight brothers. However, he was represented by his son Meiriawn who was given a share when the lands conquered were distributed among Cunedda's sons, lands which, according to the second note, extended from the Dee (*Dyfrdwy*) to the Teifi. We are left to deduce that *Meirionnydd* was called after *Meiriawn*, just as *Rhufoniog* was called after *Rhufawn*, *Dunoding* after *Dunawd*, *Edeirnion* after *Edern*, etc., i.e., eponymously after the names of Cunedda's sons.

The other tradition concerning Cunedda is also found in Harleian MS. 3859, in the *Historia Brittonum*.

> Mailcunus (*Maelgwn*), the great king, was reigning among the Britons, that is in the region of Guenedota (*Gwynedd*), for his ancestor (or, according to the meaning we give the Latin *atavus*, great-great-great-grandfather) that is Cunedag (*Cunedda*) with his sons whose number was eight, had come previously from the northern part which is called Manau Guotodin (*Manaw Gododdin*), one hundred and forty-six years before Mailcun (*Maelgwn*) reigned. And they drove out the Scots (the Irish) from those regions, who never returned to inhabit them. [63]

There are irreconcilable discrepancies between these two traditions. Furthermore, Mrs Nora Chadwick analysed these traditions in the context of ninth-century learning and compared them to other 'origin' stories; i.e. stories which relate how different dynasties came to rule different countries and how in most, if not all cases, the name of the founder of the incoming dynasty or his sons gave their names to later kingdoms. [64] Of singular interest is the story how the kingdom of the Scottish Dalriada arose as the result of an incursion from the Irish kingdom of the same name on the Antrim coast under the leadership of Erc son of Eochu and his six sons. Mrs Chadwick concludes that in dealing with stories like that of Cunedda and his sons 'we are dealing, not with historical tradition in the strict sense of the word, but with antiquarian speculations of the native class—their attempts to account for their origin and the distribution of the peoples and the kingdoms of their day.' And it is difficult to resist that conclusion. Indeed, one sympathises with Dr David Dumville's impatience with those historians who

---

[63] A. W. Wade-Evans, *Nennius's History of the Britons*, p. 80; John Morris, *Nennius*, p. 37, translates '. . . for his ancestors, Cunedda, with his sons . . .' Several attempts have been made to explain the discrepancy between the reference to Cunedda as Maelgwn's *atavus* and the reference to the '146 years' which elapsed before Maelgwn reigned. For the latest see M. Miller, 'The Foundation of Gwynedd in the Latin Texts', *Bull. Board of Celtic Studies,* XXVIII, 515-32.

[64] N. K. Chadwick *et al., Studies in the early British Church* (1958), pp. 29ff. Dr M. Miller's comment in *Bull. Board of Celtic Studies,* XXVII (1978), 515 n. 1, is: 'Mrs Chadwick's paper is concerned with literary form and fashion, and should not be quoted as historical criticism'.

have tried to give a credible background to the Cuneddan migration.[65] But we should perhaps separate the story of that migration from its accretions, i.e. from the story of Cunedda's sons and grandson and their connection with the kingdoms called after them. If the former has no basis in fact, it means that the genealogy of Maelgwn and his family as preserved by his bards has been completely and irretrievably lost, and another genealogy—a fabricated one—substituted for it. In other words, a complete break with the tradition occurred some time after Maelgwn's days, and the vacuum usually associated with the fifth century in Welsh historical scholarship has to be extended in the case of Gwynedd far into the sixth.[66] Mrs Chadwick was aware of this when, in spite of the difficulties presented by the accounts of the Cuneddan migration in Harleian MS. 3859, in the notes and the *Historia Brittonum,* she felt compelled to say: 'Yet the details suggest that there is some historical tradition behind it, linking the men of Scotland with an early Welsh dynastic group'.[67] How old that tradition was and how genuine are questions which do not at present appear to admit of any answers but they should not on that account be dismissed or ignored.

---

[65] D. N. Dumville, 'Sub-Roman Britain: History and Legend,' *History,* 62 (1977), 173-92, esp. 183.
[66] For this vacuum or void, see W. Davies, *Wales in the Early Middle Ages* (1982), p. 89.
[67] Nora Chadwick, *The Celts* (1920), p. 77.

Cultural Survival in an Age of Conquest

DAVID WALKER

WILLIAM of Malmesbury recorded an acrimonious occasion when an English bishop lost patience with a forceful and acquisitive Norman sheriff. Wulfstan, bishop of Worcester, found the Conqueror's sheriff, Urse d'Abetot, a grasping neighbour and, goaded out of all charity, he cursed the intruder: *hattest þu Urs, haue þu Godes kurs.* [1] Whether it was effective, it is scarcely possible to say. True, d'Abetot's son was disgraced and disinherited about 1110 and his office and lands passed through a daughter to the Beauchamp family. [2] But a similar fate was suffered by other Norman dynasties without the intervention of an irate churchman. Nevertheless, the incident has a symbolic quality. Not only was it a clash of personalities, involved in a quarrel about land, but it was also a clash of cultures. Wulfstan no doubt looked very much as any contemporary Norman bishop looked, but to curse his enemy he used an ancient vernacular, unfamiliar and meaningless to the intruder.

Nearly a hundred years later, in 1167, in a very different part of the kingdom, a Cistercian abbot lay dying. At Rievaulx, Abbot Aelred was wracked with pain. Stone in the kidney had been a perpetual torment for him, and he was continually in the grip of arthritis. Asceticism, discipline and illness had taken their toll of a frame reduced to little more than skin and bone, and as he drifted through bouts of fever and lucidity, he called on God for release. 'Hasten, hasten', was his incessant cry. 'And often', as his biographer wrote, 'he drove the word home by calling on the name of Christ in English, a word of one syllable in this tongue and easier to utter, and in some ways sweeter to hear.' [3] So, Aelred would call, 'Hasten *for crist love'*. As death approached, he spoke, not in the French of polite society, nor in the Latin of the world of scholarship, but in his native English.

These two anecdotes may be matched by a third. In 1188, Baldwin, archbishop of Canterbury, travelled through Wales seeking recruits for a crusade. Gerald, archdeacon of Brecon, was one of his companions and shared some of the preaching with him, using French or Latin, but not Welsh. In Cemais, the prince

---

[1] N. S. Hamilton (ed.), *Willelmi Malmesbiriensis monachi de gestis pontificum Anglorum* (R[olls] S[eries], 1870), p. 253; R. R. Darlington (ed.), *Vita Wulfstani* (Camden Soc., 3rd ser., XL, 1928), p. xxviin.

[2] E. Mason (ed.), *Beauchamp Cartulary* (P[ipe] R[oll] S[ociety], n[ew] s[eries], XLIII, 1980), pp. xx-xxi. See also *idem*, 'Magnates, Curiales and the Wheel of Fortune: 1066-1154', in R. A. Brown (ed.), [*Proceedings of the*] *Battle Conference* [*on Anglo-Norman Studies*] *II, 1979* (1980), pp. 118-40; the evidence for the Abetot-Beauchamp connection is discussed on pp. 138-9. Dr Mason draws attention to the literary parallels to Wulfstan's curse, and to the record of the curse in Gerald of Wales's 'Speculum Ecclesie', *Opera*, IV, ed. J. S. Brewer (RS, 1873), pp. 343-4.

[3] F. M. Powicke (ed.), *The Life of Ailred of Rievaulx* (1950), pp. 59-60 (cited as Powicke, *Ailred*).

of Deheubarth, the Lord Rhys, and his followers listened, first to the archbishop and then to the archdeacon whose address caused sharp comment. The prince's jester, John Spang, raised a laugh at his expense. 'Rhys', he said, 'you ought to love this kinsman of yours dearly, this archdeacon, for today he has sent a hundred of your men or more to serve Christ; and had he spoken Welsh, I doubt whether a single man would be left to you out of all this crowd.'[4] The jibe may have been aimed at Gerald's self-esteem as well as at the power of his rhetoric, but the critical element in it was the element of language, one of the principal features dividing Welsh from Anglo-Norman in border society.

Few anecdotes could be more familiar; they make their point because they are over-simplified. Yet, familiar as they are, they may reveal racial attitudes and assumptions, and they carry overtones of hatred or respect or contempt which are valuable in themselves.

Hostility and hatred between English and Norman are plain to see, whether in the early years of conquest or in the more settled conditions of the reigns of William Rufus and Henry I. A memory of widespread rape, in which Norman soldiery showed no concern for age or birth, was long-lived and was absorbed into the account of the Norman settlement in England which Orderic Vitalis was writing in the second half of Henry I's reign. It was not ill-founded. Once conditions had settled down, the Conqueror's archbishop of Canterbury, Lanfranc, was asked for a ruling: what was the position of women who had taken refuge in nunneries to escape from the Normans? They had found security by living as nuns, though they may not have made any profession. His decision was simple. Those who had taken vows must honour them and remain within the cloister; those who had sought refuge in time of danger should be released from the house and return to secular life.[5]

In no sense was Anglo-Saxon manhood held in respect. By the end of the Conqueror's reign, the greater aristocracy was in eclipse. No English secular magnate could claim any political power or curial influence. A few magnates survived as landholders of some scale in southern and midland England. Edward the Confessor's nearest kinsman, his great-nephew, survived the dangerous hazard of a strong dynastic claim to the Conqueror's throne. As recently as the reign of Cnut such a claim would have cost him his life. But he was content to exist—and be allowed to exist—as the lord of a small border lordship based on Ewias Harold. Safety lay in obscurity. Others stood in less danger, and a handful of Old English families survived with some standing into the twelfth century. Some Norman settlers strengthened their claims to estates by judicious alliances with women who were identified as heiresses of English dynasties.[6] Then in 1100,

[4] J. S. Brewer (ed.), 'De Rebus a se Gestis', *Opera*, III (RS, 1863), 77.

[5] Orderic Vitalis [*Historia Ecclesiastica*], ed. M. Chibnall, II (1969), 202; H. Clover and M. Gibson (eds.), *The Letters of Lanfranc, Archbishop of Canterbury* (1979), p. 166, no. 53. See also the penances enjoined by the legate, Bishop Ermenfrid of Sitten, in 1070: D. C. Douglas and G. W. Greenaway (eds.), E[nglish] H[istorical] D[ocuments], II (2nd ed.. 1981), 649-50.

[6] On the survival of English families, see F. M. Stenton, 'English Families and the Norman Conquest', *Trans. R. Hist. S.*, 4th ser., XXVI (1944), 1-12, reprinted in D. M. Stenton (ed.), *Preparatory to Anglo-Saxon England* (1970), pp. 325-34. On the question of marriage with heiresses, see E. Searle, 'Women and the legitimization of succession at the Norman Conquest', *Battle Conference III, 1980* (1981), pp. 159-70.

the usurpation of the throne by Henry I made a marriage into the Old English ruling house a political virtue, and English ancestry became more respectable and may have been acknowledged more openly. In rural society, over the greater part of southern and midland England, the relationship between French and English was marked by a sharp contrast in social status, and there were ample grounds for resentment and hostility on the part of the dispossessed and the disinherited. Petty revenge, exacted when isolation made a Norman vulnerable, led to the imposition of the *murdrum* fine resting on the lord of the slayer if he could be identified, or on the whole hundred if he could not. It was a heavy price to pay for casual vengeance.[7]

Even within these broad terms it would be both easy and dangerous to oversimplify. Norman settlers were not solely concerned with English claimants, whether to land or power; they had other rivals. One of the earliest expressions of Norman identity in England drew the contrast, not between Norman and English, but between different categories of Frenchmen: those who had won their place in England by conquest, and those who had settled in England during the reign of Edward the Confessor. French they might be, or even Norman, but they had not shared the hazards of conquest and they ought not to share its profits. They were to count, for fiscal purposes at least, as English.[8]

Not every Norman survivor from the Confessor's circle suffered in this way. Humphrey de Tilleul and his son, Robert, were in England before 1066, and the young Robert received knighthood from the Confessor. They had gone back to Normandy before King Edward died. After the conquest, Robert returned to the English scene in the entourage of his influential cousin, Hugh of Avranches, earl of Chester, and he was to carve a new career and a new territory for himself beyond the borders of England. Later to be identified as Robert of Rhuddlan, he dominated north Wales.[9] Another young man who settled in England as the protégé of a powerful uncle, Alfred of Marlborough, was a lucky survivor. He lived through the overthrow of Earl Godwine in 1051 and the crisis of the earl's return in the following year; he was still holding lands in Herefordshire at the end of the Confessor's reign. He found new patrons after the conquest in William fitz Osbern, earl of Hereford, and in the Conqueror himself, who confirmed Alfred in his possessions. He was a man with the capacity to get the best of two worlds.[10]

In a different context, Norman apologists discussed the succession to the English throne (in 1066 and, later, in 1087 and 1100) in personal terms, not in racial terms. The Conqueror and William Rufus used English military institutions and called on the loyalty of their English subjects with unmistakable success.[11] Once the immediate crisis of conquest was over, problems of race and

---

[7] Leges Willelmi, cl. 3: *EHD*, II, 431. *Murdrum* legislation was re-issued in the reign of Henry I: L. J. Downer (ed.), *Leges Henrici Primi* (1972), pp. 116, 234, 284-6. There is a concise definition of the whole problem in the *Dialogus de Scaccario*, ed. C. Johnson (1950), pp. 52-3; *EHD*, II, 559-60.

[8] Leges Willelmi, cl. 4: *EHD*, II, 431.

[9] Orderic Vitalis, IV (1973), xxxiv-xxxviii, 138; F. Barlow, *Edward the Confessor* (1970), p. 192; D. Walker, 'The Norman Settlement in Wales', *Battle Conference I, 1978* (1979), pp. 131-43.

[10] V[ictoria] C[ounty] H[istory] Heref[ord], I (1908), 337; J. H. Round, *Feudal England* (1895), p. 324.

[11] Perhaps the most notable example is that of Wygot of Wallingford, who saved the life of William the Conqueror at Gerberoi in 1079.

loyalty could be seen to be complex and varied. One fact had emerged with startling clarity, certainly by 1075: English magnates had no place in the corridors of power. Political authority and curial influence were no longer theirs to claim.

In city and town, conditions were very different. Before the Norman conquest, great magnates had secured valuable and lucrative rights in many English boroughs, and these claims, transferred to Norman hands, continued after the conquest. To cite only three instances from Domesday Book, French magnates had 112 houses in Warwick and 22 in Buckingham; Alan, count of Brittany, had 10 burgages in Cambridge.[12] Winchester was not included in Domesday Book, but records surviving from the twelfth century indicate that 'Norman magnates held large numbers of plots and tenements which they rented for investment'. Herbert the Chamberlain, for example, had nine houses and three other holdings, and his son, his steward, his cook, and a tenant with the French name of Ralph had tenements in the city. Herbert's full income from his properties is not recorded, but it was certainly in excess of £27.[13] Then the establishment of a castle introduced a new element in many English boroughs. The garrison itself formed an important market for local traders. The castellan was always an influential figure; where he was also sheriff, those who worked with him in local administration could be a small but powerful French élite within the town. Other Frenchmen settled in towns, not as *rentiers* and administrators, but as burgesses. Garrison, administrators and alien settlers were daily in contact with townsmen of local provenance, and in many towns they formed only a small minority of the total population.

Domesday Book provides an extensive survey of Colchester, covering 450 houses.[14] If each personal name in the list represents a separate individual, we are dealing with 294 burgesses. If, as at Canterbury, the town was surveyed by wards or, as at Winchester in the twelfth century, it was surveyed by streets, the number of householders would be smaller. There are many duplicate names, with no by-name, trade description, or family connection to distinguish particular individuals and some of these must represent multiple holdings. The names reflect overwhelmingly a pre-conquest population; scarcely more than a score of names are obviously French, and some of these are the names of magnates rather than of burgesses. That French element might represent between 7 per cent and 10 per cent of the total population of Colchester. At Hereford, an outpost on the Welsh border and in no sense a typical borough, a different balance was certainly intended and may, perhaps, have been found. There, William fitz Osbern wished to attract Frenchmen to settle in this exposed town and he offered terms which were especially favourable to French settlers. He cut through the complexity of Old English custom and offered those who would settle a much simplified system of forfeitures. In 1086, when the king held the borough, the English burgesses had their former customs while the French burgesses were quit from all their

[12] *D[omesday] B[ook]*, I, 143, 189, 238; *VCH, Warw.*, I (1904), 299; *VCH, Bucks.*, I (1905), 230; *VCH, Camb.*, I (1938), 359.

[13] M. Biddle (ed.), *Winchester in the Early Middle Ages* (1976), pp. 18, 28.

[14] *DB*, II, 104-7b; *VCH, Essex*, I (1903), 540; H. C. Darby (ed.), *Domesday Geography of Eastern England* (1957), p. 253.

forfeitures for a simple payment of 12*d*. The equation of race and privilege is unmistakable. Unfortunately, Domesday Book does not provide the material for a detailed comparison of the two racial elements in the town community. The bishop of Hereford had a substantial share of that community in the quarter around the cathedral. During the next century and a half, where there was conflict in Hereford, it was not conflict between French and English but between the burgesses of the king and those of the bishop.[15] For Southampton there are precise figures: in 1086, there were 65 French and 31 English burgesses. At Northampton and at Nottingham, Domesday Book indicates the existence of new boroughs, and it has been assumed that at each place an English borough and a new French borough existed side by side. The same pattern prevailed at Norwich, where the old borough was said to have 665 English burgesses, while a new borough certainly with 124 and perhaps with as many as 160 French burgesses was growing rapidly.[16]

For a small number of towns, lists of burgesses have survived, ranging in date from *c.* 1100 to 1207. Detailed analysis provides a basis for tentative conclusions about the cultural influences at work in these communities. In some places, at Bury St. Edmunds, Battle, Burton, King's Lynn, and Newark, we have a single list of names: the position is caught at one moment. At Canterbury, a series of rentals provides the basis for a comparative study of the city's population in the second half of the twelfth century. For Winchester, too, a sequence of lists makes comparative study possible from the last phase of the reign of Edward the Confessor to the first decade of the thirteenth century.[17] Lists do not provide actual figures for the number of householders involved, and we must be content with estimates. At Battle, there were 20 burgages in 1086; within thirty-five years that figure had increased to more than 100, a process which involved massive

---

[15] *DB*, I, 179, 181*v*; *VCH, Heref.*, I, 310, 320. The customs which William fitz Osbern gave Hereford were derived from Breteuil, the *caput* of his Norman honour. For a full discussion, see D. Walker, 'Hereford and the Laws of Breteuil', *Trans. Woolhope Nat. Field Club, Herefordshire*, XL (1972), 55-65.

[16] *DB*, I, 52, 219, 280; II, 116-18; *VCH, Hants.*, I (1900), 516; *VCH, Northants.*, I (1902), 301; *VCH, Notts.*, I (1906), 247; *VCH, Norfolk*, II (1906), 36, 46-7. H. C. Darby acknowledged the confusion in the Domesday account of Norwich and accepted the figure of 160: *Domesday Geography of Eastern England* (1957), pp. 139-40. The precise figures for 1087 are 41 Frenchmen as burgesses, with 83 burgesses/burgages belonging to other Norman magnates.

[17] Bury St. Edmunds: D. C. Douglas, *Feudal Documents from the Abbey of Bury St. Edmunds* (British Academy, Records of the Social and Economic History of England and Wales, VIII, 1931), pp. 25-44.
Battle: C. Clark, 'An Anthroponymist looks at an Anglo-Norman New Town', *Battle Conference II, 1979* (1980), pp. 21-41.
Burton: C. G. O. Bridgeman, 'The Burton Abbey twelfth-century surveys', *William Salt Society* (1916), pp. 209-310.
King's Lynn: *Pipe Roll, 13 Henry II* (PRS, XI, 1889), pp. 20-31; D. M. Owen, 'Bishop's Lynn: the first century of a new town?', *Battle Conference II, 1979*, pp. 141-53, and especially pp. 151-2.
Newark: M. W. Barley *et al.* (eds.), *Documents relating to the Manor and Soke of Newark on Trent* (Thoroton Soc., Records Ser., XVI, 1956).
Canterbury: W. Urry, *Canterbury under the Angevin Kings* (1967); the section on pp. 221-382 covers the period 1153-1206. The Canterbury lists have an added refinement: if an individual holds a number of tenements the lists indicate the house where he actually lived.
Winchester: Biddle, *Winchester in the Early Middle Ages*, pp. 1-141 (for the surveys) and 143-229 (for the discussion of personal names).

immigration. The town's burgesses were mostly English, many of them natives of East Sussex, men using the local dialect. Already by 1110, French influence was strong and an analysis of the personal names has suggested that 'a French presence in the background was substantial'. A feature, prominent in larger towns, was also discernible at Battle: French forms were appearing in by-names given to men with English Christian names.[18]

At Winchester, where the number of householders was much larger, material from three surveys has survived together with a later, ancillary document; the earliest post-conquest survey, which dates from about 1110, was based on a survey from the last decade of the reign of Edward the Confessor, probably from 1057, and covered 251 tenements on the king's fief in the city. In 1148, a survey was carried out for the bishop of Winchester which covered a total of 1,078 holdings. Then, in 1207, 389 Winchester men stood as pledges for the sheriff, and the names of 383 of these have been preserved. From these lists, Olof von Feilitzen could establish the percentages of names of different provenance, and they point to a steady increase in continental forms and influence as the twelfth century advanced. There is not sufficient material to attempt any estimate for the country as a whole, and the rate at which continental influences, and in particular French influences, affected English towns cannot be determined.[19] The steady increase observable at Winchester may have been typical of boroughs in the southern part of the kingdom, and was presumably clear but less marked in midland towns. It appears that a town population recruited substantially from the local area was supplemented by immigration from further afield in England and from northern France. When evidence becomes more plentiful in the thirteenth and fourteenth centuries, it can be seen that urban populations could not be maintained without regular recruitment from outside the borough. Many English boroughs were then reinforced by immigration from a confined local area.[20]

The inferences to be drawn from this are clear to see. The population of English towns after the Norman conquest remained largely English in stock. The social depression of English families, so characteristic of rural society, was not a feature of urban society. In some centres French settlement was intensive, and in larger cities, or perhaps in towns associated with a church or lordship in northern France, there may have been a continuing influx of French settlers. Over much of the country initial French immigration into towns was limited and the population was predominantly native. The habit, widely adopted by English urban families, of giving their children French names in place of Old English names, is enough to frustrate any attempt to measure immigration from France or from other French settlements in England. Certainly, French influence was strong, much stronger than small numbers might warrant. Borough communities found their own unity. Distinctive customs, established on a racial basis, were not maintained for their original purpose, though, as with the customs which prevailed at Hereford, they might be seen to have great advantage for the town community as a whole.

---

[18] Clark, *Battle Conference II, 1979*, pp. 28, 30.

[19] Biddle, *Winchester in the Early Middle Ages*, pp. 184-5, 188, and for a map showing the provenance of personal names, p. 197 fig. 3.

[20] Cf. S. Reynolds, *An Introduction to the History of English Medieval Towns* (1977), pp. 70, 72.

Within their own borough, English burgesses had wealth, status and power. When, in the thirteenth century, borough records become more plentiful, both English and French names may be found among the élites of town society, but the standing of these leading figures no longer had anything to do with race.

The significant feature, again, is that until the end of the thirteenth century, burgesses did not walk in the corridors of power of the English state. Their influence and authority lay in local affairs. Political influence came late. Even in a local setting, boroughs did not fit easily into a feudal order. Both in a rural and in an urban setting, we are dealing with a paradox familiar enough in the aftermath of conquest: a new élite sets the fashions and holds the positions of power, while survivors of an older society adopt the fashions but rarely manage to enter the charmed circle of the élite. In a rural context, that was true both in a national and a local setting; in an urban context, local power and local influence were often in English hands, but had no effect on a national scale.

When, if at all, does the subordinated community become articulate and give expression to the continuity of its own existence? Borough customs, with their long echoes of the past, are a clear expression of the corporate community of the borough and often provide evidence of survival. The particular characteristics of a substantial area may survive and find expression over a considerable period of time. Sir Frank Stenton's analysis of the twelfth-century charters of the Danelaw is a classic study. Place-names, personal names, and the survival of social and legal elements long after the Norman conquest establish the survival of a society with strong Scandinavian characteristics and which, as Sir Frank put it, 'presented in the early Angevin age distinctive features of the highest interest'. [21] But an articulate individual who may speak of, or for, the subordinated elements in society is rare to find.

In that setting, Aelred of Rievaulx deserves the closest attention. Aelred was English through and through: Jocelin of Furness called him 'a man of fine old English stock'. [22] Yet, while he was still a layman, he was accepted as a man of consequence. He came from a dynasty of priests closely associated with the shrine of St. Cuthbert at Durham and with a church on the remote *limites* of the English kingdom at Hexham. When the family acquired Hexham, sometime between 1023 and 1036, the church was a source of income, with son succeeding father as priest. Unexpectedly, the church became a place of refuge for them after the

---

[21] F. M. Stenton, *Documents Illustrative of the Social and Economic History of the Danelaw* (British Academy, Records of the Social and Economic History of England and Wales, V, 1920). Stenton returned to the theme in later years and made a number of contributions to the growing literature on this topic, notably in 'The Free Peasantry of the Northern Danelaw', *Bulletin de la Société royale des Lettres de Lund* (1925-6) (reprinted Oxford, 1969); 'The Danes in England', *Proc. British Academy*, XIII (1927), 203-46, and 'The Historical Bearing of Place-Name Studies: the Danish Settlement of Eastern England', *Trans. R. Hist. S.*, 4th ser., XXIV (1942), 1-24. The last two papers are reprinted in *Preparatory to Anglo-Saxon England*, pp. 136-65, 298-313.

[22] In 1921, F. M. Powicke drew a warm and attractive portrait of Aelred in a paper, 'Ailred of Rievaulx and his biographer', in *Bull. John Rylands Library*, VI (1921), 310-51. He used this as a basis for his introduction to his edition of *The Life of Ailred of Rievaulx* (1950), where his historical summary is to be found on pp. xxxiii-lxviii. His survey has been modified, but it established the approach to Aelred's life which historians have taken for some sixty years. Jocelin's comment is quoted on p. xxxiii. More recently, A. Squire has produced a fresh study, *Aelred of Rievaulx* (1969).

Norman conquest. Bishop William of St. Carilef established a community of monks in the cathedral church of Durham in 1083, and Aelred's grandfather, Eilaf, was one of the dispossessed seculars who preferred to disperse rather than be absorbed into the new monastic community. He retired to Hexham, and after the security of life at Durham the future must have seemed bleak. The church was in ruins, and for two years, as it was said, Eilaf could only support his family by hunting and fowling. No doubt the account was heightened for dramatic effect, but even allowing for some licence, life must have seemed very primitive. The family suffered the common fate of so many of their compatriots. Hexham had been drawn into the orbit of the archbishop of York, Thomas of Bayeux, who attached it to a prebend in his cathedral. Eilaf could no longer count on the principal revenues of his church and became a subordinate figure in his own patrimony. Early in the twelfth century, a community of canons was established at Hexham and Aelred's father, another Eilaf, now head of the dynasty, was responsible for housing them. He was not easily reconciled to the change in his family's fortunes. Only on his deathbed, in 1138, did he acknowledge in full the loss of his claim to Hexham for himself and for his sons. The Norman conquest had reduced his family in standing and in wealth and, however long delayed the impact, the final consequence was effectively disinheritance.

In the south there would have been little chance of recovery, but in the north, for all its wildness, resilience could bring dividends and recovery was possible. Norman settlement was less intensive and royal supervision was, at best, sporadic. In 140 years the ruling monarch visited Yorkshire and the north-east only on some twenty occasions. Government by deputy was not always efficient, until in the last few decades of the twelfth century royal influence was made stronger through the work of royal justices itinerant. Even more significant were the close links between Northumbria and the Scottish Lowlands.[23] In the ninth century, Anglian expansion had extended English cultural influences as far as the Firth of Forth, and Lothian remained in English hands. By the middle of the tenth century, a Scottish king had regained control of Lothian, perhaps by stages, with the recovery of Edinburgh in the 950s as one achievement, and with recognition by the English king, Edgar, in 973 as another substantial achievement. English cultural influences remained strong, despite the fact that political links had been broken. English stock, English language, and English influence played an important part in the process by which the Scottish kingdom was refashioned in the late-eleventh and early-twelfth centuries. Norman settlers in northern England found welcome opportunities of extending their landed interests into Lowland Scotland. Balliol and Brus were by no means the only names to become familiar in a Scottish setting under the patronage of Malcolm Canmore and his English wife, Margaret. Percy and fitz John might be barons of the English king in northern England; they were also heavily committed to the Scottish crown, and their dual allegiance could make for intense clashes of

[23] What follows may be seen in depth, though with different interpretations of evidence on major issues, in G. W. S. Barrow, *The Kingdom of the Scots* (1973), and *The Anglo-Norman Era in Scottish History* (1980), and in A. A. M. Duncan, *Scotland: the Making of the Kingdom* (1975), pp. 101-73. For northern England, see W. E. Kapelle, *The Norman Conquest of the North* (1979).

loyalty, as it did in the savage Scottish invasion of the north in 1138. The Scottish kings of the twelfth century knew what it was to be guests and hostages at the court of the Norman kings of England, and so to be pawns in the diplomatic relationship between the two kingdoms. On the credit side, they could claim that they had acquired in the process an understanding of the Anglo-Norman state, a concept of feudal kingship, and at least a veneer of French culture. In their hands, the Celtic kingdom of Scotland, with its essentially Celtic kingship, was remodelled to become a kingdom and a monarchy of the contemporary European type.

In his early 'teens Aelred found a patron in the Scottish king, David I, and was taken into the royal household. We do not know the occasion nor the means by which it was brought about. Writing in the mid-1150s, Aelred suggested that he had known David's son, Henry, not merely in adolescence but from the cradle, and it has been assumed that the priestly family at Hexham was already well-known in David's circle before Aelred entered the king's service.[24] In the royal household, the boy could grow up in a setting where English lineage and English culture were held in respect. To the basic, but limited, education which he had received from his English kinsmen, Aelred could now add the French culture available at the Scottish court. He was brought up with David's son, Earl Henry, and David's step-son, Waltheof, later to be a leading figure in the monastic life of northern England and, as abbot of Melrose, a powerful influence in the Scottish church. Aelred could take for granted skills, and some graces, acquired by the young men of the court. He himself was an official in the king's household; his function has perhaps been exaggerated in the light of his later distinction and by analogy with the power of household officers in England. He himself spoke of his work in more modest and domestic terms. Still, in his mid-twenties he was a person of standing with a future of considerable promise in the Scottish royal administration.

In 1134, Aelred was sent to York as an emissary of the Scottish king, and we are presented with an intriguing picture, rare in the literary record if not in fact. This young Englishman was entertained as a person of consequence by a leading Norman magnate, Walter d'Espec, lord of Helmsley castle.[25] Their encounter was remembered for its aftermath. Aelred was taken by his host to see the Cistercian settlement at Rievaulx, newly established by Walter d'Espec. They returned to the castle and talked far into the night. Next day, Aelred set out for Scotland, turned aside for a second visit to Rievaulx, and stayed there. As a monk, and later as abbot, he came to know Walter d'Espec closely, and a strong bond of sympathy and admiration seems to have been established between them. An Englishman who found in Scotland the opportunity to acquire something of the education and attitudes of a French ruling class could be accepted by an Anglo-Norman magnate. Perhaps it was only in the fluid conditions of the northern marchland that such social flexibility was possible. Ease of movement

---

[24] Powicke, *Ailred*, p. xxxv. Powicke overestimated the standing and influence of Aelred's grandfather, Eilaf, in northern society.

[25] Powicke, *Ailred*, pp. 12-16. For Walter d'Espec, see C. T. Clay (ed.), *Early Yorkshire Charters*, X (1955), 143-4.

across the Anglo-Scottish border, the interaction of a number of traditions, a changing pattern of loyalties, and the concentration of political and military power in the hands of a small number of Norman magnates: these created the conditions for acculturation and acceptance. Further south, the clash between two traditions marked by racial dominance and racial subordination could not provide similar fertile ground. Personal and political loyalties were more sharply defined, the distinction between race and privilege was more clearly drawn, and magnates of English stock had long since been identified as unreliable and unwilling to adapt to new conditions.

In maturity, Aelred became a monk and a scholar, and new loyalties made demands upon him, but the racial and cultural elements which contributed to his make-up remained powerful factors.[26] In 1138, the Scots invaded northern England and their campaign was marked by brutality and savagery, most of it ascribed to the wild men of Galloway. Some twenty years later, Aelred wrote an account of that invasion and of the defeat of the Scots at the battle of the Standard at Northallerton. It is written with great sensitivity.[27] The invaders are commanded by King David and his son, Henry, and Aelred will not revile his old companions. He gives a substantial part in the story to Walter d'Espec, whom he presents as a brave and wise old man, steeped in the lore of the Normans, and in a long speech which he puts into Walter's mouth he lays out very clearly the devastating effects of the Scottish incursions. He pulls no punches and makes no attempt to disguise the horrors of the story. Robert Brus, speaking as one of the defenders of the north and yet as one who had given his allegiance to the Scottish king, argued vigorously with David to persuade him to withdraw. Leading figures in Northumbria abandoned their English loyalty and went over to the Scots. These themes of Aelred's narrative are the themes of Aelred's life. He deals with them honestly but sympathetically. He will not provide a cover-up for the Scottish forces, nor will he fall back on vituperation. If he had received kindness from Walter d'Espec, he repaid it with admiration. His account of the battle of the Standard is an exercise in balance and moderation. These qualities came from within Aelred himself. The key to his careful analysis is his recognition, made explicit elsewhere, that northern England is not alien territory to be invaded by the Scots; rather, it is territory to which David has a rightful claim, and when the Scots appear in the north they are engaged in domestic politics. Yet, at the same time, Normans are not intruders.[28] Northern society and northern politics cannot be analysed in the sharp contrasts of black and white.

---

[26] After an early draft of this essay had been delivered as a seminar paper, R. Ransford's paper, 'A Kind of Noah's Ark: Aelred of Rievaulx and National Identity', appeared in *Religion and National Identity: Studies in Church History*, XVIII (1982), 137-46. We have been working in part along parallel lines, developing leading ideas in Powicke's work on Aelred.

[27] R. Howlett (ed.), *Chronicles of the Reigns of Stephen, Henry II, and Richard I* (RS, III, 1886), pp. 181-99. His account may be set against the strong prose of Richard of Hexham, who had no sympathy for the Scots: ibid., pp. 139-78, and *EHD*, II, 339-47. For R. Ransford's comments on Aelred's account of the battle, *Religion and National Identity*, pp. 138-40.

[28] This follows Powicke's reconstruction very closely: *Ailred*, p. xlii.

Aelred was not a man to leave loose ends, however complex the issues. Trusted and secure, he could analyse these issues with the confidence that he himself had been accepted and successful both as a secular figure and as a monastic leader. He sought to express in writing the integration he had found in practice, and he achieved this by a clear but simple line of thought: he moved from personal loyalty to family connection; that led him to his English past and to his Christian convictions. The death of King David in 1153 left him with a deep sense of loss. In England, the political uncertainties of the reign of Stephen appeared to be moving towards stability with the acceptance of the young Henry fitz Empress as Stephen's successor. Aelred brought both themes together in a letter addressed to the young Henry.[29] He could extol David in a lament rather than a careful piece of historical writing; he could find the promise of Henry's future in the prince's ancestry. Henry was 'the glory of Anjou, the guardian of Normandy, the hope of England', and in a less precise phrase he is 'the ornament of Aquitaine'. The positive roles which he could play in Anjou, Normandy and England, are due to his inheritance from his mother, the empress. In justification of this claim, Aelred produces a genealogy showing Matilda to be the product of a long and honourable Anglo-Saxon lineage. Then, in a series of brief sketches he demonstrates the quality of her forbears. King Alfred and Edmund Ironside are the great heroic figures in his story. Edmund has the key role since from his line there would descend St. Margaret of Scotland, her daughter, Matilda, wife of Henry I, and so the empress herself. Edward the Confessor appears as something of an intrusion; his importance lay in the fact that he had recalled Edmund Ironside's heirs to England. William the Conqueror was given scant notice. The narrative has been described, quite accurately, as 'redolent with pride in Englishness'.[30] The interesting feature about it is that there is no overt recognition of race or culture; Englishness is incidental. Aelred's concern was with personal achievements, with bravery, and with the virtues of Christian kingship. All these were now the inheritance of the young Henry, but for Aelred, they do not derive from his Norman or his Angevin ancestry.

In 1163, Aelred moved a stage closer to integration. Under the patronage of Henry II, the body of Edward the Confessor was then housed in a new shrine. A king, wholly French in outlook, who received knighthood at the hands of King David of Scotland, was honouring an English predecessor. Laurence, abbot of Westminster, had connections with Durham. He commissioned a new *Life* of the Confessor for the occasion, and he invited Aelred to write it.[31] The perfunctory treatment which Aelred had so recently given King Edward in his survey of Henry's English legacy suggests that, at this stage, he had much to learn about the Confessor. His dependence on the *Life* of the Confessor by Osbert of Clare shows clearly how he filled the gaps in his own knowledge. Yet even with this routine commission, the translation of the Confessor's remains brought together many of the strands in Aelred's life. He himself was clearly aware of the fact, and

---

[29] Roger Twysden printed the text in 1652 in his *Historiae Anglicanae Scriptores X*, cols. 347-70.

[30] Ransford, *Religion and National Identity*, p. 140.

[31] Powicke, *Ailred*, pp. xlvii-xlviii.

he saw Henry II as the key figure in the whole structure. Henry was the fulfilment of Edward the Confessor's dying prophecy: the old stock was restored, and the kingdom could once again flourish. From his father and mother Henry had inherited his throne and his noble blood. 'We rejoice in him', he wrote, 'as the cornerstone, as it might be, bringing together the walls of the English and Norman races.'[32] It was a well-turned compliment, and on the surface it might be no more than flattery. But in the setting of Aelred's concept of historical development, the agent of reconciliation could only fulfill his destiny because of his English blood and his debt to the English past. Aelred wanted explanations. There was nothing crude about him, and the explanations must be subtle, sensitive and all-embracing.

The Anglo-Welsh frontier, like the Anglo-Scottish border, was an area of conflicting loyalties. The long history of Norman settlement in the Welsh frontier zone and in Wales itself generated many of the problems with which Aelred was concerned. But there was little to soften the impact of the clash between Norman and Welsh.[33] Earlier contact between Welsh princes and the lords of Mercia had produced a useful military alliance, with no indication of social or political harmony. There had been conquest and reconquest on a limited scale along the border, and place-names point to a linguistic zone along the linear frontier; but there is little sign of mutual toleration or of the assimilation of cultures.[34] By contrast, Norman infiltration into Wales saw the displacement of Welsh princely dynasties, the establishment of Norman lordships from Gwent to Dyfed, along the mid-Wales frontier, and over long stretches of the coastal areas of north Wales. The clash of race and culture now occurred on a scale which was massive by comparison with pre-conquest experience. In the late-eleventh century and the twelfth century, the problems of this much enlarged frontier zone were sharply defined in terms of Norman and Welsh. English settlement and, in parts of Dyfed and Ceredigion, Flemish settlement, were small in scale and localised, with the long-term influence of these cultural enclaves still to be made apparent.[35] Castles formed the nuclei of towns which were overwhelmingly Anglo-Norman in population and alignment. Sparse though the evidence may be, it is clear that these garrison towns provided no setting for a Welsh enclave. One of the great nurseries of cultural survival in England was not to be matched in Wales.[36] Other

[32] Twysden, *Scriptores X*, 369; cited in Powicke, *Ailred*, p. xlvii, n. 2, and Ransford, *Religion and National Identity*, p. 143.

[33] This can be seen in the hostile attitudes of Gruffydd ap Rhydderch of Deheubarth and Gruffydd ap Llywelyn of Gwynedd in the middle decades of the eleventh century, and in the language of the *Brut y Tywysogyon*, though that owes something to the sense of conflict and hostility which marked the thirteenth century. See D. Walker, 'A Note on Gruffydd ap Llywelyn (1039-1063)', *Welsh History Rev.*, I (1960), 83-94, and *The Norman Conquerors* (1977), pp. 13-19, 50-67.

[34] These features are most effectively to be discerned in D. Sylvester's *The Rural Landscape of the Welsh Borderland* (1969).

[35] I. W. Rowlands, 'The Making of the March: aspects of the Norman settlement in Dyfed', *Battle Conference III, 1980* (1981), pp. 142-58.

[36] See H. Carter, *The Towns of Wales* (1966); R. A. Griffiths (ed.), *The Boroughs of Medieval Wales* (1978), and especially papers on three south Wales towns, R. R. Davies, 'Brecon', pp. 47-70, D. Walker, 'Cardiff', pp. 103-28, and R. F. Walker, 'Tenby', pp. 289-320. Important general claims are made in the editor's introduction (pp. 1-17) and in his essay on Carmarthen, pp. 131-63.

institutions, strong in those parts of Wales which were not affected by Norman invasion, or from which the Normans had been ousted, remained as indications and agents of cultural survival. Genealogy preserved in family and folk memory a strong sense of continuity divorced, as it was, from the present misfortunes of particular dynasties. Law and custom were enshrined in local practice. In the March, they were subjected to a process of erosion, especially in the thirteenth century, while in north Wales more radical changes were introduced by royal enactment after the Edwardian conquest. The task of interpreting the surviving texts and of drawing out of them the social and political realities of the Welsh kingdoms is a continuing process comparable to the rediscovery of Scandinavian elements in Anglo-Saxon society. Language remained the principal means of identifying and preserving Welsh culture, whether in *Wallia Pura* or in the March.

Welsh writers who might have provided an informed reaction to Norman infiltration were active early in the long history of the March. At St. David's, Rhigyfarch maintained the scholarly traditions of Bishop Sulien, but he looked back at a distant past and produced a *Life* of St. David.[37] At Llancarfan, a generation later, another group of scholarly clerics shared his interest in a remote past. How far were the virtues which they identified and admired in the early saints of Wales a reflection of what they sensed to be missing in their own community, living as it did under the pressure of battle and conquest? At a later stage, when men could look back at the recent past and informed assessment was possible, the significant literary figures were men of mixed blood. They had not only to record and report the condition of Wales and its frontier, but to resolve within themselves the tensions created by their own ancestry. Orderic Vitalis spent his boyhood near Shrewsbury until, at the age of ten, he was suddenly removed from his familiar surroundings and taken off to Normandy, dedicated to the monastic life at St. Evroul. There he was given his French name, Vital, and there, over nearly sixty years, he came to terms with the emotional trauma caused by that early separation and exile. He found much to admire in the Normans among whom he spent his adult life, and he found contentment especially in his historical studies. The memory of his childhood home always aroused deep emotion within him, and when he wrote the history of the Welsh border he brought to the task a strong sense of involvement.[38] Proud though he might be of the Normans and their achievements, he could feel and express something of the agony of conquest for those who were defeated. Exile meant that, for Orderic, this resolution of an emotional conflict within himself was something of an academic exercise, for he was never involved in the practical problems of a multi-racial society.

In terms of involvement and ability, who better to set against Aelred of Rievaulx than Gerald of Wales? Who could pose in more acute form the problems

---

[37] J. W. James (ed.), *Rhigyfarch's Life of St. David* (1967); G. Williams, 'The tradition of St. David in Wales', in O. W. Jones and D. Walker (eds.), *Links with the Past* (1974), pp. 1-20, esp. pp. 4-9, reprinted in *Religion, Language and Nationality in Wales* (1979), pp. 109-26, esp. pp. 112-15.

[38] For his own background, Orderic Vitalis, II, xiii-xvi; III (1972), 6-8, 146, 150; IV, xxii-xxiv; VI (1978), 550-6. The most extensive of his notices of Welsh affairs covers the career of Robert of Rhuddlan, IV, xxxiv-xxxviii, 135-47, but he has much to say about such figures as William fitz Osbern and Hugh d'Avranches.

of loyalty and the tensions of mixed race?[39] He was highly intelligent, clear-sighted and articulate. He was proud to be a man sprung from two races, proud to be a member of a Norman marcher family, and happy that the ruling prince of south Wales should claim him as a kinsman. Gerald was, first and foremost, a scholar. That meant long training and frequent withdrawal from practical affairs to concentrate on the particular work in hand. He was a prolific writer, capable of intensive and sustained study. He was a shrewd observer, never at a loss for lucid and sharp comment. At the same time, he was deeply involved in the ecclesiastical politics of south Wales for more than a quarter of a century. There were critical occasions when he could not escape from involvement, at the point of an election to St. David's after the death of Bishop David fitz Gerald in 1176, or again when Bishop Peter de Leia died in 1198. As commissary for Peter de Leia after 1179 and, above all, as bishop-elect from 1198, he had a continuing role to play in the diocese. His serious concern for the administration of his archdeaconry of Brecon reinforced this element of sustained involvement. He was a curial figure, with some hope of a career in royal administration. Family connections in Wales and Ireland made him well-informed about major political issues in these areas, and family pride was a powerful factor in his make-up. All this imposed upon his life an episodic pattern, marked by waves of intensity, involvement, and withdrawal. Hence the much debated questions: did he have Welsh interests and Welsh ambitions? did he sustain or abandon them? what were his loyalties? Voluble as Gerald was, he cannot be regarded as the best witness to face such a cross-examination. Immersed in conflict, he could be scathing about the English king and English administrators.[40] In old age, when he showed a strong sense of disappointment at a career which had produced more frustration than success, he might hint at ambitions in England and hopes of an English see rather than a Welsh diocese.[41] A family quarrel embittered even his association with the archdeaconry of Brecon.[42] Reflecting the attitudes of Anglo-Norman marcher

[39] The modern literature on Gerald grows steadily. M. Richter's views are to be found mainly in *Giraldus Cambrensis: The Growth of the Welsh Nation,* published originally in the *National Library of Wales Journal,* XVI and XVII, and issued in book form in 1972, and in his 'Gerald of Wales: A Reassessment on the 750th Anniversary of his Death', *Traditio,* XXIX (1973), 379-90. In his last book, issued in 1978, L. Thorpe presented a vivid picture of Gerald by way of introduction to his translation of *The Journey Through Wales/The Description of Wales* (Penguin Classics). R. Bartlett, *Gerald of Wales, 1146-1223* (1982), is a biographical study especially useful for Gerald's scholarly work. The introduction to the edition of Gerald's *Expugnatio Hibernica,* ed. A. B. Scott and F. X. Martin (Royal Irish Academy, 1978), is very perceptive. B. F. Roberts has contributed a brief study, *Gerald of Wales* (Writers of Wales Ser., 1982). For my own views, see 'Gerald of Wales, Archdeacon of Brecon', *Links with the Past,* pp. 67-88; 'Gerald of Wales: a Review of Recent Work', *Journal of the Historical Society of the Church in Wales,* XXIV (1972), 13-26, and 'Gerald of Wales', *Brycheiniog,* XVIII (1979), 60-70, where the emphasis is placed chiefly on his pastoral work in the archdeaconry of Brecon.

[40] He was critical of Henry II, especially in his *De Principis Instructione*; for a discussion, see Bartlett, pp. 69-100. He also made a dangerous enemy of Hubert Walter, archbishop of Canterbury, in the course of his attempts to gain favourable judgment from the papal curia in the causes relating to St. David's.

[41] There is a passing reference in *Invectiones*; see the edition by W. S. Davies, *Y Cymmrodor,* XXX (1920), 213. Too much is made to hang on this very slender thread: Richter, *Giraldus Cambrensis,* pp. 81, 90; Bartlett, pp. 48, 58, 61, 212.

[42] For this unhappy episode, see M. Richter, Y. Lefèvre and R. B. C. Huygens (eds.), *Speculum Duorum* (1974).

society, he might identify the Welsh as the great problem of security in the March, and see firm control as the answer to the fear of Welsh resurgence.[43] As archdeacon, he had no illusions as to the poor quality of the Welsh clergy with whom he had to deal.[44] Writing as a scholar, and seeking some detachment from the subject of his discourse, he could look at the Welsh from the standpoint of an outsider, in much the same way as he could look at the Irish. View his works as a whole and they can produce discordancies and discrepancies. That was the price to be paid for his many-sided career and for the fact that he was a representative of two races and two traditions.

Gerald's zeal for St. David's was mingled inextricably with personal ambition to hold the see, though it must be said that he jeopardised his own chances of success in the greater interests of the diocese. He feared, and reported, that Henry II would not have a Welshman—and especially so able a Welshman as himself—as bishop in west Wales. He asserted that his Welsh blood had cost him that preferment.[45] When Baldwin of Canterbury visited Wales, Gerald appeared in his company less as a Welsh figure than as one of the Anglo-Norman establishment. He himself had no doubt that his marcher kin in Ireland were marked with a double brand: to the English they were Irish; to the Irish they were English. Born and bred in the March, he felt himself to be in a similar position. He could identify marcher stock as, peculiarly, a race nourished in the March of Wales.[46] As one of that marcher breed, with the added ingredient of Welsh ancestry, could he—to use one of his favourite metaphors—hold up a mirror to Welsh society?

Certainly, his knowledge of Wales was coloured by his marcher background. His Welsh kinsmen were affected by close and continuous association with Anglo-Norman lords and with the English crown. They adapted their traditional methods of defence in an attempt to match the strength of Norman castles. The weaknesses of their military tactics could be recognised by Gerald himself or, later, by the compiler of the *Brut y Tywysogyon*: if the first assault succeeded, all was well; if it did not, the Welsh lacked the capacity to regroup and mount sustained attacks on a disciplined enemy. They could grow skilful in alliance and use diplomacy to good advantage. They do not reflect in every detail their

---

[43] This is certainly the tone of the latter part of his *Description of Wales*. He creates some problems by borrowing substantially from a parallel section in the *Expugnatio Hibernica*. Gerald adds to his text the disparaging phrase 'like all barbarous people' to describe the Welsh. This was a section of the *Description* which he did not find satisfactory. In his first version Gerald suggested recolonizing Wales or turning it into a game-preserve. Alien colonists in Dyfed and Ceredigion may have worked on a small scale, and Gerald was familiar with the use which the Norman lords of Brecknock made of the Great Forest of Brecknock for hunting. But it looks as if Gerald did not consider either remedy as a serious prospect for the country as a whole. It was omitted in his second recension, and the extensive reliance on his comments in *Expugnatio Hibernica* may suggest that he had not formed any definitive opinion on how best to deal with Wales and the Welsh. See Thorpe, *Journey/Description*, pp. 271, 273, 622; *Expugnatio Hibernica*, pp. xxvi-xxvii, xxxi, 230; and the text as edited by J. Dimock in *Opera*, VI (RS, 1868), 223.

[44] J. S. Brewer (ed.), 'Gemma Ecclesiastica' in *Opera*, II (RS, 1862); Bartlett, pp. 29-31; Walker, *Brycheiniog*, pp. 68-9.

[45] J. S. Brewer (ed.), 'De Rebus a Se Gestis' in *Opera*, I (RS, 1861), 43; the objection was generalised in *idem*, 'De Jure et Statu Menevensis Ecclesiae' in *Opera*, III (RS, 1863), 340-1.

[46] *Expugnatio Hibernica*, pp. xx, 45, 247.

Welsh counterparts in the middle decades of the eleventh century. Well aware of the power of the princes of Deheubarth, Gerald had less insight into the role of the Welsh rulers in the north. He identified towns as a product of conquest, but he underestimated the importance of trade and markets in Wales, and of nascent centres where some of the functions of an urban society were already being carried out. Underestimation and understatement may help to explain the contrast between political power in Wales as Gerald saw it and the development of princely power in Wales during the thirteenth century. Gerald is credited with identifying in advance the methods by which Edward I would one day conquer independent Wales. It is a fair criticism that he saw much less clearly the nature of the principality which Edward would overrun.

Unlike Aelred, Gerald did not have the means of achieving integration either in his life or in his writings. Inner tranquillity was beyond his experience. He could not match Aelred's personal successes, nor his unifying insight into the past. He could comment on current affairs, on family history, and on the recent past. But his great strength lay in his gifts as an observer of place and people. His topographical studies of Ireland and Wales have properly been identified as 'original attempts at topographical and ethnographical writing' which, 'in structure, scope, and detail, represented new departures'.[47]

Is not that the point at which the telling anecdote has a significant role to play? It may highlight a trait not easily described in abstract terms. It may, by analogy, indicate a change of key or tempo or mood in music. Wulfstan of Worcester recognised the inevitable soon after the death of King Harold at Senlac in 1066 and threw in his lot with William the Conqueror. For the last thirty years of his life he was a firm and active supporter of the Norman régime. Regular contact with the Norman sheriff and other Norman officials was a normal part of his life. His clash with Urse d'Abetot marked the point where irritation boiled over into anger, and Wulfstan, never one to mince words, cursed his Norman neighbour. Aelred, urbane and scholarly, experienced in the world of politics and administration and then tried in the fire of monastic discipline, found the means of harmonising his role in a Normanised milieu with his English inheritance. When he used English for his cry of anguish as he was dying he was not taking refuge in a past which he had neglected or rejected in favour of new ways. There was a unity about his life and the manner of his death. When Gerald was teased for his limited Welsh (or lack of Welsh, as it may be), the incident pointed to a major defect in his cultural armoury. Yet, the dissonance so characteristic of Gerald's life is an essential part of his equipment as an observer and recorder of the Welsh scene. The society in which he lived did not make for racial harmony or cultural interchange. The discord and tension in his own life reflect the discords and tensions of Wales and the March. If Gerald can be said to hold up a mirror to Welsh society, we must understand the mirror as well as the image it presents or our view of the past will be sadly distorted.

---

[47] Bartlett, p. 178.

Law and National Identity in Thirteenth-Century Wales

R. R. DAVIES

EDIEVAL historians have, of late, rather looked askance at the concept of national identity. They have been anxious to distance themselves from the naïvetés and anachronisms of their nineteenth-century predecessors who, consciously or otherwise, imported the nationalist values and assumptions of their own day into the study of the medieval past. The most potent ties of loyalty and obligation in medieval society, so it is now insisted, were personal and local; they were expressed in the vocabulary of personal service, not in the abstractions of national sentiment. Even when medieval men themselves paraded their sense of belonging to a common race or nation, their sentiments should be distrusted as attempts to fabricate a racial or national identity which in fact hardly existed.[1]

Nowhere do these strictures apply more forcefully than to the study of medieval Wales. Here indeed appears to be a country where the necessary and sufficient conditions for the development of national identity were truly absent. Political authority here was fragmented, and that fragmentation was further compounded by the fissiparous consequences of the custom of partibility. Political ambition and military competition were essentially dynastic and familial. In such a society loyalties were bound to be intensely local and personal. National sentiment was a rare, and largely a literary, luxury; and national unity was more frequently than not the consequence of a temporary hegemony imposed by military might.

These observations, both general and particular, have a good measure of truth in them. Yet as so often with historical spring-cleaning, our anxiety to avoid the pitfalls of our predecessors can in itself lead to distortion. National sentiment *could* be important in medieval society; it could and did co-exist with a pattern of local loyalties and with a vocabulary of personal relationships.[2] Furthermore, the growth of a sense of national identity need not be matched by or conditional upon the development of the institutions of common state authority. It is the constitutionalist and centralist bias of English historiography which has persuaded us otherwise. Kings, it is true, channelled national sentiment and prejudice to their own ends and thereby fostered a heightened sense of national awareness, as the Welsh and the Scots found to their cost under Edward I, in

---

[1] For a recent example of this scepticism, see R. H. C. Davis, *The Normans and their Myth* (1976).

[2] Two interesting recent reviews of the problem are presented by B. Guenée, 'État et nation en France au Moyen Age', *Revue Historique,* 237 (1967), 17-31, and K.-F. Werner, 'Les nations et le sentiment national dans l'Europe mediévale', ibid., 244 (1970), 285-304.

whose reign 'nationalism was born'.[3] Likewise the experience of a common governance, a common law and, above all perhaps, common taxation served to accelerate the development of national self-awareness, whilst the vocabulary of national sentiment was enriched by the revival of classical notions of 'the common utility' and the 'public good'.[4] But countries and peoples which lack a common polity and the institutions of unitary governance are not thereby disqualified from developing a sense of national identity. For national identity, like class, is a matter of perception as much as of institutions. The institutions of centralised authority are by no means its only or most powerful focus. In medieval society, it could also manifest itself in an awareness of the common genealogical descent of a people, in a shared belief in a particular version of historical mythology and prophecy, in an emotional attachment to the geographical boundaries of a country, in a heightened awareness of the distinctiveness of a common language and of common customs, in the yearning for the prospect of unitary rule, in the articulation of a 'we—they' dichotomy to express the distinction between natives and aliens. By these tokens, the ingredients of a sense of national identity were present, albeit spasmodically and unevenly, in medieval Wales, as well as in medieval Scotland and Ireland.[5] 'The people of Snowdon assert', so ran a defiant statement in the desperate winter months of 1282, 'that even if their prince should give seisin of them to the king, they themselves would refuse to do homage to any foreigner, of whose language, customs and laws they were thoroughly ignorant.'[6] In its modest fashion that statement may be placed side by side with the Irish Remonstrance of 1317-18 and the Declaration of Arbroath of 1320 as among the most dignified statements of national identity in the medieval period.

The century prior to that statement had witnessed in Wales, as elsewhere, remarkably rapid strides in the cultivation of a national identity and in the articulation of a sentiment of patriotism. The political map of *pura Wallia* was considerably simplified: the lesser princely dynasties were, in greater or lesser measure, either absorbed into the greater principalities or acknowledged a client relationship towards them, while among the greater principalities themselves Gwynedd's pre-eminence, though often resented, was rarely effectively challenged during the thirteenth century. The treaty of Montgomery of 1267, whereby the English king formally acknowledged the right of the prince of Gwynedd and his heirs to the title of prince of Wales and which conceded to them feudal control over 'all the Welsh barons of Wales', was the coping-stone on this

---

[3] F. M. Powicke, *The Thirteenth Century* (Oxford, 1953), p. 528.

[4] This whole theme has recently been much illuminated by G. L. Harriss, *King, Parliament and Public Finance in Medieval England to 1369* (Oxford, 1975).

[5] For general reviews of the question of nationality in medieval Wales, see especially G. A. Williams, 'Twf Hanesyddol Cenedlaetholdeb Cymru', *Efrydiau Athronyddol*, 24 (1961), 18-30; J. B. Smith, 'Gwleidyddiaeth a Diwylliant Cenedl', ibid., 38 (1975), 55-74; and G. Williams, *Religion, Language and Nationality in Wales* (Cardiff, 1979), esp. ch. I and VI. G. W. S. Barrow has some valuable comments on the sense of nationhood in medieval Scotland in *The Anglo-Norman Era in Scottish History* (Oxford, 1980), esp. pp. 145-56, while for early-medieval Ireland, D. Ó Corráin, 'Nationality and Kingship in pre-Norman Ireland', *Nationality and the Pursuit of National Independence*, ed. T. W. Moody (Belfast, 1978), pp. 1-35, is of prime importance.

[6] C. T. Martin (ed.), *Registrum Epistolarum fratris Johannis Peckham* (henceforth *Reg. Ep. Peckham*) (R[olls] S[eries], 1882-5), II, 471. For Llywelyn's use of the phrase 'nostra nacio' to refer to Wales, see ibid., II, 437.

remarkable process of the political unification of native Wales. That unification was more than a matter of political and military hegemony. It was in its turn grounded upon and accompanied by a growing awareness, and a deliberate cultivation, of some of the emblems of national identity, such as language, customs and geographical boundaries. When Gwenwynwyn of Powys was said in 1198 to have launched a campaign 'to restore to the Welsh their ancient liberty and their ancient proprietary rights and their bounds', or when Llywelyn ab Iorwerth of Gwynedd could appeal in 1220 for 'justice and equity appropriate to the status of Wales' (*statum Wallie*), we are given a glimpse of the vocabulary of national pride in the service of princely ambition.[7] Within Wales itself, the lines of racial division between Welsh and English (as the settler population was now increasingly indifferently called) were more clearly and consciously drawn, while the conflicts between English kings and Welsh princes were increasingly expressed in racial or national as well as in feudal or dynastic terms. It was, for example, the proclaimed intention of the treaty of Montgomery in 1267 to bring an end to 'the war and discord . . . between the English and the Welsh'.[8] The growing references in the documentation of the period to Wales (*Wallia*) as the focus of national sentiment and as the appropriate unit for political ambition are a further reflection of this increasing awareness of national identity.[9]

In the armoury of national identity, law occupied a prominent position.[10] This is hardly surprising. The twelfth and thirteenth centuries witnessed remarkable strides in the field of law: customary laws were systematized and codified; the judicial powers of kings and princes were more clearly articulated and their scope greatly extended; the boundaries of competing jurisdictional powers and their relationship to each other were more closely defined. The consequences of these developments in terms of the articulation of national identity were truly momentous. The definition of law and of those subject to it served to draw the lines of national and racial division more sharply and precisely and to draw them in legal terms. Welshmen could now be increasingly distinguished from Englishmen by the law to which they were subject.[11] Furthermore, law, especially unitary law, quickly became a focus of national pride and identity.[12] It was seen as exemplifying the character and independence of a people; and its defence, therefore, became, as in Scotland, a central feature of the struggle for national independence.[13] By the same token the imposition of foreign law and custom was now regarded—in a way which was hardly so in the twelfth century—as the necessary consequence of military conquest and political domination. Thus, King

---

[7] T. Jones (ed.), *Brut y Tywysogyon or The Chronicle of the Princes. Red Book of Hergest Version* (henceforth *Brut, RBH version*) (Cardiff, 1955), p. 181; J. G. Edwards (ed.), *Calendar of Ancient Correspondence concerning Wales* (henceforth *Cal. Anc. Corr.*) (Cardiff, 1935), p. 9.

[8] J. G. Edwards (ed.), *Littere Wallie* (Cardiff, 1940), p. 1.

[9] I hope to return elsewhere to some of the issues here touched upon briefly.

[10] Cf. J. C. Holt's comments in *History*, LXIII (1978), 106.

[11] For an early (1241) example of a Welshman claiming that he did not know how to plead 'according to the custom of England', see *Curia Regis Rolls, 1237-42* (1979), no. 1493. For the issue in general in the later middle ages, see J. B. Smith, 'The Legal Position of Wales in the Middle Ages', in A. Harding (ed.), *Law-Making and Law-Makers in British History* (1980), pp. 21-53.

[12] R. C. van Caenegem, *The Birth of the English Common Law* (1973), ch. 4.

[13] G. W. S. Barrow, *Robert Bruce and the Community of the Realm of Scotland* (2nd ed., Edinburgh, 1976), p. 187.

John was held to have imposed the laws and customs of England on Ireland in 1210.[14] Likewise the English kings were believed by contemporary chroniclers to have imposed English laws and customs on Wales in the thirteenth century and thereby to have provided a pretext for Welsh rebellions.[15] Whether the charge is true or not is not material in the present context; what is significant is that contemporaries regarded the imposition of alien law and the defence of native custom as an important, indeed often the most important, pretext for revolt. Law had clearly come to occupy a crucial rôle in the articulation of national identity during the thirteenth century.

It is against this background that we can approach the question of Welsh law in the thirteenth century. At this stage three prefatory comments may be made about the nature of native Welsh law before we proceed to discuss its rôle in the political struggles of the period.[16] It was, in the first place, in origin not a prince-made law, issued by or in the name of a sovereign ruler and enforced by the machinery of state authority. Rather was it a customary law, a *Volksrecht*, an assemblage of legal lore transmitted largely by memory and arranged, glossed and expounded by a class of quasi-professional jurists. Secondly, the law-texts as they survive are very unlikely to contain a corpus of law that was current in its usage at any one given time. They contain material that is archaic, obsolete and possibly only half-understood; they often overlook some of the most significant social and governmental changes in contemporary Wales.[17] They are thereby a very inadequate mirror of contemporary society and even of contemporary legal usage. It is well to bear this in mind, since it was on the whole the general status and validity of Welsh law as an independent corpus of law, not the particular details of the law texts as we have them today, which became a central issue in the disputes with the king of England. Thirdly, the oldest surviving manuscripts of Welsh law were probably written in the thirteenth century, the very period at issue here.[18] Too much should certainly not be made of this coincidence (especially given the fortuitous survival of many Welsh medieval manuscripts); but it might at least prompt us to consider how far native law was deliberately cultivated in the campaign for political unity and national identity within Wales.

Law and legislation have always been powerful features of the ideology of authority. It was so in the middle ages, as kings and princes preened themselves as the givers and founts of law. The inspiration of written law, it has been justly remarked of the early-medieval period, was often 'ideological rather than practical in origin';[19] its purpose as often as not was to placard the authority of the prince. So in measure was it in thirteenth-century Wales. The law, it is true,

---

[14] A. J. Otway-Ruthven, *A History of Medieval Ireland* (2nd ed., London, 1980), pp. 81-2.

[15] See, for example, Matthew Paris, *Chronica Majora*, ed. H. R. Luard (RS, 1872-83), V, 639; *Annales Monastici*, ed. H. R. Luard (RS, 1864-69), II, 89; III, 200, 291.

[16] For a recent survey, see D. Jenkins, 'The Significance of the Law of Hywel', *Trans. Hon. Soc. Cymmrodorion*, 1977, pp. 54-76.

[17] T. Jones Pierce, *Medieval Welsh Society*, ed. J. B. Smith (Cardiff, 1972), pp. 353-7.

[18] Previous suggestions as to the dating of the earliest manuscripts of the Welsh laws have now to be revised in the light of the studies of D. Huws, 'Leges Howelda at Canterbury', *National Library of Wales Journal*, 19 (1976), 340-4; 20 (1977), 95, and *The Medieval Codex with reference to the Welsh Law Books* (Aberystwyth, 1980).

[19] P. Wormald, '*Lex Scripta* and *Verbum Regis*: Legislation and Germanic Kingship, from Euric to Cnut', in P. H. Sawyer and I. N. Wood (eds.), *Early Medieval Kingship* (Leeds, 1977), p. 125.

was a customary law; but the rôle that was ascribed in the texts to the legislative genius of Dyfnwal Moelmud[20] and then to the reforming skills of Hywel Dda (and in some measure of other Welsh princes)[21] could only redound to the glory of princely power, in the present as in the past. Hywel Dda's name in particular appears with increasing regularity in the thirteenth century; he was rapidly acquiring or having bestowed upon him the reputation of a Solon or an Edward the Confessor. Likewise, the premier place given in most of the texts to the law of the king's court, the emphasis placed on 'the dignity of the king' and the position of the queen and members of the royal *familia,* and the *dicta* which proclaim that no land ought to be without a king or that ownerless property reverts to the king betoken the strong 'royalist' flavour of the law-texts as they were committed to writing in the thirteenth century.[22] It is also clear—without necessarily accepting the evidence submitted to the royal inquiry of 1281 into Welsh law at its face value—that the princes, more especially the princes of Gwynedd, had arrogated to themselves the claim to correct and amend the law, however much that claim might be qualified by reference to conciliar consent and the benefit of the country.[23] The *Volksrecht* was increasingly being overlaid with the features of a *Kaiserrecht.*

This association of prince and law was particularly clear in Gwynedd, for there Welsh law was consciously employed not only to promote princely power in general but also to further Gwynedd's claim to the political leadership of native Wales in the thirteenth century. This is manifested, for example, in the fabrication of mythological stories (such as the legend regarding Maelgwn Gwynedd) to uphold Gwynedd's claim to judicial supremacy within native Wales, or in the reference to the special insult payment (*sarhad*) due to the king of Aberffraw, or, most uncompromisingly, in the remarkable assertion that 'all the kings of Wales are to accept their land from the king of Aberffraw' and to pay him a special recognition due, *mechteyrn dyled.* 'For his word shall be a command to all the kings of Wales, but no other king's word shall be a command to him.'[24] Here indeed *lex scripta* has become the expression of *verbum regis,* and native customary law converted into a vehicle of Gwynedd's political ideology and ambitions.

The argument may be taken a step further. What was at issue in the employment of written law in the service of political apologetics was not only the supremacy of Gwynedd, but also the unity of Wales. It was indeed easy—and convenient—to slip from the one argument to the other. In a politically fragmented and dynastically divided country, law was one of the few vehicles of

---

[20] For Dyfnwal see, for example, A. R. Wiliam (ed.), *Llyfr Iorwerth* (Cardiff, 1960), §90; D. Jenkins (ed.), *Llyfr Colan* (Cardiff, 1963), §§638-9.

[21] Notably Bleddyn ap Cynfyn of Powys (d. 1075) and Rhys ap Gruffydd of Deheubarth (d. 1197): *Llyfr Iorwerth,* §82, 115; S. J. Williams and J. E. Powell (eds.), *Llyfr Blegywryd* (Cardiff, 1942), p. 154.

[22] H. D. Emanuel (ed.), *The Latin Texts of the Welsh Laws* (Cardiff, 1967), p. 111; *Llyfr Iorwerth,* §83, §43; D. Jenkins, *Cyfraith Hywel* (Llandysul, 1970), esp. pp. 30-2.

[23] 'Calendar of Welsh Rolls' in *Calendar of Various Chancery Rolls, 1277-1326* (henceforth *Cal. Welsh Rolls*), pp. 191-211, esp. pp. 196 (Einion ap David, Llywelyn ap Bleddyn), pp. 199-200 (Ithel ap Philip, Gruffydd ap Tudur), 205 (Cadwgan ap Gwyn, Robert ap Gwyn, David ap Iorwerth), 206 (Tudur ap Madoc).

[24] A. Owen (ed.), *Ancient Laws and Institutes of Wales* (Record Comm., 1841), II, 48-50; *Latin Texts of the Welsh Laws,* pp. 207, 277, 437-8 and, for discussion, ibid., pp. 49-53. Cf. D. Jenkins (ed.), *Damweiniau Colan* (Aberystwyth, 1973), §221.

national unity. As a customary law, it certainly differed markedly in substance, procedure and enforcement from one region of Wales to another; but the law-texts themselves clearly proclaim to the world that Wales, regardless of its political fragmentation, was one legally.[25] They drew a clear distinction between the Welshman and the alien (*alltud*);[26] and their definition of the essence of free Welsh status as descent from a Welsh mother and father (*Cymro famtad*) is a cardinal statement of the perception of Welsh identity in the middle ages.[27] Welsh law, so it was asserted in 1278, prevailed 'throughout Wales and the marches, as far as the power of the Welsh extends'.[28] Law clearly was a powerful platform on which to proclaim a sense of the national identity and unity of Wales.

The prologues of the law texts in particular provided an obvious occasion to proclaim the legal unity of Wales.[29] Hywel Dda, so these prologues asserted, as 'prince of the whole of Wales' had summoned 'six men from every *cantref* in Wales' to draw up the laws. The curse of 'the whole of Wales' was to be visited on anyone who failed to observe those laws 'in Wales'. The prologues became thereby the vehicles for fostering a historical mythology of the legal and even constitutional unity of the whole of Wales. Thence it was but a short step to deploy native laws in the campaign to promote the notion of the political unity of native Wales. The echoes of this all-Wales ideology are not difficult to detect in the thirteenth-century sources: just as Hywel was 'prince of the whole of Wales', so Llywelyn ab Iorwerth was said by a native chronicler to possess 'the monarchy and the principality of almost the whole of Wales'; just as Hywel had summoned an assembly at Whitland, so Llywelyn in 1216 convoked 'almost all the princes of Wales and all the wise men of Gwynedd' to Aberdyfi (the venue of Maelgwn Gwynedd's demonstration of Gwynedd's political and judicial superiority, according to the legal apocrypha); just as representatives from all the commotes of Wales were said to have assembled at the law-making assembly at Whitland, so it was claimed that 'all the tenants of all the *cantrefi* of Wales together' stood by Llywelyn in 1282.[30] Such coincidences in phrases and concepts may not have been self-conscious; but it is certainly noteworthy that the law texts, chronicles and official correspondence of the thirteenth century all partake of the phraseology of a Welsh national identity. An ideology of national unity was being forged; legal mythology was a crucial constituent in it.

---

[25] Cf. J. G. Edwards, 'Hywel Dda and the Welsh Lawbooks', in D. Jenkins (ed.), *Celtic Law Papers* (Brussels, 1973), pp. 159-60; D. Jenkins, *Trans. Hon. Soc. Cymmrodorion*, 1977, pp. 73-4.

[26] For the position of the *alltud*, see D. Jenkins, *Cyfraith Hywel*, pp. 15-17, and note in particular *Llyfr Colan*, §530 (the alien cannot act as a witness against a Welshman).

[27] For *Cymro famtad*, see especially *Llyfr Blegywryd*, p. 58; *Llyfr Iorwerth*, §87.

[28] *Calendar of Inquisitions Miscellaneous, 1219-1307*, no. 1109.

[29] The classic study of the prologues is, of course, that by Sir Goronwy Edwards, referred to in n. 25.

[30] T. Jones, ' "Cronica de Wallia" and other documents from Exeter Cathedral Library Ms. 3514', *Bull. Board of Celtic Studies*, XII (1946), 10 *sub anno* 1215; *Brut, RBH version*, p. 206 *sub anno* 1216; *Reg. Ep. Peckham*, II, 469, Cf. the statement of the *Brut sub anno* 1264 that Llywelyn ap Gruffydd was 'prince over all Wales'. Professor D. Jenkins has noted that the only two occasions on which the title 'tywysog Cymru' (prince of Wales) was employed in the law-texts are when it refers to Hywel Dda in some of the 'northern' versions of the texts: 'Kings, Laws and Princes: the Nomenclature of Authority in Thirteenth-Century Wales', *Bull. Board of Celtic Studies*, XXVI (1975-6), 454.

There was one further service which the laws could perform in the promotion of this ideology of national unity in Wales. They could be used to assert the international acceptability of that unity by claiming that the laws of Wales conformed with the legal and ethical norms of international behaviour. In a Christendom where these norms were increasingly being defined by the church and where the peculiarities of local customs were increasingly condemned as deviations, ecclesiastical sanction was imperative to sustain the status of native law. Without it, native law might be condemned as local custom rather than upheld as national law. It was precisely for this reason that St. Patrick's reputation had been summoned in the twelfth century to bolster the ecclesiastical respectability of the *Senchas Mar* against the attacks of reforming clerics. [31] Much in the same fashion, as Sir Goronwy Edwards showed in his classic study, the increasingly ecclesiastical mythology of the various redactions of the prologues of the Welsh law-texts—reaching their apogee with an account of the visit of a Welsh delegation, led by Hywel Dda himself and three Welsh bishops, to Rome where the laws were read to, and approved by, the Pope—reflects an anxiety to counter any opposition to the laws on the grounds that they were not consonant with scripture and canon law. Archbishop Pecham showed that the anxiety was not ill-founded. His tirades against Welsh law as being contrary to the Decalogue and inspired by the devil not only called in question the ecclesiastical credentials of Hywel's law; they also thereby in effect torpedoed the campaign of the princes of Gwynedd to appeal to that law as one of the major expressions of Welsh national identity. [32]

So far we have been concerned to outline briefly how Welsh law could be deliberately exploited to bolster native princely power, to further the hegemonic ambitions of the princes of Gwynedd and to foster an ideology of political unity and national identity within *pura Wallia*. But native law had one other obvious function in the political turmoil of the period: it could be cultivated as a bastion of national independence against the outsider. From the days of the earliest Norman attacks on Wales, law had begun to acquire this emblematic quality. It was 'the laws and judgements and violence of the French' which in contemporary eyes had occasioned the revolt in Gwynedd in 1098; the author of the *Gesta Stephani* likewise believed that 'the Normans imposed laws and statutes on the Welsh'; while Bishop Bernard of St. David's, himself a Norman nominee, believed that the laws of the Welsh were one of the features which distinguished them from other peoples. [33] And so no doubt the references could be multiplied. As yet, however, those references are vague and unspecific. It is not until the late-twelfth century—or so the evidence suggests—that law began to become a major issue in Anglo-Welsh relations. The chronology is not surprising. This was the period of the so-called 'Angevin leap-forward' in English royal justice, as the law of the king's court was transformed into the common law of England and into a potent instrument for the advance of royal power. It was a period when even some of the

[31] D. A. Binchy, 'The pseudo-historical prologue to the Senchas Már', *Studia Celtica*, X-XI (1975-6), 15-28.

[32] *Reg. Ep. Peckham*, I, 77; II, 475-6. Peckham probably based his comments on N.L.W., Peniarth MS. 28, which is known to have once belonged to St. Augustine's Abbey, Canterbury: D. Huws, art. cit. (above n. 18).

[33] *Brut, RBH version*, p. 38; K. R. Potter and R. H. C. Davis (eds), *Gesta Stephani* (Oxford, 1976), p. 15; Giraldus Cambrensis, 'De Invectionibus', ed. W. S. Davies, *Y Cymmrodor*, XXX (1920), 142.

princelings of Wales were attracted, as if by a magnet, to have their disputes
heard by English law or settled in the king's court. [34] It was also a period when the
jurisdictional content of feudal relationships was more closely defined and
vigorously exercised. It was in good part in response to the challenge of English
common law and of a rapidly developing royal jurisdiction that Welsh law and its
status emerged in the thirteenth century as an issue in Anglo-Welsh relations.
The parallels between Welsh law and the law and customs of the March of Wales
in this respect are close and instructive; both began to be defined and cited
frequently in the thirteenth century; both were called into service as bulwarks
against the encroachments of an intrusive royal law and justice. [35] In the
palatinates of England also, and notably in Cheshire, local law was likewise being
shaped and cited at much the same time as a defence against royal
encroachment. [36]

In the story of the emergence of Welsh law as a touchstone of national identity
and as a major issue in the relations of English and Welsh, 1201 is a very
significant date. In that year the first formal written agreement which is known to
survive between an English king (John) and a Welsh prince (Llywelyn ab
Iorwerth of Gwynedd) was concluded and in it a clear and specific distinction was
drawn between the law of England (*lex Anglie*) and the law of Wales (*lex Wallie*). [37]
The laws of the two countries were, thereby, in effect acknowledged to be unitary,
'national' laws and the question of the relationship of the two laws had been
placed on the agenda of Anglo-Welsh relations. The situation was in fact by no
means as straightforward as the treaty of 1201 suggested. Magna Carta (clauses
56-57) acknowledged as much when it proclaimed that disputes concerning
tenements in Wales should be determined according to the law of Wales and in
the March according to the law of the March. A further facet of the complex legal
situation in Wales came to light in an agreement of 1218 when Llywelyn ab
Iorwerth, on taking custody of Carmarthen and Cardigan, confirmed that he
would deal with the English of those districts according to English law and with
the Welsh according to Welsh law. [38] Between 1201 and 1218, therefore, all the
major ingredients of the 'conflict of laws' in Wales, especially as it was manifested
in the confrontation of 1277-82, had been assembled: the co-existence and overlap
of at least three laws (those of England, Wales and the March); the realisation
that the law to be applied depended (as the 1218 agreement made clear) on person

[34] One example is the attempt of Hywel ap Cadwallon and Madoc ap Maelgwn to secure a judgement
regarding the status of Maelienydd against Roger Mortimer. W. Dugdale (ed.), *Monasticon Anglicanum* (revised
ed., 1830), VI, i. 350.
[35] R. R. Davies, 'The Law of the March', *Welsh Hist. Rev.*, V (1970-1), 1-30, and idem, 'Kings, Lords and
Liberties in the March of Wales, 1066-1272', *Trans. R. Hist. S.*, 5th ser., 29 (1979), 41-61, esp. 56-61.
[36] H. M. Cam, 'The Medieval English Franchise', *Speculum*, 32 (1957), 427-42; G. Barraclough, *The
Earldom and County Palatine of Chester* (Oxford, 1953), esp. p. 22.
[37] *Rotuli Litterarum Patentium* (Record Comm., 1835), I, i, 8b. Sir John Lloyd's reference to this important
treaty (*History of Wales from the earliest times to the Edwardian conquest* [3rd ed., 1939], II, 615) is rather cursory. M.
Richter has drawn attention to the significance of the treaty in 'The political and institutional background to
national consciousness in medieval Wales', in T. W. Moody (ed.), *Nationalism and the Pursuit of National
Independence* (Belfast, 1978), pp. 37-55 at pp. 51-2; but the judicial and legal aspects of the treaty require further
emphasis.
[38] Magna Carta, *c.* 56-*c.* 57; *Rotuli Litterarum Clausarum*, I (Record Comm., 1833), 379.

and race as well as on geography; the absence of any agreed definition of what constituted 'Wales' and 'the March'; and the uncertainty, evident in the treaty of 1201, as to the nature and extent of the jurisdictional supervision which the king of England as feudal lord might exercise over Welsh princes. But what needs emphasis above all, in the present context, is that it is in the first two decades of the thirteenth century that the status of Welsh law emerges as an issue in Anglo-Welsh relations, more specifically in the relations of the king of England and the prince of Gwynedd.

After 1218 the references to Welsh law grow apace in the formal agreements and in the official correspondence relating to Wales. In general terms it may be said that the English government during these years rarely called the status of Welsh law into question, even at its moments of greatest political triumph as in 1241 or 1247.[39] Likewise, the Welsh for their part had not made the defence of their law into a major feature of their political claims. It is as yet only an occasional procedural awkwardness and the occasional defiant statement which hint at the potential for trouble inherent in the issue of law.[40] After the first of Edward I's campaigns of 1276-7, however, the situation was transformed; thence until the final war of 1282-3, the issue of law was to be at the centre of Anglo-Welsh conflict. Part of the reason for the premier importance now attached to the question of law may indeed lie in the deliberate ambiguity of the famous clause in the treaty of Aberconwy of 1277 which provided that disputes arising in the March should be terminated by the laws of the March and those in Wales according to the laws of Wales. Part of the reason may also lie, as we shall see, in the changing attitude of Edward I and some of his advisers towards Welsh law. But much of the answer also surely rests in the realisation of many of the Welsh leaders themselves that law was much the most favourable platform on which they could now conduct their struggle. Llywelyn ap Gruffydd, of course, made Welsh law into the centrepiece of his *gravamina* in these years; but in what appears to be a deliberately orchestrated campaign, the same issue of the status of Welsh law was taken up throughout Wales—in Ystrad Alun and Ceredigion, in Tegeingl and Ystrad Tywi, by the princelings of Powys Fadog and Deheubarth, even by David, Llywelyn ap Gruffydd's treacherous brother.[41] It is well to ask why.

We must certainly allow ample room in our explanation for the argument of self-interested convenience. The list of those who appealed at one stage or another to Welsh law in these years is indeed a motley one. Not only does it include, as we would expect, Welshmen such as Llywelyn ap Gruffydd himself, Rhys Fychan and Maelgwyn ap Maelgwn of Deheubarth and the sons of Gruffydd Maelor of Powys Fadog, but also more surprising company such as Adam of Montgomery, Roger Mortimer, Bogo de Knovill and even Gruffydd ap Gwenwynwyn of southern Powys, otherwise known as the greatest opponent of the application of

---

[39] As the treaties of Gwern Eigron (1241) and Woodstock (1247) show: *Littere Wallie*, pp. 7-10.

[40] As in the case of Maelgwn Fychan in 1241 (cited above n. 11) or in the statement of Owain and Llywelyn ap Gruffydd in 1249-50 that they would do justice to Maredudd ap Rhicert 'according to the law of Wales', *Cal. Anc. Corr.*, p. 33.

[41] *Reg. Ep. Peckham*, II. 447-63; J. C. Davies (ed.), *Welsh Assize Roll* (Cardiff, 1940), *passim*.

Welsh law in the Arwystli case.[42] The kings of England had also on occasion realised the political advantages of proclaiming themselves as champions of Welsh law in their attempts to exploit the fissures within the dynasty of Gwynedd and to impose the Welsh custom of partibility for their own advantage. Nor should these apparently cynical appeals to Welsh law surprise us. The co-existence of Welsh and English (and, for that matter, Marcher) law was, like every other overlap of law and jurisdiction in medieval society, a marvellous addition to the armoury of legal delays and appeals. Welsh law was a particularly adept spanner to throw into the judicial works on matters of procedure—on issues such as the acceptability of essoins, the number of permissible defaults, the citation of co-parcenors, the appropriate season for pleading, the time limit on bringing cases, the custom of giving hostages, the status of amercements and so forth.[43] It could also be used to challenge basic assumptions in substantive law, especially on issues relating to land, such as the appropriate pretext for territorial disinheritance, the rights of co-parcenors, practices relating to minority and custody, and the status of illegitimate children.[44] It is as well to recognise that in many such cases, a general appeal to the authority of Welsh law and custom need not refer to the written law of the texts.[45] Some of the statements, it is true, tally fairly closely with what we know from the law texts; but others plainly do not do so, and on occasion (as on the issue of bastardy) litigants might appeal to Welsh law to uphold mutually contradictory arguments.[46] For, truth to tell, generalized references to Welsh law were often no more than a façade for legal obfuscation, procrastination and special pleading.

That does not mean, however, that appeals to Welsh law were only prompted by self-interested convenience. Law in this respect must not be too narrowly or too specifically construed. 'Law' was often the catch-phrase of a custom-based society which resented innovation and which saw in an appeal to 'the laws, customs and usages of those parts' the best defence, short of revolt, against the new-fangled administrative, financial and judicial claims of an intrusive officialdom and an alien governance. These 'laws, customs and usages' were rarely specified. When we catch a glimpse of them in the official correspondence of the period, they often do not refer to legal and judicial matters *sensu stricto* but rather to issues such as forest rights, freedom to assart, rights of common pasture, the petty extortions of officials, the right to pay the same financial dues as in the

---

[42] *Welsh Assize Roll*, pp. 235, 275 (Adam of Montgomery), 285, 313 (Roger Mortimer, Bogo de Knovill), 149; H. Hall (ed.), *Select Cases concerning the Law Merchant, 1251-1779*, III (Selden Soc., 1932), 140-2 (Gruffydd ap Gwenwynwyn).

[43] *Welsh Assize Roll*, pp. 274, 293-4, 332 (essoins), 313 (defaults), 253, 324 (co-parcenors), 269 (period of pleading), 285 (time limit), 253 (hostages), 235, 268 (amercements).

[44] *Welsh Assize Roll*, pp. 242 (disinheritance), 244; *Close Rolls, 1247-51*, p. 236 (co-parcenors); *Welsh Assize Roll*, p. 243; *Close Rolls, 1247-51*, p. 555 (minority and custody); *Welsh Assize Roll*, pp. 255, 257, 275 (illegitimate children and rights through females).

[45] Cf. P. Wormald's comments in art. cit. (above n. 19), pp. 119-23.

[46] Thus, the legal arguments on the occasions for disinheritance are not far removed from those to be found in Welsh contexts: *Welsh Assize Roll*, p. 242; *Latin Texts of the Welsh Laws*, pp. 134, 231; *Llyfr Colan*, §§283-8. Elsewhere, however, the reference to Welsh law and custom is implausible (*Cal. Inquisitions Miscellaneous, 1219-1307*, no. 1095) or contradictory (*Welsh Assize Roll*, pp. 255, 257).

time of the Welsh princes, or the promise not to be distrained to serve overseas.[47] In other words, the appeal to law—like the appeal to 'the ancient constitution' or the 'immemorial law' in other periods—was often not an appeal to precise legal practices or texts but to a generalized body of customs as the bulwark against innovation, especially foreign innovation.

It was in part in this spirit that the princes of Gwynedd appealed to Welsh law; but there was another, tactical, reason why they came to rely so heavily on that appeal in their relations with the kings of England. The issue of Welsh law was chosen deliberately by them in order to divert attention away from the issue of feudal subjection and more particularly from the increasing measure of jurisdictional supervision and control involved in feudal subjection in the thirteenth century. Welsh princes from at least the twelfth century had not denied that they owed fealty and homage to the kings of England; what they had not bargained for was the way in which that feudal bond could be transformed into a more demanding and demeaning relationship in the thirteenth century. The nature of that transformation was heralded by the formal agreement of 1201. King John, it is true, acknowledged the separate identity of Welsh law; but in return Llywelyn ab Iorwerth committed to writing his feudal dependence and that of his greater tenants (*majores*) on the king of England and he also in effect acknowledged a measure of royal jurisdictional control over his affairs.[48] It was a thin edge of a wedge which John and his successors knew full well how to exploit. Political circumstances, it is true, did not allow them to do so often or fully; but the events of the 1240s showed how easy it might be to convert a loose overlordship into a precise and demeaning dependence, judicially and militarily.

There must have been a clear awareness in native Wales, or at least in the councils of Gwynedd, of the need to counter such developments. Most of the answer would lie, of course, in the field of practical politics and military power; but in an age of increasing propaganda and self-justification, it was also imperative to counter the arguments of feudal and jurisdictional dependence on a theoretical level. Several approaches suggested themselves, at different times. One was to seek to construe the nature of the feudal relationship as being no more than a harmless *hommage en marche* or *hommage de paix* between two near equals and by insisting on an etiquette of behaviour—such as parleys on the boundaries of the two countries—which demonstrated the mutuality of the relationship.[49] Another approach was to insist that the position of the prince of Gwynedd was not—as English analogies seemed to insist—comparable to that of an English tenant-in-chief, but rather that it approximated to the position of the king of Scotland *vis-à-vis* the king of England. The rights of the principality of Wales (as it

---

[47] *Close Rolls, 1247-51*, pp. 441-2, 541-2, 552, 566; *1251-53*, pp. 4, 143, 365, 483; *1253-54*, pp. 20-1; *1254-56*, p. 301; *Cal. Patent Rolls, 1247-58*, p. 368. These same anxieties, among others, are articulated in the communal charters of liberties of the thirteenth and fourteenth centuries: R. R. Davies, *Lordship and Society in the March of Wales, 1282-1400* (Oxford, 1978), pp. 462-4.

[48] Supra, n. 37.

[49] For *hommage de paix* and *hommage en marche*, see J. F. Lemarignier. *Hommage en marche: Recherches sur l'hommage en marche et les frontières féodales* (Lille, 1945), and J. Le Patourel, *The Norman Empire* (Oxford, 1976), pp. 208, 218-20. For such parleys see, for example, *Cal. Anc. Corr.*, pp. 2, 37.

was called after 1267) were indeed held (so it was argued) under the king's royal power, but they were 'entirely separate from those of the king's realm'. Notions of the status (*status*) of the principality, of the prince and of Wales itself were valuable ingredients in developing an ideology of the separateness of Wales which might be used to challenge English notions of feudal dependence.[50]

These, however, were arguments appropriate only to men who spoke from a position of strength. When the tide of fortune turned, especially after 1277, the appeal to Welsh law came into its own as a way to counter English interpretations of the obligations of feudal relationship. Feudal dependence could not now be denied; even some of the implications of the superior jurisdiction implicit in such dependence could not be gainsaid.[51] But it could be argued that even the king of England was bound to respect and to uphold the law of Wales in matters relating to Wales. That would at least qualify the nature of his superior jurisdiction as it was exercised in Wales. It would also divert the argument deftly from the obligations of the vassal (the prince of Wales) to the responsibilities of the lord (the king of England). But the argument had also the further advantage of escalating the issue to the level of the defence of national customs and even of international conventions. 'All Christian men have their own laws and customs in their own lands', as the sons of Maredudd ab Owain of Ceredigion provocatively put it; 'they and their ancestors likewise in their lands had their immutable laws and customs until the English deprived them of their laws after the last war'.[52] The struggle about the obligations of feudal dependence was being transformed into confrontation about the national identity of the Welsh people as manifested in the individuality of their laws. It is in this context that we must surely interpret the 'imperial' argument put forward by Welsh apologists in these years. 'Each province under the empire of the lord king', so asserted Llywelyn ap Gruffydd's attorney, 'has its own laws and customs. The Welsh, therefore, should enjoy their Welsh law and customs as did other nations (*naciones*) under the empire of the lord king.' It was an argument echoed by Llywelyn's brother, David.[53] To query the constitutional propriety or legal validity of that argument, as Sir Maurice Powicke did, is beside the point.[54] What needs to be emphasized is the political deftness of the attempt to divert the dispute from one about the jurisdictional obligations of feudal dependence to the more exalted issues of the laws and customs of nations (*jura nacionum*) and of the responsibility of an 'emperor' to respect the laws of the 'provinces' of his 'empire'.

Law was being cleverly exploited by the prince of Wales and his allies in the service of a campaign for political survival. It was also exploited by them to convert that campaign into a struggle for the preservation of Welsh national identity. In some respects law seemed to be unpromising material for such a

[50] Ibid., pp. 9 (1220), 24-5 (1224), 86 (1273). Cf. *Reg. Ep. Peckham*, II, 466 (1282).

[51] Some of the possible consequences of that dependence included an acknowledgement that land within the principality was given with the king's licence, an acceptance of a royal commission to inquire into a case in Anglesey and a claim that a litigant might take a case to the king if the prince failed to provide justice: *Cal. Anc. Corr.*, pp. 95, 111-12, 59-60.

[52] *Reg. Ep. Peckham*, II, 453-4.

[53] *Welsh Assize Roll*, p. 266: *Cal. Anc. Corr.*, p. 73.

[54] *King Henry III and the Lord Edward* (Oxford, 1947), pp. 664-70.

purpose. In spite of the declarations of the law texts themselves, it was patently clear that Welsh law did not apply throughout Wales. It co-existed with English and Marcher law; it was pock-marked with local customs and variations; in its substance and procedure it was being heavily influenced by English law and practice; and there is no reason to believe that there was an articulated pattern of jurisdiction or even a recognized curriculum of legal learning which prevailed throughout native Wales. It was not altogether clear even to contemporaries whether the applicability of Welsh law was territorial (that is, within the bounds, themselves undefined, of *pura Wallia*) or personal (that is, to be applied to persons of 'Welsh condition', however defined). It is also amply clear that the attitude of Welshmen themselves, from the prince of Gwynedd to local communities such as the men of Rhos and Ceri, towards native law was ambivalent and shifting.[55] Above all, law in Wales as elsewhere in Europe in the thirteenth century was in a state of rapid flux as it responded to political pressure, social developments and legal and intellectual influences from within and without Wales. In short, neither in its content nor in its status nor in its geographical applicability did Welsh law enjoy the monolithic and clear-cut quality that political argument bestowed upon it in the period 1277-82.

Yet it is the quality of political propaganda at all times to make light of practical difficulties and to reduce the complex to the simple, even *simpliste*. So it was with Welsh law. It was used after 1277 to couch the struggle of the prince of Gwynedd-Wales and his associates in national terms. It was the law of the people, comparable with the laws of other nations; it was 'the common law' of Wales.[56] Furthermore, it had been conceded, so it was claimed by Llywelyn ap Gruffydd and many of his allies, by Edward I to *all* Welshmen as *their* law (*omnibus hominibus Walensicis legem suam Walensicam concessit*).[57] Edward I had in fact made no such grant; but the claim was a clever propaganda ploy. It converted Welsh law into national property to be guaranteed to all Welshmen and sanctioned by royal grant. To defend it, therefore, was to partake in a national struggle, not merely in a campaign to salvage the pride of the prince of Gwynedd. To say as much is not necessarily to assert that Llywelyn ap Gruffydd and his advisers deliberately chose to provoke a quarrel over the issue of law; it was almost axiomatic in the thirteenth century that political friction should express itself in disputes about legal and jurisdictional relationships. But what is surely evident is that Llywelyn and his supporters exploited the political potential of Welsh law as an issue to divert attention from that of jurisdictional dependence on the king of England and to proclaim their cause as being ultimately that of the defence of Welsh national identity.

What was the response of the kings of England to the challenge presented by

[55] *Cal. Welsh Rolls,* pp. 196 (Gwion ap Madoc), 198 (Cynwrig ap Carwet), 199 (Ithel ap Philip), 200 (Tegwared son of John); *Cal. Anc. Corr.,* pp. 20-1.

[56] Ibid., pp. 72-3; *Cal. Inquisitions Miscellaneous, 1219-1307,* no. 1109.

[57] *Welsh Assize Roll,* pp. 266 (Llywelyn ap Gruffydd), 269 (Rhys Fychan), 258 (Owain and Llywelyn ap Gruffydd Maelor); *Reg. Ep. Peckham,* II, 446 (Dafydd ap Gruffydd).

the argument from Welsh law? From the agreement of 1201 onwards their attitude towards Welsh law, at least in official statements, was essentially one of tolerant respect. In formal treaties with the rulers of Gwynedd, including those concluded at moments of military triumph as in 1247 and 1277, they readily acknowledged the status of Welsh law; they promised Welshmen living under their direct governance, such as those of Tegeingl (Englefield), that they should be tried 'according to Welsh law and custom';[58] they consistently and repeatedly instructed their officials in the royal lands in Wales to treat Welshmen 'according to their own laws' or 'according to the law and custom of those parts'.[59] It is true that it was occasionally in the king's own political interest to cast himself in the rôle of upholder of Welsh law, especially when the Welsh custom of partibility might be used to exploit fissures within Welsh princely families or to extort concessions from them.[60] But there is no need to doubt that in general English kings, Edward I included, were indeed willing to respect the law of Wales where it could be shown to have been the law in current usage. Lack of respect was much more likely to come from insensitive, ambitious and high-handed officials in Wales itself, who might need to be reminded to 'bear themselves patiently towards the Welsh' and who were no doubt the source of the mischief-making rumour that the king wished to abolish Welsh law.[61]

It was not on the issue of law, but on the question of jurisdiction, that English policy wished to concentrate. The two issues, of course, overlapped, as the famous Arwystli case was to make evident; but in the pursuit of political control and mastery, it was the issue of jurisdiction which was the premier one from the English point of view. Thus, to take but one illuminating example from the reign of Henry III, the English government was quite willing to allow Rhys Fychan of Deheubarth to be treated in everything 'according to the law and custom of Wales which the king has undertaken to uphold', provided that he acknowledged his dependence on the king's court of Carmarthen.[62] Likewise in the relationship between the English kings and the princes of Gwynedd, it was not the status of Welsh law but the measure of jurisdictional overlordship arising out of feudal dependence which was the key issue. The degree of content given to that overlordship was the most accurate barometer of the state of Anglo-Welsh relations. Jurisdictional control was the most useful weapon in the articulation of political mastery. That is precisely what Llywelyn ap Gruffydd found to his cost after 1277. Prince of Wales he might still be, but he could be summoned to appear before the king and his justices, told to do so on days and at places appointed by them, ordered (however politely) to observe the procedures of English law incumbent on all litigants, and reminded that the king was 'debtor of justice to all' and could not therefore brook any liberty or even an appeal to precedent in

[58] *Cal. Charter Rolls, 1226-57*, p. 274; *Close Rolls, 1251-53*, p. 483.

[59] *Cal. Patent Rolls, 1232-47*, p. 430; *Close Rolls, 1247-51*, pp. 113, 236, 408, 541, 555; *1251-53.* pp. 185, 419, 483, 511; *Welsh Assize Roll*, p. 15.

[60] *Littere Wallie*, pp. 9, 52, 119; *Close Rolls, 1247-51*, p. 236; *1251-53*, pp. 419, 511; *Welsh Assize Roll*, p. 246.

[61] *Close Rolls, 1251-53*, pp. 465, 467, 483; *Welsh Assize Roll*, p. 286.

[62] *Close Rolls, 1247-51*, p. 113; *Cal. Patent Rolls, 1247-58*, p. 155.

the pursuit of that obligation.[63] The demeaning nature of jurisdictional overlordship was spelt out grimly for him in the tortuous proceedings of the next few years and reinforced by threats to send justices to hear complaints against him or to command royal officials to distrain his lands and chattels in the principality of Wales itself.[64] Jurisdictional overlordship, as practised by Edward I and his lawyers after 1277, had shattered any illusions that Llywelyn might have had that he could salvage his authority and his dignity from the settlement of 1277.

It was in the face of these shattered illusions that Llywelyn, as we have seen, concentrated on the issue of Welsh law as a way of deflecting attention from jurisdiction to law and of basing his case on a national, rather than a personal or feudal, issue. In the face of this challenge, Edward I and his advisers were in effect compelled, whether they liked it or not, to face up to the issue of Welsh law and its status. One approach was to institute inquiries to discover what were the laws and customs of Wales and the March and how, and how far, they had been applied in disputes in the past.[65] Edward I has been much berated for the *parti-pris* nature of these inquiries, for the selective use of evidence both geographically and chronologically, for the loaded character of the questions posed, for the perfunctory dismissal of inconvenient testimony, for the insensitive aggravation of delicate issues.[66] Much of the criticism is certainly well-directed; but its high moral tone is in good measure misplaced. It overlooks one primary purpose of the inquiries and searches: to establish that the legal position in Wales, especially with regard to the status and applicability of Welsh law, was by no means as simple and clear-cut as Llywelyn claimed it to be. It is in that light that the searches and inquiries are to be interpreted—as a political response, masquerading as a judicial inquiry, by Edward I to an equally political ploy by the prince of Wales. For both parties Welsh law was now in effect a political football.

Commissions and inquiries might serve to show the complexity of the issues, politically and legally. But there were other, and eventually more devastating, avenues which the king of England might explore. One was to invoke the dignity of the crown and the superior responsibility it entailed. This was a particularly effective response to Llywelyn's argument that each province of the king's realm should enjoy its own laws. Such laws could only be permitted, was Edward I's retort, if they were not derogatory to his crown or to the rights of his kingdom.[67] Archbishop Pecham made the same point rather more provocatively, as usual, by remarking that royal custom (*consuetudo regia*) must prevail over the custom of any

---

[63] *Cal. Welsh Rolls*, pp. 173-5, 211; *Welsh Assize Roll*, pp. 59-60; *Cal. Anc. Corr.*, pp. 58-60.

[64] *Cal. Welsh Rolls*, pp. 174-5; *Cal. Close Rolls, 1272-79*, pp. 506-7.

[65] Notably of course: (i) the compilation of cases from the years 1247-58 to be found in Curia Regis Roll (K.B. 26), 159, summarized in *Welsh Assize Roll*, pp. 13-30; (ii) the Grey-Hamilton Inquisition of October 1278, *Cal. Inquisitions Miscellaneous, 1219-1307*, no. 1109; (iii) the commission of inquiry into Welsh law, January-February 1281, *Cal. Welsh Rolls*, pp. 190-210.

[66] Notably by J. C. Davies in his introduction to *Welsh Assize Roll*.

[67] The memorandum of 19 May 1280 is crucial in this respect. It is paraphrased in *Welsh Assize Roll*, pp. 59-60. Some of the words in the original (P.R.O., Chancery Miscellanea [C. 47] 27/2 [19]) are now illegible; but the gist of the argument is unmistakable.

subject, including that of the prince of Wales. [68] Royal prerogative and the dignity of the crown were being summoned to put Welsh law in its place. Royal masterfulness, of which Edward I was an arch exponent, was another weapon in the king's armoury. 'The King', said a tart endorsement on a letter sent by Llywelyn, 'ought not to have a march with his man in a matter which touches the king'. That put the relationship clearly and crisply into perspective: Llywelyn was a man, a vassal; Edward a king. Edward was to use very much the same argument to put the Marcher lords in their place in the 1290s. [69] He did not change over the years: just as *dignitas corone* was the ultimate and unanswerable response to *libertas marchie,* so was it an argument which could eventually override the laws and customs of Wales.

But the ultimate royal riposte to Llywelyn's appeal to the inviolable status of Welsh law was even more devastating. The king was not merely bound to uphold the rights of his crown and kingdom; he had an even more awesome obligation to defend reason, justice and the divine law. The status and indeed the validity of Welsh law would have to be scrutinized in the light of that obligation. There had certainly been earlier adumbrations of this high moral argument. Thus, in 1241 'right' (*jus*) was rather provocatively contrasted with the custom of Wales. [70] But it was in the late 1270s, as the English Justinian began to flex his legislative muscles and as the problem of the diversity of laws and customs in his realm was brought into clearer focus that the potentialities of the argument were explored. Already in 1277 Edward had indicated his willingness to grant English laws to the Irish 'because the laws which the Irish use are detestable to God and so contrary to all law that they ought not to be deemed laws'. [71] It was an ominous precedent. It was in 1279-80 that it began to be applied to Wales. Archbishop Pecham set about with sanctimonious zeal to examine the moral and ecclesiastical shortcomings of Welsh law, probably at Edward's instigation. Arguments emphasising the need for justice to be done 'according to God and right' or 'according to God and justice' began to appear in the correspondence, as did an ominous promise to uphold such Welsh laws as were 'just and reasonable'. [72] Edward began to speak of his obligation to root out bad laws and customs; his justices dropped a hint that though the king did not intend to abolish Welsh law, it was his intention to correct it. [73] Clearly Welsh law was not inviolable; it was subject to royal scrutiny and correction. It is no doubt for the same reason that a new question, which was no part of the original questionnaire, was very significantly added to the terms of the commission of inquiry into Welsh law of 1280-1. The commissioners were empowered to inquire into the right of the

[68] *Reg. Ep. Peckham,* I, 135-37 (August 1280).
[69] *Cal. Anc. Corr.,* p. 93; *Cal. Welsh Rolls,* p. 336.
[70] *Littere Wallie,* p. 9; and for comment, Powicke, *King Henry III and the Lord Edward,* p. 633.
[71] *Foedera etc.,* T. Rymer (ed.) (revised ed., 1816-69), I, ii, 540; A. J. Otway-Ruthven, 'The Request of the Irish for English law, 1277-80', *Irish Historical Studies,* VI (1948-49), 261-70; and A. Gwynn, 'Edward I and the Proposed Purchase of English Law for the Irish *c.* 1276-80', *Trans. R. Hist. S.,* X (1960), 111-27.
[72] *Welsh Assize Roll,* pp. 59-60 (19 May 1280); *Cal. Anc. Corr.,* p. 60 (18 July 1280). The phrase used in the May 1280 memorandum is noteworthy: *si tunc a justicie linea non discordant,* C. 47/27/2 (19).
[73] *Welsh Assize Roll,* pp. 60 (19 May 1280), 286 (December 1279).

prince to amend and to improve the law. The marginal glosses referring to 'amendment of laws' and 'evil laws' in the Chancery copy of the commission's report show that the inquiry was not disinterested; Edward and his advisers were seeking a theoretical pretext to bring Welsh law under their scrutiny and to arrogate the right to amend it. [74] Their ultimate answer to Llywelyn's appeal to the inviolability of Welsh law was to invoke the rôle of the king as the guardian of reason and justice and as the interpreter of what was consonant with the Bible and Christian morality. Such an exalted claim, combined as it was with the confidence of political and military superiority, was the answer answerless to Llywelyn's argument.

The nature of the argument about the status of Welsh law in the years 1277-82 is of interest not only as providing an insight into the nature of political polemics in the thirteenth century but also because it reveals how starkly the issue between the king of England and the prince of Wales had been brought into focus in those years. The issue was not merely that of the status or validity of Welsh law, but that of Welsh law as the emblem of a Welsh national identity. Nothing less was at stake than a conflict about the identity of Wales, more particularly native Wales, *pura Wallia*. The princes of Gwynedd in the thirteenth century were intent on attempting to reshape the basis of their authority in national, Welsh terms. Their periodic assumption of the title 'lord' or 'prince of Wales' was part of that campaign; so also was the occasional appropriation by their chief official of the title of justiciar or seneschal of Wales; so also was their attempt to claim overlordship over all 'the Welsh barons of Wales' (including those of Glamorgan and even Caerleon) and to give some measure of structure and compulsion to that overlordship; so also was the convenient distinction that they attempted to draw between 'the barons of Wales' and 'the barons of England in the March'; so also was their conscious adoption of a vocabulary which spoke of Wales (*Wallia*) as the sphere of their pretensions and authority. [75] In that ambition law, an unitary law for native Wales, was crucial. Indeed, it was arguably much more crucial after 1277 because the rhetoric of the prince of Wales's ambitions—for he was still incongruously accorded the title of prince of Wales—bore steadily less relation to political realities. In those circumstances mythology flourishes. Law, along with Trojan descent, language and customs, was becoming an inextricable part of the mythology of Welsh independence. It was an issue which could be made to appear to bind the prince of Gwynedd and the people of native Wales together. It was a touchstone of national identity.

It was this issue that, sooner or later, the English king would have to broach. The outlines of the royal response to Gwynedd's version of the identity of Wales came to the surface time and again in the thirteenth century—in the insistence that the prince of Gwynedd was no more than one of the magnates of Wales, in the crown's claim to the direct feudal dependence and jurisdictional control of those magnates, in the insistence that the new-fangled principality of Wales as forged by the house of Gwynedd was not coterminous with Wales, not even with

[74] The question was added to the original list of fourteen questions at the second sitting of the commission at Rhuddlan on 24 January 1281.

[75] Some of these themes are discussed in T. Jones Pierce, *Medieval Welsh Society*, ch. I, and M. Richter, op. cit., pp. 37-55.

native Wales.[76] But it was after 1277 in particular that the question of the definition of the identity of Wales came into clear focus. It came so in part because the Arwystli case, for all the casuistry that was involved in the arguments, called forth from Gruffydd ap Gwenwynwyn a counter-definition of the identity and status of native Wales to that advanced by the house of Gwynedd and one which was much closer to the interests of royal policy. It also came into focus because Edward I's exercise of judicial overlordship in Wales, on the one hand, and Llywelyn's appeal to Welsh law as the hallmark of Welsh identity, on the other, escalated the issues onto a plane where victory or submission seemed the only alternatives. For it can hardly be doubted that what was at stake in the tortuous legal and judicial proceedings of 1278-82 was not, in Powicke's phrase, a 'conflict of laws' in a narrow sense but a conflict of power—over the identity and mastery of Wales.

It was Edward I who emerged victorious from that conflict. The coping-stone on his victory was the statute of Rhuddlan of 1284. In it Edward dealt magisterially with the two intertwined issues which had come into such sharp focus since 1277—the status of Welsh law and the identity of Wales. 'We . . . have caused to be rehearsed before us and the nobles of our realm the laws and customs of those parts hitherto in use; which being diligently heard and fully understood, we have . . . abolished certain of them, some thereof we have allowed, and some we have corrected; and we have likewise commanded certain others to be ordained and added thereto.' In those resonant phrases—echoing, appropriately enough, Justinian's seventh *Novella*—Edward I disposed imperiously of the appeal to Welsh law as a national law, a badge of Welsh identity. Even such features of the law as were allowed to continue hereafter did so only after royal scrutiny and by the King's grace and favour.

He dealt equally imperiously and briskly with the question of the identity and status of Wales. 'Divine providence', so proclaimed the Statute with rotund certainty, 'has . . . entirely transferred under our proper dominion the land of Wales with its inhabitants, heretofore subject to us in feudal right; . . . and has annexed and united the same into the Crown of the . . . realm (of England)'. The use of the word 'Wales' in this famous passage is both inappropriate and significant. It is inappropriate since Edward's conquest had brought into his direct control only the lands of the prince of Gwynedd/Wales and of his allies; it is also inappropriate in as much as the detailed clauses of the Statute of 1284 applied only to the king's lands of north Wales and the county of Flint. It is again inappropriate in that the settlement of 1284 did not impose institutional or legal unity on the whole of Wales; instead, Edward I in effect allowed the division of Wales into the March and native Wales (*pura Wallia*) to be perpetuated, albeit under new terms. Inappropriate as it is, the recurring use of the phrase Wales—and it is used time and again in the body of the Statute as well as in its preamble and it is also echoed by other contemporaries, such as Archbishop Pecham when he referred to 'the church of Wales' (*ecclesia Wallie*) and to 'the governance of Wales' (*gubernacula Wallie*)[77]—is surely significant and self-

---

[76] *Littere Wallie*, introduction, *passim*.
[77] *Reg. Ep. Peckham*, III, 774.

conscious. 'Wales' had been a key catchphrase in the policies of the princes of Gwynedd, especially of Llywelyn ap Gruffydd; it summed up in a word their pretensions to the political leadership of the whole of native Wales and their ambition to create it into a single political unit. By appropriating the phrase 'Wales' Edward I was therefore annexing, as it were, the political terminology of the prince of Gwynedd/Wales. It is ironic that Edward I should thereby be, as it were, the residuary legatee of the political ambitions and phraseology of the princes of Gwynedd.[78] Ironic, but appropriate; for their attempt to assert and to promote the national identity of Wales—of which Welsh law was an essential part, and especially so after 1277—had ultimately to be countered by annexing and uniting 'the land of Wales' into 'the Crown of the realm of England'. That for Edward I was the final solution of the question of the identity and status of Wales.

[78] Cf. J. G. Edwards, *The Principality of Wales, 1267-1967. A Study in Constitutional History* (Caernarvonshire Historical Society, 1969).

Medieval Severnside:
The Welsh Connection

RALPH A. GRIFFITHS

THE distance between the opposite shores of the Severn estuary ranges from about one mile at the modern Severn Bridge to about twenty miles between Worms Head in Gower and Ilfracombe in Devon, and reaches fifty miles between Pembroke and Hartland Point. It may have been rather less in Neolithic times, to judge by the submerged forests located along the south Wales coast at Barry, Cardiff, Port Talbot and Swansea; whilst the Somerset, Devon and Glamorgan cliffs then stood further out in the channel. Even in more recent times, sand and other deposits have created coastal flats in Gwent, at Merthyr Mawr, Kenfig and Aberafan, and further west in Carmarthenshire too.[1] Be that as it may, throughout historic times the distance has been regarded as short. For this reason, one might think that (to take one example) Somerset's historians would have given direct attention to the impact of their county's people on the northern side of the channel and, too, would have considered the contribution which Welshmen have made to west-country development. Yet as a gauge of such interest, the volumes of the Somerset Archaeological and Natural History Society for the last thirty years are a disappointment. True enough, in 1950 the president of the Society, Sir Cyril Fox, addressed its members on the subject of 'Somerset from a South Wales viewpoint', and Sir Cyril had, appropriately enough, been director of the National Museum of Wales from 1926.[2] Since 1950, this salient theme has had no attention paid to it in these distinguished volumes, with the single unflattering exception of a brief note on a pigsty found at Berrow village, on the coast just north of Burnham, which is judged to be of a traditional Welsh type common in the counties of Monmouth, Glamorgan and Carmarthen.[3]

By contrast, the links between the two shores were well appreciated by England's earliest antiquarians. In the fifteenth century William Worcestre, that busy traveller and selective recorder who was born in Bristol in 1415 and never lost his affection for the city, was familiar with the Welsh countryside he could see across the Severn and with the shipping facilities and traffic of the river itself. Some of his information was gleaned from Welsh acquaintances: from William Powell of Tintern; the bibliophile canon of Exeter, Dr Owen Lloyd; an old Bristol merchant, John Gryffyth, who had retired to the college at Westbury-on-Trym,

---

[1] F. J. North, *The evolution of the Bristol Channel* (Cardiff, 1929), pp. 51-61, 64-7.

[2] *Proc.*, XCV (1950), 53-62.

[3] Ibid., CVII (1962-3), 108; I. C. Peate, *The Welsh House* (Liverpool, 1944), pp. 42-5. The Somerset example is thought to be anything between 100 and 300 years old.

where Worcestre visited him; and from John Smyth, bishop of Llandaff and sometime archdeacon of St. David's and vicar of Tenby. Worcestre also travelled to south-east Wales himself on at least one occasion, in September 1478 when he spent time at Chepstow and Tintern.[4] Three-quarters of a century later, in Henry VIII's reign, that footloose topographer and voracious note-taker from London, John Leland, the 'king's antiquary', spent a good deal of time in the west country and on his travels in Wales. One noteworthy feature that struck him time and again was the connection between the two shores of what he described as the 'Severn Se'; and it was Leland who coined the word 'Severnside'.[5] For him the cliffs at Aust in Gloucestershire stood guard over the ferry that crossed to Beachley and afforded access to the Forest of Dean and the Gwent countryside to the west—'the key of those countries' [Wales], as the ferry was described in 1644. What he found worth recording about the river Thaw in Glamorgan was 'the next passage to' Minehead which it offered. And among Leland's surviving papers is a note emphasising the value of the tiny haven of Colhuw, near Llantwit Major, because from there the Severn sea could be crossed direct to Dunster and Minehead.[6] The significance of these cross-channel connections was identified in similar terms by Dr Thomas Phaer, the lawyer and physician who, though brought up probably in Norwich, settled at Cilgerran and round about 1551-3 compiled an official report on the harbours, ports and customs administration of Wales. Cardiff, for him, 'lieth agenst Asshewater [the River Axe] and Bridgwater in Somerset'; Barry 'lieth agenste Mynet [Minehead] and Bridgewater'; Aberthaw was 'A drie haven for small vesselles and daily passage to Mynet and Donster'; and even Porteynon, with 'no haven', had 'a pyer and commen passage from Wales into Cornewall and Devon'.[7]

More recently, historians have seen the Severn and other seas around Britain as separating features, even in some cases as defensive barriers with Englishmen's pride in their island race swelling as the centuries passed and Welsh historians, for their part, anxious to see the uniqueness of things west of Offa's Dyke and north of the Severn channel. But, as prehistoric man discovered, if seas and channels proved navigable, then they could unify peoples and forge cultural links between them. Archaeologists have demonstrated how, before and after the Roman invasion, the Irish sea facilitated the evolution of a 'culture province' that included Ireland, Wales, northern Britain, Cornwall and even Brittany.[8] Though in a more limited way geographically (but therefore, perhaps, more intensive culturally), the Severn sea has done much the same at many points in the past, especially during the middle ages. As a historian of the late-medieval

---

[4] J. H. Harvey (ed.), *William Worcestre: Itineraries* (Oxford, 1969), pp. 39, 67, 75, 117, 119; Worcestre's topographical description of Bristol is in J. Dallaway (ed.), *Antiquities of Bristow in the middle centuries* (Bristol, 1834), which notes (p. 23) Worcestre's visit to Tintern. For Lloyd and Smyth, see A. B. Emden, *A Biographical Register of the University of Oxford to A.D. 1500* (3 vols., Oxford, 1957-9), II, 1153-4; III, 1716.

[5] L. T. Smith (ed.), *The Itinerary of John Leland* (5 vols., London, 1907-10), *passim*; for Severnside, *idem*, *The Itinerary in Wales* (London, 1906), p. 15.

[6] Ibid., pp. 22, 42; *Itinerary*, II, 63, 68-9; V, 238; *Cal. State Papers, Dom.*, *1644*, p. 528.

[7] W. R. B. Robinson, 'Dr. Thomas Phaer's report on the harbours and customs administration of Wales under Edward VI', *Bull. Board of Celtic Studies*, XXIV (1972), 485-503; *DNB*, XLV, 140.

[8] C. Fox, *The Personality of Britain* (4th ed., Cardiff, 1952), p. 44, for the term.

church and of the Reformation in Wales, and as general editor of *The Glamorgan County History,* Professor Glanmor Williams has shown a rare awareness of the influence of the Severn waterway on the development of south Wales—not least as the commercial channel whereby the teachings of religious reformers reached ports such as Carmarthen—and of the role of Welshmen in the growth of Bristol's metropolis. [9]

It must be admitted that, short though the distance may be, the channel crossing is not always an easy one and the coastline, as it narrows rapidly into a funnel, makes for formidable tides and eventually, near the mouth of the river Wye, the Severn Bore. [10] On the other hand, the numerous rivers and havens of the northern shore, and the low-lying vales of Glamorgan, Carmarthenshire and Pembrokeshire provide reasonably good anchorage and sheltered harbours. This is less true of the southern shore: the rivers there are fewer, the cliffs often uninviting and the anchorages (except for Bristol, Bridgwater and Barnstaple) of smaller account. By Roman times a landward link had been established through Glevum (later Gloucester), but the journey westward was long and often difficult, especially through the dense Forest of Dean. The Romans quickly learned the value of Severn ferries: their road from Bath ran directly to Abone on the Avon (now Sea Mills) and from its harbour, which can still be seen beside the Portway, boats could ferry across to the legionary fortress of Isca at Caerleon and to the Roman capital of the Silures tribe, Caerwent, through its ferry stage at Caldicot Pill. [11] A little further upriver, the 'Old Passage' at Aust is thought to have a Roman ancestry as Augustus's Passage to the Roman fortresses and villas of Gwent and Glamorgan. [12] In fact, most of the movements of peoples and cultures have been from the southern to the northern shore of the Severn. The reasons for this are partly physical: the view from Exmoor across the channel to Glamorgan's vale and the lowlands further west was— and is—rather more enticing than that from the Gower peninsula to the dark and daunting cliffs of north Somerset and Devon; the medieval mariner in his small sailing craft, running before prevailing south-westerly winds, would have found it easier and safer to put into a Welsh harbour than to search for an anchorage along the southern coast. Other reasons for these predominantly northern movements are political, not least the waves of conquerors, including Romans and Anglo-Normans, advancing from the west country into Wales. And yet others are cultural, with new fashions and innovations most frequently spreading westward from the continent, or at least from lowland England.

[9] 'Carmarthen and the Reformation, 1536-58', in T. Barnes and N. Yates (eds.), *Carmarthenshire Studies* (Carmarthen, 1974), pp. 139-40; *Religion, Language and Nationality in Wales* (Cardiff, 1979), ch. VIII ('The Welsh in Tudor England').

[10] F. Rowbotham, *The Severn Bore* (London, 1964); I. Gray, 'The Severn Bore: an 18th-century description', *Trans. Bristol and Glos. Arch. Soc.,* XCVII (1979), 123-6, where it is called 'Head of Tide'.

[11] For an even earlier crossing, protected by an Iron Age camp, V. E. Nash-Williams, 'An early Iron Age coastal camp at Sudbrook, near the Severn Tunnel, Monmouthshire', *Arch. Camb.,* XCIV (1939), 42-79.

[12] V[ictoria] C[ounty] H[istory], *Glos.,* X (1972), 50, 52, 62; I. D. Margary, *Roman roads in Britain* (3rd ed., London, 1973), pp. 138-9; A. H. Smith, *The Place-names of Gloucestershire,* III (E[nglish] P[lacename] S[ociety], XL, 1964), 127-8.

The historical occasions when such movements took place were many. In prehistoric times, people evidently found the Severn no great obstacle. Stone Age man took his skills in building megalithic tombs (known in Wales as cromlechs) from the Severn-Cotswold area to the Vale of Glamorgan where, to take one example, the chambered tombs at Tinkinswood, near Cardiff, have parallels on the other side of the channel. [13] Similarly, in the Bronze Age beaker finds and axes have been located in Somerset which show strong resemblances to others unearthed in the Vale. Later still, the Iron Age civilisation straddled the Severn, so that multivallate hill forts like the one at Llantwit Major have their counterpart at Worlebury in Somerset and elsewhere. [14] Nor should this surprise anyone who thinks of the colossal effort required to transport the famous blue-stones of the Presely mountains in Pembrokeshire to their present resting-place at Stonehenge. Cross-channel trade and travel were routine in this early period and inspired a common cultural development which has left traces even today. When Romans arrived in the west of England, the legionary fortress at Glevum was soon matched about AD 75 by another at Isca; between them ran ferries as well as a Roman road which sped westwards to Carmarthen and beyond. It is hardly surprising that Isca should have had stone from the vicinity of Bath in its walls. [15]

In the fifth and sixth centuries, after the Roman legions had withdrawn, Celtic Christian communities, fired with missionary zeal, are thought to have embarked on Christianising endeavours in the west country; and this may have been the direction from which the countryside of the southern shore embraced the faith of Christ anew. Place-name scholars and students of the later *Lives* of these Celtic 'saints' (few of which can be dated earlier than the eleventh or twelfth century) are much more sceptical nowadays about accepting Professor E. G. Bowen's bold reconstructions of the personal itineraries of these holy men or *peregrini*. [16] Nevertheless, religious communities and simple hermitages on one side of the channel often felt an affinity with similar settlements on the other side and declared their common attachment to the memory of a particular Celtic pilgrim. The havens of Gwent and the Vale of Glamorgan were at their service, and from the distinguished monastic community at Llancarfan monks could travel to the nearby harbour of Aberthaw to cross the Severn; from the ancient monastery at Llantwit Major the crossing was direct through Colhuw. Remnants of their activities included relics of supposedly sixth-century Celtic saints which were still in reliquaries at Glastonbury and Tewkesbury in the twelfth century. [17] Churches in Somerset and Devon were dedicated to these saintly Welshmen and in some cases the dedications still survive, even if the original Celtic names have become distorted in later dialects. St. Cyngar may have given his name to Congresbury in Somerset, St. Petroc his to the church at Timberscombe, near Dunster, and to

[13] A. Fox, 'The dual colonisation of East Glamorgan in the Neolithic and Bronze Ages', *Arch. Camb.*, XCI (1936), 100-17.

[14] *Idem*, 'Hill-slope forts and related earthworks in south-west England and south Wales', *Arch. Journal*, CIX (1952), 1-22; J. Forde-Johnston, *Hillforts of the Iron Age in England and Wales* (Liverpool, 1976), esp. ch. IX; and in general, W. F. Grimes, *The Prehistory of Wales* (Cardiff, 1951).

[15] D. Moore, *Caerleon: Fortress of the Legion* (Cardiff, 1970), p. 41.

[16] E. G. Bowen, *The Settlements of the Celtic Saints in Wales* (2nd ed., Cardiff, 1956).

[17] G. H. Doble, *Lives of the Welsh Saints*, ed. D. S. Evans (Cardiff, 1971), p. 134.

another in Pembrokeshire; St. Brioc is remembered at St. Breoke in Cornwall, Brixham in Devon, St. Briavels in Gloucestershire, and at Llandyfriog in far-off Cardiganshire; and St. Keyne, reputedly the daughter of Brychan, ancestor of almost all the saints of south Wales, is commemorated at Keynsham, near Bristol, Llangeinor in Glamorgan, and perhaps at Ffynnon Gain, near St. Clears in Carmarthenshire. Yet few of these church dedications can be dated earlier than the eighth century, and indeed some may be more plausibly associated with the literary activity of south Wales monasteries in the eleventh and twelfth centuries or with the appropriation of churches and property in Wales by the Anglo-Norman conquerors and settlers.[18]

For all their destructive raiding, the Vikings who came to the Severn region *via* Ireland added a new dimension to the development of both sides of the channel and demonstrated how valuable were the sea-ways as avenues of cultural communication. Scandinavian settlements on the south Wales coast are hinted at in place-names, and not only those of physical features indentifiable at sea (like Skomer and Sker and Steep Holm). Their raids, like those of 914 when a bishop of Llandaff was captured in Archenfield and landfalls were made near Watchet and Porlock and on Steep Holm, and others in the last two decades of the tenth century when the Severn coasts of Wales, Devon and Cornwall were ravaged, are attested by the Anglo-Saxon Chronicle.[19] In the place-names of the west country, too, their impact is discernible, albeit dimly. It is true that there are only a few such place-names in Gloucestershire, Devon and Cornwall; but Sveinn Forkbeard, who is traditionally believed to have given his name to a river island in south Wales (Sveinn's 'ey', which became Swansea), landed on Lundy Island and advanced on the Somerset and Devon coast in the early-eleventh century.[20] Severnside shared a common Viking experience. It has been suggested by Professor H. R. Loyn that these Scandinavian forays led to the establishment of staging-posts, even of Norse trading communities, at such places as Milford Haven, Swansea and Cardiff, and at Bristol and elsewhere on the Severn's southern shore.[21] There is no denying that for these Vikings the Severn sea was an inviting channel, certainly of communication and pillage, and possibly of trading and settlement too.

Far greater and more indelible was the impact of the Anglo-Norman conquerors, who forged newer links between the two shores which were

[18] C. A. Ralegh Radford, 'The church in Somerset down to 1100', *Proc. Somerset Arch. Soc.*, CVI (1961-2), 33-9; G. H. Doble, 'Saint Congar', *Antiquity*, XIX (1945), 32-43, 85-95; *idem, S. Nectan, S. Keyne and the children of Brychan in Cornwall* (Exeter, 1930), pp. 34-48. But see W. N. Yates, 'The "Age of the Saints" in Carmarthenshire: a study of church dedications', in *Carms. Antiquary*, IX (1973), 53-81, and S. M. Pearce, 'The dating of some Celtic dedications and hagiographical traditions in south-western Britain', *Trans. Devon. Assoc.*, CV (1973), 100-7.

[19] D. R. Patterson, *Early Cardiff* (Exeter, 1926), pp. 8-9; B. G. Charles, *Old-Norse relations with Wales* (Cardiff, 1934); *idem, Non-Celtic place-names in Wales* (London, 1938), pp. xxxiii-xxxiv, 292-5; D. Whitelock (ed.), *English Historical Documents*, I, *c. 500-1042* (2nd ed., London, 1979), pp. 212, 232-3, 236.

[20] J. E. B. Glover *et al.*, *The Place-names of Devon*, I (EPS, VIII, 1931), xxvi-xxvii, 19, 308, 519; II (EPS, IX, 1932), 687; Smith, *Place-names of Glos.*, IV (EPS, XLI, 1965), 44-5; W. H. Jones, *History of the port of Swansea* (Carmarthen, 1923), pp. 1-2. Swansea could equally well be a combination of Old Scandinavian 'Sveinn' and 'saer' (sea): Charles, *Non-Celtic Place-Names*, p. 130.

[21] H. R. Loyn, *The Vikings in Wales* (London, 1976).

strengthened progressively during the ensuing middle ages. Shortly before 1100, the coastal lowlands of Gwent and Glamorgan were invaded and overrun by Norman knights either from Bristol, using the well known ferry routes, or overland from Gloucester under Robert FitzHamon and his tenants. FitzHamon and his successors as earls of Gloucester were west-country barons, and even after the Vale of Glamorgan had been occupied and settled by this relatively small group of knights, their new lordship continued to be governed from Bristol and Gloucester, as well as from Cardiff, by a group of clerical administrators that moved easily through the earls' estates. Among the knightly tenantry was at least one member of the de Bonville family, from Minehead and Chewton in Somerset; he was certainly in Glamorgan by the middle of the twelfth century and his holding not far from Cardiff came to be known as Bonvilston.[22] Gregory de Turri, on whom Earl William (1147-83) of Gloucester depended, had property in Bristol as well as in Newport and, further to the west, at Kenfig in Glamorgan—holdings that effectively charted the advance of comital authority across the Severn estuary.[23] One of Earl Robert (1122-47)'s tenants in Devon, Richard de Granville, seems to have sailed independently across the Severn sea in about 1129 to establish a lordship west of the river Neath; it was accordingly cut off from the primary settlement of the earls and their other tenants further to the east by Welsh commotes.[24] For more than two centuries, the close relationship between the earldom of Gloucester and the lordships of Gwynllwg and Glamorgan had social, administrative, economic and religious dimensions that meant much to their inhabitants astride the Severn channel. The earls looked on those who lived in their territories as a single community, frequently addressing them collectively in charters—and not only those charters that concerned lands in Wales—as 'all our faithful French, English and Welsh'.[25]

The abbeys of Gloucester, Tewkesbury and St. Augustine's, Bristol, which were handsomely patronised by the earls, acquired churches, burgages and other property in Newport, Cardiff and Bristol, where their monks were freed from tolls. The new religious houses in south Wales that were nurtured by the earls and their men, Neath, Margam, Caerleon and Tintern among them, had their own properties in Bristol. Margam, for instance, occupied land in Small Street and elsewhere, and had several stalls in the market place and in Goldsmith's Place; only in the 1480s did the abbot dispose of this valuable commercial interest by leasing it to Tewkesbury abbey.[26] The burgesses of each of the boroughs within the earls' regional dominion enjoyed special reciprocal privileges in the others.

---

[22] G. O. Pierce, *The Place-names of Dinas Powys Hundred* (Cardiff, 1968), pp. 11-13; R. B. Patterson (ed.), *Earldom of Gloucester Charters* (Oxford, 1973), pp. 17, 19, 26.

[23] Ibid., pp. 46-7, 120-1, 162.

[24] For this and other examples in Glamorgan, see R. A. Griffiths, 'The Norman Conquest and the Twelve Knights of Glamorgan', in S. Williams (ed.), *Glamorgan Historian*, III (1966), 153-69.

[25] Patterson, op. cit., *passim*.

[26] Ibid., pp. 116 (Margam), 90-1, 170 (Caerleon), 176 (Goldcliff); G. T. Clark (ed.), *Cartae et alia munimenta de Glamorgancia* [henceforward *Cartae*], I, 126; III, 886-7, 890-4 (Margam); W. de Gray Birch, *History of Margam Abbey* (London, 1897), pp. 202-4; D. H. Williams, *The Welsh Cistercians* (Pontypool, 1969), p. 70.

And these arrangements long outlasted the personal and administrative links between south Wales and the earldom of Gloucester. [27]

Further west, the coastal plains of Carmarthenshire and south Pembrokeshire were similarly penetrated by Anglo-Norman adventurers from Devon and Somerset, though this time at the behest of William Rufus and Henry I. William FitzBaldwin arrived from Devon on the king's commission in 1094 and built a fortress near Carmarthen. [28] Henry I seems to have encouraged a number of Flemish immigrants to settle in Pembrokeshire, some of them from Devon where they kept their estates even after acquiring others across the channel. The Wide de Brian who can be observed at Rosemarket, near Haverfordwest, in the mid-twelfth century is probably to be identified with Wido de Brionna, a tenant of the honor of Okehampton in 1166. It is instructive to note that when the Cluniac priory of St. Clears was founded in the mid-twelfth century, it was attached to a house in Paris, St. Martin des Champs, which was also the mother house of Exeter and Barnstaple priories. [29]

The ecclesiastical bond became even closer when the invaders donated Welsh estates to their favoured monasteries in the west country, and when they attached churches and monasteries in south Wales to great abbeys like Tewkesbury (in the case of Llantwit Major, Llanbleddian, Newcastle and Kenfig churches in Glamorgan, and St. Mary's church, Cardiff), Gloucester (which received the ancient Celtic house at Llancarfan and the newer one at Ewenny, and St. Gwynllyw's church, Newport), Bristol (whose monks on Flat Holm were granted the advowson of Rumney and St. Mellon's churches in Gwent), Montacute (granted Malpas church, Gwent, in 1132), Glastonbury (which acquired Bassaleg as a daughter house), and Sherborne (which became the mother house of Kidwelly priory in 1114). [30] Even the new Welsh houses were given English properties by their Anglo-Norman patrons. St. Dogmael's priory acquired land in Devon in this way, whilst Whitland abbey enjoyed property in Bristol that enabled its agents to trade freely in the town. [31] Neath, founded by the Devonshire knight. Richard de Granville, and patronised by the Mohuns of Dunster, was endowed with substantial lands in Devon and Somerset as well as in Glamorgan. The Somerset lands were at Hornblotton, Exford and near Watchet, and on one occasion in the late-1190s it was even proposed to move the mother abbey to its grange at Exford, where there would be greater room for expansion than at Neath, which was situated not many miles from Margam and Ewenny. But the project came to nothing because plans were already afoot to found a

---

[27] T. B. Pugh (ed.), *Glamorgan County History*, III: *The Middle Ages* (Cardiff, 1971), ch. VII.

[28] R. A. Griffiths (ed.), *Boroughs of Medieval Wales* (Cardiff, 1978), p. 138.

[29] I. W. Rowlands, 'The making of the march: aspects of the Norman settlement in Dyfed', in R. A. Brown (ed.), *Battle Conference III, 1980* (Boydell Press, 1981), pp. 148-50.

[30] Patterson, op. cit., *passim*; W. Rees, 'Accounts of the rectory of Cardiff and other possessions of the abbey of Tewkesbury in Glamorgan for the year 1449-50', *South Wales and Mon. Record Soc.*, II (1950), 127-86; *Two Cartularies of the Augustinian priory of Bruton and the Cluniac priory of Montacute* (S[omerset] R[ecord] S[ociety], VIII, 1894), pp. 182-4. Probably in the fourteenth century, the dean and chapter of Llandaff secured the farm of Bassaleg from Glastonbury in perpetuity: A. Watkin (ed.), *The Great Chartulary of Glastonbury*, III (SRS, LXIV, 1956), 707-9.

[31] Rowlands, op. cit., p. 150; D. H. Williams, *Welsh Cistercians*, p. 70.

monastery on donated land some ten miles away: Cleeve abbey was opened by monks from Revesby in Lincolnshire in 1198, despite a vigorous protest from Neath to the general chapter of the Cistercian order.[32] Unlike Hornblotton (which was exchanged for Walterston in Gower) and the acres at Watchet (which were abandoned), Exford remained in Neath's possession until the Reformation, but gradually the monks' direct interest in their grange waned and it eventually became indistinguishable from any other west-country manor; in 1322 it was leased to Sir John Inge for life.[33]

Within the dominion of the earls of Gloucester especially, these great abbeys and their extensive estates astride the channel became a convenient source of patronage for the clerically-trained administrators who organised the earls' affairs. Accordingly, the personnel of this Anglo-Welsh church reflected the growth of a close-knit clerical community in medieval Severnside. William of Saltmarsh, near Bristol, moved easily across the estuary when, as prior of St. Augustine's, Bristol, he was elected bishop of Llandaff in 1184. Nineteen years later, a new bishop of St. David's was appointed, Geoffrey de Henlow, who had lived in Bristol earlier in his life and had been prior of Llanthony priory since about 1189. The new monasteries founded in south Wales naturally recruited manpower from the west country: William, Thomas and Elias of Bristol, monks of Margam, were prominent members of their community in the first century of the abbey's existence.[34]

Once the initial phases of conquest and settlement were passed, more peaceful activities were able to flourish, offering opportunities for a common heritage in church, state and commerce to evolve. And in an age of demographic growth, in the steps of the conquerors came traders, migrants and settlers, especially to the new colonial boroughs founded alongside the Anglo-Norman castles. Well before the end of the thirteenth century, Carmarthen, probably the largest town in medieval Wales, was attracting Bristolians like Thomas Bolpenne and John Winter, and Devonshire men like Simon Bideford, all of whom became reeve of the town in Edward I's reign. Members of the family of Thomas de Chippenham in the Gwent village of Chippenham had presumably brought their name with them from Wiltshire.[35] John de Kenfig was a burgess of Bristol by 1253 when he served as reeve of the town; though he lived in Tucker Street, his cherished

---

[32] D. Knowles and R. N. Hadcock, *Medieval Religious Houses, England and Wales* (2nd ed., London, 1971), p. 117; F. G. Cowley, 'Neath versus Margam: some 13th century disputes', *Trans. Port Talbot Hist. Soc.,* III, no. 1 (1967), 11. Other property near Bideford had been exchanged for land in Glamorgan not long after Neath's foundation: Patterson, op. cit., p. 172.

[33] W. de Gray Birch, *A History of Neath Abbey* (Neath, 1902), pp. 109, 123; F. G. Cowley, 'The Cistercian economy in Glamorgan, 1130-1349', *Morgannwg,* XI (1967), 10-11. A dispute between the rector of Exford and the abbot and convent of Neath in 1348 referred to Exford as a manor to be cultivated or leased, and the dispute was settled at Bridgwater by the dean of Wells and confirmed by the prior of Bath and the bishop of Bath and Wells: T. S. Holmes (ed.), *The Register of Ralph of Shrewsbury, bishop of Bath and Wells, 1329-1363* (SRS, X, 1896), p. 558: Glam RO., CL Deeds 1/8 (the prior's notification).

[34] D. Knowles and C. N. L. Brooke, *The Heads of Religious Houses, England and Wales, 940-1216* (Cambridge, 1972), pp. 155, 172; *Cartae,* I, 159; II, 363-4; V, 2290; D. Williams, 'Fasti Cistercienses Cambrenses', *Bull. Board of Celtic Studies,* XXIV (1971), 181-229.

[35] R. A. Griffiths, *The Principality of Wales in the Later Middle Ages,* I. *South Wales, 1277-1536* (Cardiff, 1972), pp. 331-2; Charles, *Non-Celtic Place-Names,* p. 262.

emotional (and commercial?) ties with Glamorgan prompted him to patronise Margam abbey round about 1261.[36] It is a distinct possibility, too, that Earl William of Gloucester's tenants in Glamorgan, the de Cardiffs, were also his tenants at Walton (soon to be Walton Cardiff) in his honor of Gloucester by 1166; and by the next century members of the family had settled in Bristol, where John de Cardiff was reeve in 1231-2 and a later John was steward in 1280-1 and a resident of Tucker Street. The Bristol field name of 'Kerdyfiscroft' which appears in the city charter of 1373 doubtless records this family's prominence.[37] These men had no reason to disavow the surname which their new neighbours presumably gave them.

Trading links within medieval Severnside multiplied. The characteristic products of both shores were channelled to the homes, offices and churches of those who could afford them. By the thirteenth century, Welsh hides, leather, wool and fish were finding their way out of Tenby, Carmarthen and Kidwelly to the growing port of Bristol; timber, iron and coal were carried from the Forest of Dean down to Chepstow, Bristol and Gloucester and then out into the channel; and tradition has it that Somerset freestone was transported all the way to the little port of Aberarth, en route to the new abbey of Strata Florida (re-founded in 1184) in remote Cardiganshire.[38] Ships from Bristol carried this valued Dundry Hill freestone from Somerset to south Wales on other more melancholy occasions—in the 1240s for tomb effigies in Margam abbey and St. Peter's church, Carmarthen, and in 1284-5 for the carving of tombs at Carmarthen for two English esquires slain in the king's service.[39] There was, too, a vital commercial link at times of emergency: in 1188 famine in south Wales was partially alleviated by the abbot of Margam securing a licence to import corn from Bristol for the hungry at his gate. A generation or so later, Neath abbey undertook to obtain corn from the west country in not dissimilar circumstances.[40] Commercial contacts of the boroughs and religious houses of south Wales with Bristol and the Devon and Somerset ports had been regularised by this stage and, it is likely, were an established feature of burghal and monastic life.

In these stabler conditions, there were opportunities in local government for Englishmen and Welshmen to serve on either side of the channel. The English

[36] Bristol RO, Museum Deeds, 5139 (452); *Cartae*, II, 648-9.

[37] The critical connections seem to be made by William de Cardiff at Llantriddid in 1126 and Walton in 1166 (*VCH, Glos.*, VIII [Oxford, 1968], 238), his sons Richard and Simon in Glamorgan *c.* 1147-83 (Patterson, op. cit., *passim*), his other sons Robert and Roger in Glos. *c.* 1182-1202 (*VCH, Glos.*, VIII, 238), Robert's son William in Glamorgan, Glos. and Bristol by *c.* 1230 (Bristol RO, Museum Deeds, 5139 [185]; W. St. Clair Baddeley, 'Early deeds relating to St. Peter's abbey, Gloucester', *Trans. Bristol and Glos. Arch. Soc.*, XXXVIII [1915], 44). See also L. T. Smith (ed.), *The maire of Bristowe is kalendar, by Robert Ricart* (Camden soc., n.s., V, 1872); Bristol RO, All Saints deeds, HS E 1(8) MS 2, 3 (Bristol Deeds 168, 79); *Cartae, passim*; F. W. Weaver (ed.), *A Cartulary of Buckland Priory* (SRS, XXV, 1909), p. 76; Smith, *Place-Names of Glos.*, III, 97.

[38] H. C. Darby, *An historical geography of England before AD 1800* (Cambridge, 1951), pp. 282-92; J. W. Sherborne, *The Port of Bristol in the Middle Ages* (Bristol, 1971), p. 4; *Arch. Camb.*, XCIV (1946-7), 146 (comment by T. Jones Pierce).

[39] A. C. Fryer, 'Monumental effigies made by Bristol craftsmen (1240-1550)', *Archaeologia*, LXXIV (1925), 2-3; Griffiths, *Boroughs*, p. 148 and n. 56.

[40] D. H. Williams, *Welsh Cistercians*, pp. 21, 71; *Close Rolls, 1227-31*, p. 203; *1231-4*, p. 360; *1242-7*, p. 430; *Cal. Patent Rolls, 1232-47*, p. 69.

rulers of Wales understandably relied heavily on men from the border shires to staff the more responsible positions in Wales's administration. Walter de Pederton, who probably hailed from either North or South Petherton in Somerset, held high office in the king's employ in south Wales and Ireland during Edward I's reign as one of his more dependable officials at a crucial phase in the settlement of the country.[41] A few years earlier, in 1271, the abbot of Tintern, a monastery with extensive Severnside interests through its recruitment and endowment, was detailed to assess royal taxes imposed on Bristol.[42]

Despite the bitterness which the military conquest had generated, attacks from one side of the channel on the other were relatively few in number and mainly piratical in character. The occasional raid from Glamorgan on the Somerset coast was not unknown; probably in 1242 outlaws from Lundy Island, protected by the abbot of Margam, descended on Devon, and a little later in the century there was a Welsh attack on Minehead. But the pirates who infested most open waterways in the middle ages did not, in the case of the Severn, seriously damage more peaceful links. The nest of pirates established on Lundy in the 1230s was soon cleared by the government, and although Henry Stradling was captured in the channel by a Breton pirate as late as 1449, this episode did not disrupt the long-standing communication between the Stradlings' Somerset estates at Combe Hawey and the family castle at St. Donat's.[43]

It might be thought that the efforts to repel Welsh assaults on the castles and towns of south Wales and to suppress the periodic and more widespread rebellions would have undermined—even severed—the regular and profitable communications that had been established across the channel. Yet in one important respect they strengthened them. As early as 1193 Bristol castle was used as the supply-base for troops despatched by Richard the Lionheart to relieve a besieged Swansea castle, and Bristol had a similar role to play in munitioning and supplying Carmarthen and Cardigan castles during the crises of the following decades.[44] But it was during Edward I's decisive campaigns in Wales that Severnside's military, maritime and commercial resources were put to most effective use. Soldiers and tradesmen from Bristol channel ports were frequently drawn to assembly-points in south Wales in these years—and some of them even sustained the current of migrant settlers. King Edward, in the last decades of the thirteenth century, often relied on Somerset for the knights and archers needed for his armies in Wales: in 1276 twenty of the county's knights were summoned to Worcester, and in 1294 twenty-eight were assembled in Cardiff. Such forces had to be fed and supplied while on the march, and in 1277 Bridgwater sailors were amongst those responsible for carrying provisions across the water for the troops engaged in Edward's first Welsh war. The suppression of Rhys ap Maredudd's

---

[41] Griffiths, *Principality*, I, 93-4, and references cited there.

[42] F. G. Cowley, *The Monastic Order in South Wales, 1066-1349* (Cardiff, 1977), p. 218.

[43] F. M. Powicke, *King Henry III and the Lord Edward* (Oxford, 1947), pp. 747-58; R. A. Griffiths, 'The Stradlings of St. Donat's', *Morgannwg*, VIII (1963), 25-6. Sir Edward Stradling and his son were called 'merchants of the county of Somerset' in 1339: *Cartae*, IV, 1233.

[44] D. M. Stenton (ed.), *Pipe Roll, 5 Richard I* (Pipe Roll Soc., n.s., III, 1927), pp. 113-14, 148; *Close Rolls, 1231-4*, p. 394; *Cal. Liberate Rolls, 1251-60*, p. 43; *Close Rolls, 1253-4*, p. 63.

revolt in Carmarthenshire in 1287-8 and of the larger scale rebellion of 1294-5 was partly sustained by armaments and other resources sent from Bristol to the ports of south-west Wales. [45]

Edward's castle-building at Aberystwyth between 1277 and 1283 presented logistical problems which were solved by relying on Bristol as the assembly-point for the carpenters and masons (almost 500 in six years) recruited in Devon, Somerset, Dorset, Wiltshire and Gloucestershire for despatch by sea to Carmarthen, Cardigan and on to Aberystwyth. John of Bedminster, a Bristol suburb, was hard at work repairing Carmarthen castle in 1288-9, while fifty years later Roger de Devonshire had succeeded him as mason. [46]

Again, at the height of the Glyndŵr rebellion a century and more later, supplies and recruits from Devon, Dorset, Somerset and Gloucestershire were transported to Carmarthen, Cardiff and elsewhere from Ilfracombe, Bridgwater, Dunster, Uphill and, above all, Bristol. [47] Two Bristol merchants in particular, Thomas Saunders and John Stevenes, filled something akin to the role of contracted suppliers of wines and foodstuffs to royal armies and hard-pressed castles in south Wales during 1404-5. [48] Others, however, put profit—and perhaps blood—before royal injunctions. Efforts were made to starve the rebels in Wales of supplies provided by normal commercial intercourse, but it is quite evident that some Bristolians were still plying their trade across the Severn estuary in April 1404. And at least one Barnstaple merchant and former mayor, Thomas Hertescote, was charged that same month with supplying the rebel leader by sea; that this accusation ultimately proved to be maliciously inspired by a disgruntled rival in Barnstaple cannot disguise the seriousness with which it was regarded in the north Devon port. [49] The punitive legislation of Henry IV's early parliaments, which was intended in part to disable Welshmen from civic office in English and Welsh towns, was equally ineffective in medieval Severnside. By 1395 John Kidwelly was residing in Bridgwater, where he was a burgess and clerk to the urban community; he and a handful of other prominent townsmen of Welsh origin continued to live there throughout the rebellion and Kidwelly did

[45] *VCH, Somerset*, II, 185; J. E. Morris, *The Welsh Wars of Edward I* (Oxford, 1901); E. B. Fryde (ed.), *Book of Prests for the King's Wardrobe for 1294-5* (Oxford, 1962), pp. xxxi *et seq.*; M. Prestwich, *War, Politics and Finance under Edward I* (London, 1972), p. 117; R. A. Griffiths, 'The revolt of Rhys ap Maredudd, 1287-88', *Welsh Hist. Rev.*, III (1966), 133.

[36] Griffiths, *Boroughs*, p. 148; M. Sharp (ed.), *Accounts of the constables of Bristol Castle in the thirteenth and early fourteenth centuries* (Bristol Record Soc., XXXIV, 1982), pp. 42-6; A. J. Taylor, 'Castle-building in Wales in the thirteenth century: the prelude to construction', in E. M. Jope (ed.), *Studies in Building History* (London, 1961), ch. VII, with maps on pp. 107, 111, reproduced in P. Smith, *Houses of the Welsh Countryside* (London, 1975), pp. 428-31. For Bristol castle's role as a prison for Welsh princes and other rebels after 1283, Sharp, op. cit., pp. xxx-xxxii, 17, 44, 46, 63, 66.

[47] *Cal. Patent Rolls, 1401-5*, pp. 296-7, 440, 439 (1403), 310 (1404); *1405-8*, pp. 163 (1406), 362 (1407); *Cal. Close Rolls, 1405-9*, p. 29 (1406). See in general T. W. Williams, 'The Glyndŵr rebellion: a military study' (unpublished Wales M.A. diss., 1979), pp. 19-23.

[48] *Cal. Patent Rolls, 1405-8*, pp. 63, 67; F. Devon (ed.), *Issues of the Exchequer, Henry III-Henry VI* (Record Comm., 1835), p. 299.

[49] N. H. Nicolas (ed.), *Proceedings and Ordinances of the Privy Council of England* (7 vols., Record Comm., 1834-7), II, 83: *Cal. Patent Rolls, 1401-5*, p. 135; Barnstable Borough Records, 441.

not even lose his influential position in the town's government.[50] Periodic strains such as these between the thirteenth and the fifteenth centuries were no more than temporary threats to a Severnside society that was developing common interests and some sense of social identity.

All these circumstances and historical contexts facilitated contact across the Bristol channel, and offered opportunities for the interchange of ideas and habits, fashions and families. The nature of the society which resulted at least in part from these centuries of contact was distinctive enough to warrant the description of medieval Severnside as a 'culture province'.

For one thing, they had an appreciable effect on how people spoke and how their dialects developed, particularly in south Wales. It was said of Coychurch parish, near Bridgend, towards the end of the seventeenth century, that 'the language is partly English, partly Welsh, our tradeing being for the most parte with Summer and Devon Shires which spoiles our Welsh'. A little later, an English traveller in Glamorgan noted the scarcity of Welsh-speaking people in Llantwit Major, where 'their dialect [is] approaching nearer to a broad Somersetshire than to any other'.[51] Further west, the best available opinion on the peculiarity of south Pembrokeshire's dialect is that it owes little to the famous Flemish settlers there in Henry I's reign and much more to reinforcements of migrants from south-west England.[52] This extension of the use of an English tongue in south Wales has been plausibly dated in Glamorgan's case—and the same would go for Gower and Pembrokeshire—no earlier than the Anglo-Norman conquest and settlement, predominantly directed from the west country.[53] Precious little work has been done on the place-names of Somerset whereby these phenomena can be examined, and although a few studies have been made on the Welsh side, the region as a whole is not as well served in this respect as other parts of the country. Still, it is suggested that many place-names in south Wales mirror the history of migration, for names that incorporate the non-Welsh personal names of medieval landowners are known to be paralleled in Devon and Somerset. The distribution of non-Celtic place-names in Wales before 1715 shows an overwhelming preponderance in south Pembrokeshire, south Gower, and in the vales of Glamorgan and Gwent.[54] Gloucestershire, particularly between the rivers Severn and Wye, has more Welsh elements in its place-names than most other counties, and whereas a number of these are likely

[50] T. B. Dilks (ed.), 'A Calendar of some medieval manuscripts in the custody of Bridgwater Corporation', in *Collectanea*, III (SRS, LVII, 1942), 33-6; idem, *Bridgwater Borough Archives, 1400-45* (SRS, LVIII, 1945), nos. 499, 587, 590.

[51] Pierce, *Dinas Powys*, pp. xv-xvi.

[52] Griffiths, *Boroughs*, p. 320.

[53] Charles, *Non-Celtic Place-names*, pp. xxviii-xxix; B. L. James, 'The Welsh language in the Vale of Glamorgan', *Morgannwg*, XVI (1972), 16-18; H. Tucker, 'The dialect speech of Gower', *Gower*, III (1950), 26-9; W. G. V. Balchin (ed.), *Swansea and its region* (Swansea, 1971), pp. 160-1, 199-200, and map p. 152. In 1511 Cardiff seemed a good place for an apprentice cabin-boy to learn English: J. Bernard, *Navires et gens de mer à Bordeaux (vers 1400-vers 1550)* (3 vols., Paris, 1968), pp. 531, 641.

[54] Smith, *Houses*, pp. 340-54.

to be survivals from Anglo-Saxon times when a British population still clung to the Cotswold area, others are certain to indicate continuous Welsh immigration in the middle ages, even to the east of the river Severn.[55] Between Glamorgan and Somerset common elements may be seen in Swansea and Swayneswick, Penarth and Pennard, and there may be an equally close relationship between Dollaston (in Pembrokeshire) and Loosedon Barton (Devon), both of which perhaps owe their origin to 'lollard'.[56] The Dumballe, the low-lying marsh or moorland between Cardiff's south gate and the sea, has place-name elements in it which can also be identified in Gloucestershire and Somerset, where they describe flat and muddy meadowland beside river courses. In the other direction, the sixteenth-century name for Cardiff's borough prison, the Cockmarel (or Kwchmoel) was in use in the next century in the west country as Cockmoil, indicating a bare cell.[57]

Social customs, too, seem to have pursued a common development on both banks of the Severn. The practice of ultimogeniture, whereby the youngest son inherited a father's property rather than his older brothers, was a custom followed in the Vale of Glamorgan, southern Gwent and in Somerset; and when peasants were settled by Anglo-Norman colonists on the plains of south Wales, between the lordship of Pembroke and the coastal manors of Gwent, they ploughed a customary acre whose size had been familiar to them in Devon and Cornwall.[58] Intermarriage may have been common then; it certainly was later. In 1329, William Berd, of Huish-by-Highbridge in Somerset, concluded a business agreement with John Lovel of Kenfig in Glamorgan; it provided that William's son, Ralph Berd, should marry John's daughter, Joan Lovel. She would receive from her father the Lovel lands at Kenfig for her lifetime; but in fact the Welshman proved the more astute of the two fathers, for his lands were not made over to his son-in-law, and while the couple lived under his roof in Glamorgan for four years, John Lovel had custody of the Berd property in Somerset.[59] To take another example: John Beauchamp, of Hatch in Somerset, died in 1361 and left as his heiress a sister, Cecilia. She was already a widow and now much wealthier as a result of her brother's death; she crossed the channel to marry Sir Gilbert Turberville of Coity five years later.[60]

The houses in which men lived and the churches in which they worshipped and were buried were often constructed by Severnside architects who practised their craft on both sides of the channel. Long houses that have survived from the fifteenth century and have been carefully studied in Carmarthenshire and on the Brendon Hills and elsewhere in Somerset, Devon and Dorset show close affinities

[55] Smith, *Place-Names of Glos.,* IV, 23-30, 203, 216.

[56] Glover, *Place-Names of Devon,* II (EPS, IX, 1932), 373.

[57] T. Jones, 'The place-names of Cardiff', *South Wales and Mon. Record Soc.,* II (1950), 45-6, 48.

[58] H. J. Randall, *Vale of Glamorgan* (Newport, 1961), pp. 93-4; W. Rees, *South Wales and the March, 1284-1415* (Oxford, 1924), p. 155; B. E. Howells, 'The distribution of customary acres in south Wales', *National Library of Wales Journal,* XV (1967-8), 227-32.

[59] T. B. Dilks (ed.), *Bridgwater Borough Archives, 1200-1377* (SRS, XLVIII, 1933), pp. 81-2. For the later history of both properties, Dilks, *Bridgwater Archives, 1400-45,* no. 674 (1437); cf. ibid., no. 700.

[60] E. H. Bates (ed.), *The Cartularies of the Benedictine Abbeys of Muchelney and Athelney* (SRS, XIV, 1899), p. 193.

in the principles of their roof-construction.[61] More opulent stone-vaulted houses from an earlier time in south Pembrokeshire and Somerset have common features, and there is evidence that Master Thomas de la Bataile was employed at Caerphilly castle by Hugh Despenser in the 1320s and on the Despenser reconstruction of Tewkesbury abbey.[62] Severnside church architecture exhibits the same tendency, as the similarities between Llandaff Cathedral, St. John's church in Cardiff, St. Mary's in Tenby, Dundry, Bridgwater and St. Stephen's, Bristol, illustrate. It is thought that the Bristol stonemason named Hert was responsible for the towers at both St. John's and St. Stephen's in the late-fifteenth century.[63] Professor Glanmor Williams has noted the correspondences in architectural conception and stylistic detail between the novel work at St. Augustine's abbey, Bristol, and at other great churches in the west midlands and west country, and Bishop Henry Gower's building enterprises (1328-47) at St. David's cathedral and palace. Gower and Edmund Knowle, abbot of St. Augustine's (died 1332), were friends and the former seems to have used west-country masons at St. David's and Lamphey palace, and perhaps at other churches in Pembrokeshire (notably Carew, Hodgeston and Monkton). The architects, masons and carpenters who worked on such buildings were patronised by great figures, such as the king and his court and abbots and bishops like Knowle and Gower who moved in the same circles. Just as Bataile is known to have done work on Tewkesbury and Caerphilly, so Master Nicholas de Dernford was engaged on Burton abbey and Repton priory, and also at St. Augustine's under Knowle's direction before he was engaged on the royal castle at Beaumaris in the early-fourteenth century. Dernford probably came from the west midlands, and it is not impossible that he or one of his craftsmen was engaged by Bishop Gower at St. David's where the palace shows certain similarities with the plans of Edward I's castles and with the chequered stone-work design at Beaumaris. Dernford was master mason in north Wales from 1323 to 1331, though he may have been at work on Beaumaris by 1316; but in 1327 the royal castles in south Wales (all of them, significantly, lying within the diocese of St. David's) were placed in his charge and this appointment was confirmed in 1331. His expertise would have been easily available to Bishop Gower.[64] Other, more modest, churches carry a waggon or barrel type of wooden roof which is almost as common in Carmarthenshire parish churches as it is in those of the west of

[61] Peate, op. cit.; Smith, *Houses,* ch. III and pp. 362-3, 376-9.

[62] Ibid., pp. 372-4; *idem,* 'Historical domestic architecture in Dyfed: an outline', in Barnes and Yates, *Carms. Studies,* pp. 43-109; W. G. Thomas, 'The architectural history of St. Mary's Church, Tenby', *Arch. Camb.,* CXV (1966), 134-65; R. Morris, 'Tewkesbury Abbey: the Despenser Mausoleum', *Trans. Bristol and Glos. Arch. Soc.,* XCIII (1974), 151-3.

[63] W. G. Thomas, 'Medieval church building in Dyfed', in D. Moore (ed.), *The Land of Dyfed in early times* (Cardiff, 1964), pp. 27-30; R. Merrick, *A Booke of Glamorganshires Antiquities,* ed. J. A. Corbett (London, 1887), p. 93. For the will of William Hert, burgess of Bristol (d. 1493), PRO, PCC, 28 Doggett, where two sons, William and John, are also mentioned.

[64] 'Henry de Gower (?1278-1347): bishop and builder', *Arch. Camb.,* CXXX (1981), 9-16; J. Evans, *English Art, 1307-1461* (London, 1949), pp. 23-4, 67; A. J. Taylor, 'A petition from Master Nicholas de Derneford to Edward II', *Trans. Bristol and Glos. Arch. Soc.,* XCVIII (1980), 171-3; H. M. Colvin (ed.), *The History of the King's Works: The Middle Ages* (2 vols., London, 1963), I, 405, 469-70; II, 1057. Dernford's petition is calendared in W. Rees (ed.), *Calendar of Ancient Petitions relating to Wales* (Cardiff, 1975), pp. 165-6.

England. Inside some of them were placed memorial figure sculptures carved in stone by highly regarded craftsmen from the Bristol workshops of the mid-thirteenth century and later. They supplied effigies of knights and civilians alike for Margam abbey and St. Peter's, Carmarthen, and the style of their work can be paralleled in St. James's priory church and in the hospital of St. Mark, Bristol, as well as at Iddesleigh in Devon and Tickenham in Somerset. In other cases, and a little later, in Pembrokeshire as well as in Gwent, Welsh ateliers modelled their work on Bristol exemplars, using local stone in place of the Dundry Hill freestone. [65]

Factors such as intermarriage helped to make the pattern of landownership in Wales and the west country a complex and interlocking one. At first, opportunities presented by conquest led to an influx into south Wales of aristocratic Anglo-Norman and English proprietors; but as time passed and more peaceful conditions prevailed, the movement became a two-way one. A south Walian named John married Alice, daughter and heiress of Peter de Evercy of Brimpton, by about 1324; he thereafter enjoyed the Somerset estates of his wife and took to living on the southern side of the Severn, where he was given the surname of 'de Glamorgan'. It is no judgement on the wisdom of this instance of social mobility that their offspring, John, was born an idiot. [66] This cross-fertilisation had an ecclesiastical dimension, too, so that the Severnside church, despite falling within at least four dioceses, became a community of clerics, monks and institutions that transcended county and diocesan boundaries, political frontiers and the hazards of road and water travel. Severnside abbeys like Margam, Neath, Tintern, Goldcliff, Glastonbury and Montacute retained estates in several counties; they continued to recruit monks from all parts of the region, English and Welsh, and for those who administered the abbey lands, there was an annual circuit from estate to estate. To speak of individuals, one may mention those priests who exchanged benefices with one another, or bishops of Llandaff who were employed by bishops of Bath and Wells as assistants or suffragans, or Welshmen such as Thomas of Exeter, vicar of St. Michael's, Pembroke, in 1350, who established themselves in west-country benefices. And Richard Hore, provost and canon residentiary of Wells at the time of his death, remembered in his will of 1449 eight churches and two friaries in the diocese of St. David's where he had served as precentor and canon of the cathedral at an earlier stage of his career. Miles Salley was successively abbot of Abingdon and Eynsham in Oxfordshire, but he also rebuilt St. Mark's hospital church in Bristol and became bishop of Llandaff in 1500; he erected his own tomb in St. Mark's before he died in 1516, and yet he directed in his will that his heart be buried in Mathern church, near Chepstow, where bishops of Llandaff had a residence, and that certain

---

[65] Fryer, *Archaeologia*, LXXIV (1925), 1-72.

[66] T. S. Holmes (ed.), *The Register of Ralph of Shrewsbury, bishop of Bath and Wells, 1329-63*, II (SRS, X, 1896), 477, 725; H. C. Maxwell-Lyte (ed.), *Two registers formerly belonging to the family of Beauchamp of Hatch* (SRS, XXXV, 1920), p. 94 n. 2; E. Green (ed.), *Feet of Fines, 1 Edward III* (SRS, XII, 1898), p. 242.

building work at his cathedral church should be financed from his estate.[67] On the other hand, these trans-channel experiences were not always quite so effortless. When John Soyer, the prior of St. Clears in Carmarthenshire, was elected prior of Barnstaple priory in 1333, the bishop of Exeter strenuously protested—though his reason for doing so was the notoriously dissolute life that the Welshman led and the fear that it would prove contagious.[68]

The cosmopolitan character of this Severnside culture is especially apparent in the merchant community, and in the towns and ports of the region. As early as 1155 Bristol and its merchants had been accorded the privilege of trading in Wales free of tolls and irksome customs duties; while Pembroke's men enjoyed similar freedoms in Bristol, Gloucester, Devon and Cornwall.[69] By 1356, the mayor and commonalty of Carmarthen were so eager for 'good accord and good friendship between the good people of Barnstaple and our Burgesses' of Carmarthen that they made formal arrangements for Barnstaple men to recover debts owed to them by Carmarthen's burgesses.[70] The Wysmans of Tenby had a tenement in Small Street, Bristol, by the early years of the fourteenth century, and in Cardiff men from Bristol and Somerset had acquired tenements and other property before the end of the century.[71] Those in south Wales seeking the best trading apprenticeships might cross the water to find them, and this, no doubt, was why John Taylor, a young man from Swansea, was indentured by his father to an experienced Bridgwater tanner, John Davy, for three years in 1426 to learn his trade. Davy, who may well have been of Welsh origin himself, had a flourishing connection with several Neath merchants too.[72] Indeed, a number of Welshmen involved in the cloth industry chose to set up business in Bridgwater, among them by the 1460s William Somer and his son David, who were fullers from Neath, and William ap Howell, a weaver and tailor who had secured a tenement in the Somerset port by about the same time.[73] David Cornysshe, a Somerset merchant living at Combwich in the Parret estuary, who was anxious to be buried at nearby Cannington church and had strong commercial associations with Bridgwater up-river, nevertheless had cultivated a prosperous interest in the Glamorgan coastal belt around Neath: in 1524 he left oxen, cows and sheep to three churches in the vicinity of the borough and to his brother John he bequeathed all his burgages in Neath itself.[74] Nor was it unknown for ships to be

---

[67] T. S. Holmes (ed.), *The Register of Nicholas Bubwith, bishop of Bath and Wells, 1407-24*, I (SRS, XXIX, 1914), 95-6, 100; 'Pembrokeshire Parsons', *West Wales Hist. Soc. Trans.*, III (1912-13), 234. For Hore, Emden, II, 962, and his will, misdated by a century, in F. W. Weaver (ed.), *Somerset Medieval Wills, 1501-30* (SRS, XIX, 1903), pp. 353-4; for Salley, Fryer, *Archaeologia*, LXXIV (1925), 40; G. Williams, *The Welsh Church from Conquest to Reformation* (2nd ed., Cardiff, 1976), pp. 455, 504, and for his will, *Cartae*, VI, 2388.

[68] Cowley, *Monastic Order*, p. 133.

[69] N. D. Harding (ed.), *Bristol Charters, 1155-1373* (Bristol Record Soc., I, 1930), pp. 3, 5, 107. Tenby's burgesses were relieved of paying various duties in Bristol in March 1423: Griffiths, *Boroughs*, p. 308.

[70] J. R. Chanter and T. Wainwright, *Reprint of the Barnstaple Records*, I (Barnstaple, 1900), 150.

[71] E. Owen (ed.), *A Catalogue of the Manuscripts relating to Wales in the British Museum*, III (London, 1908), 547-8; *Cartae*, IV, 1434.

[72] *Bridgwater Archives, 1400-45*, nos. 628, 687.

[73] Ibid., *1445-68* (SRS, LX, 1948), nos. 786, 818, 854; R. W. Dunning and T. D. Tremlett (eds.), ibid., *1468-85* (SRS, LXX, 1971), nos. 941, 1013, 1065.

[74] Weaver, *Somerset Wills*, pp. 230-1.

jointly owned by men from both sides of the channel. In the 1440s the balinger *Mary* was owned by William Nerbere of St. Athan in Glamorgan and John Bere of Barnstaple, though admittedly the arrangement did not work uniformly smoothly.[75]

Above all, it was Bristol, a city and county since 1373, which exemplified the distinctive cultural unity of medieval Severnside. By the fifteenth century, Welshmen were taking a full part in its trade with Ireland, France, Spain and Portugal; imports to Bristol frequently arrived in Welsh ships and were unloaded on a quay that became known as Welsh Back. In nine months during 1479-80 at least nine ships docked there from both Tenby and Chepstow, with others from Haverfordwest and Milford Haven.[76] In 1494 alone cheap Welsh cloth to the value of £816 was sold in Bristol, whilst a sizeable quantity of imports was re-shipped from the metropolis by Bristol merchants, Welshmen doubtless among them.[77] Other ships called at ports like Neath and Swansea *en route* for La Rochelle: in their holds lay coal from the mines that were already being developed along the coastal belt of south Wales.[78] Chepstow had a vital role to play in this international trade of Bristol's, for as early as 1387 ships were regularly taking on cargoes of cloth, beans and corn, and discharging wines, at its wharves or to lighters in the channel in order to avoid customs duties that were certain to be imposed in Bristol itself. Official attempts to close this loop-hole and extend efficient customs collection to Chepstow produced an outcry in parliament which ensured that little by way of administrative reform was achieved.[79]

In the 1530s and 1540s, when John Smythe's detailed business ledger allows us to observe the commercial dealings of a prominent Bristol entrepreneur, merchants, smiths and others from practically every Welsh port and haven between Milford Haven and Chepstow—and from a few inland towns like Abergavenny, Cowbridge and Caerphilly as well—were frequenting the bustling streets of the city, purchasing iron and wine especially from Bordeaux and the Iberian peninsula.[80] Between 1532 and 1565, when figures become available, Welshmen from the shires between Monmouth and Pembroke formed a sizeable proportion (between 15 and 20 per cent) of the apprentices registered in Bristol, many of them learning trades connected with the manufacture and marketing of

[75] D. M. Gardiner (ed.), *A Calendar of Early Chancery Proceedings relating to West Country shipping, 1388-1493* (Devon and Corn. Record Soc., n.s. XXI, 1976), p. 66.

[76] Dallaway, op. cit., pp. 73, 111; Sherborne, op. cit., pp. 15, 21-4; cf. H. Bush, *Bristol Town Duties* (Bristol, 1828), pp. 17-25 (based on accounts for 1437-8).

[77] Darby, *Historical Geography*, p. 291. For Welsh cloth exports from Bristol, G. Connell-Smith, *Forerunners of Drake* (repr., Connecticut, 1975), pp. 208-12; W. R. Childs, *Anglo-Castilian trade in the later middle ages* (Manchester, 1978), pp. 45, 79, 110, 156, 167, 207-8.

[78] J. Vanes (ed.), *Documents illustrating the overseas trade of Bristol in the sixteenth century* (Bristol Record Soc., XXXI, 1979), pp. 103, 135.

[79] Ibid., pp. 20, 42, 45, 79-82, 91; *Cal. Close Rolls, 1389-92,* pp. 528-9, 532, 542 (1391-2); *Rotuli Parliamentorum*, III, 330 (1394-5); F. B. Bickley (ed.), *The Little Red Book of Bristol* (2 vols., Bristol, 1900), I, 129-32; Bernard, *Navires,* p. 780.

[80] J. Angus and J. Vanes (eds.), *The Ledger of John Smythe* (Bristol Record Soc., XXVIII, 1975). Smythe's father had himself come from near Lydney and his mother was the daughter of Lewis John, a Bristol merchant who may have been of Welsh descent.

cloth. [81] The guilds of Bristol had members who were evidently of Welsh ancestry, some of them, as in the religious guild of Kalendars, serving as chaplains and officers, and others occupying the messuages and tenements that were owned by the guilds. [82] The Llandogo Trow, well known to thirsty theatre-goers at Bristol's *Old Vic,* is a reminder of the Welsh commercial tradition of the city.

The presence of Welshmen living and trading in late-medieval Bristol is attested by the fortunes of several of the Rede family, who were as familiar in the streets of Carmarthen as they were on the quayside at Bristol, for they were residents of both towns. Thomas Rede spent much of his time on government business in south Wales, and when he died in 1412 he arranged to be buried in St. Peter's church, Carmarthen; but his will was drawn up in Bristol and two of his executors were Bristolians. His son William maintained the family business in the two centres and his personal seal may still be seen among the Bristol city archives; but his trips to Bristol were not always without incident, for on one occasion he attempted to rape a worthy Bristol lady. [83] These merchant-burgesses of Welsh origin were fully integrated in Bristol's urban and mercantile society: they did not live in one particular quarter of the city—certainly not in any ghetto—and their burials were not concentrated in one particular city church. Yet they frequently cherished their Welsh connections, retained property in Wales and, when death approached, remembered their native heath in their wills. Thomas Wellys, for example, died in 1405 and was buried in St. Mary Redcliffe; but he had kept two tenements in Caerleon as well as 'le Werhouse' which had doubtless played a part in his commercial operations. He made a bequest to St. Cadog's parish church and, as the good merchant he was, earmarked a sum of money for the repair of the road between Caerleon and Newport. John Benett, another Bristol merchant, who composed his will while on a trading expedition to Spain in 1507, left twenty marks to the church at Mumbles, 'beyonde Sowaynse', where he had been born. [84]

The pilgrimage industry, focussed on the famous shrine of St. James at Compostela in northern Spain, two visits to which ranked with one to Rome itself, is another example of the co-operative enterprises that made Bristol the entrepôt of medieval Severnside. With its strong links with English Gascony and the Bay of Biscay, Bristol co-ordinated many of the pilgrim sailings from Ireland, Wales and the west of England. The commemorative scallop shell, the badge of St. James, appears on the tombs of late-medieval pilgrims at Llangynin in

---

[81] D. Hollis (ed.), *Calendar of the Bristol Apprentice-Books, 1532-1542* (Bristol Record Soc., XIV, 1949), p. 197; E. Ralph and N. M. Herdwick (eds.), ibid., II (1542-52) (Bristol Record Soc., XXXIII, 1980), 152; A. Yarbrough, 'Geographical and social origins of Bristol apprentices, 1542-1565', *Trans. Bristol and Glos. Arch. Soc.,* XCVIII (1980), 113-29.

[82] N. Orme, 'The guild of Kalendars, Bristol', ibid., XCVI (1979), 46-52. For John Vaughan, vicar of Bedminster and chaplain of the first chantry of the guild in 1499, Emden, III, 1941.

[83] Griffiths, *Principality,* I, 113-4, 135-6, and references cited there. William also repudiated some of his father's debts in Bristol in 1416: Bristol RO, Museum Deeds 5139 (497).

[84] PRO, PCC, 8 Marche, p. 61; Vanes, op. cit., p. 135. See in general G. H. Nicolson, 'The medieval wills of Bristol, with special reference to those of the merchants' (unpublished Birmingham M.A. thesis, 1970).

Carmarthenshire, Haverfordwest and in Glamorgan, and on sculptures in St. Mary's church, Tenby, as well as in churches of the west country.[85] Even in those great Bristol enterprises of the late-fifteenth century, the north Atlantic discoveries, Welshmen had a role to play. One of the earliest ventures of this kind, in July 1480 in search of the so-called Isle of Brasil, was probably financed by Bristol merchants and undertaken by a Welsh captain from Bristol, John Lloyd, who was acknowledged by William Worcestre to be 'the [most] competent seaman of all England'.[86] Even more distinguished was Roger Barlow, a Bristol merchant who was the brother of the prior of Haverfordwest (1534-5) and later bishop of St. David's (1536-48), William Barlow; another brother, John, was archdeacon of Westbury-on-Trym. When Roger decided to retire from sea-faring by 1538, it was at Slebech in Pembrokeshire, in the diocese of St. David's, that he settled; three years before, Brother William had leased to him some tenements and property not far from Haverfordwest. During an active life, he engaged in trade with Spain, and also in exploring ventures from Bristol to the Azores and the West Indies, translating a Spanish account of other discoveries in the same field.[87] John Cabot was residing in Bristol by the late-1490s, in St. Nicholas Street; round the corner in Baldwin Street were the premises of Henry Vaughan and John Vaughan, both of whom were among the most prominent of city merchants.[88] The Vaughans seem to have hailed from Cardiganshire, to judge by Richard Vaughan (d. 1503), who remembered Aberystwyth church in his will. Richard's wife Cecily was buried in St. Stephen's, Bristol; his brother David was sheriff of the city in 1498-9 and another brother, William, was sheriff in 1516.[89] John, Thomas and Henry Vaughan are likely to have been relatives, all of them merchants of the city. In his day—and he was trading in Bristol by 1463—Henry was Bristol's most successful and respected merchant, trading overseas especially in broad cloths to Spain and Portugal, and importing mainly wine from France and Spain. He was bailiff of Bristol in 1469-70, sheriff in 1477-8, mayor three times, in 1483-4, 1485-6 and 1493-4, and MP for the city in 1487 and 1496; he had already constructed his tomb in St. Stephen's well before his death in 1499. In some ways, Henry Vaughan was the obvious man to whom the common council should turn in an emergency when, on 11 October 1485, the newly elected mayor suddenly died. Four days later, Henry was elected in his place, though the common council carefully stipulated that after the end of his

[85] G. Hartwell Jones, *Celtic Britain and the Pilgrim Movement* (*Y Cymmrodor*, XXIII, 1912), pp. 252-63; E. Laws and E. H. Edwards, 'Monumental effigies, Pembrokeshire', *Arch. Camb.*, 6th ser., XII (1912), 1-6; Williams, *Welsh Church*, pp. 498-9. See in general M. D. Hewitt, 'Cultural contacts between Spain and Celtic Britain during the middle ages' (unpublished Wales M.A. thesis, 1978), ch. II and Appendix B.

[86] Harvey, *Itineraries*, p. 309; J A. Williamson (ed.), *The Cabot Voyages and Bristol discovery under Henry VII* (Hakluyt soc., 2nd ser., CXX, 1962), pp. 19-21; below p. 90.

[87] F. Green, 'The Barlows of Slebech', *West Wales Hist. Soc. Trans.*, III (1912-13), 119-24; *Dictionary Welsh Biography*, pp. 25-6; Connell-Smith, op. cit., pp. 10, 19, 60-1, 70-4, 91; D. B. Quinn, *England and the discovery of America, 1481-1620* (London, 1974), pp. 148-51. For Barlow's writings, E. G. R. Taylor (ed.), *A Brief Summe of Geographie* (Hakluyt soc., 2nd ser., LXIX, 1932); and for his lease of property, Glam RO., CL Deeds 1/3716.

[88] St. Clair Baddeley, 'A Bristol rental, 1498-9', *Trans. Bristol and Glos. Arch. Soc.*, XLVII (1925), 123-9.

[89] F. Green, 'Early wills in West Wales', *West Wales Hist. Soc. Trans.*, VII (1917-18), 153ff; for the officers, *Ricart's Kalendar*, pp. 44ff, and A. E. Hudd, 'Two Bristol calendars', *Trans. Bristol and Glos. Arch. Soc.*, XIX (1894-5), 108-33.

term he should not be eligible for re-election in view of the fact that he had already held the office as recently as 1483-4. His election on this second occasion came only weeks after England's first Tudor monarch, the part-Welsh Henry VII, ascended the throne.[90] Bristol may also have risen to the occasion, through pride or circumspection, by thrusting to the fore one of the leaders of its Welsh community. When King Henry visited the city in 1486, he could well have been welcomed in more than one of the several native tongues of his immediate ancestors!

[90] Sherborne, op. cit., p. 28 (using the 1479-80 customs accounts); Childs, op. cit., pp. 207-8 (1485-7 accounts); E. W. W. Veale (ed.), *The Great Red Book of Bristol,* I (Bristol Record Soc., IV, 1933), 216-17, 233-4; II (Bristol Record Soc., VIII, 1937), 108-9; J. C. Wedgwood, *History of Parliament: Biographies of the Members of the Commons House, 1439-1509* (London, 1936), p. 901. Richard Vaughan was supervisor of Henry's will (PRO, PCC, 38 Horne), and for John Vaughan's will (1492) see ibid., 9 Doggult, p. 65.

Wales and the West

DAVID B. QUINN

ARLY westward expansion from the British Isles has usually been
thought of in terms of the actions of English monarchs, of citizens and
sailors of Bristol and London and of the restless and enterprising gentry
of, mainly, the English south-west. But there was no insurmountable
impediment to the participation of ports like Galway or Milford, Waterford or
Carmarthen, Cardiff or Wexford, to take examples of active, if small, merchant
and fishing communities in Wales and Ireland, sending ships out to search for
fishing grounds and islands in the wide Atlantic. Both areas were regularly
sending fishing ventures into the deeper waters of the continental shelf before
America was found. Galway, for example, was deeply involved in the Iceland
trade, though we do not know if this was through the medium of Bristol vessels
only or whether Irish vessels also took part in the fifteenth-century Iceland
voyages. Nothing of this sort is so far known for Wales itself, but Bristol had an
active Welsh community, which was concerned in some degree in the earliest
English Atlantic enterprises and continued to concern itself with later ones. A
Welsh community in London also was not backward in such activity as marked
the early faltering years of official enterprise. However, the essential factor in the
absence of independent Welsh expansion westward—except latterly in the
Newfoundland fishery—was the comparative backwardness of the Welsh
economy and the lack of disposable capital except among a small section of the
gentry class. In general, it is Welshmen who had migrated to England or men of
Welsh descent established there for a generation or more who are, with a few
exceptions, to be found in the meagre records of early westward enterprise from
England, Wales and Ireland. There was, too, the question of nomenclature. How
are we to say that a particular Jones or Thomas or Davies, or such like, was
indeed Welsh when such names spread over much of England and were especially
frequent in the English border counties and in the south-west? The answer must
lie in many cases in guesswork rather than proof, with, however, the occurrence
of a Welsh forename as being one useful guide. Anglo-Welsh names offer their
own problems.

In the first recorded voyage of exploration westward from Bristol, made in 1480
to 'the island of Brasylle in the western part of Ireland', the ship's master,
described as 'the most knowledgeable seaman of the whole of England', was
named by William Worcestre, in his draft chronicle, as '[blank] Thloyde'. We are
entitled to conclude that this was a Welsh seaman called 'Lloyd', the 'Th' being
an attempt to reproduce the Welsh double 'l'; but there was a Thomas Lloyd in
Bristol at this time and the form of the name may therefore represent someone
whose Welshness was not, at least, recent. The expedition did not find the

supposed island, though another in 1481 perhaps did so, in the shape of a glimpse of Newfoundland, though this is not certain. Whether Lloyd was involved in this too is not recorded. [1] But under the part-Welsh monarch, Henry VII, many more Welsh men and women made their way to the capital and elsewhere in England. It was then that the successful voyage of John Cabot was made in 1497, the Newfoundland fishery begun in 1502, and much of the North American coast explored by 1509. Richard Ap Meryke (or Merrick) was customer of Bristol at the time and he was undoubtedly Welsh. On the strength of his association with the payment of John Cabot's pension between 1497 and 1499 and of his name, A. E. Hudd made the audacious assumption that the name America derived from him and not from Amerigo Vespucci, [2] even if the evidence to sustain this claim has not found acceptance, but for a time it was a potential feather in the Welsh cap. A John Thomas was certainly involved in the Bristol voyages of the early years of the century, but who is to say that he or his forebears came from Wales?

Though under Henry VIII westward voyaging (except for the development of the Newfoundland fishery, the growth of which is very obscure but which was actively pursued by the 1530s) was infrequent and intermittent, it may be that the Welsh trans-Atlantic fishery began then, since we have an example of a Waterford ship being engaged in it in 1537 and there is no reason why Milford, for example, should have lagged behind. But hard evidence has still to be produced. Certainly men with Welsh names who were members of the Mercers' and Drapers' Companies of London—Philip Meredith and John Appowell in the Mercers and Master Vaughan, Thomas Howell, Robert Ap Raynolds and David Greffeth among the Drapers—proved willing to support a venture by Sebastian Cabot to sail through a Northwest Passage to trade with China, even if sufficient support for it was not obtained and it remained a project only. [3] In what little we know of the participants in North American voyages in 1527 and 1536 no Welsh-sounding name stands out. The only well-researched group of merchants for the mid-Tudor period are those who were involved in the Muscovy Company in 1550: [4] among them were Davie Appowell, a mercer, Philip Gunter, born at Dyffryn, Monmouthshire, a skinner, and Anthony Gamage of Coity, who accumulated extensive lands in Wales which, by the marriage of his grand-daughter Barbara Gamage to Robert Sidney, passed into the hands of that family. While both Gunter and Gamage were active in new branches of foreign trade, neither seems to have had any connection with American ventures, except very indirectly. The Muscovy Company indeed claimed to have a monopoly of venturing to the north-west as well as the north-east, and the London merchant Michael Lok had difficulty in getting recognition by the Company of the venture he sent out under Martin Frobisher in 1576. Mineral finds led to the formation of

[1] For the early Bristol enterprises, see D. B. Quinn, *North America from First Discovery to Early Settlements* (1977), pp. 112-35; *idem, England and the Discovery of America* (1974), pp. 5-24, 47, 144; D. B. Quinn, A. M. Quinn, S. E. Hillier (eds.), *New American World*, I (1979), 91-127.

[2] See A. E. Hudd, 'Richard Ameryk and the name America', in H. P. R. Finberg (ed.), *Gloucestershire Studies* (Leicester, 1957), pp. 123-9.

[3] Quinn *et al., New American World*, I, 174, 177-8.

[4] T. S. Willan, *The Muscovy Merchants of 1555* (Manchester, 1953), *passim.*

the Company of Cathay in 1577 and its activities brought to England in 1577 and 1578 much ore soon found to be worthless. William Williams, assay master at the Tower, is likely to have had Welsh associations. He astutely condemned the ore brought in 1576 as only 'marsquasite stone' but was over-ruled. He was involved in further assays of ore from America between 1577 and 1583 on which he returned mixed reports. There were a few subscribers with Welsh-sounding names such as Thomas Owine, and some of the humbler men may also have been Welsh: for example, Thomas Philips, who was to have been left as a miner-colonist on Baffin Island in 1578 (fortunately he did not have to stay), and in the ship *Aid* that year were sailors Robert Owen, Thomas Price, William and Harry Davies.[5] Whether this adds up to Welsh participation or not is debatable, but it illustrates the problem of assessing Welsh contributions to western enterprise.

From the middle of the sixteenth century, at least, the coasts of south Wales and southern Ireland were extensively used in the course of one of the most profitable 'trades' of the time, piracy. It might seem that whereas most of the shipping employed in stealing at sea was English, there was a Welsh element amongst its crews. Prize goods, taken from French, Spanish and Portuguese ships, as well as English, were brought to south Wales and Irish ports to be disposed of illegally. Sometimes the prize mart might be an Irish port like Kinsale, but the ultimate destination of the goods might perhaps be Cardiff, coming through the hands of Welsh middlemen. Valuable African goods from Portuguese ships were coming in this way before and after 1560. Some of the prize marts were in south Wales itself, perhaps the most blatant at Penarth. The first serious crack-down on this pernicious trade was made by a special commission in 1577, which seized ships, goods and men at Penarth and Cardiff, hanged some of the pirates and hoped the example would stamp out the trade. Instead, it temporarily diverted some of the shipping and men, and the backing which they evidently had from a number of Welsh gentlemen to an overseas venture designed both to penetrate and rob in the West Indies and also to reconnoitre a site for a colony on the shores of eastern North America. The inspirer of this was Sir Humphrey Gilbert, a Devonshire gentleman, fanatically hostile to Spain but also bitten with the desire to occupy the vast untenanted lands (so far as he knew) of North America.

In June 1578 Queen Elizabeth gave him a patent which was a blank cheque to seize and occupy land hitherto untouched by Spain in the west. Through the efforts of Henry Knollys, son of the queen's vice-chamberlain, and Simao Fernandes, the Portuguese pilot who had escaped hanging by selling his presumed knowledge of North America to Sir Francis Walsingham, Gilbert's backer, a number of former pirate vessels were enrolled. Among the ships which assembled at Plymouth (though we do not know whether or not she had had a career in piracy) was the *Red Lion*. Her captain was Miles Morgan of Tredegar, who had been high sheriff of Glamorgan a few years previously and who had mobilised a number of Welsh gentlemen to serve under his command. A vessel of 110 tons, well-gunned, carrying fifty-three sailors and soldiers, her master, John

[5] V. Stefansson (ed.), *The Three Voyages of Martin Frobisher* (2 vols., 1938), I, cxi, cxvi; II, 83-4, 112-13, 117-18, 217, 221.

Anthonie, had a good south Wales name, while his mate was Risa (Rees) Sparrowe (and the master's mate Black Robin, surely a stateless pirate!). The gentlemen – adventurers came from gentry families in Monmouthshire and Glamorgan: Edward Herbert, Edmond Mathew, Charles Brady (Bradney?), Risa Lewis, John Martin, Thomas Nycholas, John Amerideth, and Lewes Jones.[6] In making his will before leaving on the voyage, Miles Morgan (a son of John Morgan of Tredegar, and married to Catherine Morgan, daughter of Rowland Morgan of Machen)[7] stated that 'I . . . do intend and purpose by God's goodwill and sufferance to travel by sea in the company of Sir Humphrey Gilbert' and wished to 'order his affairs' before he did so. It may be noted that he left an annuity of 3s. 4d. to Rees Lewis, gent. (the Risa Lewis above), 'only if the said Rees Lewis do go with me to the seas this voyage in the company of Sir Humphrey Gilbert Knight'. This involvement of such a company in westward enterprises could have been a significant pointer to further participation if it had not had fatal consequences. Knollys and Gilbert quarrelled over their objectives and tactics, and Knollys took part of the squadron to sea to plunder off the coasts of Spain. Miles Morgan commanded one of the vessels which remained with Gilbert on his intended course, when they set out on 19 November 1579, for the Americas. But this squadron was soon scattered by storms and each vessel was left very much to its own devices. Gilbert himself with the flagship, *Ann Auger,* took refuge with some other ships in Irish ports. The crank old *Falcon* sailed south to the Canaries and evidently attempted to make westwards but was forced to turn back. The *Red Lion* evidently fell in with some of Knollys's ships and joined him in piratical attacks on friendly vessels, French ships, the *Marie* and the *Margerite,* on their way from Spain to Le Havre, robbing them of woollen and linen cloth belonging to Spanish merchants and said to be worth £2,700. Part of the spoil was put on board the *Red Lion* 'afore the aforesaid Master Morgan with the ship and goods were cast away'. The *Red Lion* sank and, evidently, her captain and crew with her. Gilbert, after he returned to England, heard of and mourned the 'loss of a tall ship' and (more to his grief) of a 'valiant gentleman, Miles Morgan'.[8] Though Gilbert was to sail again in 1583, annex Newfoundland, and be lost himself on the way back, the only Welsh subscriber we can trace in his venture was Sir William Morgan of Pencoed.[9] The loss of the ship and so many Welsh gentlemen-adventurers prejudiced the landed class in south Wales against direct participation in such ventures for many years.

The Newfoundland fishery, after it had been pioneered by Bristol ships at the opening of the sixteenth century, remains an obscure subject for over half a century. It seems that it expanded mainly in the hands of fishermen of Devonshire and drew in others from the Severn estuary; although when the first Welsh

[6] The book of pirates, 1577, PRO, SP 12/112; D. B. Quinn (ed.), *The Voyages and Colonising Enterprises of Sir Humphrey Gilbert* (2 vols., 1940), I, 198, 212; *New American World,* III, 191.

[7] G. B. Morgan (ed.), *Historical and Genealogical Memoirs of the Morgan family* (London, privately printed, 1891), pp. 112-18; G. T. Clark, *Limbus patrum Morganiae et Glamorganiae* (1886), p. 311.

[8] Thomas Churchyard, in the poem he composed before the expedition set sail (*A discourse . . . Whereunto is adjoined a commendation of Sir H. Gilbert's ventrous journey* [1578]), wrote 'Miles Morgan gaynes good fame'; Quinn, *Gilbert,* I, 202, 390; *New American World,* III, 204-9.

[9] Quinn, *Gilbert,* II, 332.

participation began we cannot say, by the 1560s it had started. Sir John Perrot was the leading figure in Pembrokeshire before he became involved in Ireland in 1570 and he was one of the first of the Anglo-Welsh gentry to be involved in the overseas fishery. His ship, the *Bark Perrotte* of Milford, 50 tons, David Wogan master, sailed from the Pembrokeshire coast to Newfoundland (though we do not know to what harbour) in 1566. She brought back the respectable lading of nineteen thousand cod (reckoned at 120 to the hundred) to Milford on 4 September. These were probably wet salted fish, some of which may have been shore dried before being exported. Consigned to Perrot himself and to Wogan, it was probably five thousand of these that were reconsigned to Bristol on 27 September, along with some friezes, in the *Turtaile* of Milford, Arnold Williams master, by John Synet (Synnot) of Haverfordwest. But this was not the first Welsh sponsored voyage to the fishery. On 31 March 1566 the *Michaell* of Laugharne brought a mixed cargo for Robert Toy of Carmarthen for Bristol, including six hundreds of 'Newfoundland fish' which are likely to have been the product of a 1565 voyage by a Laugharne- or Carmarthen-owned vessel. The *Turtaile*, rated at only 16 tons, was typical of the small coasting vessels in the Severn trade at this time, too small itself to have been at Newfoundland, but the fact that Perrot's ship was only rated at 50 tons shows how small were the vessels crossing the ocean at this time. [10]

Even earlier we find not only that there were Welsh-owned vessels at Newfoundland but also that they and their owners were closely tied in with the Devonshire fishery to the extent of employing a Plymouth master for a Tenby ship. On 13 April 1562, James Barret, gentleman, John Philkyn, John Pallmer and John Kibery, merchants of Tenby, owners of the *Jesus* of Tenby, whose master and 'governor' was John Garret of Plymouth, made an agreement with William Philpott of Tenby, James Barret of Tenby and William Lougher, apparently of Plymouth, victuallers. The *Jesus* was to sail from Tenby Quay 'to the Newfoundland with the first wind and weather', return with a full cargo and unload within twenty days, the catch to be divided in thirds between owners, victuallers and the ship's complement, a usual arrangement then and later. The ship duly set sail, made her lading, and was on her way back when she was caught in an Atlantic storm, driven northwards and was making her way, the long way round by the Orkney Islands, when pirates relieved her of her cargo but eventually allowed her to sail home intact. [11] The fact that when she sailed she was armed with artillery, shot and powder, bows and pikes (since piracy was so common) makes her easy looting a little suspicious. Was her lading sold off at the Orkneys or elsewhere or was it seized? We cannot tell, but owners and victuallers got nothing. What the document reveals is that Tenby was at this time engaged in a sophisticated manner in the fishery and may well have gone on trading in this way.

After Perrot returned from his first assignment in Ireland (1570-3), he appears to have built up a small fleet of vessels based on Milford. These may have been

[10] E. A. Lewis (ed.), *Welsh Port Books, 1550-1593* (1927), pp. 79, 85, 56.
[11] Quinn, *New American World,* IV, 99, with additional references in PRO, High Court of Admiralty, HCA 24/34, 90-3, 234-5, 272, 290; HCA 24/35, 208.

partly engaged in the fishery, but more likely in piracy. However, as relations with Spain worsened, open piracy gave way to 'reprisals': the seizing of Iberian ships and goods in retaliation for goods seized in Spain or, after 1580, when the kingdoms were joined, by Portugal. Perrot was evidently in close touch with a leading Southampton shipowner and merchant, Henry Oughtred (who had lost property, he claimed, at Spanish hands). Oughtred's *Susan Fortune,* 200 tons, Richard Clerke master, was joined with Perrot's *Popinjay,* 60 tons, Henry Taylor master, on a cruise to seize Iberian ships and their cargoes by way of reprisal at Newfoundland. At the harbour of Renews, in south-eastern Newfoundland, there were three Portuguese ships anchored, their crews out in boats, shore-fishing. Clerke decided to seize them, but the *Susan* was too large to enter the harbour. He, himself, with thirteen men 'besides the said Taylers whole companye' in the *Popinjay* sailed in to attack. There was no resistance and substantial quantities of fish and train oil (from the cod livers) were transferred to the *Popinjay* (some 120 thousand of fish and 3 or 4 tuns of train). Moreover, prize crews were placed on board and the ships were sailed to a nearby harbour, Fermeuse. There and at the Isle of Boys, a little farther north, two other Portuguese vessels were brought into the net. All five were stripped of everything of value, and much of the spoil was packed on one of them, so that the two raiders and their prize set out for Southampton on 31 August, leaving the Portuguese fishermen in a very perilous position. Relations between the English fishermen and the Portuguese at Newfoundland had hitherto been uniformly friendly. A number of English fishermen gave evidence in the High Court of Admiralty against Perrot and Oughtred when Portuguese representatives brought a case for damages against them, though the result of the case is not known.[12]

This aggression did not at once bring to an end the triangular trade between Newfoundland, the Iberian countries and the British Isles. By the 1580s the north Wales ports, in association with Chester, were engaged in the trade. In 1582 the *Victory* of Beaumaris (44 tons), fitted out at Chester, sailed from Beaumaris to Newfoundland, brought her lading of fish to Lisbon ('Lisburne in Spain') and was back in June 1583 with 350 barrels of salt (some perhaps designated for future fishing voyages), 400 pounds of Castile soap and 6 pecks of barley malt for a Manchester merchant, Henry Hardie, based at Beaumaris.[13] This is our sole glimpse so far of an interesting involvement of north Wales in a trans-Atlantic development of some significance. But the triangular trade with the Iberian countries was brought to an end by the Spanish seizure of English ships in Spanish ports in May 1585, though a few may have continued the triangular trade to Marseilles and Leghorn. Perhaps some Welsh vessels may some day turn out to have done so too.

The south Wales-Newfoundland fishery at Newfoundland continued, however, during the war years though, it might appear from surviving records, only on a small scale. We mostly hear of it at the redistributive end. Thus, on 4 November 1585 the *Margaret* of Carmarthen (18 tons) left Carmarthen for Bristol with a

[12] The story is outlined in Quinn, *North America* (1977), p. 363, and the documents printed in *New American World,* IV, 13-20.

[13] A. Eames, *Ships and Seamen of Anglesey* (Llangefni, 1973), pp. 27-8 (his note reference being faulty).

cargo including 4 hundreds of Newfoundland fish and 6 hogsheads of train oil, evidence of a returning fishing vessel in that year. The same voyage may have been responsible for the one tun of train brought on 14 February 1586 by the *Elizabeth* of Tenby for Walter Hooper of Bristol. A 1586 voyage, too, presumably lay behind the lading on 3 February 1587 on the *Mathewe* of Milford, John Fortune master, of two hundreds of Newfoundland fish for Bristol. [14] The arrival and lading of ships engaged directly in fishing off Newfoundland did not normally attract the attention of officials, since such fish entered without paying custom though sometimes customs officers mentioned the fact.

We have no further published records until 1600, when on 27 February the *Moises* of Cardiff (50 tons) landed at Cardiff 9 hogsheads of train oil, presumably going to Bristol or another port to unload her fish. Finally, just after the end of Queen Elizabeth's reign, the *Nicholas* of Milbrook (30 tons, but possibly really of 300 tons) landed no less than 500 tuns of train oil at Milford for Morgan Powell of Pembroke and Thomas Powell of Haverfordwest. [15] This was not normal cargo. Perhaps the *Nicholas* was a 'sack' ship, which went out to buy from fishermen at Newfoundland rather than to fish and render down oil, and had purchased oil in this quantity from English, or more likely French Basque, vessels (the quantity suggests whale oil from the strait of Belle Isle, rather than oil from the cod fishery).

No further records for the early-seventeenth century have yet been published, but it is clear that, in the later sixteenth century, ships of Welsh or Severn Channel ownership were engaged in most branches of the complex international trans-Atlantic trade in fish, train oil (possibly some of it whale or walrus oil), salt and other products. The extent of the capital and shipping available in ports like Tenby, Milford and Carmarthen for such enterprises is as yet unknown. The fishery, however, did much to widen Welsh horizons across the ocean.

The question of the emergence of the statement that Madoc ap Owain Gruffydd made a voyage across the Atlantic and that he established a Welsh colony in America has been treated in sufficient detail in the early part of *Madoc. The Making of a Myth* (1979), [16] to make it unnecessary to go into it in detail, but it forms an essential part of the Welsh contribution to western enterprise which must at least be noticed. Whether the myth of Madoc was constructed out of folk-memory, myth, lost medieval literature or wholesale invention must remain somewhat controversial. Its begetter appears to have been the antiquary Humphrey Lhoyd (Llwyd) who died in 1568, and who set it out in a preface prepared for his translation of a chronicle attributed to Caradoc of Llancarfan, of which John Dee, an enthusiast for ancient Britain, who was of Welsh descent if not birth, had a copy. It was not brought into the open, we think, before Dee in 1578 put it forward to Queen Elizabeth as a reason for challenging Spanish claims to the first discovery of America. The idea spread. Sir George Peckham, who as a

---

[14] Lewis, *Welsh Port Books*, pp. 111-12, 118, 140.

[15] Ibid., p. 234.

[16] G. A. Williams, *Madoc. The Making of a Myth* (1979), pp. 36-49, 55, 61-7. The classic piece of demolition remains T. Stephens, *Madoc* (1893), though the invention of the myth can now be surveyed within a wider context even if it remains one.

Catholic had little taste for impugning the papal division of 1493 between Spain and Portugal, seized on it after talks with Dee, and it appears as evidence for English rights to colonize North America in his tract, *A true reporte of the late discoveries . . . by Sir Humphrey Gilbert,* in 1583.[17] By this time, Dee had been joined by the Revd Richard Hakluyt, from a Herefordshire family with Welsh sympathies, and possibly as early as this by William Camden (though he is not known to have been a believer in the tale), and most actively by David Powel, whose edition of Llwyd's work, with his 'Madoc' preface, and further notes by Powel appeared as *The historie of Cambria* in 1584. This remained one of the primary printed sources on the Madoc myth down to the nineteenth century, though it was elaborated by Sir Thomas Herbert in *A relation of some yeares travaile* (1634). In 1584 it was brought before Queen Elizabeth in a more weighty form by Richard Hakluyt in the report on North American prospects, 'A particuler discourse concerninge the great necessitye and manifolde comodyties lately attempted' (now known less cumbrously as his *Discourse of Western planting*).[18] Here it was made, alongside the discoveries of John and Sebastian Cabot, part of the materials for an English challenge to the Iberian claim, at least so far as North America was concerned. Hakluyt continued to assert it, but it cannot be said to have done more than bring together a small group of imperialist (and pro-Welsh) intellectuals in London, rather than influenced Welsh activity in the west on which it had, at that time, no observed effect.

A side issue, which was to have a longer and stranger life, as Gwyn Williams has shown, was the myth of the Welsh-speaking Indians. In Newfoundland fishermen, some of them Welsh, encountered the strange flightless bird, the Great Auk, which was extensively killed for food. They gathered that the local Beothuk Indians called it 'Pengwyn', or something like it, which was translated as Welsh 'White Head' (in fact the oval white patch on the Great Auk covered more of its neck than its head).[19] So home came the tale that the Indians spoke Welsh, a slight base indeed. (The name 'penguin' was transferred to the birds of the southern continent in the seventeenth century.) Peckham publicised it, along with some Welsh-sounding 'Indian' words invented by the lying David Ingram, whose tales about his travels in North America in 1568-9 were for a time believed by Peckham and by Hakluyt, though by few others. Thus, Welsh visitors or settlers in America thereafter, who had probably never heard of Madoc, continued to repeat the more enduring myth about the Welsh-speaking Indians.

Gilbert's death in 1583 led to his patent being transferred to the more cautious and intelligent Walter Ralegh, his half-brother, under whose auspices five expeditions to North America were launched between 1584 and 1590, two of which led to the earliest English colonising experiments we know of in North America. No major Welsh participation in them can be traced, but that Welshmen were involved in both and Welsh women in the second is highly

[17] Reprinted in Quinn, *New American World,* III, 34-60.

[18] Reprinted in ibid., III, 74-123; a critical edition is in preparation by D. B. and A. M. Quinn.

[19] G. A. Williams is puzzled by the 'Pengwyn' story since penguins of the modern sort do not have white anywhere on their heads, but his knowledge of earlier natural history is at fault. For a century the Penguin was the Great Auk, and perhaps in northern waters for much longer.

probable though we have only the guess-work of names to go by. On the
reconnaissance voyage of 1584 there is only the name of John Hewes as
conceivably Welsh. In the colony which was left to explore the land and estimate
its possibilities for permanent settlement (it spent from July 1585 to June 1586
mainly on Roanoke Island), there are more possibilities: among the gentlemen
Captain (John) Vaughan, among the men (soldiers and labourers) Thomas and
William Philippes, John Evans, Rowland Griffyn, David Williams and Hans and
William Walters. But we know nothing of how they behaved, some well and some
ill, in the year's course, until Sir Francis Drake took them all back to England in
July 1586. The 1587 colony was to be a more serious affair, a community of
families which would make a living for themselves in America, a first real colony
of settlement. Certainly Gryffen Jones was Welsh. John Jones and Jane Jones
(probably wife to one or the other) may have been, while there was also an
Edward Powell—not a very convincing group, but a possible one, among the
hundred-odd men, women and children that the governor, John White, left in
August 1587 to speed supplies and never saw again, nor any other white man so
far as we know. When White arrived back only in 1590 the Lost Colony had
vanished, though some may have survived some fifty miles to the north for nearly
twenty years. [20] Welsh association with these earliest colonising ventures remains
tenuous in the extreme.

The privateering war against Spain and Portugal from 1585 to 1604 brought
shipping from England to almost all parts of Spanish and Portuguese America,
west coast as well as east. Amongst those manning the privateers there were,
undoubtedly, a number of Welsh seamen. One ship from a south Wales port was
the *Wheel of Fortune* of Carmarthen, Richard Nashe captain, which in 1589 took
wines, calicoes, pepper and other goods from a French vessel laden with Spanish
goods. [21] She may have been only one of a number of Welsh origin. 'Mr.
Myddelton the merchant, of Tower Street', as the late A. H. Dodd called
Thomas Myddleton, merchant, [22] and ultimately lord mayor of London and a
knight, as well as many times a MP, based his many overseas activities on
London and Weymouth, roping into them many of his relatives from Galch Hill
and Llansannan, near Denbigh, and investing his great profits substantially in
Welsh estates. He was active over the whole period of the war, and at a more
peaceful level right through to his death in 1631. His 'Journal' in the National
Library of Wales gives us much detail of his manifold enterprises. His brother
Peter, his cousin William, and a nephew were all involved in expeditions which
he financed in Atlantic waters. He emerges as one of the most enterprising and
astute of the London merchants who invested in the cargoes of sugar, hides and
bullion seized in the Caribbean or coming from Brazil. The list of them would fill
a page. But he lost as well as gained. The voyage of Richard Hawkins to the

[20] Quinn, *New American World*, III, 281, 288, 321-2.
[21] K. R. Andrews, *Elizabethan Privateering* (1964), p. 261.
[22] A. H. Dodd, 'Mr. Myddleton the merchant of Tower Street', in S. T. Bindoff, J. Hurstfield, and C. H.
Williams (eds.), *Elizabethan Government and Society* (1961), pp. 249-81; K. R. Andrews, *Elizabethan Privateering*
(1964), pp. 113-18 (*passim*); 'A Jurnal of all owtlandishe accompts, 1583-1603', National Library of Wales,
Chirk Castle MS. Fr. 12,540.

Pacific in 1592-3 was partly financed by him and he lost much when Hawkins was captured by the Spaniards; similarly, his investment in the last voyage of Drake and Hawkins to the West Indies in 1595-6 was a dead loss. He was quick to involve himself in peaceful trade with the West Indies as the privateering war ran down and his *Vineyard* made a successful trading voyage there as early as 1603. He was, too, an active participant in the Virginia Company when colonising restarted from 1609 (perhaps earlier) down to 1622. He demonstrated that if Welsh gentry and merchants were to engage in major commercial enterprises in peace or war their base had to be in London, not in Wales itself. But there were not many who could touch him for shrewdness and capacity for taking calculated risks which very often paid their way.

There was, after 1587, a long gap in English planning and attempts at colonisation in North America. The fishery alone went on in Newfoundland waters. The sea war was partly fought in the Caribbean by privateers and some larger expeditions, but the Spanish war made a hiatus in what might have been a continuous pattern of commerce and attempted colonisation. Before the war was quite over, indeed, ventures were made to what we know as New England. Bartholomew Gosnold planned a fur-trading post off the shores of southern Massachusetts, but his men would not chance staying. A Bristol venture in 1603, under Martin Pring, may have had some Welsh participants but we cannot be sure. His two small ships, *Speedwell* and *Discoverer,* were forced by contrary winds to put into Milford Haven; they stayed for a fortnight and may have made contact with some of the old Newfoundland fishermen of the port. There, before setting out, they heard on 10 April of the death of Queen Elizabeth, the end of an era. In 1605, again, Sir Thomas Arundell of Wardour, hoping to capitalize on the explorations of 1602-3 which had been valuable, sent George Waymouth to find a site for a mainly Catholic colony in the area recently reconnoitred. In 1605 the *Archangell* explored the islands off the Maine coast and the St. George River into the mainland. James Rosier, the later Jesuit priest, who was to collect materials on Abenaki Indian language and customs, was aided by a young man who was almost certainly Welsh, Owen Griffin. He was supposed to remain with the Indians and it was presumably thought he would make rapid progress with their language, if indeed they spoke Welsh or anything like it. As it was, none of the words he and Rosier collected had any similarity to Welsh. They were just another branch of the Algonquian languages spoken from modern North Carolina all the way to Cape Breton.[23]

A curious episode concerning persons from north Wales occurred in 1606-7. Rowland Bulkeley had at Beaumaris a 30-ton pinnace with which he contemplated a 'viadge in trade to the Indies for tobacco', since the illegal trade was developing in the West Indies. He went to Chester to buy commodities with which to trade and encountered there Sir Ralph Bingley, a Flintshire gentleman, who had collected a number of men for a voyage (he claimed) to Virginia. Bulkeley and his crew of five were given £13 to convey them to Dublin. On the journey Bingley persuaded Bulkeley to join him. He had a number of vessels lying off Drogheda, and it might seem that there was a plan to transport some settlers

[23] Quinn, *New American World,* III, 360, 372, 384-6.

from Ireland to North America just at the time the Virginia Company was organising its first voyages, but the whole thing may have been from the first a cover for a piratical venture. Previously, Bingley had induced a group of London fishmongers to appoint him captain of the ship *Triall,* which was to join him in Irish waters and take part in an expedition which its owners considered should bring them information on possible fishing bases on the Maine coast. It so happened that the master, Arthur Chambers, who was to bring the ship to Dublin, was a rascal and spent much of 1606 wasting his time and his masters' substance in visits to south-coast English ports. By the time the *Triall* reached Dublin, most of the other vessels had dispersed, giving up the voyage. But, according to Bulkeley, his pinnace was seized by Bingley and brought into Dublin Bay and eventually to Kinsale. There Bingley openly associated with pirate ships and from him Bulkeley made his escape, coming to Cardiff and eventually to London, to report that Bingley had in fact gone to sea but only to rob and seize Spanish ships in European waters. After Bingley's return, legal actions taken against him failed for want of evidence, his defence being that he ran out of supplies and could not get to Virginia. As both the lord deputy of Ireland, Sir Arthur Chichester, and the earl of Salisbury were prepared to overlook his crimes, he got away with them: the *Triall* was eventually recovered by her owners, but Bulkeley lost his pinnace and, perhaps, his taste for maritime adventure. His deposition in the High Court of Admiralty on 29 April 1607 constitutes a valuable sidelight on the confused situation after the end of the Spanish war, when Irish ports—and it seems Welsh as well (since Cardiff comes in marginally to the story)—were being used with the connivance of the local authorities to carry on a maritime war of plunder against all-comers. At this stage the cover of a voyage to Virginia could be used to disguise such operations. The London charterers of the *Triall* were genuine enough, but it is doubtful if Bingley ever was, or indeed if Rowland Bulkeley was as innocent as he made himself out to be. [24]

If Owen Griffin was employed in 1605 to collect information and a vocabulary from the Eastern Abenaki of the Maine coast, we might expect to find a Welsh element in the attempt by the Plymouth division of the Virginia Company (Bristol was involved as well) to establish a post on the Kennebec River in 1607, but it is not easy to do so with any certainty. What is clear is that two men, their surname both 'Davies' and 'Davis', were prominent in it, though research has not so far pinned them down to a Welsh origin. James was captain of Fort St. George on the Sagadahoc (Kennebec) River from August 1607 to the evacuation of the post late in 1608. He left a journal but this has been lost. Robert Davies is somewhat more prominent. He had evidently had experience both as a soldier and at sea. He was pilot of the *Mary and John* on the outward voyage in 1607 and, as master of the vessel (though his military rank was sergeant-major and he was a member of the

---

[24] D. B. Quinn, 'The voyage of Triall, 1606-1607: an abortive Virginia venture', *American Neptune,* XXXI (1971), 85-103; *idem, New American World,* III, 396-402. Bulkeley's deposition is printed in full in D. B. and A. M. Quinn (eds.), *The English New England Voyages, 1602-1608* (1983). The first full study of Bingley is R. J. Hunter, 'Sir Ralph Bingley, *c.* 1570-1627', in P. Roebuck (ed.), *Plantation to Partition: Essays in Ulster History in Honour of J. L. McCracken* (Belfast, 1981), pp. 14-28, 253-6.

council), he explored the Maine coast to the south with Captain Raleigh Gilbert, the second-in-command of the expedition. He also accompanied him on boat searches upstream when the lower reaches of the Kennebec were explored. He commanded the *Gifte of God,* the larger vessel, back to England between October and December 1607, and the surviving journal, which is almost certainly his, is our main source of information on the activities of the settlers up to his departure. In England he reported on the rather poor prospects of the colony and later in 1608 was sent out in the *Gifte* to bring it aid. Instead, the settlers insisted on evacuating the fort, so that he conveyed them back to England late in 1608, a Virginia Company venture which set back the colonisation of New England for more than a decade. But we know no more about him. Perhaps he will appear when we learn more about the individuals, Welsh and non-Welsh, who took part in these early American ventures. [25]

When serious attempts at colonisation began we might expect to find traces of Welsh participation under the activities of the London division, which was charged with the settlement of the Chesapeake Bay area, and the Plymouth division, whose responsibility was modern Maine. Jamestown was established in May 1607. Settlers arrived between then and the end of 1608 in three separate groups. Among them we find names of men who were or could have been Welsh, mostly in humble positions: David Ap Hugh, artisan; Edward Morris, gentleman; David Ellis, carpenter; James Watkins, labourer,—William, labourer; and Hugh Winne, of whom we know nothing else. A young man, whose surname we do not know (he was called Thomas 'Savage'), was sent to live with the Indians and pick up their language and customs (which he did so well that he won his surname for his success); since it was still supposed the Indians might speak a kind of Welsh, his linguistic capacities might have been those of a Welsh boy, though Algonquian dialects soon revealed they had no Welsh elements that could be discerned. The only significant figure we can cite is Captain Peter Winne (Wynne), active among the first settlers and eventually appointed to the council of the colony but dying before he could take up office. Accompanying Captain Christopher Newport in the first expedition beyond the falls where modern Richmond stands, he penetrated the country of the Monacan or Siouan Indians and was one of the first to make contact with them. On returning to Jamestown, he wrote to his Yorkshire friend, Sir John Egerton, on 26 November 1607 that after going upstream on the James some 120 to 140 miles, 'afterwards I travelled between 50 or 60 myles by land, in a country called Monacan, who owe no sujection to Powhatan [high chief of the Indians lower down the river] . . . The people of Monacon speak a farr differing language from the subjectes of Powatan, theyre pronunciation being very like Welch so that the gentlemen in our Company desired me to be theyr Interpreter.' He had no success, yet it is clear that the myth was strong at Jamestown and that to a Welshman their language had some similarities *in sound* to Welsh. Unfortunately,

[25] Quinn, *New American World,* III, 429-37; D. B. and A. M. Quinn (eds.), *English New England Voyages, 1602-1608, passim.*

Winne died too soon to enlighten us further, and no echo of his efforts to speak and interpret Welsh to the Indians of the interior is on record. [26]

An amusing episode in 1614, however, illustrates how little the people of Pembrokeshire knew about what was going on across the Atlantic. The earliest Jesuit mission in north-eastern America, first started in 1611 at Port Royal, had only recently been re-established on Mount Desert Island when the Virginia Company of London sent Samuel Argall in 1613 to root it out as they did not want French Catholic competition along the Atlantic coast. He took some of the Jesuits and French civilians to Jamestown and brought two Jesuits back with him on a second raid in 1614 to show where the French civilian settlement at Port Royal was located (this he destroyed but did not catch its occupants who were away hunting). One of the vessels he had seized, with the two Jesuits on board, got separated from Argall and crossed the Atlantic eastward, putting into Milford Haven and remaining there for some time. In his *Relation de la Nouvelle-France* (1616), Father Pierre Biard S.J. recalled the visit. Though he labelled the captain of the ship, William Turner, a pirate and claimed he, along with his companion, Father Jacques Quentin, had been ill-treated at sea, he was anxious to impress himself on the local population as an educated man who was a victim of circumstances. He and Quentin were brought before the vice-admiral of Pembrokeshire at Milford, whom he names as Nicholas Adams, to explain their presence. When Adams heard the story he took them into his protection, had them lodged in the mayor's house and waited until he could hear from the authorities in London what should be done with them. In the meantime, the Jesuits in their habits had become a source of curiosity to the people of the locality. Even a member of the privy council, he tells us (who could he have been?), came to talk to them. The high point was when some local Anglican clergy were brought together to have a disputation with them, presumably with an interpreter present. Biard was amazed, he said, that so much of the traditional liturgy and ceremonial had been retained and that the hierarchy had remained unchanged (there was even an archdeacon present). We could do with a report from the Welsh side of their discussion but it was evidently more an informative talk than a theological wrangle. The people of Milford were able to hear at first hand something of what the French had been doing in Acadia (modern Nova Scotia and northern Maine) as well as learning some of the main points of difference between Anglican and Catholic. Finally, word came to send the Jesuits to London, where they were soon after repatriated. The basic irony of the situation was that, according to the laws in force at the time (strengthened in 1606 after the Guy Fawkes plot), any Jesuit landing in England or Wales was automatically liable to be tried as a traitor and to suffer as such. It was well for Biard and Quentin that knowledge of this law had not effectively penetrated to Pembrokeshire, and was not in fact being enforced by James I.

[26] P. L. Barbour (ed.), *The Jamestown Voyages, 1607-1609* (1969), I, xxv-xxviii, 245-6; Quinn, *New American World*, V, 285.

It is only recently that Biard's letter to the general of his Order, written in Latin shortly after the Milford episode, has been published.[27] The relief, and the irony, expressed in it may appear from the original:

> In Wallia capitaneus noster, cum ad urbem Pembrochium excendisset victus petendi causa, ob certa quaedam indicia, velut pirata captus est ac detentus. Ille enimvero, ut se liberaret, negat se piratam argumentumque innocentiae suae profert iesuitas duos, quos in navi haberet quosque si placeat accersere exipsis cognosci posse veritatem. O artificium divinae Providentiae! Erat tum hyens adulta et omnia in navi deerant. Ideoque, nisi provisum nobis fuisset, et frigore et malis peribamus. Quid multa! Extemplo accersuntur iesuitae et in urbem mirantibus omnibus deducuntur. Iubemur pro testimonio dicere. Nos enimvero quae vera erant proferimus: capitaneum scilicet nostrum officiarum esse regium non piratum, et quae in nos fecisset parendi necessitate magis quam voluntate fecisse. Ita capitaneus noster liberatus est, et non cum ipso in urbe, usque dum Londin[i]o responsum acciperetur, perhumaniter retenti sumus.

There is no evidence whatever that this episode, however illuminating to those who encountered Fathers Biard and Quentin, had any effect on Pembrokeshire's contribution to the western enterprise, which was confined no doubt, as before, to the Newfoundland fishery.

Much of the interest displayed by Welshmen in America in the early-seventeenth century was directed farther north. Sir Robert Mansel, again, was a leading figure in the North-West Passage Company, chartered in 1612 to develop Henry Hudson's discovery of the bay which took his name in 1611. Captain Thomas Button, an associate of Mansel's in naval affairs and another Glamorgan man, took two ships to explore the Bay in 1612 and managed to winter at the mouth of the Nelson River. His explorations revealed the outlines of the Bay but showed it to be a cul-de-sac. He did, however, import the names New North Wales and New South Wales to North American soil, though they did not remain there as long even as Button's Bay, which was his name for Hudson Bay. (The re-naming of Mount Desert Island in Maine as Mount Mansel, after Sir Robert who had thought of settling there in the 1620s, had no longer lease of life.)[28]

It was not until 1609 that nationwide support was sought and found for the Virginia Company of London and its Jamestown colony. Most of the money was drawn from the London merchant and craft companies (many of which had Welsh members) and also from individuals in the city, at court and from the nobility and gentry represented in parliament. How far systematic attempts were made to raise money in the outlying parts of England and Wales is by no means clear—probably none at this point. A wider range was drawn on in the next big subscription in 1612 and thereafter there was some countrywide participation in the annual lotteries which, until 1621, made up much of the effective income of the Company. It was not until it launched its new programme of expansion in

---

[27] Biard's *Relation* was published at Lyon in 1616; it is reprinted in I. Campeau (ed.), *La Première mission d'Acadie (1602-1616)* (Monumenta Novae Franciae, I, Quebec, 1967), pp. 595-7; the letter of 16/26 May 1614 to Father Claude Acquaviva, general of the Jesuit Order, is on p. 420.

[28] E. S. Dodge, *Northwest by Sea* (New York, 1961), pp. 129-34. There is a useful summary of Mansel's American involvement in A. Brown, *The Genesis of the United States*, II (1890), 573-4.

1618 that opportunities for speculation and employment in Virginia proliferated. Land was distributed to investors who would take it up themselves or induce others to take it off their hands, but most significantly private syndicates were empowered to receive large portions of land on which they could settle free farmers, craftsmen or, mostly, indentured labourers. In 1619 Sir Thomas Myddleton and Alderman Robert Johnson (the latter having been active in Virginia affairs from the start) combined to apply for a 'particular plantation' on which they might plant tobacco-growing colonists. Needless to say, neither Myddleton nor Johnson proposed to go himself, but under the care of Captain Peter Mathew (who appears as Mathewe and Mathewes but was almost certainly a member of the Glamorganshire gentry family of that name) a group of colonists was sent out. How many came from Wales we do not know, but at the very least some of the many dependents of the Myddletons would have gone, together with a selection from the London Welsh, and since south Wales was not prosperous at the time, we may suspect a number of labourers (who could indeed have been craftsmen or farmers in a better time) went too. The land assigned to them was well up the James River, three miles north of the second town in Virginia, Henrico. Its Indian name seems to have been Harrowhatock, and it is described as 'one of the best seats'. From November 1619 to March 1622 it appears to have had good fortune, though we know little or nothing about its internal development as yet. At Martin's Hundred, south of Jamestown, thanks to the excavations of Ivor Noël Hume in recent years, a comparable plantation is known to have established an extensive agricultural base and built a village, Wolstenholme, which bore every sign of developing prosperity. But then on 22 March 1622 came disaster for many of the colonists. The Powhatan Indians made a stand, too late indeed, as they saw their land being overrun by settlers now numbered in their thousands. Their rising killed more than 350 colonists but by luck, skill and good judgement (or a combination of all three) Captain Mathew kept his Anglo-Welsh plantation unscathed. Jamestown itself was spared and readied to begin a counter-attack: Captain Mathew's land was too near the frontier for safety and he and his men were called back. Though Mathew himself received a new grant and probably took most of the members of the plantation there, we do not know just where they went; perhaps some dispersed, since labour was short and indentures could not for a time be firmly enforced. Mathew himself was soon enrolling a force which he was to lead to destroy the Indian settlement of Tanx Powhatan, some way to the north of where the plantation had been. He went on to play a distinguished part as a member of the colony's council before and after the collapse of the Company and the setting up of the royal colony. More can no doubt be written about the Welsh in early Virginia but we at least know that they were present and active. [29]

Newfoundland was something different. There Welshmen had long fished and there they attempted to make their mark as organisers, proprietors and settlers, though with mixed success for some years and ultimately failure. A few Welshmen may have subscribed to the Newfoundland Company after it was

---

[29] S. M. Kingsbury (ed.), *Records of the Virginia Company of London*, III (Washington, 1933), 227, 246, 264, 570; V (1935), *passim*.

chartered in 1610, but none have been found among John Guy's settlers at Cupids Cove from 1611 onwards. It was not until the Company disposed of much of its right to lands in the peninsula to the south of St. John's Harbour from 1616 onwards that Wales took a stake in the country.

The man who is most closely associated with Newfoundland is William Vaughan, second son of Walter Vaughan of Golden Grove, Carmarthenshire, who after his marriage settled at Llangyndeyrn in 1605, and resided there until his death in 1641. But from 1616 to 1631 he focused much of his attention on Newfoundland. In his early moralising work, *The Golden Grove* in 1600, enlarged in 1608, he had noted the sufferings of poor farmers, oppressed by rising population and enclosures, and this was reflected in his works on Newfoundland, the first in Latin, *Cambrensium Caroleia* (1625), assuring the new king that almost all the ills of his kingdom would be solved by colonising Newfoundland; then *The Golden Fleece* (1626), under the poorly-concealed pseudonym of 'Orpheus Junior', assuring his public that by colonisation there 'we should performe miracles, and returne yearly into Great Britain a surer gain than Jason's Golden Fleece from Colochos' [sign, B3*v*.]; and descending to *The Newlanders cure* (1630), which dealt, prosaically for him, with the ills to which seamen and settlers were heir.

The extent to which practice accompanied (preceded or followed) theory has been debated. According to most Welsh historians, Vaughan visited Newfoundland in 1622 and 1628: later views suggest he never crossed the seas. He did indeed acquire a large tract of the southern part of the modern Avalon Peninsula from the Newfoundland Company in 1616, from Caplin Bay to Placentia Harbour, which was called Cambriola (the second territory to be named after Wales). From 1617 onwards he supplied John Mason, who was engaged in mapping the island (Vaughan printed his map in 1625 and 1626), with names like Glamorgan, Vaughans Cove, Golden Grove, Colchos, Pembrok, Cardigan and Brechonia for bays and capes already known by other names. But this was a smokescreen only. We now know that he sent his first settlers out to Aquafort (later transferred to Lord Falkland) in 1617. Nothing is known of how many there were or who led them, but they lived miserably in the huts the fishermen had built during the summer. In 1618 Vaughan appointed the experienced Captain Richard Whitbourne as governor for life of his colony and sent him out with fresh colonists. Whitbourne moved the first settlers and his new associates to Renews, a better fishing harbour. But he sent many of them home as unsuitable. One of their ships was despoiled by robbers. Finally, he left only six men to winter at Renews and came home to quarrel with Vaughan and to look for other means of colonising Newfoundland. In 1619 the survivors at Renews gave up—'the welch Fooles haue left of', said another colonist unkindly. The latest summary of his involvement is given by Professor Gillian T. Cell:[30]

---

[30] G. T. Cell (ed.), *Newfoundland Discovered: English Attempts at Colonisation, 1610-1630* (Hakluyt Soc., 1981), p. 25. The documentation on which she bases her conclusions will be found in this volume. However, D. W. Prowse, *A History of Newfoundland* (2nd ed., 1896), pp. 110-12, gave his authority to the placing of the Vaughan colony at Trepassy and said Vaughan lived there for some years. This was taken up subsequently by Welsh historians, notably A. H. Dodd, whose *Studies in Stuart Wales* (Cardiff, 1953), put him at Trepassy, considered that ill-health prevented him from making the crossing in 1622, but sent him there later. G. T. Cell, in her *English enterprise in Newfoundland, 1577-1660* (Toronto, 1969), pp. 83-92, put forward the view that the settlement at Trepassy never took effect, though Vaughan was planning it as late as 1630. In her *Newfoundland Discovered*, pp. 25-6, she gives a critical account of the significance of his writings, which for all their oddity make him significant as a pioneer propagandist for Welsh settlement in Newfoundland.

So William Vaughan's brief and unfortunate attempt at colonisation came to an end. There is no evidence that he ever sent out any more settlers to Renews or any other site. In his writings he refers only to the two groups of men and women whom he had despatched in 1617 and 1618, as well as to his hopes of reviving the venture and even of visiting the island in person. There is no good evidence that he ever achieved either of these goals, whether because of ill-health . . . or because of the financial difficulties to which Vaughan himself refers.

He continued to puff and blow about Newfoundland for some years, but his airy notions were at least based on the assumption that the real wealth of Newfoundland lay in its fish even if he built castles of air over this prosaic topic.

It may be true, however, that one or two of the men whom Vaughan was responsible for sending to Newfoundland, under other direction, became significant figures for a few years. At the instigation of his eldest brother, the earl of Carbery, Vaughan transferred in 1620 a small part of his grant to Sir George Calvert, who was interested in preparing the way for a Catholic settlement in Newfoundland, finally choosing Ferryland which had formed part of the original Vaughan territory. His chief agent was Captain Edward Winne who is not unlikely to have come over to Calvert from the Renews settlement when it dispersed. In 1620-1 Winne had created, with the assistance of men sent out by Calvert, a substantial building at Ferryland and had begun to grow crops by the time he wrote *A letetr* [sic] . . . *to Sir George Calvert, from Ferryland in Newfoundland, the 26. of August, 1621,* printed in London by B. Alsop with the date 1621. This was excellent work. Whitbourne, who had gone into the service of Lord Falkland's colony a little further north, published in a second edition of his *A discourse and discovery of New-found-land* in 1622, a further letter from Winne to Calvert reporting that a large house had been completed, timber cut for winter and various crops planted and now flourishing. Daniel Powell, almost certainly another Welshman, wrote on the same day to describe the country round Ferryland in flattering terms. Winne remained there until at least 1624 and laid foundations which impressed Calvert (now Lord Baltimore) that settlement was possible. So there was an indirect Welsh contribution to Newfoundland settlement after all.[31]

Over the whole field of Welsh activity in the early discovery, exploitation and settlement of the trans-Atlantic world we cannot say that Wales or Welshmen took an outstanding part, yet they touched on its successive manifestations at many points, even if largely peripherally. Welsh merchants, sailors and intellectuals in Bristol and London probably played a greater part than Welshmen in Wales. Yet this was not wholly true. Welsh fishermen from south Wales took part in fishing voyages to Newfoundland at least from the beginning of Queen Elizabeth's reign (and we still require to know much more of what they did before and after that reign). Welsh gentry in Monmouthshire and Glamorgan

[31] Vaughan, in *Cambrensium Caroleia.* For the Calvert colony, see Cell, *English Enterprise,* pp. 92-5, and full documentation in her *Newfoundland Discovered,* pp. 250-306. L. Codignola, *Simon Stock, Propaganda Fide e la colonia di Lord Baltimore a Terranova* (Venice, 1982), has interesting things to say about Vaughan and Calvert. For a general perspective on Newfoundland, see D. B. Quinn, 'Newfoundland in the consciousness of Europe in the sixteenth and early seventeenth centuries', in G. M. Story (ed.), *Early European Settlement and Exploitation in Atlantic Canada* (St. John's, Newfoundland, 1982), pp. 9-30.

were attracted by the possibility of combining penetration of the Spanish zone in the Americas with robbery. A few seem to have considered early settlement. But Wales was relatively poor. It was not until the early-seventeenth century that an appreciable number of Welsh gentry turned to the west. Perhaps this was because it was now fashionable in England to do so; perhaps it was because they had more mobile capital to expend on speculative ventures; possibly it was because the economic situation at home in the early-seventeenth century was uncertain and overseas investment and even settlement might prove more profitable than investment nearer home. In all, the Welsh commitment down to about 1630 did not amount to a great deal, but it was pervasive. We would like to know why it was not more so. This is not likely to be possible until much more systematic research on Welsh social and economic history of the period has been published. Perhaps it may then be possible to present this topic as an integral part of the history of Wales rather than as a series of largely isolated and only casually related episodes. [32]

---

[32] Glanmor Williams, 'The Welsh in Tudor England', in *Religion, Language and Nationality in Wales*, pp. 171-99, touches brilliantly on cognate topics. We still lack not only further research on Welsh people overseas in this period, but also on the Welsh in Ireland.

Wales in Parliament, 1542–1581[*]

G. R. ELTON

THOUGH one of the best known provisions of the so-called Union of Wales with England in 1536 equipped the twelve counties with twenty-four representatives at Westminster, we now know that the first elected members sat only in 1542.[1] Their presence and influence may well have contributed to the very large statute of the next session which at long last attended to the unfinished business of turning the intentions of 1536 into something like a settled order, for that the act incorporated Welsh demands and proposals is clear enough from its contents.[2] Wales thus seemed well placed to share in the expanding use of parliamentary statute for personal, local and national purposes which characterized the years from 1530 onwards; one would expect to find bills promoted by Welsh knights and burgesses as one finds them promoted by other identifiable interests. A study of such bills, so far as the evidence survives, for the first forty years of Welsh participation should therefore prove illuminating, though it can be said from the start that the tally is not impressive, reveals no determined exploitation of the possibilities, and must call in doubt whether an entity to be called Wales had much reality in the middle of the sixteenth century. Wales was never so prominent again in the business of the English Parliament as it had been in the nine years following upon Thomas Cromwell's decision to reduce the region beyond Offa's Dyke to order; nothing like the remarkable sequence of acts beginning with 26 Henry VIII, c. 6 (which created a system of law-enforcement modelled on that of the English shires), and ending with the 1543 Statute of Wales already mentioned, was ever seen again during the century. Those acts, however, testified to government policy, however much they may have been influenced by representations from Welsh interests; we turn to what those Welsh interests did with the opportunities that government had thus prepared for them.[3]

The evidence, as usual in such matters, leaves a good deal to be desired. Before 1547 we have only the Journal of the House of Lords to tell us of bills in the

---

[*] I am grateful to Professor R. A. Griffiths whose advice most generously enlightened my ignorance.

[1] P. S. Edwards, 'The parliamentary representation of the Welsh boroughs in the mid-sixteenth century', *Bull. Board of Celtic Studies*, XXVII (1977), 425-39. The 1536 act set up one knight for every shire but two for Monmouth, and one for every shire town except in Merioneth, deemed to have no such centre.

[2] 34 & 35 Henry VIII, c. 26. For the history of the settlement of Wales, extending from 1534 to 1543, cf. P. R. Roberts, 'The "Acts of Union" and the Tudor Settlement of Wales' (unpublished University of Cambridge Ph.D. thesis, 1966).

[3] For an earlier attempt to investigate more or less this question, cf. A. H. Dodd, 'Wales's Parliamentary Apprenticeship (1536-1625)', *Trans. Hon. Soc. Cymmrodorion* (1944 for 1942), pp. 8-72. Dominated by the concepts of the Notestein/Neale school of parliamentary history, Dodd concentrated on men rather than measures; he also made quite a few mistakes and misunderstood aspects of parliamentary procedure.

Parliament, and even when thereafter the more informative Journal of the House of Commons is added we rarely get more than a brief description of a bill's purpose, sometimes in terms that leave us baffled. If a bill passed we can study its text, but we rarely know anything about its prehistory or inner history. These are the familiar problems of Tudor parliamentary history, aggravated in this instance by the paucity of private materials surviving from mid-Tudor Wales. Making what we can of this unsatisfactory state of affairs, we may first note that Welsh activity in Parliament was extraordinarily unsystematic: what look like energetic initiatives peter out with distressing regularity. Thus, the first session for which we know of bills in both Houses (1547-1 Edward VI) was also the session in which most bills touching Wales were promoted: eight in all. Only two more appeared in the remaining five years and four sessions of Edward VI's reign, one in 1549 and another in 1553. In the five sessions of Mary's reign we find only four such bills, three of them in the opening Parliament and none at all after 1554. It looks as though the Marian régime offered little encouragement to Wales. Under Elizabeth activity revived, there being only the surprise meeting of 1572, called to deal with Mary, queen of Scots, which found all Wales unprepared to submit even one bill; in 1566, a very active session altogether, five such appeared. Even so, only sixteen out of the approximately 770 bills and acts before the parliament in the years 1559-81 were specifically Welsh bills and acts, and though perhaps one should pay some regard to the rare occasions on which specific reference to Welsh shires was made in general acts, it does not seem that the principality in its recast state found its novel connection with the sovereign legislature of the realm particularly interesting. Alternatively, it discovered that the consequences of the laws made for all the queen's dominions were quite enough to have to live with.

This small harvest of legislative initiatives nevertheless deserves a closer look. Some quite simply dealt with the consequences of the Henrician settlement—loose ends that wanted tying up. The newly-arrived representatives of 1542 seem to have discovered that the payment of members' wages, long settled in England, needed sorting out for Wales: so in the next session they obtained an act which constructed a complex contributory system for raising the money—not a system which was to work smoothly. The act started in the Commons, where its history is unknown; it passed the Lords without difficulty.[4] Other consequences of the reorganization took longer to work out. In the Parliament of 1554-5, the remnant of lords marcher put in a petition to remedy a defect in the first 'Act of Union'. That act had saved the (largely financial) rights of lay lords touching the holding of courts, collection of forfeitures, and so forth, but had failed to extend that protection to bishops who happened to have marcher rights or to the heirs of lords in possession in 1536. The statute of 1 & 2 Philip & Mary, c. 15, introduced in the Lords, remedied this defect. Which bishops might be concerned the statute does not tell us, but the fact that Thomas Goldwell, about to bring the pope back to St. Asaph, was favourite with both Queen Mary and Cardinal Pole may have

---

[4] 35 Henry VIII, c. 11 (*Statutes of the Realm* [hereafter *SR*], III, 969-70). For the problems of payment, cf. P. S. Edwards, op. cit.

significance.[5] Much later still, in 1566, the county of Merioneth woke up to an insult hidden in the 1534 act which had reorganized the trial of crimes in Wales. It accepted that, like the rest of Wales, it might have to see its criminals tried in the nearby English shires, but protested that an accident of drafting had empowered also neighbouring Welsh shires (Caernarvon and Anglesey) to sit upon criminals from Merioneth. The protest produced a soothing Council bill rapidly passed through both Houses, and though all it got was a private act the shire was seemingly satisfied.[6] Since the bill started in the Lords, it would seem that the grievance was presented through a patron there rather than through the knight for the shire. A last afterglow of Henry VIII's reign is found reflected in the act of his son's first Parliament which reversed the attainder of Rhys ap Gruffydd, victim, in 1531, of obscure faction struggles at court.[7] There is nothing unusual about this act, except perhaps the fact that it was the only restitution in blood called for in Wales by the attainders of Henry VIII's bloodstained reign.

A much more immediate and widely felt consequence of the Tudor 'Union' sprang from one of Parliament's foremost purposes—general taxation. Incorporated in the realm, represented in Parliament, Wales had for the first time become liable to the subsidies and fifteenths and tenths regularly voted to the Crown—regularly, that is, in Henry VIII's last years and from 1559 onwards. Until the Union, Wales—old principality and future shire ground—quite properly did not contribute to supply voted in Parliament (no taxation, they no doubt reasoned, without representation). The fact that Wales was still exempt in 1540, together with Ireland and Calais, supports the view that the 1536 act did not constitute a complete reform in itself.[8] In 1543, however, following the completion of the incorporation, Wales dropped from the list of exemptions, and it was also made to pay the last Henrician subsidy, in 1545.[9] Things changed in the less stringent atmosphere of Edward VI's reign. The act for the extraordinary tax of 1549, called the relief, included two provisos added by the Lords which exempted spiritual persons from certain charges and for the first time used the ancient customary payments due in Wales to a new king or prince to postpone the liability of Welsh taxpayers until those 'mises' had been collected.[10] The

[5] *SR*, IV, 262; *Journals of the House of Lords* [hereafter *LJ*], I, 483, 489 (the first reference being to a 'lord marshall' of Wales, an editorial error). The bill passed the Lords on 3 January 1555 but did not return from the Commons until the 16th, the last day of the session (*Journals of the House of Commons* [hereafter *CJ*], I, 40-41). Dr Roberts (thesis cited, pp. 369-70) refers to the bishops of St. David's and Hereford as prelates with marcher interests.

[6] 8 Eliz. I, c. 20 (*SR*, IV, 522), given a chapter number because it was printed in later collections. Its omission from the sessional statute of 1566 defines it as private; its short-formula enacting clause suggests Council initiative (cf. my remarks in E. W. Ives *et al.* (eds.), *Wealth and Power in Tudor England* (London, 1978), esp. pp. 81-2; and *Bull. Institute Hist. Research*, LIII (1980), 183ff.). For the parliamentary history of the act, cf. *LJ*, I, 657-8, 663; *CJ*, I, 80. Private acts left without a chapter number in *SR* are here referred to by the number inscribed on the O[riginal] A[cts] in the H[ouse of] L[ords] R[ecord] O[ffice].

[7] 1 Edward VI, OA 19, mentioned in the Journal only on the occasion that it returned to the Lords after passage in the Commons (*LJ*, I, 312).

[8] *SR*, III, 824. Calais had had burgesses at Westminster since 1539; its continued exemption probably arose out of its known bankrupt state.

[9] Ibid., pp. 950, 1031.

[10] Ibid., IV, 93.

precedent having been set, the principle reappeared in the next regular subsidy, in 1553. Once again, interestingly enough, it was the Lords and not the taxpayers' proper representatives in the Commons who moved for it, asking the Lower House to substitute their proviso for one (now lost) that had been in the subsidy bill. [11] On this occasion, the (as yet) unpaid relief, held over from 1549, was made the pretext. This curious rolling exemption—no relief because of mises, no subsidy because of the relief—continued for some time. In 1555 the new mises due to Philip and Mary did duty; in 1558, the unpaid subsidy postponed by those mises served its turn; and on both occasions the proviso was in the Commons' bill. [12]

The year 1558 brought a new queen with new mises due, but the bill as passed by the Commons (and prepared by the Council) attempted to ignore the (by now) no doubt 'traditional' rights of the Welsh. Once again it was in the Lords that attention was drawn to the exception, by means of a petition (no names preserved) addressed to that House which, favourably impressed, obtained a statement from the queen that neither subsidy nor mise should be collected in a year in which the other was payable. The necessary proviso appeared in a schedule attached to the 1559 act. [13] For once Elizabeth kept her promise, and the exemption clauses appeared in 1563, 1566 and 1571. [14] Thereafter, however, the view seems to have been taken that old obligations had been discharged, and from 1576 onwards Wales no longer enjoyed freedom from subsidies. [15] Mises next became payable at the accession of James I, but his first subsidy act (1606) only postponed payment by a short period without remitting it altogether. [16] In the most palpable manner imaginable, through their pockets, the inhabitants of Wales joined the realm of England in 1576.

It remains to consider what they tried to make of their membership: what matters did they, or some of them, try to achieve by parliamentary legislation? The bills and acts in question may be divided by content into matters economic, legal reform, and the pursuit of spiritual improvement. The harvest was small in all three respects, but not so small as to be without significance. Wales used Parliament only a little, but it used it.

Like many districts of England, Wales contained its clothmaking interests who hoped to profit from protection by statute. Like their English counterparts, they found the business very frustrating: bills for cloth, clothiers and clothworkers are among the most regular failures in mid-Tudor Parliaments. The Welsh makers of cottons and friezes (cheap and light woollens) put a bill into the Commons in 1547 which never progressed beyond second reading. [17] Discouraged for twelve years, they tried again in Elizabeth's first Parliament (1559) and this time with greater persistence. The bill passed the Commons easily, but the Lords, after three

---

[11] Ibid., p. 189; *LJ*, I, 436; *CJ*, I, 24.
[12] *SR*, IV, 312, 348.
[13] Ibid., p. 396; *LJ*, I, 549.
[14] *SR*, IV, 478, 518-19, 581.
[15] E.g. ibid., pp. 651 (1576), 697-8 (1581), etc.
[16] Ibid., p. 1126.
[17] *CJ*, I, 3.

readings in three days, voted it down.[18] In the cutthroat competition between clothmaking districts which doomed one bill after another, this failure at the last hurdle is less surprising than that the bill ever got so far. In 1566, when Welsh woolgrowers hoped to improve their trade with the rest of the realm, they apparently thought to demonstrate a lesson learned by starting in the Upper House; on this occasion the roles were reversed, and the Commons on second reading dashed the bill readily passed by the Lords.[19] Much more obscure is the subject of yet another failure, a bill promoted in 1547 'for the nursing and fostering of children in Wales and divers exactions'. This title—all we have of the bill—makes it impossible to know just what the measure might have achieved. However, it met with success in the Commons who passed it right at the end of the session, so that there was no time left for the Lords even to receive it.[20] The odd thing, quite contrary to more usual practice, is that a bill which had got that far was never brought in again in a later session. Perhaps it represented a private move by some individual who did not serve in another Parliament. Whoever he was, he may even have got the notion on the spur of the moment, after hearing the two readings given to a bill 'for bringing up poor men's children'; if so, he proved himself something of a novice, for this was the bill *pro forma*, read at the opening of the session, which no one really intended to pass.[21] All this, of course, is conjecture: but why not?

However, four bills of economic import did pass in these forty years. The first of them is in some ways the most interesting—the act of 1544 which empowered a large number of towns in Wales and elsewhere in the realm to override private rights in the interest of rebuilding decayed houses.[22] Such collective acts, evidently promoted by some municipalities and then attracting other interested parties once the bill got going, had been used in 1536 and 1540 to tackle the much complained of urban problems of the day, and the first such measure had probably originated with the towns of the Welsh border country.[23] The 'Union' allowed this sensible movement of reform to cross into Wales itself, though whether the powers obtained were ever used is something that local investigation would have to study. Another of Thomas Cromwell's reform measures attracted Welsh attention in 1554 when the powers created by the 1532 statute of sewers were extended to provide protection to the seacoast of Glamorgan against the encroachment of tide-borne sands. A privately-promoted bill, it achieved public act status, even though the earl of Shrewsbury, one of the better known marcher lords, recorded his dissent in the Upper House.[24] Both these acts, in their

---

[18] Ibid., pp. 59-60; *English Hist. Rev.*, XXVIII (1913), 537-8.

[19] *LJ*, I, 642-5; *CJ*, I, 77-8, 81.

[20] Ibid., pp. 3-4.

[21] Ibid., pp. 1-2. The bill disappeared after second reading on 24 November; the Welsh bill was read a first time on 15 December.

[22] 35 Henry VIII, c. 4 (*SR*, III, 959-60). It was the Lords who wished to add to the Commons' bill a proviso for the inclusion of Radnor and Presteigne (*LJ*, I, 250); since these towns are listed currently in the text of the act, the Commons seem to have preferred to write it out afresh.

[23] G. R. Elton, *Reform and Renewal: Thomas Cromwell and the Common Weal* (Cambridge, 1973), pp. 108-9.

[24] 1 Mary, stat. 3, c. 11 (*SR*, IV, 235); *CJ*, I, 36; *LJ*, I, 461-2.

different ways, testify to opportunities taken to benefit from the new relationship between Wales and the laws made by the Parliament of England.

The other two successful economic measures concern the maintenance of bridges; one of them reflects local conflicts which we may often suspect lurk behind a bill but are only very occasionally able to unravel. Thus, we have no evidence that the act for the bridge at Chepstow in Monmouthshire caused any problems or roused any concern, but since it implied the possibility of local rates it may well have done. [25] It was a private bill, [26] put up in petitionary form and in the name of 'the greatest part of the inhabitants of South Wales', which professed to remedy an accidental defect in the bridges and highways act of 1531 (22 Henry VIII, c. 5). That act, it was claimed, did not apply to areas then not shired and thus made no provision for the old marcher lordships. Since 1536, however, Chepstow stood in shire ground, and the bill therefore expressly extended the provisions of 1531 to it, placing the responsibility for maintaining Chepstow bridge on Monmouthshire and Gloucestershire jointly. This act, too, started in the Lords and passed both Houses with rapid ease. [27] Of course, it only created powers to levy money for a future contingency, whereas the case stood very differently at Cardiff, where a bridge had actually collapsed and money was needed at once to rebuild it. This led to a prolonged dispute, which has been fully discussed elsewhere, [28] between the town and the shire, each trying to unload the responsibility onto the other.

It appears from the correspondence between the contending parties that a first effort to promote a bill for raising the necessary money was made in 1576, though the silence of both Journals indicates that it never reached even first reading. It looks, therefore, as though the immediate protests from the shire succeeded in stopping proceedings and prevented the town's promoters from handing the bill in. The next four years were filled with acrimonious discussions over the distribution of the costs between town and county, but in 1581 Cardiff (with the support of the knight of the shire, one William Matthew) got its act with surprising ease. Or so would be suggested by the Journals, which record nothing but smooth and rapid progress. [30] A private diarist, who distinguished himself by supposing that Cardiff was in Montgomeryshire, [31] also notes only the readings of the bill, and the original act indicates that no changes were made during passage. However, there survives evidence of frenzied efforts to stop the proceedings. Some twelve months before the Parliament met, but when there was reason to suppose that it would not again be prorogued, the county interests prepared a

[25] 18 Eliz. I, c. 18 (*SR*, IV, 629).

[26] PRO, SP12, vol. 107, fo. 144.

[27] *LJ*, I, 734-6, 742; *CJ*, I, 107-9.

[28] P. Williams, 'Controversy in Elizabethan Glamorgan: the Rebuilding of Cardiff Bridge', *Morgannwg*, II (1958), 38-46. My account is much indebted to this article, and I have provided references only for such points as I have been able to add.

[29] Ibid., pp. 39-40.

[30] *CJ*, I, 123, 128, 130-1; *LJ*, II, 43, 45, 46-7. The act is 23 Eliz. I, c. 11 (*SR*, IV, 673-4). A private bill, it achieved printing and thus public act status for no known reason—except perhaps favour; as Dr Williams has shown, the settlement had the backing of the earl of Pembroke.

[31] T. E. Hartley (ed.), *Proceedings in the Parliaments of Elizabeth I* (Leicester, 1981), I, 533, 538.

case against the expected legislation,[32] while on the same day two privy
councillors who supported the town (the earl of Pembroke and Sir Henry Sidney)
mobilised the sheriff on the other side.[33] When the bill was actually before the
Parliament, the protesters moved rather belatedly: they sent out letters of appeal
on 24 February 1581, four days after the bill had been ordered to be engrossed
after passing its second reading. By then it was rather late for the sort of elaborate
statements or points against the town, with detailed (and generally convincing)
replies, which survives and which, we may therefore presume, was intended to
persuade the Upper House to stop the bill;[34] though not too late for a pompously
solemn self-defence by William Matthew, who (rather unconvincingly) asserted
that he had been solely moved by the justice of the case.[35] The victory of the
town, whose bill compelled the shire to contribute rather more to the rebuilding
than an earlier compromise proposal had offered, derived from the fact that it
commanded the better interest at court and therefore in the Parliament. One
point of interest may be noted: in presenting the case, the town relied heavily on
the precedents set in 1576, when not only Chepstow but also Rochester had
obtained similar acts for the rebuilding of bridges. Evidently recent precedents,
which the 'Union' had made relevant, could override such ancient customary
arrangements as those upon which the shire gentry tried to rely.

Wales, in effect, shared the common experience that matters of the law were
easier to get through the Parliament than matters of trade, as well as the
experience that even in law reform the number of failed bills greatly exceeded
those that passed. Two private acts, transferring the county capital in Anglesey
from declining Newborough to rising Beaumaris (1549), and arranging for the
county days in Cardiganshire to alternate between Aberystwyth and Cardigan
(1553), testified to careful local preparation: unless all parties were satisfied, such
bills usually got quashed by protests from the unsatisfied.[36] The first bill was a
petition put forward by Beaumaris, but once again the Welsh preference for
working through the Lords manifested itself, though the Commons added a
proviso which the Upper House accepted; this freed Newborough from
contributing to the wages of the parliamentary burgess for Anglesey and was
obviously obtained by representations from the de-throned shire town.[37]

Four more general bills were introduced in the first Parliament of Edward VI;
of these three failed, leaving us with only a brief title to indicate what they may
have been about. The Commons gave two readings to a bill 'to avoid the office of
ragler in Wales', apparently an attempt to abolish that ancient local officer, the

---

[32] For some reason, these found their way into the Percy archives at Alnwick: Historical Manuscripts
Commission, *Third Report*, App. 47b.

[33] *Cal. State Papers, Dom., 1547-1580*, p. 638.

[34] PRO, SP12, vol. 148, fos. 33-4.

[35] Ibid., fos. 35-6.

[36] 2 & 3 Edward VI, OA 54; 1 Mary, stat. 2, OA 23 (not the non-existent 1 Philip & Mary, c. 8, as in Dodd,
op. cit., p. 10, n. 3).

[37] *LJ*, I, 347-8, 351, 353; *CJ*, I, 9-10. For the second bill, only the third reading in the Commons is recorded
(ibid., p. 30); the Lords Journal does not mention it. I am grateful to Mr David Dean for ascertaining the
details of 2 & 3 Edward VI, OA 54.

rhaglaw or constable of the commote. [38] Of two bills read for a first time on the same day in the Lords, one which in some way meant to reform forest jurisdiction in Wales was committed to the attorney-general and not heard of again; the other—'for courts to be held in Wales', a title which tells us nothing—slept after being read once. [39] A successful bill, which started in the Commons, remedied a deficiency created by a gap in the Union laws. It dealt with a problem arising out of the processes of the common law—the process known as exigent and outlawry, that is to say, the instruments available for getting a recalcitrant defendant into the Westminster courts. Writs of exigent (warning a man to attend) followed, if disobeyed, by a public proclamation making the defaulter an outlaw (and therefore unable to engage in any litigation and in theory deprived of all his movables), were in particular employed against persons accused of felony at the Crown's suit, but also against debtors who sought to defraud their creditors. An act of 1512 had tried to ensure that the subject of the exercise became aware of this process against himself by decreeing that proclamation should be made not in the county in which the suit had arisen but in that in which the defendant resided. [40] The legislation for Wales, while creating the necessary shrieval machinery, had failed to remove the pre-Union provision (whereby no such machinery existed) that outlawries in Wales should be proclaimed in the adjoining English shire, an anomaly which the bill of 1547 set itself to remove. It started in the Commons but had no easy passage there. First, it was decided to amalgamate it with a similar bill introduced by Chester, which faced the same problem. The fact that the new bill formed the sole item before the House for one whole sitting day, after which yet another new bill was brought in, proves the occurrence of prolonged debate, much hesitation, and repeated redrafting. The likelihood is that behind these difficulties there lay apprehensions among lords with interests in Wales and the Marches: in the Upper House it was opposed to the last, though in vain, by three prominent marcher lords including the earls of Arundel and Derby. In the end the Lords added a rather meaningless proviso saving the rights of marcher lords, which the Commons accepted. [41]

Bills of this sort, straightening out differences between England and the newly incorporated parts, evidently stood the best chance of getting through. The principle applies to the act of 1563 which extended a reform of 1544 to Wales, Chester, Lancaster and Durham. [42] That measure had dealt with the not uncommon problem raised at assizes when a jury empanelled by the sheriff upon a precept issued to him by the court either failed to turn up in full or got attenuated by challenges from the parties. In order to avoid trials being protracted by such means, the act authorized the court to complete the jury *de circumstantibus*—that is, from other qualified persons who happened to be present. The bill which extended this useful device to Wales and the rest passed the Commons with ease, was in the Lords given to the chief justice of Common Pleas

---

[38] *CJ*, I, 1; cf. Roberts, thesis cited, p. 364.
[39] *LJ*, I, 303.
[40] 4 Henry VIII, c. 4, made permanent by 5 Henry VIII, c. 4.
[41] 1 Edward VI, c. 10; *CJ*, I, 2-3; *LJ*, I, 311-13.
[42] 5 Eliz. I, c. 25: 35 Henry VIII, c. 6, sect. 3.

to revise, and was accepted with the Lords' amendments by the Lower House. Though most of the amendments touched only details of phrasing, it was actually the Lords who added Durham to the bill's beneficiaries.[43] The bishop of Durham, James Pilkington, owner of the franchise affected, was present on the two days that mattered; one would like to know how this earnest prelate took the inclusion of his special charge.

Altogether, the chief problem exercising reponsible people in Wales concerned the effectiveness of law enforcement in a region which had only so very recently been provided with the organization long available in England, and a region, moreover, which everybody—insiders as well as outsiders—regarded as exceptionally lawless. In view of the difficulties which the established English system notoriously encountered in preventing neglect or abuse of the law, the apparent trust in reforming bills for Wales must nevertheless strike one as a trifle naïve. Still, earnest men in Wales tried several times. In Edward VI's last Parliament a bill to compel outlaws and fugitives to surrender when proclaimed—a bill, that is, which would give teeth to the act of 1547—was committed on second reading, understandably enough because such a law must have raised many points of substance and form. The chairman of the committee was an eminent lawyer, Francis Morgan, serjeant at law and later a judge, whose name suggests Welsh connections but who actually sat for Northampton.[44] After revision, the bill again reached second reading but only four days before the dissolution of the Parliament. Since Morgan sat again in the next Parliament (Mary's first),[45] the bill came forward once more, this time to be read once and not heard of again.[46] An attempt to put an end to those potential sources of resistance and lawlessness, the customary popular gatherings known as *commorthas,* also ended after a single reading in 1571.[47] A major effort to reform criminal trials (gaol deliveries and quarter sessions) in Wales actually passed both Houses in 1566, after considerable revision and discussion, only to be vetoed by the queen. Seeing that the bill proposed to terminate the trial of Welsh crimes in adjoining shires, and that during its passage provisos safeguarding the sessions at Shrewsbury and Hereford were added, one may perhaps conjecture that the government received protests from the Council in the Marches, apprehensive that control might slip from its hands. This caused the Privy Council to block the bill by applying the veto, a device quite common at the time when it was thought that more time for reflection and discussion might resolve difficulties and disagreements.[48] The bill was indeed reintroduced, perhaps altered, in the next session (1571) when it passed the Commons easily. However, governmental doubts evidently remained, for the powerful Lords' committee which took charge of the bill (including, among others, Burghley, Leicester, Bedford and Hunsdon)

[43] *CJ,* I, 64, 66-7; *LJ,* I, 598, 600, 611-12, 615. The Lords' amendments appear on the OA in HLRO.
[44] *Official Return of Members of Parliament* (1878), I, 382.
[45] Ibid., p. 386.
[46] *CJ,* I, 24-7.
[47] Ibid., p. 90.
[48] Ibid., pp. 77-80; *LJ,* I, 660-3.

recommended a conference with the Lower House which was unfortunately prevented by the closing of the session. [49]

The approach of the next session roused the reformers once more. Advice was received from Sir John Throckmorton, chief justice of Chester, [50] as well as from Richard Price, a Brecknock gentleman who told Burghley (on 31 January 1576) that he was offering counsel because 'the Parliament going forwards, whatsoever cannot otherwise conveniently, may there be redressed by your wisdom and furtherance'. [51] Price, in fact, produced a fine collection of necessary reforms, some of which called for action by Parliament, though it appears from the comments noted on it that the document did not reach the Lord Treasurer until after the session of 1576. [52] For in that session an act had passed which followed up a suggestion of Throckmorton's and anticipated one of Price's reforms: evidently the matter was in the air. This was the act appointing a second judge to each of the four circuits in Wales in order to ensure that there should be no lapse in law enforcement or needless delay in the trial of civil suits. [53] To judge by the enacting clause, the bill was drawn up privately, but it was introduced in the Lords, perhaps from Welsh habit but more likely in order to take advantage of the ground prepared beforehand with Burghley; it caused no difficulties. [54] Price had been anxious always to have two experts on the bench, serving in person and not by deputy, though he allowed for the possibility of illness, when the clerk of assize was to join the bench. The act says nothing on either point, but since justices of assize in England could not in any case appoint deputies to sit for them, explicit provision may have been regarded as superfluous. Anyway, the adviser who went over Price's proposals thought them fully answered by drawing attention to the act just passed. It appears that the reform did not become actual until 1579; [55] when it did, it must have helped to make assizes in Wales more effective for both criminal cases and *nisi prius* actions.

That, however, was the sum total of legal reform—accommodating Wales to English practice in respect of the proclamation of outlawries and the filling up of deficient juries, and giving Welsh circuits two expert judges where one was thought enough in England. Two other bills for Wales pleased the Commons but got shipwrecked in the Lords. One of 1566 wished to set up record offices in every Welsh shire, an excellent proposal whose failure the historian, not served in such fashion until the 1950s, must deeply regret. [56] Another, of 1579, would have improved the handling of a very common form of land transaction (conveyancing by fine and recovery), probably by better record-keeping at least in Wales; the Lords, who deliberately 'stayed' the bill after reading it only once, decided on a conference with the Lower House which once again was arranged too late in the

[49] *CJ*, I, 89-92; *LJ*, I, 695-7. Cf. *Proceedings*, ed. Hartley, I, 252-4.

[50] P. Williams, *The Council in the Marches of Wales under Elizabeth I* (Cardiff, 1958), p. 263.

[51] H. Ellis (ed.), *Original Letters Illustrative of English History*, second ser., III, 42-8.

[52] PRO, SP12, vol. 107, fos. 2-3, 5-33, 43-54, endorsed as coming from 'Mr Price'. Annotations (fo. 13) point out that what Price wanted done had been achieved 'by an act of the late Parliament'.

[53] 18 Eliz. I, c. 8 (*SR*, IV, 618-19).

[54] *LJ*, I, 736, 738, 743; *CJ*, I, 109-11.

[55] Williams, *Council in the Marches*, p. 264.

[56] *CJ*, I, 77, 79-80; *LJ*, I, 660-1.

session actually to take place. One suspects that the judges raised immediate difficulties, though lacking the bill we cannot even guess what these might have been.[57]

After these sordid, and largely unsuccessful, efforts to exploit the Parliament for profit and advantage, it is some relief to turn to endeavours to promote more spiritual causes—few indeed, but with a much higher incidence of success. In fact, there were three such bills, of which two passed, leading to one further abortive bill for the repeal of one of the successful measures. On 19 December 1547 a bill was introduced (again in the Lords) for the founding of a grammar school at Carmarthen. It was evidently meant to secure the continued existence of the school which Thomas Lloyd, precentor of St. David's, had established there four years earlier, and which his death early in September 1547 threatened with closure. Lloyd had hoped to preserve it by provisions in his will, but his executors got entangled with the town authorities, and the money set aside for the school was soon converted to other uses. We may guess that the bill was the work of Lloyd's friends, and we may further guess that the introduction in the Lords reflects the lack of enthusiasm for the school encountered in the town. The fact that the bill foundered after only one reading indicates that no one much cared for the preserving of Lloyd's foundation, and Carmarthen had to wait for its school until 1576.[58]

The shire harboured some who cared about spiritual well-being, and in 1559 they got an act which improved their chances of salvation for the parishioners of Abernant.[59] The bill was a private petition, with a handsomely decorated initial letter (in this sort of document, a hallmark of the amateur), from the parishioners themselves. It explained that their existing parish church lay six miles distant from the nearest habitations within the parish, and was in addition too small to accommodate all the congregation. At their own expense, therefore, the parishioners had enlarged a convenient chapel at Cynwyl Elfed, previously annexed to the parish church but much better placed to serve the needs of the parish, and they now asked for an act that would turn this chapel into the parish church. They saved the right of the patron, who was to present to the new church in the same way as he had done to the old. Before the Reformation the living had been in the gift of the Austin priory of St. John at Carmarthen, and at the Dissolution the advowson fell to the Crown which still held the patronage in the 1550s—a fact which underlines the wisdom of the saving clause.[60] Precautions, however, failed to satisfy everybody: someone, perhaps the patron, tried in 1566 to have this sensible act of 1559 repealed, though he got no further than a single reading in the Lords.[61]

---

[57] *CJ*, I, 109-11; *LJ*, I, 741-2. When listing the bills left in his hands, the clerk of the Lords included this one among those he described as stayed (PRO, SP12, vol. 107, fo. 190).

[58] *LJ*, I, 309; Glanmor Williams, 'Thomas Lloyd his Skole: Carmarthen's first Tudor Grammar School', *Carms. Antiquary*, X (1974), 49-62.

[59] 1 Eliz. I, OA 35.

[60] *Valor Ecclesiasticus*, IV, 410; E. Yardley, *Menevia Sacra*, ed. F. Green (London, 1927), 396.

[61] *LJ*, I, 649. With 2,000 souls the parish was a large one, and the building operations at Cynwyl Elfed must have cost a fair penny.

Of greater import was the crown of Welsh parliamentary lobbying in this period, the well-known act of 1563 for a Welsh translation of the Bible and the Prayer Book.[62] Glanmor Williams, who has so well illumined the roles of Richard Davies, bishop of St. David's, and William Salesbury, scholar and translator, in this momentous translation,[63] may like to hear a little more about the parliamentary history of this measure which is not without interest. The bill, clearly the work of its promoters though a professional job, was put into the Commons; the act, though now printed in the *Statutes of the Realm*, was not the sessional statute and must therefore have been a private one, paying its quite considerable fees to the officers of both Houses. Its relatively slow passage in the Commons, from 22 February to 27 March, reflects the common fortunes of private bills which needed urgent promoting and regular fee-paying if they were to get on, rather than any objections; it was not, for instance, committed. Rather it looks as though the promoters worked with insufficient zeal, perhaps because the most enthusiastic among them sat in the Lords, or just ran into too much business; certainly this was a very busy session. The bill authorized five bishops (of Hereford, Bangor, St. Asaph, St. David's and Llandaff) to license a Welsh translation of the Scriptures and the Book of Common Prayer, pleading that the English translation had proved the supreme virtue of a vernacular version in the spiritual life of the nation but that in Wales, 'no small part of the realm', an English Bible served no vernacular purpose. The bishops were to see to it that a Welsh translation was available by 1 March 1565.

In this form the bill reached the Lords, who made some changes.[64] Most of these were verbal, but it was the Upper House who changed the date in the act from 1565 to 1567, a sensible decision seeing that even by that date the translators were able to produce only the Prayer Book and the New Testament, even though Salesbury had translated most of the latter as early as 1551.[65] Furthermore, the Lords added the proviso which is now the last clause of the act and which ensured that not only the Welsh Bible but the English version also should be placed in every parish church in Wales. This proviso maintained that there were people in Wales who could read only English and also hoped that others would find the possibility of comparing the two versions conducive to learning the English tongue. Who was responsible for this piece of English chauvinism? Of the five bishops, Hereford, Bangor and Llandaff did not attend the House at all in this session, and St. Asaph was not there on the day that the proviso was read. Only St. David's—Richard Davies himself—attended on all the relevant days.[66] He, who worked so much in harness with Salesbury and shared in the work of translation, may well have urged the later and more practical date, but it seems improbable that he, who was so eager to improve and preserve the Welsh tongue, should also have been behind the less friendly proviso. At any rate, the change of

---

[62] 5 Eliz. I, c. 28.

[63] Glanmor Williams, *Welsh Reformation Essays* (Cardiff, 1967), pp. 155-205.

[64] The OA carries a list of Lords' amendments.

[65] Williams, *Welsh Reformation Essays*, pp. 196-7.

[66] *LJ*, I, 610-13.

date strongly suggests that Davies had not been consulted in the drafting of the original bill and that Salesbury had been too optimistic.

The real mystery, however, touches the first question of all: why was the act promoted and passed at all? That mystery is deepened by the printing history of the translations called for. The various efforts, dating back to 1537, to provide an English Bible for exhibition in parish churches had never bothered with a statute, such authorization as seemed necessary being conveyed in royal proclamations.[67] The act in effect did three things. It called for the making of the two translations; it empowered five bishops to act as approvers and therefore licensers; and by omitting all reference to the Bible-printing monopoly held by the queen's printer prepared the way for breaking it. And broken it was, without protest from Richard Jugge and John Cawood, who held the patent at the time. It would appear that Salesbury first came to terms with John Walley, a leading member of the Stationers' Company, who some time in the summer of 1563 paid 4*d.* for a licence to print a Welsh litany (that is, the translation of the Prayer Book).[68] Most likely it was also Walley who, conscious as he was bound to be of the queen's printer's claims, suggested that the two of them should obtain a monopoly patent for printing and selling Welsh translations of the Bible, the Prayer Book and the Book of Homilies; a draft of such a patent was sent to William Cecil for his consideration and approval. The draft took care to mention the bishops' licensing powers created in the act, but it overstepped the mark when it added a monopoly for producing any work of scriptural commentary in Welsh or English. This was a piece of overreaching ambition which would really have harmed Jugge and Cawood who, one may well suppose, had little interest in printing for the restricted Welsh market; it is quite likely that this was the reason why the patent failed to get approval and never passed the great seal.[69]

Before Salesbury and Davies were ready with their translations, Walley in fact lost interest and wrote off his 4*d.* The volumes which appeared in 1567 were printed by Henry Denham for Humphrey Toy, who were well enough known London printers and booksellers, Toy paying 3*s.* 4*d.* for entering the Prayer Book in the Stationers' Register but only 12*d.* for the New Testament.[70] Interestingly enough, when a complete Welsh Bible at last became available in 1588, the

[67] E.g. it was by proclamation that Thomas Cromwell was given power to approve an English Bible: P. Hughes and J. F. Larkin (eds.), *Tudor Royal Proclamations* (New Haven, 1964-9), I, 286-7.
[68] E. Arber (ed.), *A Transcript of the Registers of the Company of Stationers of London* (London, 1875-94), I, 209.
[69] The draft is in British Library, Lansdown MS. 48, fo. 75; it is printed in W. W. Greg, *A Companion to Arber* (Oxford, 1967), 113-14. Greg called it a certified copy of what he took to be a patent issued. Against this view are these facts: no such patent was ever enrolled; there are several signs of unfinished drafting in the document; it lacks the dating clause, one thing that would certainly have been transcribed for a certified copy. The name appended (which Greg correctly identified as that of a clerk of the Signet but wrongly supposed to be the certifier) was that of the man responsible for writing out what would have become a Signet warrant to the Privy Seal Office if the queen had approved the application; certified copies of letters patent had to be got from the Chancery. Furthermore, contrary to Greg's printing, the endorsement is not dated. The dorse carried two modern and quite unauthoritative dates—1563 and 1582, in different hands—but in view of Walley's action in the Stationers' Register, 1563 may well be a right guess. 1582 is certainly wrong.
[70] Arber, *Stationers' Registers*, I, 336. The books' title-pages confirm the part played by Toy and Denham (Greg, *Companion*, p. 8), for whom see R. B. McKerrow (ed.), *A Dictionary of Printers and Booksellers . . . 1557-1640* (London, 1910).

queen's printer (by this time Christopher Barker's assigns) asserted his patented rights to the production.[71] But it seems that the five bishops failed to do what the act demanded of them; we hear nothing about approval for the 1567 New Testament, whereas the Prayer Book is explicitly stated to have been 'authorized' by the bishop of London, that is Edmund Grindal. It is to be hoped that he obtained a clean bill from someone capable of checking a Welsh text, but perhaps he contented himself with a reassurance from his brother of St. David's, who was so deeply involved in the work of translating.

In a way, this best known and most respectable of all the parliamentary measures promoted for Wales in the years 1542-81 confirms the impression left by its less illustrious companions. An unnecessary act whose provisions were only partially observed just about fits as a symbol for the efforts made by the newly represented region to put its contacts with the legislative institution to use. On the other hand, the act was exceptional in being the only one of all the bills to concern itself with the needs of the true Welsh; the rest really attended to the needs and ambitions of the governing sort, many of whom were surely English or Anglicized enough. Their needs and ambitions as a rule extended to the establishment of a settled order which to the ranks below them must too often have looked like the destruction of old habits and customs.

One further point deserves a summarizing comment. We have noted that, except in 1547, the majority of Welsh bills started in the Upper House. When it came to promoting their interests, the Welsh gentry and boroughs looked not to the men they sent to Westminster but to noble patrons, more particularly perhaps to the house of Herbert, so influential in Elizabeth's Court and Council. It is surely significant that Welsh activity in Parliament stood at its lowest ebb in the reign of Mary, when the earl of Pembroke, having just about managed to survive his prominence under Edward VI, carried least weight at Court. If this reliance on noble favour was considered policy, as it very much seems to have been, the 'battle of Cardiff Bridge' shows how well participants understood the position. What use was William Matthew to the shire that had elected him? Like the city, he looked to Pembroke who thus directed both the members of the Lower House concerned in the business. This structure of politics, of course, was by no means peculiar to Wales. The English country gentry carried more weight than the Welsh squirearchy, and English borough interests knew how to push bills through the House of Commons; but in the end favour in high places would do more for a man or an interest than historians of that somewhat overrated House may like to think.

---

[71] Greg, *Companion*, p. 8.

Hall, Tower and Church: Some Themes and Sites Reconsidered

PETER SMITH

I N *Houses of the Welsh Countryside* (1975), I surveyed the historical domestic architecture of Wales.[1] Since publication, certain discoveries have been made which have a bearing on the work. Some of these discoveries relate to the medieval (i.e. pre-Elizabethan) period, including the remarkable parallels which have emerged between the architectural detailing of church and house. The place of these Welsh building traditions will be considered not only in a British setting, but also in a broader European context. I trust that Glanmor Williams, who as Commissioner for Ancient Monuments was one of the sponsors of my original venture, will find this collection of second thoughts an appropriate tribute.

GENERAL

In my original study, I divided medieval houses into hall-houses, on the one hand, and first-floor halls and towers on the other, an antithesis that is fundamental and most revealing in terms of social and political history.

A study of the Welsh house should begin with the hall. Indeed, in southern Britain the hall-house is the earliest house to survive in quantity. Hall-houses built before the mid-sixteenth century, when the storeyed house became fashionable, abound in much of what I have previously called the *lowland* and *intermediate* zones (Fig. 1).[2] These halls include not only the halls of the upper classes but also the halls of lesser people. The majority of these lesser halls appear to be early Tudor in date, suggesting that during this period, these zones were producing economic surpluses sufficient to finance durable buildings not only for the church, the lords, and the merchants, but also—and for the first time— for a significant number of the common people as well.

There is, indeed, good archaeological evidence that a major improvement in housing standards was taking place as the middle ages drew to a close. Very little peasant architecture antedates the Tudors, but a great wealth of farmhouses can be assigned to the period between the battle of Bosworth and the accession of Elizabeth I. It is revealing that whereas Elizabethan storeyed houses often contain the framework of previous Tudor halls, these halls themselves rarely incorporate structures from *their* predecessors. The absence of pre-Tudor material in early Tudor houses suggests that nothing had been thought worth re-using and that a

---

[1] HMSO, 1975.
[2] P. Smith, 'The Architectural Personality of the British Isles', *Arch. Camb.*, 1980, pp. 22, 28.

remarkable transformation in building standards had taken place. The permanent had replaced the impermanent peasant home.

It is important to stress that the area in which this transformation had occurred extends into eastern Wales, Devon and the southern Pennines. Beyond these regions, however, early peasant hall-houses are hard to find, while even the halls of the upper classes become rarities. In the north of England we find a countryside more and more dominated by the needs of defence (Fig. 2). As we move westwards into Ireland or northwards into Scotland, we enter regions that had changed even more slowly, where medieval conditions endured as late as the seventeenth century and where lairds lived not in undefended halls but in defensive towers. Here pre-Reformation instances of peasant building simply do not exist. In this outer highland zone few peasant houses antedate the eighteenth century, while the majority are later still. Here the durable peasant house appeared centuries later than in the south. [3]

Most hall-houses of the lowland and intermediate zones were half-timbered (Figs. 3-4). In the south-east the box-frame predominates. In the midlands and Wales cruck frames encasing generally smaller buildings form a significant proportion of the whole. A characteristic feature of the south-east is the crown-post, collar-purlin roof, while in the 'mid-west' the side-purlin roof preponderates. In the former region the bayed roof is a late development, while in the latter it is a fundamental idea.

The significance of these contrasts has been much debated. According to some, structural ideas so distinct must go back much earlier than the first surviving examples and may be related either to ethnic divisions, or to a 'lowland' or 'highland' demarcation, an idea which receives much support from distribution maps. Others argue that some of the most marked geographical contrasts are comparatively recent. [4] For example, a map of early crown-post roofs shows a more even spread than a map showing all crown-post roofs, which indicates a south-easterly concentration. Likewise, R. A. Cordingley regarded the tenon-purlin as derived from the 'lowland' non-bayed roof, and it is true that a map including all such would again show a south-easterly concentration. [5] Yet this would obscure the important fact that a significant number of medieval Welsh gentry houses incorporate a tenon-purlin roof, while the majority of medieval Welsh church roofs are either of tenon-purlin or of non-bayed construction. In these circumstances, the argument for diffusion from a point of maximum

[3] It must be admitted that within the lowland and intermediate zones there are variations, not always explicable, in the quantity of early peasant houses still extant. The wealth of Kent, Sussex and Suffolk is legendary, and the west midlands are richly endowed. In comparison with these, the east midlands seem poor and compare unfavourably with the Welsh border counties. It is perhaps arguable that a limited area of Cumberland and Northumberland has a number of early-sixteenth-century peasant houses in the form of strong houses, first-floor halls containing a refuge for cattle on the ground floor. The social standing of their builders is not clear, but would probably include the equivalent of the builders of the better cruck-framed halls in the west midlands and Wales. For alternative views, see H. G. Ramm, R. W. McDowall and E. Mercer, *Shielings and Bastles* (HMSO, 1970), and Philip Dixon, 'Tower-houses, Pelehouses and Border Society', *Archaeological Journal*, 1979, pp. 240-52.

[4] E. Mercer, *English Vernacular Houses* (HMSO, 1975), pp. 82-5.

[5] R. A. Cordingley, 'British Historical roof-types and their members', *Trans. Ancient Monuments Soc.*, new ser., IX (1961), 73-118.

concentration is clearly open to challenge. But even if these qualifications are introduced and even if it has to be conceded that the origin of the contrasting structural systems remains a mystery, there is no denying the existence of the contrast. Nor can the existence by the end of the middle ages of recognizable south-eastern and middle-western, as well as of south-western and northern, schools of carpentry be denied.[6]

Common features of almost all hall-houses are the cross-passage at one end of the hall and the 'dais' partition at the other. In great halls there was a raised dais where the lord and the most honoured members of his household sat. But even those peasants who lacked a raised platform evidently regarded this end of the hall as an area of status. Here they would sit with their backs to the 'dais' partition in imitation of the life-style of their lords.

Beyond these common features, variations in the placing and design of the secondary rooms are legion. A prime distinction should be made between those houses in which the rooms at the passage end were domestic and those which contained a byre (Figs. 3-4). The latter is normally associated with peasant houses on the westerly and mountain fringes. There is, however, some evidence to suggest that such a design reached higher social levels and was not entirely confined to the mountains. But it is certain that little trace of this design has been found either in the south-east where the house-plan is exclusively domestic or, oddly enough, in north-west Wales.

Close continental parallels to the hall-houses of England and Wales at either the peasant or the gentry level are difficult to find. Indeed, there can be few parts of northern Europe with such a concentration of pre-Reformation peasant houses as the lowland and intermediate zones of Great Britain. Here the durable peasant house emerged at a remarkably early date, with all that this means in terms of social and economic development. Among European peasant houses, the best documented are the North German/Dutch *hallenhäuser,* vast aisled structures entered longitudinally from their end walls, quite unlike the hall-house in England and Wales entered transversely by the cross-passage.[7] In northern France and middle Germany, where the houses seem to have a similar span and similar entry position to our own, it is difficult to find clear evidence for the open hall, because the roof space was used for storage. The north European box-frame differs from that of England and Wales in that the tie beams (Ger. *Ankerbalken*) project through the walls which they hold by means of wedges. This construction is unknown here, but it is paralleled in the rows of iron plates which tie Dutch and Belgian brick walls to their interior beams.[8] There is little on the continent to

---

[6] J. T. Smith, 'Medieval roofs: a classification', *Archaeological Journal,* 1958, pp. 111-49; see also *idem,* 'Timber-framed building in England, its development and regional differences', ibid., CXXII (1965), 133-58.

[7] K. Baumgarten, *Das deutsche Bauernhaus* (Akadamie Verlag, Berlin, 1980); *Hallenhäuser in Mecklenburg* (Akademie Verlag, Berlin, 1970). For the very different peasant houses of middle Germany, see also G. Eitzen, *Das Bauernhaus im Kreise, Euskirchen* (Euskirchen, 1970).

[8] There was one example in Wales of this derivative of the continental box-frame. At Sir Richard Clough's Flintshire house, Bachegraig, built in 1567, were a series of iron plates holding the house together and confirming the tradition that the house had been built by Flemish workmen. Those plates were in the form of letters and numerals, a common Flemish practice. They appear to have been moved to Plas Clough when Bachegraig was demolished.

correspond to the alternative cruck construction which is so widespread in mid-western Britain and clearly linked with the open hall, because it is unsuited to storeyed building.

At the gentry level one gets the impression that on much of the continent the first-floor hall, tower-castle tradition is strong, and that this, rather than the hall-house, prevailed among the upper classes until the emergence of pure Renaissance designs in the late-seventeenth century. The mould of the hall-house ancestor can easily be detected in the classic H-plan sub-medieval English manor house (Pls. I-III). Such a mould is difficult to discover in sixteenth-century French *manoirs* (Pl. IV), which were built like small castles before Richelieu and Mazarin asserted the power of the French monarchy.

The notion that England and Wales are architecturally *sui generis* gains force if the ornate open roof is considerd. This roof, so characterstic of the English and Welsh hall-house, appears to be as alien to continental architecture as the Perpendicular style and the four-centred arch. The ornamental roof is typical of both 'lowland' and 'highland' carpentry. A Kentish crown-post and a Denbighshire arch-braced cruck may appear to have little in common. But they are linked by a common intention, namely, to create out of the roof structure itself a thing of beauty, a perfect match of form and function. While continental church and house roofs were utilitarian structures, hidden above vaults, boarded floors or flat ceilings, in England and Wales the roof was often exposed for all to see—a conscious work of art (Pl. VI).

The skills which in the medieval hall-house had been expended on the roof were transferred in the Elizabethan storeyed house to the ceilings, whose beams and joists were richly carved. These mouldings seem to be unknown in Scotland, where the ceilings were often painted as if to make up for the lack of carving. The plainly wrought but painted ceiling is also characteristic of the continent (Pl. VIII).

Even in southern Britain the distribution of ornate structural carpentry varies. In Wales the ornate roof is more strongly represented in the domestic work of the north-east than the south-west. This northerly emphasis recalls patterns of cultural contact which can be traced as far back as the movement of craftsmen following the Edwardian Conquest described by Dr A. J. Taylor.[9] It should also be considered in relation to the geography of church building. After all, what is a church but a great hall? Indeed, the medieval church and the medieval house have much in common. Both have open, strongly directional interiors. The artistic development of one is reflected in the artistic development of the other. It is not surprising, therefore, that many variations in church design anticipate variations in house design. In church, as in house, many features are largely confined to one side of the Machynlleth-Newport line. For example, all wooden porches (Fig. 8) and bell-frames lie to the north-east of this line, while vaulting, particularly of towers, lies mainly to the south-west of it. More immediately relevant is the fact that the prevailing type of nave roof in north Wales is an open, heavily bayed truss-and-rafter roof in which the braces and

[9] A. J. Taylor, 'Castle-building in Wales in the later thirteenth century: the prelude to construction', in E. M. Jope (ed.), *Studies in Building History* (1961), p. 107.

struts are often cusped, a type of roof that achieves its finest expression in the hammerbeam roofs of Denbighshire (Pl. VI; Figs. 5, 7). In south Wales the trussed rafter is more common, many in the barrel form where panels conceal the roof structure (Pl. VII; Fig. 6). Here windbraces are rare and cusping is unknown. It is no accident that most ambitious house roofs occur in the north-east where the ornate open bayed church roof is predominant. The trussed-rafter roof is almost unknown in Welsh domestic work and in south Wales, where the trussed-rafter church is common, truss-and-rafter roofs over the houses tend to be less ornate than in the north, where both church and house had roofs of the truss-and-rafter type.

Interesting examples of the ornate roof tradition of north-east Wales occur in the aisle-truss houses. This group deserves re-examination, not only for its carpentry but also for light it can throw on the planning of the upper-class hall-house.

Aisle-truss Houses

An aisle-truss supports the roof by posts within the external walls rather than on the external walls themselves. The distribution of aisled building in the British Isles is markedly south-easterly, a distribution which admittedly receives great emphasis from large numbers of aisled barns, many built as recently as the eighteenth century. However, aisled domestic (as opposed to agricultural) building began to lose favour in the south-east from the fourteenth century, when forms of truss were devised that dispensed with the aisle posts and left an unobstructed floor space. The classic illustration of the change in taste occurs in Westminster Hall, where Richard II's vast hammerbeam roof replaced the aisled colonnades of William Rufus. It is remarkable that at about this time aisled construction began to enjoy fashionable acclaim in the north-west. This is another good illustration of how architectural fashions drifted north-westwards and of the time-lag that was involved.[10]

I became interested in the aisle-truss house when I discovered five around Wrexham in the course of a single week's fieldwork. I already knew Glamorgan sufficiently well to be sure that a similar search there would not yield a similar result, and indeed no subsequent fieldwork either in Glamorgan or in south-west Wales has discovered a single aisle-truss house.

Although my previous studies of aisle-truss houses produced a distribution pattern that is unlikely to be challenged, a number of other problems were far from satisfactorily resolved: the use of secondary rooms; the date; the relationship between the partly aisled houses and their presumed precursors, the fully aisled houses, and their presumed successors, the single aisle-truss houses. The discovery of one further example and the reconsideration of a few others may throw some light on these problems.

Probably all the aisle-truss houses were built to the classic three-unit large hall-house plan, that is, the hall between a unit at the dais end (the inner unit) and the unit at the passage end (the outer unit). Unfortunately, rebuilding has made the nature of these units difficult to ascertain. There appeared to be two alternative

---

[10] P. Smith, *Arch. Camb.*, 1980, pp. 6-13.

arrangements for the inner unit, both storeyed. In the first, a rather narrow bay housed on the ground floor two small rooms, a cold parlour and a store room side by side. This is the arrangement at Pen-y-bryn (Llansilin) and Egryn (Llanaber), and is evident in large numbers of Welsh yeoman houses (Fig. 3). An alternative provided a single large room, a parlour, occupying the whole of the ground floor but again with a chamber over, an arrangement common in the houses of south-eastern England (Fig. 4). Mr Brooksby's recent discovery of Upper House (Painscastle) offers a third pattern, that is, a large parlour *open to the roof,* heated by an open hearth—a mini-hall, as it were (Fig. 11).[11] A single-storey parlour open to the roof may also have occupied the whole of the dais unit at Tŷ-mawr (Fig. 15). The roof is heavily smoke-blackened and such smoke could only have come from a hearth below because the roof is cut off by the dais partition from the fire in the hall.

At Llwyncelyn (Crucornau Fawr) there was probably another open parlour (Figs. 12-13). I had hitherto assumed that the present plan of first floor chambers over store rooms had been the original layout. However, Mr Brooksby convinced me that here was another open parlour, for again the roof was heavily smoke-blackened, which could only have resulted from a fire below since the roof of the cross-wing was completely separated from the hall roof by a valley. At Llwyncelyn, alongside the open parlour was a storeyed bay containing a chamber over a store room.

Another house with a parlour cross-wing was Horsemans Green Farm, Halghton (Fig. 14). The wing is divided into two rooms, over one of which is an open, archbraced truss. The structure suggested that here originally was another open parlour with store-room and chamber alongside on the pattern of Llwyncelyn.

One might well ask if houses with an open parlour at the dais end had a standard plan at the passage end. Unfortunately, nothing survives of the medieval passage-end at either Upper House or Horsemans Green Farm. But at Llwyncelyn and Tŷ-mawr, where the passage-ends do survive, they are completely different. The passage partition at Llwyncelyn incorporates ornately carved twin doorways side by side, indicating the buttery and the pantry (Fig. 16). But at Tŷ-mawr the partition had two long openings which S. R. Jones has suggested in another context can only be explained as part of a feeding walk for cattle tethered in the room beyond (Fig. 15). In other words, this great house was a long-house.[12] If so, it shows that there were remarkable contrasts in the life-style of the Welsh privileged classes in the late-medieval period. Both Llwyncelyn and Tŷ-mawr were finely wrought buildings implying a high social position. Both were similarly situated in the foothills of the Welsh mountains, yet very close to the great midland plain. Llwyncelyn suggests a design for living like that of neighbouring midland proprietors. Tŷ-mawr implies a life-style not very different, though more ornately framed, from that of an upland peasant farmer who could see the tethered heads of his herd from his bench against the dais partition.

[11] H. Brooksby, 'The Houses of Radnorshire', *Trans. Radnorshire Soc.,* 1978, pp. 20-6.

[12] S. R. Jones, 'Cil-Eos-Isaf', *Montgomeryshire Collections,* 1969-70, pp. 115-31.

The second problem posed by the aisle-truss houses is their date. The houses were all heated by open hearths and therefore preceded those upper-class hall-houses built with enclosed fireplaces in the early-sixteenth century. But a starting date was lacking. I had been inclined to date some as early as the fourteenth century. The discovery of Upper House has cast doubt on this early dating. It is the site of this fine hall which is critical. Built in the moat at Painscastle against the earthen rampart of the fortress, it must date from a time when the castle's military role had ceased, and that cannot have been before the early-fifteenth century, after the suppression of Glyndŵr's rebellion. Although there is no record of a siege at Painscastle, Richard Beauchamp, earl of Warwick was ordered in 1403 to put Painscastle in a state of defence against Glyndŵr.[13] A large wooden house against the wall of the castle would have been an intolerable hazard. The house must, therefore, postdate the rebellion. Indeed, it may have been built as part of a programme of post-war reconstruction. Its situation close to the castle indicates that it had assumed the mantle of the castle as the administrative centre of the lordship.

If Upper House is post-Glyndŵr, it raises the question of the age of the other aisle-truss houses and its place in the series. Upper House is 'lowland', built without ridge-beam and with tenon purlins, features which are incorporated in about half of the aisle-truss houses. Seven houses have 'lowland' details; seven have clear 'highland' details, while not enough of the remainder survives to be certain (Fig. 9). As a means of establishing dating relatives, the highland/lowland analysis does not greatly advance the argument since the two systems appear contemporary. However, Upper House impresses by its sheer massiveness and by the simplicity of the ornament. It is without cusping. This indicates that the house is early in the series, an argument supported by the distance between the aisle posts and the outer wall, hinting that the house is close to the original aisled idea. But in spite of this, it is not a fully aisled hall. The central truss of the hall is a base cruck (Fig. 11). It belongs to a small group in which each hall truss (apart from the central truss) is aisled, and thus stands half-way between the fully aisled prototype and a large group in which a single aisle-truss survives by the passage.

So far, the only fully aisled house known in Wales is a fragment, Hafod (Llansilin). All that survives is the upper part of the dais partition and the upper part of the central hall truss; but slight though the remains now are, they are enough to show that this was once a magnificent fully aisled hall (Fig. 10). Horsemans Green Farm, Halghton, might have been a second (Fig. 14). The very fine surviving aisled truss must have formed the screens, while the lost passage partition must also have been aisled. The mortices in the arcade-plate leave no room for doubt. The central truss spanning the hall is clearly missing. The square-set arcade plates indicate that this truss must have been either a base cruck or an aisled truss. There seems no good reason why a base cruck should have been removed. Base crucks are substantial, difficult to remove, and do not obstruct the floor. But an aisle-truss would be an obstruction. At Hafod the shafts of the aisle posts have been removed, leaving only the superstructure. Perhaps at Horsemans Green

---

[13] *Cal. Close Rolls, 1402-5,* p. 111. I am grateful to Mr C. J. Spurgeon for this reference.

Farm the whole framework was removed. This, then, is our only other possible fully aisled hall.

Clearly, the fully aisled house was a great rarity in Wales. Even in the west midlands, where there are also a number of partly aisled houses, only two fully aisled examples have been identified: Upton Cresset in Shropshire and the much older Romanesque bishop's palace in Hereford.[14] Allowing for losses, the group can never have been very large.

It is possible to construct more than one hypothesis to explain the development of the various forms of aisle-truss house and their distribution. One envisages three schools of aisled building, each originating independently of the others: first, a lowland, south-eastern school, based on the trussed rafter roof and originally without ridge-beam or purlin; second, a 'highland' northern school, based on the king-post supported ridge-beam and trenched-purlin; finally a Welsh/west midland school incorporating elements of both 'highland' and 'lowland' carpentry. Thus, each school of aisled building could be seen as an independent local development, functional in origin, in which the aisled element was reduced by stages as alternative support systems were devised to replace the obstructing aisle posts. In the end, these were reduced to the single aisled element, the screens by the passage.

An alternative theory would argue that the very rarity of these buildings, particularly in their fully aisled form, shows that they were not independent local developments, but a series of intrusions from the lowlands into the highlands, where the predominant structural forms were not aisled. The incentive was not utility but display, which is very evident in the single aisle-truss house, the only type in the remoter north-west. It is unlikely that either view can be proved, but the second seems preferable.

First-floor Halls and Towers

Not the least important aspect of the aisle-truss houses is the way they establish that the hall, rather than the tower, was the favoured residence of the upper classes as well as of the peasantry. Although the first-floor hall and the tower are uncharacteristic of Wales, a small number has come to light, mainly in Glamorgan and Pembrokeshire. However, one recent discovery in Merioneth deserves special mention as the only instance of the type in the county.

On the quay at Barmouth is a stone house known as Tŷ-gwyn (Fig. 17). At a casual glance it is not very different from other houses in the old quarter of this little port that were built in the late-seventeenth or early-eighteenth century. Yet there has long been a tradition that Tŷ-gwyn is much older than the rest and is a medieval building with Tudor associations going back to the fifteenth century. This tradition arises from a poem by Tudur Penllyn praising the house of his patron, Griffith Vaughan. It describes a house by the shore at Barmouth, and the question is whether the house is still standing, a question so far answered in the

---

[14] Upton Cresset, *ex. inf.* J. W. Tonkin; for the bishop's palace, see S. R. Jones and J. T. Smith, 'The Great Hall of the Bishop's Palace, Hereford', *Medieval Archaeology*, 1960, pp. 69-80. See also C. A. R. Radford, E. M. Jope and J. W. Tonkin, 'The Great Hall of the Bishop's Palace, Hereford', *Medieval Archaeology*, 1963, pp. 78-86.

negative. The poem was known to Thomas Pennant, who failed to recognize Penllyn's Tŷ-gwyn, which he assumed had been destroyed.[15]

Shortly before 1914, Barmouth was investigated by the Royal Commission on Ancient Monuments. Among the notes in the Commission's files is one referring to a manuscript dated 1654 and said to be at Peniarth. The transcript states: 'Gruffydd [Vaughan of Corsygedol] . . . built a convenient house at Barmouth, close to the entrance of the river into the sea, which now remains in good order and is called Tŷ-gwyn yn Bermo'. Medieval Tŷ-gwyn was thus reported to be still extant in 1654. However, the Merioneth *Inventory* preferred a sixteenth-century date for the ground floor of the present building and a later date for the first floor.[16] Even more sceptical was the present-writer, who stated 'of Tudur Penllyn's Tŷ-gwyn yn Abermo . . . not one stone remains'.[17]

A recent re-examination of Tŷ-gwyn indicates that tradition was right and the pundits, from Pennant onwards, were wrong. This revision was the result of an examination of the roof structure previously inaccessible. The late Col. A. K. Campbell, long interested in the identity of Tudur Penllyn's house, heard that the trusses were of unusual interest. These quickly led us to the conclusion that this was more than just another seventeenth-century or eighteenth-century vernacular house. The roof consisted of four (originally six) collar-beam trusses of unusual design. Each pair of principals had curved braces at the feet and met in a vertical butt-joint which did not carry a ridge-beam, while the purlins, instead of resting on the principals, were threaded through them. These apparently minor details are of historical significance. In north Wales a 'lowland' ridgeless, tenoned-purlin indicates a roof of considerable age. Before the Reformation trenched-purlins (resting on the backs of the principals), tenon-purlins and occasionally (though only in churches) trussed-rafter roofs can all be found, but after the Reformation the 'highland' trenched-purlin predominates. The tenon-purlin construction at Tŷ-gwyn is a strong argument for an early date. The plan produced supporting evidence. Clearly the house was always on two main floors with a small basement, the first floor being the more important. It is, indeed, a first-floor hall and a building perhaps of some defensive capability. The walls are over three feet thick and the only early windows to survive are narrow loops.

The two main floors were entered separately. The entry to the ground floor was by the doorway in the end wall facing the sea, its position doubtless determined by ease of access for supplies. The present first-floor entry is modern and may replace an earlier entry on the opposite side, obscured when the adjoining houses were built.

---

[15] T. Pennant, *Tours in Wales*, ed. J. Rhys, pp. 253-4. The poem is published by T. Roberts, *Gwaith Tudur Penllyn ac Ieuan ap Tudur* (1958), pp. 27-8. The poem specifically refers to Barmouth, but does not use the term Tŷ-gwyn but rather Tŵr Gwyn (in itself significant). I am indebted to Miss Nancy Jones for correlating the different MS versions of the poem in the National Library of Wales. The earliest MS (Mostyn 148), which dates from *c.* 1594, does not carry the title, *I'r Tŷ-gwyn*, but this is borne by all the seventeenth-century MSS, the title being either copied from earlier MSS since lost, or used because the most prominent building in seventeenth-century Barmouth bore this name and was by tradition associated with the poem.

[16] *RCAM, Merioneth Inventory*, p. 5.

[17] *Houses of the Welsh Countryside*, p. 136.

The poet compares his house to Rheinallt's Tower, that is, Broncoed near Mold, which still survives, albeit heavily restored.[18] This is a fortified first-floor hall with vaulted ground floor and cellar, and is shown by an early water-colour as having a castellated wall-walk. The fact that the poet chose to compare his Barmouth house with a known first-floor hall elsewhere strongly supports the identification of the present Tŷ-gwyn with the poet's house, because no other house in Barmouth suggests the analogy. However, Tŷ-gwyn has a closer resemblance to another Flintshire first-floor hall, the house previously called Llyseurgain, Northop, but which is better known as Plas Llaneurgain.[19] Although a more ambitious building than Tŷ-gwyn, with two vaulted floors, its plan recalls the Barmouth house: a short basement and a long narrow ground and first floor, both heated like Tŷ-gwyn by fireplaces in the end wall. It is significant that all three houses appear to be acknowledged in fifteenth-century poetry, and each has the tenon-purlin roof (see Fig. 18).[20]

Only in two Welsh counties, Glamorgan and Pembrokeshire, do examples of the first-floor hall and tower traditions occur in significant numbers. In both the pure hall tradition is poorly represented. Both are in the south-western half of Wales, where building traditions are perceptibly different from those in the north-east. It is arguable that the major concentration in Pembrokeshire illustrates the principle that changes occur in proportion to the remoteness of a locality from London, an idea also illustrated by a number of quasi-fortified houses in Cornwall, as well as by the great concentrations of towers in Scotland and Ireland. In Pembrokeshire one is half way to Ireland in more senses than one.

One of the most interesting of Wales's few tower-houses is Candleston Castle (Merthyr Mawr) in Glamorgan, a small tower with first-floor hall attached and alongside a fortified barmkin, the whole now under assault from encroaching sand. Early drawings suggest that nearby Tythegston Court, built at a safer distance from the coast, was once a strong house, though it is not immediately recognizable as such. Another fine Glamorgan house in the first-floor hall tradition is Garn-llwyd, Llancarfan (Fig. 19). Though not obviously fortified, it is closely related to the tower house. In Pembrokeshire the number of towers and first-floor halls slowly accumulates. Recent discoveries include Sandyhaven House (St. Ishmaels), at the centre of which is a tall narrow tower, and Sisters' House (Minwear), a small tower with vaulted basement. But the most thought-provoking of all recent discoveries is the vaulted tower now used as a farm building at Kingston Farm (St. Michaels).[21] This tiny building is not larger than West Tarr Farm (St. Florence) and Carswell (Penally), previously described in *Houses of the Welsh Countryside*. The purpose of these buildings, as well as the social standing of their occupants, remains a mystery, but they may be likened perhaps

[18] Ibid., p. 139.

[19] Ibid., p. 138. I am grateful to Mr R. M. Wilkinson of the Clwyd Photographic Survey for suggesting that Plas Llaneurgain is an historically more correct name for Northop Hall Farm than Llyseurgain.

[20] Tŷ-gwyn has been purchased by Meirionydd District Council for a local museum, a purpose it will admirably fulfil.

[21] For Sandyhaven and Sisters' House, I am indebted to Mr A. J. Parkinson who discovered them in the course of his work for the NMR. For Kingston, I am indebted to Dr Siân Rees, who discovered it in the course of her work for the Welsh Office, Ancient Monuments Branch.

to the smallest of the Irish £10 towers, which after all are not so far away across the water.

Kevin Danaher has recently published a detailed distribution map of these Irish towers and made a number of points which bear on the present discussion.[22] His map of individual sites corroborates our more generalised map of tower-houses, showing the greatest concentration of towers in the south of Ireland and the least in Ulster.[23] Mr Danaher suggests that the Irish tower arose from continental models and had no direct link with Scotland. He argues that Irish towers were built in peaceful times and that their purpose was not primarily defensive.

Certainly the distribution of the Irish towers would not point to Scotland as their source, nor would their details—lacking many of the refinements of the Scottish towers (particularly the raised round towers of the Franco-Scottish style)—suggest close cultural links. Nevertheless, an explanation which would account for the popularity of the tower-house in one half only of the British Isles is needed and the military explanation is the only one possible, though it is an explanation that Danaher rejects. Certainly a tall defensive building became a symbol of status, and would be built at a certain level of society as a badge of rank once the type had become established. But this explanation does not provide a root cause. The government of Henry VI thought towers were militarily useful and promoted them in Ireland with a £10 subsidy, surely one of the most successful housing subsidies ever devised![24] No one who has seen the gun ports in the later Scottish towers, or observed their walls chased in a disfiguring way to provide a better field of fire for their guns would easily be convinced that they did not have a serious military purpose. Surely the whole tower development reflects an insecure society in which those who could afford to do so built houses of defensive strength. This was manifestly the case in the north of England, Scotland and Ireland. It now seems to have been the case on the continent as well. On a recent tour of Normandy, I formed the impression that the landowners' house reflected the castle and tower tradition until the middle of the seventeenth century. These late castle derivatives, very tall in their proportions and with several quasi-military features, were quite different from the most characteristic south British sub-medieval manor houses, which consist of a central block flanked by cross-wings, a type evidently derived from the hall (Pls. I-III). I startled our French guide when I told her that the *manoirs* I had seen in Manche and Calvados reminded me more strongly of distant Scotland than of neighbouring Wessex. Indeed, I went on to substantiate my argument from philology. The French *château* describes both castle and mansion, structures which English and Welsh differentiate. As R. T. Jenkins observed, 'Gair anghyfiaith braidd yw *château* yn y cyd-destun hwn; nid yw ''castell'' na ''phlas'' yn hollol gyfleu ei ystyr. Castell wedi ei droi'n blas, amddiffynfa wedi tyfu'n dy annedd—dyna'r syniad.'[25]

---

[22] C. Ó Danachair, 'Irish Tower Houses and their Regional Distribution', *Béaloideas*, vols. 45-7 (1977-9), pp. 158-63.

[23] *Houses of the Welsh Countryside*, p. 338.

[24] H. G. Leask, *Irish Castles*, pp. 76-7.

[25] R. T. Jenkins, *Casglu Ffyrdd*, pp. 123-4.

How different is the hall or hall-derivative of the typical English or Welsh squire! These indicate not only a more peaceful society but also an evolutionary tempo much faster than that of France, Scotland or Ireland, where disorder lingered on. Here the Tudor government had made such towers as Tŷ-gwyn, Broncoed, and Candleston obsolete a century before such buildings would be obsolete elsewhere. For the Tudors had achieved effective authority a century ahead of Richelieu and Mazarin, and that authority was made subservient to the will of parliament a century ahead of Mirabeau and Danton. Just as Cromwell preceded Napoleon, so did the English revolutions, both political and industrial, precede the French. The architectural *indicia* are clear that in the early-sixteenth-century Tudor kingdom the stage was already set for the emergence of the most politically advanced state in Europe and for the subsequent meteoric rise of Great Britain to become for a brief but decisive period of history the greatest industrial, naval, and colonial power on earth.

Acknowledgements. I wish to express thanks to the following: for Plate I, RCAHM (England); for Plates II, III, VI, VII and VIII (top), RCAHM (Wales); for Plates IV and VIII *e*, L'Inventaire Général (Archives de la Manche) and Editions Heimdal; for Plate V, RCAHM (Scotland); for Plate VIII *d,* Scottish Office; for Figs. 3, 10, 15 and 18, RCAHM (Wales). I wish also to thank the following colleagues: Mr H. Brooksby, Mrs Jane Durrant, Miss L. M. Evans, Mr R. G. Nicol, Mr D. J. Roberts, Mr H. J. Thomas, Miss D. M. Ward and Mr I. N. Wright for assistance of various kinds.

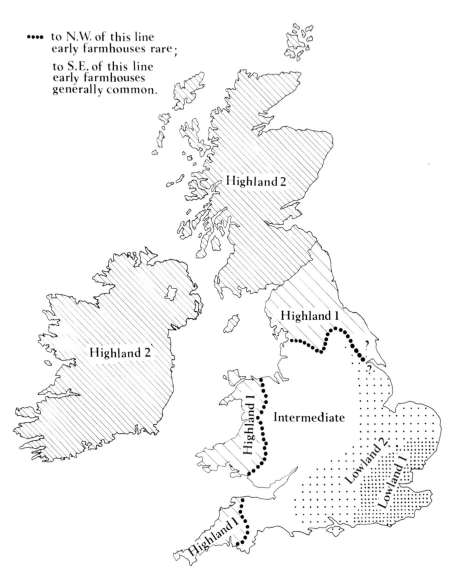

•••• to N.W. of this line
early farmhouses rare;

to S.E. of this line
early farmhouses
generally common.

Highland 2

Highland 2

Highland 1

Highland 1

Intermediate

Lowland 2

Lowland 1

Highland 1

Fig. 1 Building Regions of the British Isles. This map is intended to suggest that the 'Personality of Britain' consists not so much of the simple lowland/highland duality but more of a series of subtle gradations between the inner lowland zone on the one hand and the outer highland zone on the other. Peasant houses dating from before the Reformation can be found in quantity in most of the lowland and intermediate zones but only rarely in the highland zones.

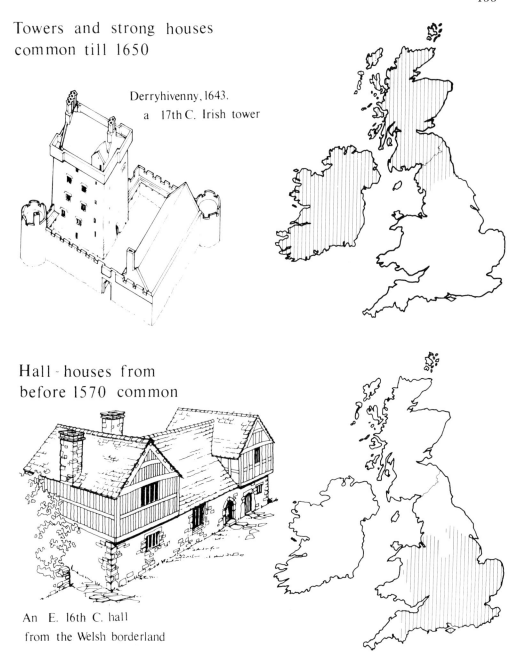

Towers and strong houses
common till 1650

Derryhivenny, 1643,
a 17th C. Irish tower

Hall - houses from
before 1570 common

An E. 16th C. hall
from the Welsh borderland

Fig. 2   Hall-houses and Towers. This map shows roughly those regions of the British Isles where the residence of a proprietor in the early-sixteenth century would normally have been a hall and those where it would normally have been a tower. It is clear that the hall is the type of dwelling associated with the politically more advanced regions and the tower with the more retarded.

Fig. 3   Rhos-fawr (Llanfyllin, Mont.), an early-sixteenth-century Welsh yeoman house. Cruck-framed hall-houses survive in considerable numbers in the Welsh border counties, though few are as complete as Rhos-fawr. The building (sited characteristically down the slope) consists of an open hall between two small inner rooms at the 'dais' end and a single large room, probably a byre, at the passage end, each secondary unit being floored over to form chambers on the first floor.

    The house is of considerable structural interest as it incorporates both the 'highland' crucks and the 'lowland' box-frames in the same building, although the trenched side purlins are 'highland'. The curved windbraces and the arch-braces to the central truss add a touch of class, and result in an interior of considerable artistic distinction.

Fig. 4   Bayleaf (Bough Beech, Kent), a 'Wealdon' house now re-erected in the Weald and Downland Museum at Singleton. Like its Welsh contemporary *opposite* the house consists of a hall between inner and outer units, but the plan is transposed so that the small rooms are at the passage end and the large room is at the dais end. Here the small secondary rooms appear to be buttery and pantry while the large room is a parlour. In both houses the only heating is by an open hearth in the middle of the hall floor which has blackened the roof timbers.

The roof construction is completely lowland and consists of box-frames on which rest crown-posts supporting an otherwise unbayed trussed rafter roof by means of a collar purlin. The crown-post provides an ornamental embellishment in addition to the arch-braces of the central box-frame.

The house is considerably larger than its Welsh opposite number. The fact that over two thousand pre-Elizabethan houses survive in Kent alone illustrates the great wealth of this south-eastern corner of England.

138

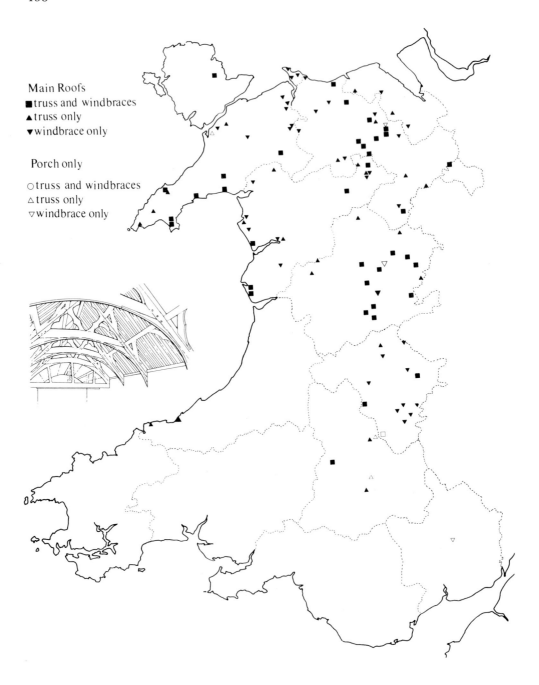

Main Roofs
■ truss and windbraces
▲ truss only
▼ windbrace only

Porch only

○ truss and windbraces
△ truss only
▽ windbrace only

Fig. 5   Cusping in Welsh church roofs. It is evident that the marked north-easterly concentration of this feature in houses (see *Houses of the Welsh Countryside,* Map 20) is also reflected in ecclesiastical work. Even those churches of the south which have the open, bayed, purlin roof do not bear this characteristically northern embellishment. The roof illustrated is in the parish church of Llansilin.

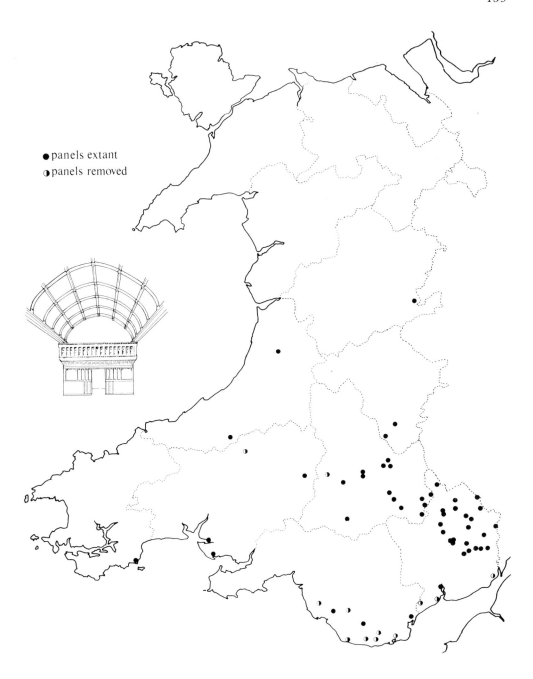

●panels extant
◑panels removed

Fig. 6 Barrel roofs in Welsh churches. Here, in contrast, a trussed rafter (*sans* purlin) superstructure was concealed by plaster or wooden panels. The boarded bays over the altars of the churches of north Wales are not held to be comparable and are not shown here. Although my survey of south Wales is not yet complete it is clear that the barrel roof is predominant in Monmouthshire and well represented in Glamorgan.

140

Fig. 7 Hammer-beam roofs. The hammer-beam represents the culmination of the ornate roof tradition. Here the distribution pattern first explored in the domestic field is generally repeated in the ecclesiastical. The roof illustrated is in the parish church of Llangollen and is a particularly fine example.

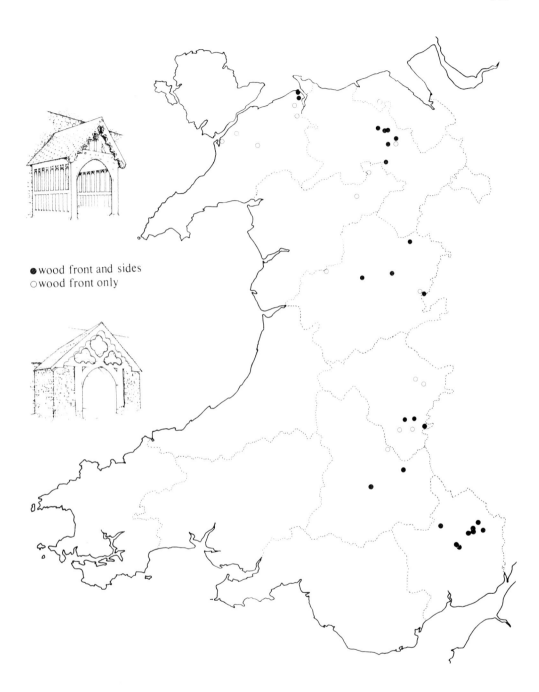

Fig. 8   Wood porches in churches. The wooden porch is well represented in eastern Wales in those areas where half-timbered houses are also found in quantity. The spread of the idea west of the Conway parallels a number of eastern domestic features which penetrated north-west but not south-west Wales (as illustrated by Fig. 9 *overleaf*).

142

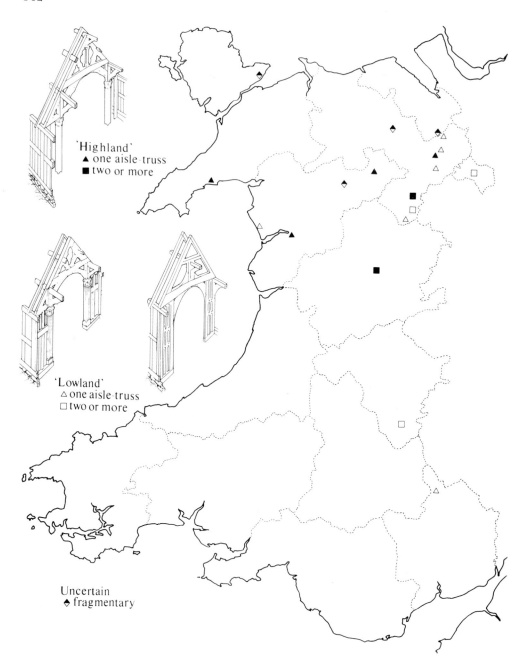

'Highland'
▲ one aisle-truss
■ two or more

'Lowland'
△ one aisle-truss
□ two or more

Uncertain
◆ fragmentary

Fig. 9 Aisle-truss houses. This map, based purely on domestic work, has a distribution pattern comparable with various ecclesiastical features previously illustrated. It also shows that certain 'lowland' features, such as the threaded (or tenon) purlin roof and the associated construction of the ridge without a beam, occur extensively in the highland areas at an early date, though falling afterwards into disuse as 'highland' detailing—the trenched purlin and ridge-beam—achieved an absolute predominance.

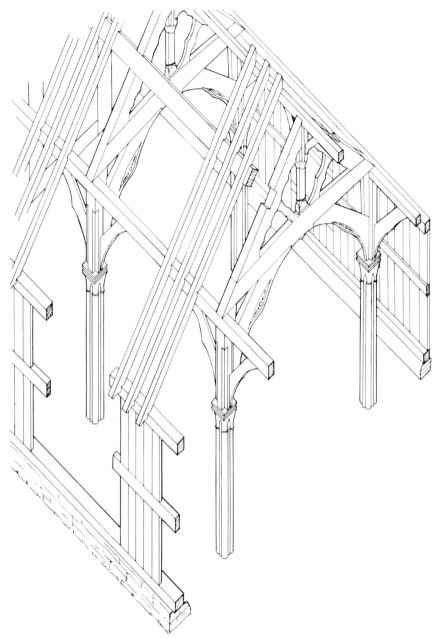

Fig. 10 Hafod (Llansilin, Denbs.). This is the only house in Wales so far discovered where it is certain that the central truss of the hall was aisled. A second aisled truss has been conjectured assuming a screens partition between hall and passage, but is is possible that the hall was of two bays only, built before the great elaboration of the screens which characterised some late medieval houses. Note the 'highland' trenched purlin and ridge-beam construction. In terms of craftsmanship this is perhaps the finest and possibly the earliest of the aisle-truss houses. One would give much for the name and standing of whoever built it and whether he was a contemporary of Owain Glyndŵr next door at Sycharth.

Fig. 11 Upper House (Painscastle). This remarkable hall-house was built in the castle ditch and thus must post-date Glyndŵr's rebellion. It illustrates the second phase of aisled building where the central truss of the hall was not aisled, but where a base cruck, a feature commonly associated with aisled construction, was used instead. Although the construction is extremely massive, it exemplifies, in contrast with Hafod (Fig. 10), 'lowland' detailing—the purlins tenoned into the principals and no ridge-beam. The single-storeyed open parlour cross-wing at the dais end should be noted. The appearance of the unit at the passage end is pure conjecture, as this end was completely rebuilt in the seventeenth century when an enclosed fireplace was placed in the passage, and a floor inserted over the hall.

Fig. 12 Llwyncelyn (Crucornau Fawr, Mon.) represents the third phase in the evolution of the aisle-truss house. It has an aisle-truss by the passage only. Moreover this truss itself is but nominally aisled as the posts do not directly support the roof whose stability would be little affected were they to be removed. The roof has 'lowland' details—the purlins tenoned into the principals, and the rafters supporting each other at the ridge without the help of a ridge-beam. Llwyncelyn is the most complete of the aisle-truss houses as the units at both passage and dais end survive in their entirety. The passage end has twin doorways indicating buttery and pantry while the dais end is similar to Upper House *opposite* in that it was partly single-storeyed and contained an open parlour. The discontinuity between the parlour and hall roof has been noticed in halls in the west of England. This discontinuity establishes that the blackening on the parlour roof can only have come from a fire on the gound below and cannot have come from the hall. Llwyncelyn is one of a minority of aisle-truss houses to have had stone containing walls.

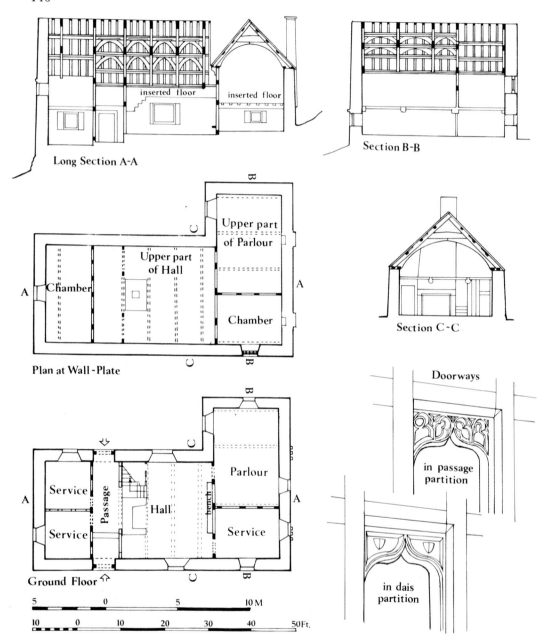

Long Section A-A

Section B-B

Plan at Wall-Plate

Section C-C

Ground Floor

Doorways

in passage partition

in dais partition

Fig. 13 Llwyncelyn, plan and section. Apart from the window fittings in the containing walls this late medieval hall-house survives almost in its entirety and would be a worthy object of conservation. The features indicated by faint lines are seventeenth-century insertions, i.e. the floor over the hall and parlour, and the fireplaces. Although clearly not a long-house Llwyncelyn has a marked downhill (platform) siting. Note the bench against the dais partition still surviving, and also the boldly carved partition doorways.

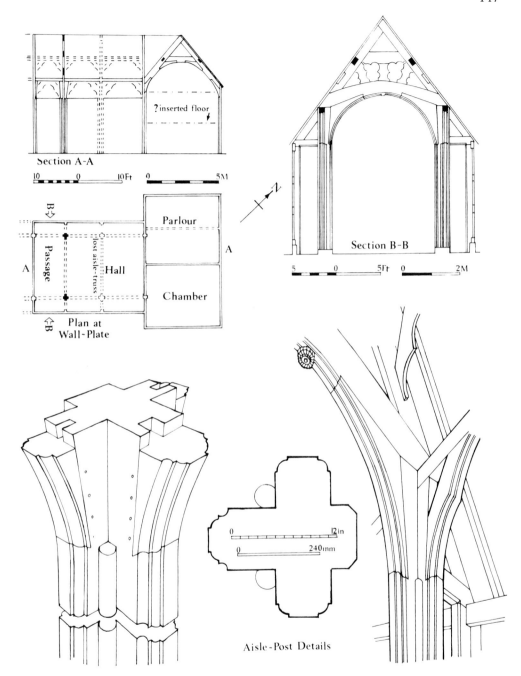

Section A-A

10   0   10Ft   0   5M

Parlour

A

Passage   Hall   lost aisle-truss

A

Chamber

B
Plan at
Wall-Plate

N

Section B-B

5   0   5Ft   0   2M

?inserted floor

Aisle-Post Details

0   12in
0   240mm

Fig. 14   Horsemans Green Farm (Halghton, Flints.). Only the aisle-truss by the screens now survives; clear evidence exists for a second by the passage partition, while a third aisle-truss dividing the hall into two equal bays has been hypothesised. Internal evidence suggests that the cross-wing at the dais end was single-storeyed containing an open parlour as at Llwyncelyn (*opposite*).

Fig. 15 Tŷ-mawr (Castell Caereinion, Mont.). This interior view shows a remarkably fine base-cruck and aisle-truss hall—obviously a house of seigneurial status (as the name itself indicates). However, the passage partition is quite unlike that of Llwyncelyn *opposite*. The long open panels suggest that the room beyond may have been a byre and the cross-passage a feeding-walk. If this interpretation is correct it means that the long-house reached much higher levels of society than had previously been thought probable.

Fig. 16 Llwyncelyn (Crucornau Fawr, Mon.). This interior view shows another fine hall, again indicating a house of high social status. However, the passage partition has the twin doorways associated with service-rooms at the passage end, in complete contrast with the partition at Tŷ-mawr *opposite*. Unlike the passage partition, the speres partition is obscured by the inserted fireplace and the detail has had to be conjectured.

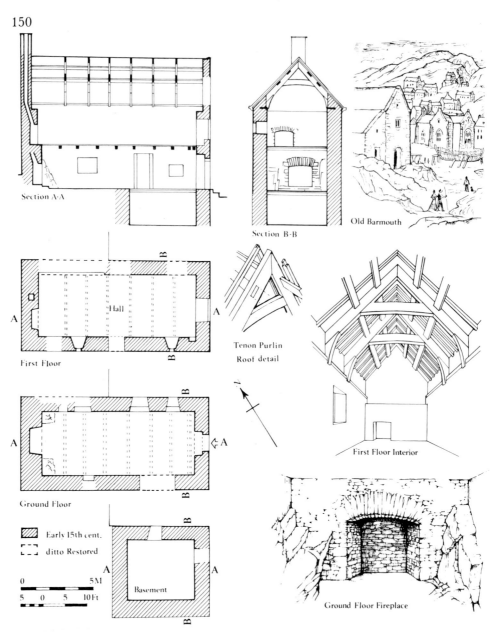

Section A·A

Section B·B

Old Barmouth

Hall

First Floor

A   A

B

B

Tenon Purlin
Roof detail

First Floor Interior

A   A

B

B

Ground Floor

Early 15th cent.

ditto Restored

0   5M

5   0   5   10Ft

Basement

A   A

B

Ground Floor Fireplace

Fig. 17   Tŷ-gwyn (Barmouth). In contrast to the ground-floor halls previously illustrated this is a first-floor hall. Literary evidence indicates that it must date from the early-fifteenth century, a date not inconsistent with the threaded purlin roof and the rafters self-supporting at the ridge, a construction that contrasts oddly with the cruck-like apex of the principals. The thick walls and surviving slit windows suggest the elements of a strong house here. Although small in scale compared with many other buildings in the tower tradition it no doubt rose high above the single-storey cottages which would have constituted medieval Barmouth. In such surroundings it would have appeared not unworthy of the *cywydd* of Tudor Penllyn likening its walls to those of Calais! It is not possible to trace beyond Pennant the tradition that Henry VII secretly met his Welsh supporters here when planning the invasion of 1485, but it may (according to H. T. Evans, *Wales and the Wars of the Roses*) have been used by Jasper Tudor in his flight from Wales after the Lancastrian débâcle of 1464.

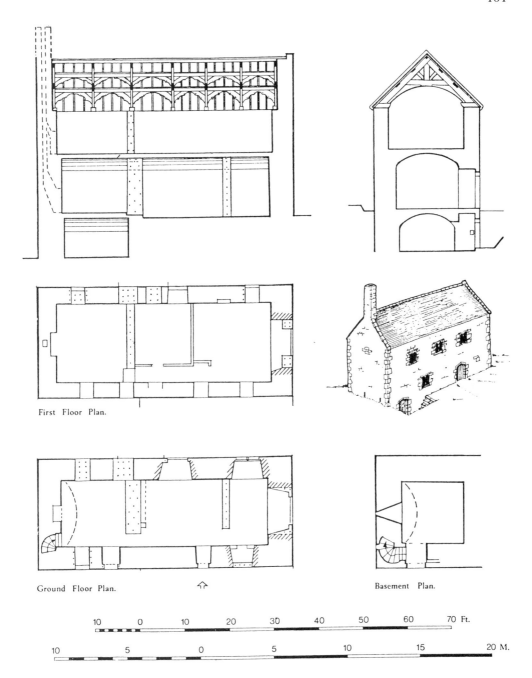

First Floor Plan.

Ground Floor Plan.

Basement Plan.

Fig. 18 Llaneurgain (Northop, Flints.) provides a remarkable parallel to Tŷ-gwyn *opposite* in its general plan and section, the open hall on the first floor and the basement extending under only part of the ground floor as well as the fireplaces in the end wall. It is, however, a more ambitious building with dressed stone vaults.

152

Fig. 19 Garnllwyd (Llancarfan, Glam.) is a more ambitious first-floor hall than Tŷ-gwyn (Fig. 17). It consists of hall over kitchen probably with retiring rooms in the projecting turret alongside. Remarkable features are the mural stair rising behind the fireplace, the arch-braced roof complete with carved boss, and the gallery at one end of the hall. Although not obviously defensive its proportions are those of a tower. It may be compared with Candleston Castle (Merthyr Mawr) where the first-floor hall constitutes an annexe to a small tower, and where the outworks include a definitely defensive barmkin wall.

I Cothay Manor *above* and Montacute House *below* underline the continuity of the hall-house tradition in England. Cothay is a large medieval hall-house. Montacute is the storeyed house of an Elizabethan grandee. However, symmetrical exterior and classical detailing do not disguise the descent of this great house from its hall-house ancestors, whose gabled cross-wings it retains as well as the screens passage (albeit translated into the classical idiom) dividing the entry from the hall.

II-III Wales is also primarily a land of the hall-house and its descendants. The characteristic central hall block flanked by gabled cross-wings is evident at Penarth (Newtown, Mont.) *opposite* as well as Pentrehobyn (Mold, Flints.) *above*. The former was a base-cruck hall but this was reconstructed on two floors in the sixteenth century. Date inscriptions claim a date of 1540 for Pentrehobyn which has always been a storeyed house. The detailing, however, would suggest an early-seventeenth-century mansion. Nevertheless it retains the entry to one side giving on to a cross-passage—clear evidence of hall-house ancestry.

IV In complete contrast are two sixteenth-century *seigneurs'* houses from Normandy. Clearly representative of the *tower* tradition are Le Château de la Cour (Marcilly) *above* and Le Château de la Cour (Chaulieu) *below*. The latter M. Jean Barbaroux dates to the reign of Henri IV, an epoch 'qui vit se couvrir le Mortinais de petites forteresses'. A royal edict of 1591 requiring their demolition was not made effective until the administration of Richelieu.

V Not unlike the French châteaux *opposite* is Balcardine Castle (Argyllshire) built in 1609. The similarity of the details in the Scots lairds' houses to those of the French *noblesse* has been attributed to the 'auld alliance'. Perhaps more fundamentally important is their similarity in basic conception which suggests that sixteenth-century France and sixteenth-century Scotland were producing similar buidings not so much because one was influencing the other but because they had both reached the same stage of social and political development.

VI   The churches of Llanrhaeadr-yng-Nghinmeirch (Denbs.) *above*, Bangor-on-Dee *below left* and Llansilin (Denbs.) *below right* exemplify types of open roof common in north Wales. Note the hammer-beam construction *above* supporting a panelled ceiling, and the windbraces *below*. Each roof has cusped ornament, and a canopy of honour over the altar. Such canopies, restricted to one bay only, once embellished with religious paintings, are characteristic of north Wales.

VII   In contrast are the ceiled 'barrel' roofs of Llandefalle (Brecs.) *above* and the stone vaulted roof of St. Twynnells (Pembs.) *below*, which conceal the main roof structure. Although the open purlin roof does occur in south Wales it rarely achieves the elaborate development of the north. It is clear that the *sans* purlin roof *above* where the panels are carried on closely-spaced trussed rafters is predominant in Monmouthshire and Breconshire.

VIII   In the age of Elizabeth I the moulded ceiling perpetuated the medieval tradition of ornate carpentry as at Corsygedol (Llanddwywe, Mer.) 1576 *top*, Maes-y-castell (Caerhun, Caerns.) 1582 *above left*, and Perthewig (Trefnant, Denbs.) 1592, *above right*. In contrast are the unmoulded but elaborately painted ceilings of contemporary France and Scotland as instanced by Le Logis de Montgommery, Ducey (*bottom right*) and Huntingtower, Perthshire (*bottom left*).

'The Sweating Astrologer': Thomas Jones the Almanacer

GERAINT H. JENKINS

I
T was once observed that the study of history demands a sense of the past, common sense, and a sense of the ridiculous. In our anxiety to clothe the past in statistical abstractions we may well be in danger of forgetting that Welsh history is a pageant of colourful episodes enacted by equally colourful, often fallible, but always profoundly human beings. It could be argued, too, that we take the study of history too seriously. One fine day someone will sit down to prepare a study of the remarkable array of oddities who litter our past. Many of these bizarre men can be observed coming in from the wings of history from the seventeenth century onwards. One thinks of Arise Evans, Edmund Jones 'the Old Prophet', Iolo Morganwg, William Owen Pughe, Talhaiarn, William Price—each, in his own way, a suitable case for treatment. What would surely emerge from such a study is not only a catalogue of the quirky idiosyncracies of such men, but also the enormous contribution which they made to the cultural, religious and social life of Wales. One figure who has strong claims for inclusion in such a pantheon is Wales's first almanacer, Thomas Jones (1648-1713), a tailor's son from Tre'r-ddôl, near Corwen in Merioneth. Resourceful and versatile by nature, he became a celebrated printer, publisher, bookseller, journalist, almanacer, astrologer, satirist, poet and quack. A man of great ingenuity and seemingly inexhaustible energy, his favourite scriptural maxim was the Protestant ethic writ large: 'the soul of the sluggard desireth, and hath nothing: but the soul of the diligent shall be made fat'. [1]

Since at least Tudor times, Welshmen had been attracted by the glitter of London's lights. Isolated in remote provincialism and frustrated by the stifling ennui of rural life, the Welsh gentry had needed no second bidding to escape to the capital to find scope for their enterprise and ambitions. During the Stuart period, however, men of humbler stock, with scarcely a penny to their name, were also induced to strike out new paths by the pressure of overpopulation, famine and unemployment. [2] To them, London was a magical city. Welsh poets claimed that its streets were paved with gold. [3] Some of the shrewdest migrants profited financially. Others swiftly discovered that London was not the fairest city on earth. Yet others learned enough evil to last them the rest of their days. In the

---

[1] Thomas Jones, *Y Gymraeg yn ei Disgleirdeb* (1688), sig. S8v.

[2] C. Hill, *The World turned Upside Down* (1975), pp. 73-81; E. Jones, 'The Welsh in London in the Seventeenth and Eighteenth Centuries', *Welsh Hist. Rev.*, X, no. 4 (1981), 465-70.

[3] T. Jones, *Newydd oddiwrth y Seêr* (1684), sig. B1v-B2v; G. Jones, 'Bywyd a Gwaith Edward Morris, Perthi Llwydion' (unpublished University of Wales M.A. thesis, 1941), p. 386.

wake of the Great Fire in 1666, Thomas Jones joined the stream of masterless men who were hopeful of finding a secure niche in Europe's leading city. How successfully he pursued his living as a tailor we cannot tell, but by the mid-1670s he had ventured into the bookselling trade.[4] The end of the decade brought a welcome twist to his fortunes. On 1 January 1679 he was granted a royal patent which conferred upon him sole rights for the compilation, printing and publishing of an annual Welsh almanac.[5] In spite of a host of trials and tribulations which would have tried the patience of a saint, Thomas Jones succeeded in publishing an annual Welsh almanac from 1680 until his death in 1713.

Despite his dramatic rise to fame, Thomas Jones was ill at ease in London. The London rebuilt after the Fire was more luxurious, decadent and hedonistic than before, and Jones was repelled by the standards of indecency and immorality flaunted by city gentlemen. He soon tired of the raffish 'bohemian' society of Grub Street, finding that his own austere moralism was scarcely consonant with the outlook of the shady, impoverished, claret-drinking hack writers, scribblers, journalists and almanacers who loitered in taverns of ill repute.[6] Jones was obliged to struggle hard to keep his soul untarnished amid the poverty and degradation of his environment. Moorfields, where he lived, was a hotbed of vice and debauchery, and Jones lived in daily fear of its rising tide of violent crime.[7] His business life, too, was riven with problems. The perversity, poor workmanship and fraudulent practices of London printers and booksellers stirred his ire.[8] Moreover, the politico-religious crimes of the 1680s brought him to the brink of despair. He became convinced that God would visit the capital with His wrath and destruction.[9] As life in London became wholly distasteful to him, Thomas Jones grew increasingly restive and longed to renew his provincial roots. His opportunity came in 1695 when the Printing Act, which had restricted the publication of books to the master-printers of the Stationers' Company, the two Universities and the archbishop of York, was allowed to lapse. It now became legally permissible for any journeyman with sufficient capital and enterprise to establish a printing press in the provinces.[10] Thomas Jones packed his bags with alacrity and by mid-winter he had set himself up as a printer and publisher in Shrewsbury. Shrewsbury was an ideal base for a Welsh printing press: it was a thriving, populous town of some seven thousand inhabitants, and was considered by Defoe to be 'one of the most flourishing towns in England'.[11] It was also the economic capital of mid-Wales. Welsh farmers, drapers and flannel merchants sold their produce and wares there, and on market day the predominant language heard on its streets was Welsh. Thomas Jones settled in the fashionable

[4] *The Character of a Quack-Doctor* (1676), title-page.

[5] Stationers' Company Court Book, 1 March 1679; T. Jones, [*Almanac*] (1703), sig. A8r-B1r.

[6] P. Pinkus, *Grub Street stripped bare* (1968), pp. 24-5.

[7] W. Denton, *Records of St. Giles', Cripplegate* (1883), pp. 102-8, 162; P. Rogers, *Grub Street. Studies in a Subculture* (1972), p. 49.

[8] *Y Gymraeg yn ei Disgleirdeb*, sig. X8r.

[9] T. Jones, *Newydd oddiwrth y Sêr* (1685), sig. B7v; *idem, Y Gwir er Gwaethed Yw* (1684), pp. 23-6.

[10] G. A. Cranfield, *The Press and Society from Caxton to Northcliffe* (1978), p. 31.

[11] D. Defoe, *A Tour through the whole island of Great Britain,* ed. G. D. H. Cole and D. C. Browning (2 vols., 1962), II, 76-7.

residential area of Hill's Lane, earned a name for himself as 'Thomas Jones the Stargazer', and made Shrewsbury the printing capital of Wales.[12]

The country air, however, seems to have done nothing for his health. For a period of six years during the 1690s his body was racked with violent pains and 'distempers', probably both real and imagined.[13] He contracted as many ailments and maladies as a porcupine has quills, ranging from dropsy to palpitations, vapours to scurvy, and rheumatism to quinsy. Lord Tennyson would surely have been proud to have made his acquaintance! Thomas Jones's most notable malady, however, was a curious form of sweating sickness which obliged him to change his shirt six times daily and which prompted his enemies to christen him 'the Sweating Astrologer'.[14] Even when his physical health improved, he remained tormented by lingering mental instability. In fact, from 1700 onwards his life was one of inconsolable melancholy and paranoia. His personal life was poisoned by suspicion and mistrust. The 'knavish tricks' of apprentices and rival almanacers forced him to rule his printing house like a grenadier. Indeed, his almanacs suggest that his life was an endless saga of furious quarrels. But although personal ill-health, domestic strife and business upheavals all cast shadows over his life, he remained extraordinarily resilient and energetic. He laboured prodigiously under almost intolerable strain, chivying authors, translating books, compiling almanacs, correcting proofs, hounding errant printers, cudgelling rivals, stumping the countryside in search of subscribers, and selling his wares in fairs and markets. His life was an unyielding round of beaver-like toil.

Although Thomas Jones was the driving force behind the substantial flow of cheap, popular devotional books, prayer books and catechisms in Welsh in the period following the collapse of the Welsh Trust in the early-1680s, he was best known in his day as Wales's premier almanacer. The seventeenth century was the golden age of English almanacs. During the Restoration decade, some 400,000 copies of English almanacs were sold annually, and throughout the late-Stuart period the almanacs of Cardanus Rider, Andrews, Coley, Gadbury, Goldsmith, Saunders, Trigge and Wing did a roaring trade.[15] Always prepared to seize his main chance, Thomas Jones committed himself to catering for Welsh interests in this same field. No other publication of his managed to stir as much curiosity, admiration, frustration, envy or resentment. Like many of his fellow-almanacers, Thomas Jones had received no formal training in astrology. He described himself as 'a lover of Learning, and Student in Astrology, and Autodidactus'.[16] His great idol was William Lilly, the most celebrated English almanacer of the seventeenth century, and Jones quoted his aphorisms and prognostications with generous approval.[17] He diligently ferreted out a wide range of information from various

[12] Shropshire RO, Assessment Rolls, 1698-1702, Box VII, no. 278; E. Rees, 'Developments in the Book Trade in Eighteenth Century Wales', *The Library*, XXIV (1969), 33.

[13] T. Jones, *Newyddion Mawr oddiwrth y Sêr* (1699), sig. A1v-7r.

[14] G. H. Jenkins, *Thomas Jones yr Almanaciwr, 1648-1713* (1980), pp. 131-6.

[15] C. Blagden, 'The Distribution of Almanacks in the Second Half of the Seventeenth Century', *Studies in Bibliography*, XI (1958), 115; B. Capp, *Astrology and the Popular Press: English Almanacs, 1500-1800* (1979), p. 23.

[16] T. Jones, *An Astrological Speculation of the late Prodigy* (1681), title-page.

[17] T. Jones, [*Almanac*] (1708), sig. C7r.

sources, often looting the almanacs of his English colleagues with shameless insouciance. At best, he was an eager novice, anxious to learn and, in times of stress, grateful for divine assistance:

> Teach me figures fair to frame
> Of sundry sorts in sight,
> That I may ascend the Heavens high,
> And bring hidden things to light. [18]

Thomas Jones's annual almanac was a curious amalgam of miscellaneous information. Usually entitled *Newyddion oddi wrth y Sêr* (News from the Stars), it comprised twenty or twenty-four leaves. Jones was highly sensitive to public taste and, in order to avoid staleness, he constantly discovered new material and dreamed up new devices and ideas to catch and maintain the interest of his readers. The main body of the almanac offered an astronomical and astrological guide over a twelve-month period. The most heavily-thumbed section was *Y Sywedyddawl Farnedigaeth,* which teemed with fascinating political and religious speculation. Due attention was accorded to the conjunctions and oppositions of the sun and moon, the timing of solar and lunar eclipses, the dates of fixed and immovable feast days, a table of ebbs and floods, the rules for blood-letting and purging, advice on agricultural matters, and prognostications of future health and well-being. These cardinal and ever-present features were supplemented by a wide range of sundry items: lists of fairs and markets in Wales and the borders, samples of Welsh poetry and literature, a chronology of pivotal historical events, a guide to reading Welsh and casting accounts, a list of the law terms, the names of Welsh bishops (much-needed in a land of absentee prelates!), and a curious hodge-podge of advertisements which informed readers where they might buy books, paper, ink, violin strings, sealing wax, spectacles, false teeth, glass eyes and a range of patent medicines which purported to be 'as infallible as the Pope'.

'Many believed strongly in the Almanac', observed Robert Jones, the Methodist commentator, as he surveyed popular beliefs in pre-evangelical Wales. [19] In many ways, the almanac reflected the traditional superstitions and magical practices which were dear to the hearts of many Welshmen. It tells us a great deal about the ignorance, curiosity, imagination and fears of common people. Clearly, a sub-culture based on superstition and magic flourished beneath the veneer of orthodox Protestantism. [20] The attempts of successive Protestant campaigns to root out lingering deposits of Catholicism and paganism, and to eliminate belief in occult forces had fallen short of expectations. Common Welshmen still adhered to ancient ways by carrying charms, amulets and talismans to ward off evil. They conversed with fairies, spirits and goblins, were vividly conscious of the immediate presence of the Devil, visited the cunning man regularly, and lived in fear and awe of the *maleficium* of the witch. In remote rural areas there were many thousands who scarcely retained 'any right Notions or

[18] *An Astrological Speculation,* sig. A3r-v.

[19] R. Jones, *Drych yr Amseroedd,* ed. G. M. Ashton (1958), p. 25.

[20] G. H. Jenkins, 'Popular Beliefs in Wales from the Restoration to Methodism', *Bull. Board of Celtic Studies,* XXVII (1977), 440-6.

Ideas of True Religion'[21] and who placed their faith primarily in magical influences. Thomas Jones himself had been born and bred in a notoriously dark corner of the land, where the boundary between superstition and religion was blurred and where the very name of a Puritan saint was scorned.[22] A whole tissue of semi-pagan, 'popish' customs and magical beliefs still survived, many of which were deeply woven into the social fabric. The lingering credulity of the Welsh was a common theme for lament among religious reformers who launched periodic campaigns against 'bad habits'[23] which diverted man's attention from more significant concerns. Fear of the unknown dogged the daily lives of peasant peoples. As they grappled with the mysteries and tragedies of life, it was a natural reflex on their part to ascribe the inexplicable event to the influence of malignant, supernatural forces. Many of them believed that their fate was inextricably bound up with the constellation of the stars, the movement of the planets and the phases of the moon. It was, they insisted, 'as natural and unavoidable as the course of the sun and river, or the growth of the grass in the field'.[24] Deprived of adequate educational facilities and thereby insulated from current scientific discoveries, men's horizons were narrow, and the task of weaning them from age-old habits of thought was a daunting one. It was not until the publication of Simon Thomas's *Hanes y byd a'r Amseroedd* (1718) and Dafydd Lewys's *Golwg ar y Byd* (1725) that 'uneducated' monoglot Welshmen were informed of the significant gains achieved in the field of scientific discovery. Even learned Welsh scholars such as Rowland Vaughan, Charles Edwards and Ellis Wynne were still wedded to the Ptolemaic theory that the earth was a solid focal point around which all else moved. In his almanacs, Thomas Jones confirmed and reinforced the popular belief in geocentrism: 'the world stands in the middle of the heavens like the yolk in the middle of an egg, and the Sun and Moon and Stars in the heavens turn constantly around it'.[25]

One of the many paradoxes of Thomas Jones's career is that although he was seldom afraid of taking new initiatives in the field of publishing, he was essentially a purveyor of old values in the sense that he perpetuated hackneyed astronomical and astrological assumptions. Although much of the astrological data presented in his almanacs was highly complex and was probably designed as much to puzzle as to impress readers, it still served to strengthen people's faith in magical beliefs. Thomas Jones's almanacs, in fact, provided a rationale for many popular superstitions and traditional lore. Popular astrologers pillaged his almanacs for material which would enable them to frame horoscopes, to list propitious days, and to follow the directions of the Anatomical or 'zodiacal' man. Moreover, some of Thomas Jones's ephemeral publications, notably *The Famous Fortune-teller, or the Manifestation of Moles* (1683) and *Artemidorus: Gwir Ddeongliad Breuddwydion* (1698), were clearly designed for the cunning man's consulting room. The

[21] H. G. Jones, 'John Kelsall: a study in religious and economic history' (unpublished University of Wales M.A. thesis, 1938), p. 101.

[22] N[ational] L[ibrary of] W[ales] MS. 11440D, f. 14.

[23] H. Evans, *Cynghorion Tad i'w Fab*, ed. S. Hughes (1681), p. 57.

[24] NLW MS. 10B, p. 80.

[25] NLW MS. 6146B, pp. 179-86.

credulity of his fellow countrymen meant that he was free to peddle a wide range of astrological material in the sure knowledge that an expectant audience was to hand.

One of the most popular utilitarian functions of Thomas Jones's almanacs was to provide a detailed weather forecast. Here, more than anywhere, almanacers skated on thin ice. But there was a constant public demand for weather predictions and farmers, in particular, took note of his prognostications. Our seventeenth-century forebears were far more conscious of weather conditions, and indeed were more dependent upon them, than we are today. Prior to the development of the steam engine, the agricultural cycle was largely determined by sun, wind and rain. The harvest was the heart-beat of the Welsh economy: its success was crucial to the well-being of the overwhelming mass of the people. In a subsistence economy governed by the natural elements, a serious harvest failure was as welcome as the plague. A run of bad harvests could prove calamitous; by driving up food prices and increasing unemployment, poor harvests were ultimately responsible for sending thousands of penurious peasants to an early grave. There is no doubt that farmers carefully scrutinised the almanac's predictions in order to prepare for likely eventualities. In his early days, Thomas Jones nursed fond hopes of being able to print precise, even bold, weather forecasts. But he soon found himself batting on a sticky wicket. His problem was twofold: having to prepare his predictions twelve or fifteen months beforehand, and having to convince irate readers that the Welsh climate was so fickle that whereas it might rain in Merioneth on a particular day, the sun might also shine without pause on that same day in Montgomeryshire. Under heavy fire from his critics, he commented wearily: 'the wind bloweth where it listeth'.[26] Nevertheless, he scored a number of successes in the 1680s and it may be, as Reginald Scot once observed, that whenever astrologers achieved dramatic success people would 'believe whatsoever they say'.[27] A number of disastrous predictions in the following decade, however, forced him to take refuge in much woollier language. As the years rolled by, he became increasingly reluctant to print copious weather forecasts.[28] His prognostications became more and more ambivalent, as if his intention was to obscure rather than to intimate the most likely outcome. By the end of his days, his weather predictions, though still widely read and heeded, carried something of the air of an academic exercise.

Ordinary folk also paid close attention to the movement of heavenly bodies. Diarists fastidiously recorded solar and lunar eclipses, lightning, comets and blazing stars. The more credulous claimed to have seen terrifying phantoms, horrifying monsters or fiery dragons in the heavens. A special significance was attached to the nature and changing phases of the moon. The moon was the queen of the stars and was believed to be capable not only of influencing the ebb and flow of tides, the weather and the growth of vegetation, but also the mental and physical characterstics of man. 'The children of the moon', claimed Morgan Llwyd, 'are angry and fickle like the whirlwind . . . unfaithful, contentious,

[26] T. Jones, *Newydd oddiwrth y Seêr* (1684), sig. A3v; *idem, [Almanac]* (1708), sig. C7r.
[27] K. Thomas, *Religion and the Decline of Magic* (1971), p. 336.
[28] *[Almanac]* (1708), sig. C7r.

jealous and uncivil'.[29] 'Many superstitions were practised at full moon',[30] claimed Robert Jones, and one of the merits of the almanac was that it reminded readers when to plough and sow crops, when to geld animals, and when to let blood. Eclipses were also a constant source of wonder to uneducated country folk, for they were considered, along with most meteorological anomalies, as portents of imminent calamity. But foretelling the precise timing of solar and lunar eclipses was no easy task, as Thomas Jones found to his cost. In 1683 he chanced his arm by prophesying that an eclipse of the sun would occur on May Day four years hence, that it would persist for three hours and ten minutes, and that it would be a harbinger of mischief and woe.[31] Shortly prior to the event, many of his readers prepared for the impending darkness by herding sheep and cattle to shelter and by postponing the fairs, markets, dances and recreations which were traditionally linked with a festival which marked the end of winter. It is more than likely, too, that many fearful spinsters cowered under their beds. Indeed, the reaction of Welshmen to Thomas Jones's prediction was itself an indication of the public's faith in the power of astrological prophecy. On the appointed day, however, the sun shone brilliantly in a cloudless sky. Obloquy and abuse were showered upon Thomas Jones for many months afterwards, but, like every self-respecting almanacer, he refused to shoulder full responsibility for his error. He reminded his readers that the stars do not compel, that astrologers simply suggested likely tendencies, and that God was both able and likely to intervene directly in the affairs of men. In this case, God, in His infinite wisdom, had chosen to stay His hand.[32] Despite this disclaimer, however, Thomas Jones had clearly learnt his lesson. Henceforward, his solar and lunar predictions were either frustratingly enigmatic or desperately confusing.

Thomas Jones lived in an age of religious upheaval and political controversy, and his almanac was an ideal forum in which to discuss the burning issues of the day and to air his most cherished prejudices. There was a heightened interest in political and public questions in the late-Stuart period and it was natural for Thomas Jones's readers to nurse a desire to ascertain precisely what the future held in store for them. On the whole, Jones's political prognostications were a healthy mixture of good and bad tidings. Some of his predictions were so equivocal that he was able to claim after the event that his prognostication had come true in precisely the way he had foretold. He proudly publicised his successes, claiming to have predicted the Rye House Plot of 1683 and the downfall of the duke of Monmouth and his rebels two years later.[33] One of his favourite ploys was to expose the errors of his English colleagues, and seldom did he confess his dependence upon them for guidance. He was also particularly adept at shrugging off embarrassing failures and, sometimes, the most egregious blunders. He was tempted on several occasions during the 1690s to prophesy the impending demise of Louis XIV, king of France. 'Farewell to the old man', he

[29] M. Llwyd, *Gwyddor Vchod* (1657), p. 12.
[30] R. Jones, op. cit., pp. 25-6.
[31] T. Jones, *Newydd oddiwrth y Sêr* (1683), pp. 27-8.
[32] *Idem, Almanac am y flwyddyn 1688* (1688), sig. A2r-A3r.
[33] *Idem, Newyddion Mawr oddiwrth y Sêr* (1694), sig. B2v.

exclaimed in his prophecy for February 1691, 'it's time for him to die.'[34] In spite of the Welshman's imperatives, the Sun King proved an unconscionable time a-dying. Many of his readers lost patience and held him up to ridicule. Once more, however, Thomas Jones's happy knack of extricating himself from the most awkward situations had not deserted him. He claimed that he had been wrongly informed of the date of Louis's birth and that it was not surprising, therefore, that his calculations of the future prospects of his *bête noire* had gone awry.[35] The sniggers of his critics often induced severe fits of depression and rage. 'If I err once', he thundered, 'I'm called a knave by some, but if I told the truth always I'd be called a devil by others.'[36] And as he grew older and wiser, it became much harder both to pin him down and prove him wrong. His predictions became riddled with clichés and generalities. Some prophecies, such as 'old men will die' or 'a famous prince will stumble into his grave', were deliberately frivolous. Other pearls of wisdom were formulated with a stunning lack of clarity: 'doubtful and worrying things will be explained soon and will turn out to be either good or bad'.[37]

In spite of these infelicities and frivolities, however, Thomas Jones's almanacs fulfilled a serious rôle in stimulating readers' interest in political affairs, in conditioning their religious and political values, and in helping them to understand the wider world. Thomas Jones made no secret of his deep-seated prejudices against the enemies of the established Church. He equated Dissent with enthusiasm, turbulence and sedition. The civil war, and especially the treatment suffered by fellow-royalists in Merioneth, continued to arouse painful reverberations in his memory long after the Restoration.[38] The prospect of a further rule of the saints or of a left-wing rebellion filled him with dread, and he seized every opportunity in his almanacs to rally support for the cause of the Anglican Church. However, it was the shadow of Popery which fell most heavily and most often across the pages of his almanacs. Thomas Jones was an anxious, self-doubting, profoundly pessimistic man, and he shared the obsessional fear of Popery which pervaded most men's lives. His almanacs probably did more than any other contemporary publication to instil in Welshmen an awareness of the false and cruel nature of the Roman Catholic faith. He fostered a stridently anti-Popish animus by reminding readers of the devilish stratagems of Irish 'barbarians' and Jesuit 'bloodsuckers'. His historical 'chronologies' raked up tales of Popish 'atrocities' committed since the days of Bloody Mary, and these did much to sustain the Protestant stereotype of the evil Papist who was capable of perpetrating acts of most fiendish character.[39] He convinced readers that foreign conquest would usher in the three badges of slavery: Popery, rape and wooden shoes. He planted within Welshmen a fanatical hatred of Catholicism and ensured that the dark prospect of arbitrary foreign rule loomed clearly before their

---

[34] *Idem, Newyddion Mawr oddiwrth y Sêr* (1691), sig. A8r.
[35] *Idem, Y Cyfreithlawn Almanac Cymraeg* (1706), sig. C6r.
[36] *Idem, Y Lleiaf o'r Almanaccau Cymraeg* (1692), sig. A8r.
[37] *Idem, [Almanac]* (1709), sig. C1r.
[38] *Idem, Y Cyfreithlawn Almanac Cymraeg* (1706), sig. C8v.
[39] *Idem, Newyddion Mawr oddiwrth y Sêr* (1691), sig. A2r.

eyes. He believed that Louis XIV was a politically adroit, ruthless and sacriligeous despot, a 'grand robber' whose ambitions were as boundless as his greed and who threatened everything which a true-born Briton held most dear. When the Edict of Nantes was revoked in 1685, Thomas Jones was outraged and he maintained that henceforward the defence of British soil against the king of France was a religious duty to be fulfilled by every citizen. As early as 1681, in predicting 'approaching woes', he had warned his countrymen to 'take heed that you be not found sleeping and unprepared'. [40] That solemn litany rang down the decades in successive almanacs.

Thomas Jones, through the medium of his almanacs, became the first political and war correspondent to write in Welsh. He lived through two major wars, the War of the League of Augsburg (1688-97) and the War of the Spanish Succession (1702-13), major dramatic conflicts which both haunted and enthralled him. A torrent of pamphlets, newspapers and journals flowed from the English printing presses during this period and helped to create an informed reading public. Thomas Jones was anxious that his fellow countrymen should not be deprived of sensational war news in their native tongue. He was well qualified for the task, having served his apprenticeship as a journalist in London by publishing *The London Mercury* (later called *The Lacedemonian Mercury*), a newspaper written by the prince of Grub Street satirists, Tom Brown. [41] Indeed, had it not been for the reluctance of Welsh shopkeepers and booksellers to co-operate with him, Welsh readers would have received a monthly newspaper in Welsh—the first of its kind—from December 1690 onwards. [42] Thwarted in this ambition, Thomas Jones was forced to be content with suffusing his almanacs with graphic and captivating accounts of the war effort on the continent. Prior to the publication of his almanacs, news-hungry Welshmen, far distant from the capital, had had to rely for political information on snatches of gossip overheard in taverns and country houses, on sermons preached in the parish pulpit, on public announcements and proclamations made by town-criers, and on eye-witness reports retailed by soldiers and sailors returning from the battle-scene. From the early-1690s onwards, the Welsh almanac was read with eager anticipation and obvious relish. The Popish threat, the imminence of a French invasion, and the stirring continental campaign waged by William III and his generals whetted the appetite of Thomas Jones's readers for news and information. Indeed, he was at times barely able to gratify the popular craving for graphic accounts of battles, campaigns, sieges, voyages and disasters. In 1701 he apologised profusely—a rare event in itself—for having failed to 'burden your ears with sufficient war news in Welsh' in his previous issue. [43] The cost of waging such huge wars was crippling, but the government's task of keeping the public's spirits buoyant was at least as important as marshalling the country's resources. In producing almanacs which were highly jingoistic and stridently anti-French, Thomas Jones helped to create a

---

[40] *An Astrological Speculation*, p. 6.

[41] Bodleian Library, The Introduction to *The London Mercury*, nos. 1-7 (1692).

[42] T. Jones, *Newyddion Mawr oddiwrth y Sêr* (1691), sig. A2v; *idem, Y Mwyaf o'r Almanaccau Cymraeg* (1692), sig. A1v.

[43] *Idem, Newyddion Mawr oddiwrth y Sêr* (1701), sig. B5r-6r.

mood of self-confidence. He bent all his energies towards stiffening his countrymen's resolve by urging them to stand by king, church and country through thick and thin, by conjuring up horrifying images of the enemy, and by reminding them that God had promised to destroy the forces of Antichrist. Thomas Jones took great pride in recounting the heroic exploits of the British army in thwarting the designs of 'the French monster' and in teaching Irish rebels a sharp lesson. He gloried in particular in the dramatic victories achieved over Papist Irishmen on the Boyne in July 1690, the crippling of the French fleet at La Hogue in May 1692, and the spectacular, if bloody, successes at Blenheim, Ramillies and Oudenarde. No other Welsh publication did as much as the almanac to arouse antipathy towards Rome, nourish francophobia and foster patriotic sentiments.

Unlike the almanacs of his English contemporaries, Thomas Jones's almanacs had a substantial literary content. Thomas Jones was profoundly concerned at the plight of the Welsh language, its poetry and literature. He was convinced, as were many scholars, that his native tongue lacked status and prestige in the eyes of the Welsh gentry as well as of Englishmen. Having moved in Grub Street circles, he knew that many Englishmen believed that the Welsh language was an uncouth, ungenteel patois, a relic of barbarism spoken by a squalid, comical people who inhabited 'the fag-end of the Creation'.[44] Furthermore, as in most parts of Europe, the upper class in Wales was slowly but surely abandoning popular culture to the lower classes. In Languedoc, French was the adopted language of the nobility, whilst craftsmen and peasants remained wedded to Occitan. German became the language of the nobles of Bohemia; only peasants spoke Czech.[45] Similarly, in Wales the gentry, especially those who lived in south and east Wales, no longer judged it worthwhile or fashionable to identify themselves with the native language, poetry and historical traditions of their land.[46] Bewitched by things English, their pride in their Welshness was evaporating swiftly. Professional bards were a thing of the past by the 1680s. The myth of the 'glorious British past' was a standing joke in intellectual circles. Crucially, too, 'the old and most excellent British language',[47] as Thomas Jones liked to call it, was believed by the gentry to be old, decrepit and eminently dispensable. Thomas Jones believed that their disparaging attitude towards their native tongue was nothing less than blasphemy. 'Can a man own God, and yet be ashamed of that language which God himself chose first? It would far better become the Welsh men to uphold and extoll their own language than to cast it away through undervaluing of it.'[48] The Welsh, he observed, had almost been 'blotted out of the Books of Records',[49] the Welsh poetic tradition was in a torpid state, and Welsh literature had been allowed to decay simply because the gentry no longer identified themselves with native culture.

[44] N. Ward, A Trip to North-Wales (1701), passim.
[45] P. Burke, Popular Culture in Early Modern Europe (1978), pp. 270-2.
[46] P. Morgan, The Eighteenth-Century Renaissance (1981), p. 19.
[47] T. Jones, Almanac am y Flwyddyn 1681 (1681), sig. A2r.
[48] Idem, Newydd oddiwrth y Seêr (1684), sig. A1r-A3r.
[49] Y Gymraeg yn ei Disgleirdeb, sig. A3r.

Fired by ardent patriotism, Thomas Jones never tired of reminding his countrymen that the Welsh language was one of the mother tongues of Europe. He was filled with a burning desire to preserve, enrich and revivify the language 'that God himself spake to Adam and others for about two thousand years after the creation'. [50] In order to compensate for the lack of gentry patronage, he gave prominent coverage in his almanacs to Welsh poetry, both old and new. Welshmen, as Erasmus Saunders put it, were 'naturally addicted to poetry', [51] and John Prys, one of Thomas Jones's successors, was convinced that poems and songs were more popular than any other part of the almanac. [52] Thomas Jones numbered himself among the growing band of amateur poets, many of whom were clergymen, freeholders and craftsmen, who were anxious to breathe new life into a sickly and tottering profession. For the first time in their lives, amateur poets were able to see their work in print. The works of leading poets such as Huw Morys, Dafydd Manuel and Owen Gruffydd were printed cheek by jowl with the sorrier efforts of lesser lights. As a result, the almanac became a convenient medium through which major poets and aspiring apprentices could publish their work and maintain contact with each other. It was through the good offices of Thomas Jones's almanac that the Welsh eisteddfod was revived from 1701 onwards. [53] It became common thereafter for poets to gather together annually in a tavern in a market-town to discuss common problems in a convivial atmosphere, to formulate a rubric of regulations applicable to the bardic fraternity as a whole, and to show off their skills in verse. The quality of their work often left a good deal to be desired, but by printing the fruit of their labours Thomas Jones was able to bind them together as a fraternity, to stimulate a desire within them to cultivate and refine the art of poetry, and to promote and exchange ideas and topics of mutual interest. In a land that lacked a centralised court and national institutions, and now was shorn of noble patronage, the rôle of the almanac as a focus for the literary endeavours of the bards was of crucial importance.

Much of the attraction of Thomas Jones's almanac lay in its author's gift for plain speaking. Thomas Jones was a forthright, even cantankerous, man. He had a talent for invective and feared neither 'the dispraise of the Learned' nor 'the scurrilous aspersion of the illiterate and barbarous'. [54] At a time when most humble folk were semi-literate, voteless and with no voice in their own destiny, Thomas Jones was more than usually explicit in articulating their resentments and grievances. He was a constant thorn in the flesh of the Welsh gentry and despised the obsequious flattery which his fellow authors showered upon them in their prefatory addresses and dedications. He fiercely criticised the pride, snobbery and vanity of the gentry, their love of lengthy pedigrees, their concern for outward appearance, their lack of moral fortitude and the mocking tones in which they disdained their mother tongue. He satirised the foibles and

[50] T. Jones, *Newydd oddiwrth y Seêr* (1684), sig. A8v.
[51] E. Saunders, *A View of the State of Religion in the Diocese of St. David's, 1721* (1949), p. 33.
[52] J. Prys, *Wybrenawl Gennadwri neu Almanacc Newydd* (1744), sig. A1v.
[53] T. Jones, *Newyddion Mawr oddiwrth y Sêr* (1701), sig. C8v.
[54] *Y Gymraeg yn ei Disgleirdeb*, sig. A4v.

affectations of the Dic Siôn Dafyddion (those who believed themselves to be 'too gentlemanly to read Welsh') as piercingly as Gruffydd Robert had done a century earlier and as Jac Glan-y-gors would do a century later. Thomas Jones took great pride in his caustic, indiscreet tongue and once confessed, with an impenitent chuckle, to having been 'too saucy' towards pompous gentlemen.[55] His pen was never sharper than when voicing the resentment of smaller landowners, tenant farmers and squatters towards acquisitive Leviathans who delighted in grinding the faces of the poor. Many landed Titans in late-Stuart Wales were busily carving out great estates for themselves, often with scant regard for the wishes and sentiments of their impoverished and helpless neighbours. Such rapacity provoked bitter and widespread resentment, and it is significant that much of the religious verse published in Thomas Jones's almanacs bristled with barbed criticisms of 'covetous mighty gentry', rack-renting landlords and bullying stewards.

Jones was also, like many of his humble contemporaries, deeply distrustful of the professions. He poured derision upon apothecaries and physicians, and upbraided pettifogging lawyers for their duplicity, avarice and venality. Any humble man, he argued, who plucked up enough courage to challenge the 'proud gentry' was judged 'a shameless knave' in the courts and was liable to find himself reduced to beggary. 'It will be a hard task to ensure that justice is done', he thundered, 'when everyone is given his just deserts, mark it down!'[56] Many gentlemen must have found Thomas Jones's acid comments not only disconcerting but also subversive of every canon which had been dinned into the heads of common Welshmen since time immemorial. In a deferential society, which conceived of God's grand design as a hierarchy of orders or degrees of men, the mass of the populace had been conditioned to accept social distinctions and the inequalities which stemmed from them as belonging to the nature of things. For that reason alone, many underprivileged and oppressed people who had traditionally suffered in silence would have looked forward to buying Thomas Jones's almanacs in order to read sentiments which they themselves felt but dared not voice within their own communities. Welsh almanacs were suffused with words of comfort for the poor, and many underprivileged readers must have searched as much for consolation as for instruction within them.

Although Thomas Jones was essentially a sombre man who took life seriously, his almanacs were not devoid of flashes of wit, especially those published before ill-health robbed him of his sense of humour. In his almanacs for 1681 he urged the reader to ensure a plentiful supply of food, warm clothes and a 'lively bedfellow' in readiness for a cold January.[57] In 1688 he suggested that hot weather in July was the most propitious time for a man to test the love of a lady, 'for if she lies close to her husband during this month, he cannot doubt that she will also do so during cold weather.[58] Such nuggets of wry humour disappeared when he was afflicted by a series of debilitating illnesses during the 1690s, the

[55] T. Jones, *Almanac am y Flwyddyn 1693* (1693), sig. Alv.
[56] *Idem, Newyddion Mawr oddiwrth y Sêr* (1695), p. 37.
[57] *Idem, Almanac am y Flwyddyn 1681* (1681), sig. A11r.
[58] *Idem, Almanac am y Flwyddyn 1688* (1688), sig. C8r.

symptoms of which were vividly depicted in his almanacs and presumably were designed to win readers' sympathy for his plight. The likelihood is, however, that the detailed descriptions of his maladies, notably the sweating sickness which drew twenty-eight barrels of sweat from his body over a six-year period, evoked shrieks of mirth rather than compassion. 'Thomas knew everything about the heavenly worlds', giggled William Morris, 'having set himself such difficult tasks it's no wonder he sweated so many gallons.'[59]

Like most enterprising almanacers of his day, Thomas Jones was sensitive to public tastes and anxious to satisfy people's thirst for entertainment. His most popular Welsh ballads were those which focused on natural disasters, gruesome murders, monstrous births, romantic love-affairs and spectacular scandals. He knew full well that startling and controversial material was good for business, and that running battles between rival almanacers attracted a considerable following. English almanacers were constantly at each other's throats, and charges of ineptitude, plagiarism and slander were legion. William Lilly embroiled himself in a lengthy and vituperative battle of wits with his protégé, John Gadbury.[60] Arise Evans, the curious self-styled prophet and dreamer from Llangelynnin, Merioneth, dared to mock Lilly as 'a cunning sophister' who 'hath no more wit than a Goose'.[61] George Parker derided his great rival, John Partridge, as a 'silly and ill-bred buffoon', whilst Partridge replied in kind by dubbing his adversary a humble cutler, a wife-beater and a Papist. Ned Ward, the satirist, made great capital of the celebrated feud between Parker and Partridge by publishing *The World Bewitched, a Dialogue between two Astrologers and the Author* (1699), and a graphic account of a mock-trial held at 'the Kings's Bench Bar'.[62] From the early-1680s onwards, conflict of some kind seems to have dominated Thomas Jones's life. When he was first granted the right to publish an annual Welsh almanac his privilege was stiffened by a commitment by the Stationers' Company to protect his interests by prosecuting any persons who dared to compete in the same field. As it turned out, Jones himself was personally prepared to guard his monopoly jealously. Scenting conspiracies under every bush, he pursued his rivals with paranoid persistence. He raised a hue and cry whenever shameless pedlars made off with the profits accrued from selling his almanacs, and waged war on 'predatory misers' who infringed his copyright by distributing 'seditious libels' merely 'for the Lucre of thy money'.[63] He regarded every potential rival as a gross interloper bent on undermining his most profitable and popular publishing venture. Prior to his removal to Shrewsbury, Thomas Jones managed to quash the aspirations of counterfeiters and pirates, but following the freedoms conferred upon the press in 1695 more and more competitors arrogated to themselves the right to publish Welsh almanacs. However often Thomas Jones might brandish his royal warrant before them, they were able to argue forcefully that the relaxation of the licensing laws had rendered his copyright nugatory in

[59] J. H. Davies (ed.), *The Letters of Lewis, Richard, William and John Morris of Anglesey* (2 vols., 1907-9), II, 157.

[60] *Dictionary of National Biography*, s.n. Gadbury.

[61] A. Evans, *The Voice of King Charls the Father, to Charls the son* (1655), pp. 41, 43.

[62] H. W. Troyer, *Ned Ward of Grub Street* (1968), pp. 51-2.

[63] T. Jones, *Almanac am y Flwyddyn 1681* (1681), sig. A2r.

spirit if not in letter. Jones, however, was unwilling to abandon his monopoly without a struggle. He pursued each rival with unflagging zeal, interpreting each challenge to his rights as a personal affront, and urging his readers to be faithful to 'their old servant' by keeping a vigilant eye open for charlatans. His almanacs contained an animated and lively account of each dispute, notably the long-running and bitter feud which broke out in 1698 between him and John Jones, a respectable and fairly learned Dissenter and almanacer of Caeau, Wrexham. Although John Kelsall believed that John Jones blatantly copied most of his material from Charles Leadbetter's almanacs, he was sufficiently confident to challenge Thomas Jones's primacy in the field by publishing an annual Welsh almanac, *Cennad oddiwrth y Sêr* (A Message from the Stars), from 1701 onwards.

Much to the amusement of his readers, Thomas Jones presented his side of the dispute with characteristic gusto and prickly sarcasm. He poured scorn on the 'bilious farrago' peddled by 'this knavish spoiler', and baited him unmercifully by exposing his family connections with Puritan saints.[64] 'Fanatick Jack', he gloated, 'can Imbrace occasional Conformity so far for the Lucre of Mamon, or deal in that which he hates for the Love of Money.'[65] He exposed the errors in his rival's astrological computations with malicious glee, claiming that his predictions made as much sense as 'the dog who barked at the stars'. Thomas Jones even engaged the services of leading poets such as Huw Morys and Dafydd Manuel to defend his honour, to speak well of his achievements, and to tease his rival in satirical verse. Not to be outdone, John Jones abused his antagonist as 'a sour, lying, idle servant', and poked fun at his delphic predictions and bumbling inadequacies.[66] Thomas Jones's business problems lent added fuel to the fire. His apprentice, Ellis Edward, betrayed his master by conspiring—'like Judas'—with 'Sionyn o'r Tŷ yn Cau' to defraud him of printing equipment and manuscripts.[67] Stung by these setbacks, Thomas Jones continued to launch annual onslaughts in racy, vigorous and often intemperate language against his major rival. His readers were entertained in these self-justifying outbursts with the petty jealousies, prejudices and bombast of a man who believed himself more sinned against than sinning. For twelve years the veteran and the *arriviste* studded their respective almanacs with accusations and counter-accusations, calumny, innuendo, threats and abuse, thus ensuring that their dispute was a saga as compelling to their readers as are modern soap-operas to television addicts.

Although they were often hastily prepared and shoddily bound, Thomas Jones's almanacs commanded a regular and wide readership. Together with Welsh ballads, they were easily the cheapest and most heavily thumbed commodities on the market. Thomas Jones lived up to his reputation as a shrewd businessman by establishing a highly effective network of agents and distributors, including professional booksellers, grocers, mercers and ironmongers, to ensure that his almanacs were available not simply in the major market towns but also in

---

[64] *Idem, Y Cyfreithlawn Almanacc Cymraeg* (1706), sig. C8r.

[65] *Idem,* [*Almanac*] (1708), sig. C8r.

[66] *Idem, Y Cyfreithlawn Almanac Cymraeg* (1712), sig. B8r-v.

[67] E. Rees and D. Nuttall, 'Baddy Vindicated or Jones v. Jones', *Journal Welsh Bibliographical Soc.,* X (1970), 131-4.

remote rural parishes.[68] Literacy rates were clearly rising in Wales in this period and there was a growing demand for popular reading material. From the early-1680s onwards itinerant hawkers and pedlars could be heard crying 'Prynwch eich almanac newydd' ('Buy your new almanac') in all the major fairs and markets of Wales. Sold at twopence each, or 1s. 11d. per dozen, they were deliberately tailored to suit the needs of humble, underprivileged tenant farmers, craftsmen and peasants. Literary scholars might despise almanacs as 'sorry stuff',[69] but Thomas Jones was anxious to cater for the taste of those who were 'too poor to enter the market of English and Latin to double their caps with learning'.[70] He was particularly eager to ensure that the common man should have the opportunity of buying reading material which was both edifying and entertaining. In a society in which the burdens of sustained agricultural labour forced men and women to seek relaxation and distractions from care, it was natural that the almanac should find a ready audience among the 'uneducated common Welshman'. In sheltered communities bereft of radio, television and newspapers, the almanac provided a happy blend of entertainment and instruction. It provided an escape, especially for those who were 'as credible of tales as ye Indians and Negroes are',[71] from the tedium, penury and squalor of daily life. As winter deepened in remote rural parishes, families would gather round the hearth to tell what James Owen disparagingly called 'lying old tales' and 'monkish fables'.[72] The almanac clearly infused this oral culture with fresh material. At a time, too, when people's consciousness was shaped by the annual cycle of agricultural pursuits, the almanac was indispensable to farmers who were anxious not only to record weather predictions but also to keep an accurate check on the days of the week and months of the year. Furthermore, almanacs brought the literate and illiterate together in reading groups. During the 1680s the only literate parishioner in the parish of Llanfihangel Tre'r-beirdd in Anglesey was Siôn Edward, a cooper, to whom the local youths used to flock to learn to read Thomas Jones's books and almanacs. Among them was the father of the famous Morris brothers, whose thrusting enthusiasm lay behind the cultural revival of the eighteenth century. 'Who knows', wrote William Morris to his brother Richard, 'but that you and I would be illiterate were it not for that old fellow of Clorach who taught our father . . . and so started the blessed gift.'[73] Welsh poets also lavished praise upon Thomas Jones for fostering literacy among deprived social groups and for tempting young children to cultivate reading habits.[74] William Morris, who sniggered often enough as he thumbed Thomas Jones's almanacs, was still forced to admit that he was 'an old fellow who did a lot of good despite his ignorance'.[75] At popular levels, therefore, the almanac fulfilled a variety of

---

[68] G. H. Jenkins, *Literature, Religion and Society in Wales, 1660-1730* (1978), pp. 247-50.

[69] *Morris Letters*, I, 81.

[70] T. Jones, *Y Lleiaf o'r Almanaccau Cymraeg* (1692), sig. A8r.

[71] G. J. Williams, 'Dyddiadur William Thomas o Lanfihangel-ar-Elái', *Morgannwg*, I (1957), 19.

[72] J. Owen, *Trugaredd a Barn* (1715), sig. A4v.

[73] *Morris Letters*, I, 198.

[74] T. Jones, [*Almanac*] (1686), sig. C3r; *idem*, [*Almanac*] (1704), sig. F2r; *idem*, *Newyddion Mawr oddiwrth y Sêr* (1699), sig. C7v.

[75] *Morris Letters*, I, 198.

functions. It served as a diary, a calendar, a reference-book, an astrologer's guide, a periodical, a newspaper, a song-book and a primer. Doubtless too, as in England, it was used as lavatory paper, for lighting tobacco and 'stopping of mustard pots'.[76]

Over three decades Thomas Jones succeeded in compiling an annual almanac which was far more lively and interesting than any of those produced by his successors in the eighteenth century. Nevertheless, he attracted more than his share of criticism and abuse. Almanacers were judged fair game by contemporary satirists. Tom Brown enjoyed exposing the social background of prominent astrologers: 'Gadbury we know was no more than a country butcher, before he was admitted as a tenant into the twelve houses; and Partridge was no more than a London cobler, before he was made running footman to the seven planets'.[77] Ned Ward pungently described them as 'a parcel of Illiterate and Scandalous Deceivers of the Common People':

> Poor Taylors, Weavers, Shoe-makers, and such
> Illit'rate Fools, who think they know too much,
> Are the chief Senseless Bigots that Advance
> A foolish Whim to further Ignorance.[78]

Similarly, Thomas Jones was the despair of many Welshmen, especially men of letters, who cast doubts on his credentials and portrayed him as a plausible rogue who earned his living by gulling innocent readers. Moses Williams, one of Edward Lhuyd's acolytes, despised his idle boasts and seized every opportunity to deflate his pretensions by calling him 'Tom the tailor' and 'Tom-ass'.[79] John Jones of Caeau was no more complimentary: he averred that his rival was better qualified to sew old sacks than to interpret the influence of the planets.[80] Clergymen and Dissenters, too, often reminded him that God can do what man cannot, and urged his readers to submit their destiny to the inscrutable providence and will of God. Even after his death, Thomas Jones's reputation suffered badly from the calumnies of the Morris brothers of Anglesey. Small wonder, then, that Wales's first almanacer was forced on many occasions to admit wearily that the lot of a prophet was indeed hard: 'unless an astrologer is as wise as God Himself, his craft will be despised by many people'.[81] By the summer of 1713, Thomas Jones was a sickly, whining, misanthropic old man, his body worn out by unstinting labour and his energy spent in emotional upheavals and sterile disputes. Tired of criticism and abuse, and well aware of the frailties and fickleness of man, he was rather more worldly-wise then when he first ventured into print in 1680. During his last hours on 6 August 1713, he might well have mused wryly over the capricious twist of fate which had decreed that he was to

---

[76] Capp, op. cit., p. 66.

[77] T. Brown, *Works* (4 vols., 8th ed., 1744), p. 227.

[78] N. Ward, *The London—Spy Compleat* (1924), p. 365.

[79] See Williams's personal copy (NLW, W.S. 50).

[80] T. Jones, [*Almanac*] (1704), sig. F1v.

[81] *Idem, Newydd oddiwrth y Seêr* (1684), sig. A3v; *idem,* [*Almanac*] (1710), sig. A2r; *idem, Y Cyfreithlawn Almanacc Cymraeg* (1712), sig. A1v.

predecease his sworn enemy, the king of France. Carlyle's words may serve as a fitting epitaph of this well-meaning prophet:

> Trouble us not with thy prophecies, O croaking Friend of Men: 'tis long that we have heard such; and still the old world keeps wagging, in its old way.

Marriage and the Ownership of Land[1]

H. J. HABAKKUK

IN one of his few references to Wales in the *Wealth of Nations,* Adam Smith makes an interesting observation: '. . . very old families, such as have possessed some considerable estate from father to son for many successive generations, are very rare in commercial countries. In countries which have little commerce, on the contrary, such as Wales or the highlands of Scotland, they are very common.'[2] This is the only comparison known to me of Wales with England—for it was presumably England he had primarily in mind as the pre-eminent commercial country. But observations to the same broad effect—that landed society was more stable in the remoter parts of the kingdom—are to be found in the seventeenth century. Thomas Fuller, writing shortly after the Restoration on the mobility of families in various English counties, remarked on the rapid turnover of families in Middlesex, Berkshire and Bedfordshire and the stability of families in Cumberland and Northumberland.[3]

There is no reason to suppose that Fuller and Smith, in making these comparisons, were conforming to a tradition or a convention of observations. It is safe to assume that the observations were independent and that the differences to which they testify really existed. Nor is there any reason to doubt the explanations which they gave for the broad contrasts in the mobility of landed property: the turnover of land was greater in commercial societies because land, like other commodities, was more commonly bought and sold. Fuller certainly implied that property was more stable in the remoter counties because landowners there were less likely to acquire expensive tastes, compared with those who lived 'southward near London in the warmth of wealth and plenty of pleasures'. Landowners in the more remote counties also found it more difficult to borrow to finance extravagance. They were therefore less likely to run into debt and be forced to sell their estates. As Sir John Dalrymple wrote of Scotland in the eighteenth century: 'in a country where there is little luxury or opportunity for expense a family may last for ages without an entail'; and there is no reason to suppose that this judgement would not apply to most parts of eighteenth-century Wales.[4] Thus, in so far as indebtedness was a major cause of sales, the supply of estates on the market was relatively smaller.

---

[1] Except where another reference is given, statements on Glamorgan families are based on the evidence in G. T. Clark, *Limbus Patrum Morganiae et Glamorganiae* (1886); *Inventory of Ancient Monuments in Glamorgan, vol.* IV, Part I: *The Greater Houses* (Cardiff, 1981); *The High Sheriffs of the County of Glamorgan* with notes by G. Williams (Cardiff, 1966).

[2] A. Smith, *Wealth of Nations,* ed. R. H. Campbell and A. S. Skinner (Oxford, 1976), I, 421.

[3] T. Fuller, *The History of the Worthies of England* (London, 1662), pp. 99, 171, 187, 223, 310.

[4] Sir J. Dalrymple, *Considerations upon the policy of entails in Great Britain* (Edinburgh, 1764), p. 158.

The demand for estates in the remoter parts of the kingdom was also less. The greatest single source of demand was London. From the sixteenth century to about the middle of the eighteenth, few new fortunes of substantial size were made outside London. There was always some demand for estates among the newly rich of country towns and particularly of provincial ports, but until the 1760s and 1770s it was very modest in comparison with that of London. This concentration of new fortunes in the capital did not necessarily mean that the demand for estates to establish new landed families was concentrated in the counties near London. Some men who made their fortunes in London sought to acquire estates in their native counties, even when these were far from London. But the Londoners who bought in remote places were a minority. The force of London demand tended to peter out within, say, 100 to 150 miles of London.

Thus, both supply and demand were relatively low in the remoter parts of the kingdom. How supply and demand interacted is not clear. There may have been some landowners in the remoter parts whose decision as to whether or not to sell was influenced by the price they could get; the shortage of estates for sale may in some measure have resulted from lack of demand. Possibly, too, if estates had been cheaper in the remoter parts more Londoners would have been tempted to buy there. Most probably, however, supply and demand were not very sensitive to price. The main determinant of the volume of sales was the level of landed indebtedness. The preference of the newly rich for estates not too remote from London was too strong to be seriously modified by price. As a result the market in estates in the remoter parts was limited and was dominated by local men, so that much of the buying and selling that took place resulted in shifts in the relative position of existing landed families rather than in the introduction of new families.

Thus, it is possible to construct a simple version of the land market in the areas distant from London which applies from, say, the mid-sixteenth to the mid- or late-eighteenth century and one in which the level of transactions in land was low, and families established by 'new men' were relatively rare. How does this apply to Wales and in particular Glamorgan? This essay is primarily concerned with Glamorgan, but only in so far as, in respect of the influences on the distribution of property, it may shed light on other parts of Wales.

There are no estimates of the number of estates available for sale in Glamorgan and in the absence of manorial descents it is difficult to compile them. There are very few private acts for sale of Glamorgan estates, and though this may possibly reflect a looseness in family settlements and therefore less need for such acts, it also suggests a relative paucity of estates for sale.[5] Perhaps the best evidence, however, comes from the genealogies of Glamorgan landed families which show how rarely the mainly family estates changed hands by sale. There are signs of increasing activity in the closing decades of the eighteenth century, but until then, though there was considerable trade in parcels of land and some sales of outlying properties, the families who were compelled by economic necessity to part with the central core of their property seem to have been few.

---

[5] There also seem to be few deeds of bargain and sale of Glamorgan property on the Close Rolls; between 1701 and 1725 there were eighteen enrolments, of which some related to the same transaction.

There were, of course, some spendthrifts and some victims of political misfortune. The Vaughans in the 1640s sold Dunraven—and also their Wiltshire estate—primarily because of the Civil War. In the later-seventeenth century, Sir Robert Thomas of Llanmihangel, son of a royalist, got into financial difficulties. The Turbevilles of Sker were recusants and their property was heavily mortgaged before its sale in 1685-7. The fortunes of the Bassetts were damaged by the Civil War and further injured by extravagance and misfortune after the Restoration, and Philip Bassett was forced to sell Beaupré and St. Hilary in 1709.[6] The Thomas family of Wenvoe shed Rhiwperra in 1706 and Wenvoe in 1775, the sale of the latter being due to excessive expenditure by Sir Edmund Thomas (1712-67) on estate improvement and on his political career.[7] Duffryn St. Nicholas, the estate of the Button family, fell into the hands of the mortgagee in the 1730s and was sold. Robert Jones of Fonmon (d. 1793) mortgaged a large part of his estate and spent many years on the continent to escape his creditors; though the main estates of the family escaped, he was forced to sell land.[8] There were no doubt other extravagant landowners in Glamorgan. But to anyone who comes to the history of Glamorgan families after studying the midlands, what is striking is the relatively small number who were forced by financial pressure to sell the main family estate. Examples of spectacular squandering of estates are, Major Francis Jones concludes, 'comparatively rare among Welsh landed families'.[9]

A related feature of the history of landownership in Glamorgan is the relatively small number of new families from outside the county who were established in the county as a result of purchase. Of the new men who were so common in the home counties and the English midlands, there were few. David Jenkins, a lawyer of local origins, bought Hensol in 1614. Another lawyer, Humphrey Wyndham, a younger son of the Wyndhams of Orchard Wyndham, and without any local connexions that I have been able to trace, and his son John, also a lawyer, bought Dunraven in 1642. Around the middle of the century Col. Philip Jones, who came from Llangyfelach, bought a substantial estate from the St. John family and also acquired property belonging to the marquis of Worcester. In the years after the Restoration, Sir Leoline Jenkins, secretary of state in 1674-84, bought the manor of Moulton and surrounding properties.[10] In 1685 Sir Humphfrey Edwin, merchant and lord mayor of London, whose father came from Llandeilo, bought the Llanmihangel and Bettws estates and his son Samuel in 1718 added the Coity estate. In 1715, Abraham Barbour, a London lawyer, bought property at and around St. George's-super-Ely, settled there and made further purchases in the

[6] Beaupré was sold to Christopher Brewster. D. B. Hague, *Old Beaupré Castle* (Official Guidebook, 1965). I have not identified Brewster; but this seems one of the very few instances of the disintegration of a substantial gentry estate.

[7] R. Denning, 'The Thomas family of Wenvoe', S. Williams (ed.), *The Garden of Wales* (Cowbridge, 1961), pp. 106-15.

[8] Glam. RO, D/DF L/106.

[9] F. Jones, 'The Old Families of Wales', in D. Moore (ed.), *Wales in the Eighteenth Century* (Swansea, 1976), p. 40.

[10] W. Wynne, *Life of Sir Leoline Jenkins* (1724).

same area in 1724 from Viscount Windsor.[11] In 1749, William Bruce, of Mark Lane, London, a navy agent and banker, bought an estate at Duffryn near Aberdare and, about the same time, a property in Llanbleddian where he went to live. Both purchases were modest: Duffryn cost £1,800 and Llanbleddian was valued at £2,000.[12] In 1775, Peter Birt of Armin in Yorkshire, who had made a fortune from the Aire and Calder Navigation, bought Wenvoe. Even in the later-eighteenth and early-nineteenth centuries, when the market in estates was more active, there were few newcomers from outside. Sir Samuel Romilly acquired the manor of Barry in 1813, and part of the estates of Francis James Mathew, second earl of Llandaff, in 1818.[13] In 1811, Henry Grant, of Warmley in Hertfordshire, bought the old Mackworth estate at Gnoll.[14] And in 1820 Thomas Penrice, second son of a Yarmouth family, bought Kilvrough.

This does not purport to be a definitive list, but it is clear that there was not a large number of newcomers from a distance. The paucity of genuine newcomers in these three centuries is not really surprising. The county lay far from London: it was thus less attractive to wealthy Londoners as a place in which to settle. There were very few wealthy Londoners of Glamorgan origin for whom the attractions of return to their native county might have compensated for the distance. Moreover, when information about properties for sale was mainly spread by individual contacts, distance from London meant that there was a restricted market for estates far from the capital. Then again, few of the Glamorgan estates which were for sale were sufficiently large to attract the attention of the new man of great wealth who was prepared to range over a very wide area in his search for a suitable property. So far as the small estates were concerned, an occasional one was bought by a Londoner of modest fortune, for example, William Bruce and Abraham Barbour, attracted possibly by the cheapness of land in Glamorgan or possibly by some local contact of which the record is lost. But most small estates were bought by local families mainly to extend the main family property or to provide for younger sons. It was not until the later-eighteenth century, when indigenous fortunes were made from exploitation of minerals, that a large number of estates were acquired for the establishment of new families.[15]

It is therefore reasonable to regard Glamorgan from the sixteenth to the later-eighteenth century as an area where the sale and purchase of estates had a very limited effect on the distribution of landed property, and in particular did not provide the basis for the establishment of many new families by *nouveaux riches* originating outside the county. If we are interested in changes in landed property

[11] For Barbour's purchases, see deeds enrolled on the Close Rolls, PRO, C54/5240, 5262; Glam. RO, D/D MBN 21-33.

[12] Glam. RO, D/D Br. 75-79, 83-84, 122/1-5, 129/1-21; D/DE 549.

[13] Glam. RO, D/D Mat. 138-40: Survey of Lord Llandaff's estate in Llandaff and Whitchurch.

[14] Glam. RO, Gnoll Estate Records, D/D Gn 123-51, D/D Gn/E/170/26.

[15] Though in the longer term the greatest of these fortunes were expended on the purchase of properties outside the region—the Crawshays bought at Caversham and the Guests at Canford—initially the aspiring landowners bought where their fortunes were being made.

in Glamorgan, it is primarily to inheritance that we must look, and to the effects it produced in an age when expectation of life was low on the average but where the dispersion of individual experience around the average was considerable. There were many different patterns of succession: an estate might be inherited by a younger brother, or an uncle or a cousin; it might remain in the main male line but be enlarged by the generosity of a bachelor or spinster relation; it might be extended when its owner married an heiress or merged when it was inherited by a daughter and joined to the estate of her husband. The course of events on any particular estate depended partly on chance: death winnowed the families of landowners—like any other families—very arbitrarily. Some families inherited large properties as the result of a series of fortuitous events unforeseeable at the time of the marriage which was ultimately responsible for the inheritance. Some estates grew simply as a result of demographic luck.[16]

But it was not all fortuitous. The number of children born to a landowning family depended partly on the age of the marriage, and this was often influenced by calculation. Whether or not a younger son married was not simply a matter of individual temperament. Whether or not a bachelor uncle or cousin left his property to the main family line was certainly influenced by the state of family feeling prevailing in the social group. Above all, perhaps, the choice of brides was dominated by calculation.

It is primarily with the transmission of property *via* claims established by marriage that the rest of this essay is concerned, and in particular with the effect of marriage on the ownership of Glamorgan estates by families originating outside the county. It is not necessarily the most important question, but it is one which occurred naturally to a schoolboy in Glamorgan in the 1920s when the marquis of Bute, the Mackintosh of Mackintosh, the earl of Dunraven and the earl of Plymouth were still great names.

It is clear from the most casual inspection of the genealogies of Glamorgan families that there were many estates in the county which at some time passed into the hands of an heiress and that several did so more than once. Boverton, for example, passed by marriage in the sixteenth century from the Voss family to the Seys and in the eighteenth century from the Seys to the Jones of Fonmon. Ewenny went from one branch of the Carne family to another in the seventeenth century by marriage, to the Turbervilles by another and to the Picton family by two further marriages. Tythegston went from the Turbervilles to the Loughers, then to a branch of the Turbervilles and by another marriage to a Bristol family. The Bassetts acquired Beaupré in the middle ages by marriage with an heiress; and the main addition to the estates came from the marriage of Richard Bassett with a local heiress. The Mansell estates at Oxwich and Penrice, though extended by the purchase of former monastic property, were initially built up by marriage to heiresses. The examples could be multiplied many times.

In a great many of these marriages, both bride and bridegroom came from Glamorgan families. But in many ways the most interesting marriages are those

---

[16] I have not attempted to cover all accidents of succession, *e.g.,* those which resulted in the partition of the Stradling estates in Glamorgan and Somerset after the death of Sir Thomas Stradling in 1738 and the inheritance of St. Donat's by the Tyrwhitt-Drake family of Shardaloes (P.A. 27 & 28 Geo.II [1755] c. 9).

between the heiresses to Glamorgan estates and bridegrooms from outside the county. Such marriages can, of course, be found at any period. One of the most significant took place in 1492: that between Sir Charles Somerset and Elizabeth, only daughter and heir of William Herbert, second earl of Pembroke, which brought to the Somerset family the Welsh property which, as earls of Worcester and, later, dukes of Beaufort, they held for many centuries. The Dunraven estate passed from the Butlers to the Vaughans of Bredwardine by marriage in the early-sixteenth century. The most famous Glamorgan heiress of the sixteenth century—Barbara Gamage of Coity—married into an English landed family; in 1584, after complicated negotiations with several other possible husbands, she married Robert the younger son of Sir Henry Sidney and later earl of Leicester. But in many ways this is not typical of the fate of Welsh heiresses in the sixteenth century or indeed in the seventeenth. It was not simply that Coity was a very substantial property. The Gamage family was already linked by marriage with influential political interests and thus the 'clash over the hand of Barbara' not only involved local rivalries but was in part 'a struggle between court factions'.[17] There were other, less spectacular, marriages of Glamorgan heiresses to English families in the late-sixteenth and early-seventeenth centuries. Sir John Popham (died 1607) of Littlecote married the heiress of Castleton (St. Athan) and Llandow; Sir William Dodington of Hampshire married Mary, only child of Sir John Herbert (younger brother of Sir William Herbert of Swansea) and their son inherited Neath Abbey.

But, although marriage with outsiders was nothing new, there seems to be, in the later-seventeenth century, a perceptible increase in marriages between the heiresses of Glamorgan estates and husbands from outside the county. After the Restoration there was a series of marriages which had the effect of carrying substantial Glamorgan properties into the hands of non-Glamorgan—in most cases English—families.

In 1677 Bridget, a daughter of Walter Vaughan of Porthaml, married John, first Lord Ashburnham. Bridget was the heiress of the Vaughans of Dunraven in Glamorgan and Pembrey in Carmarthenshire. The family had sold Dunraven earlier in the century but they retained some Glamorgan property, and Bridget also brought Pembrey into her husband's family as well as Porthaml in Breconshire, which came from her mother, the heiress of Sir Thomas Knollys.[18] In 1686 Mary, the only surviving child of Sir Herbert Evans of the Gnoll, Neath, married Humphfrey Mackworth, second son of a Shropshire squire. In 1703 Charlotte, daughter of Philip, seventh earl of Pembroke and heiress to his Glamorgan estates, married Thomas Windsor, first son of the second marriage of the first earl of Plymouth. In 1705 Jane, sister of Sir Charles Kemys of Cefnmabli, married Sir John Tynte of Halsewell, Somerset, and when Sir Charles died a bachelor in 1735 the Welsh estate came to the Tyntes. In 1708 Cecil, daughter and heiress of Charles Matthews of Castell y Mynach, and ultimately heiress to her uncle, Richard Jenkins of Hensol, married Charles Talbot, the future lord chancellor.

---

[17] G. Williams (ed.), *Glamorgan County History*, vol. IV (Cardiff, 1974), ch. III, pp. 183-6.
[18] T. Jones, *History of Brecknock* (enlarged Glanusk), III (1911), 43.

Thomas Wyndham, a younger son of Francis Wyndham of Cromer (*c.* 1686-1752), married two heiresses to Glamorgan estates. He married, first, a remote cousin, Jane, and as a result of this marriage he acquired the Dunraven estate, bought by Humphfrey Wyndham on the eve of the Civil War, and also a substantial estate at Clearwell in Gloucestershire. Jane died in 1723. He married, secondly, Anne Edwin, grand-daughter of the Sir Humphfrey Edwin who had bought Llanmihangel in 1685, and ultimate heiress to the extensive Edwin estates not only in Wales but in Surrey, Northamptonshire and Sussex. The properties of both wives went to Charles, the son of Thomas by the second marriage who took his mother's name of Edwin. [19]

In 1730 Elizabeth, only daughter and heiress of Thomas Lewis of St. Fagans and of Soberton in Hampshire, married Other, third earl of Plymouth. In 1752, Anne, the illegitimate daughter and heiress of Jocelyn, seventh earl of Leicester, married Henry Streatfield of an old Kentish family and brought to his family property in Glamorgan. In 1756 Cecil, only daughter and heiress of William, Earl Talbot, married George Rice of Newton—the representative of the long established Carmarthenshire family and later raised to the peerage as Lord Dynevor—and brought with her the Hensol estate. In 1757 Barbara, daughter and heiress of the fourth Lord Mansell, who inherited the Briton Ferry estate on his death in 1750, married the second Lord Vernon. [20] In 1766 came what proved to be the most rich in consequences of all these marriages: Charlotte, first daughter and eventually sole heiress of Herbert, Viscount Windsor, married John Stuart, eldest son of the third earl of Bute, who thus ultimately acquired the Welsh estates which had come into the Windsor family as the result of the marriage of another Charlotte in 1703. On a lower scale, sometime in the eighteenth century, Cecil Bassett, sister and heiress of William Bassett, of Meisgyn and Maes-y-felin, married Stephen White, a Bristol merchant. In 1708 Cecil, daughter and heiress of Richard Lougher of Tythegston, married Edward Turberville of Sutton and their daughter and heiress married Robert Knight of Bristol, who established himself at Tythegston. [21]

There was another marriage which ultimately led to the inheritance of estates in Glamorgan by a family whose base was outside the county. Mary, daughter of Thomas, first Lord Mansell, married John Ivory Talbot of Lacock Abbey in Wiltshire; when the male line of the Mansell family came to an end on the death of her brother, the fourth Lord Mansell, in 1750, the main family estates at Penrice

---

[19] Thomas acquired these properties as a result of his marriage with Jane, but the exact process is not entirely clear. The usual account is that she acquired the Glamorgan estates from her father on the death in childhood of her two brothers; and the *History of Parliament,* ed. R. R. Sedgwick, vol. II, p. 561, says that she inherited Clearwell from her uncle, Francis Wyndham. But it appears that on the death of Jane's father, in 1696 or 1697, when she was nine years' old, the Glamorgan estates passed to her uncle, Francis Wyndham of Clearwell, and that on his death in 1716 all the estates passed to his son John. In December 1724, shortly before his death, John left all his estates, in St. Bride's Major and Llanbleddian and in Clearwell, to Thomas Wyndham, the husband of his cousin Jane, who had died in September 1723 (Glam. RO, B. Cow 164/165).

[20] The only child of this marriage died before her mother, who in 1786 left the Briton Ferry estate, but subject to a life interest to her husband, to her cousin's second son, then aged six, on whose death in 1813 it came to the main line of the Jersey family.

[21] Robert Knight was the son of Sir John Knight, MP for Bristol.

and Margam passed by the will of the third Lord to the second of Mary's sons, the Revd Thomas Talbot.

In the later-eighteenth century there were fewer marriages which brought the estates of Glamorgan heiresses to landed families originally based outside the county. But there were a number. In 1779, Margaret, the only surviving child of William Bruce, the purchaser of Duffryn (Aberdare), married John Knight who is said to have come from Barnstaple.[22] The widow of the last Mackworth, who inherited the Gnoll property, brought it by marriage to Capel Hanbury Leigh of the Pontypool family. Mary, the heiress of the Dawkins family, inherited the family estate at Kilvrough and in 1791 married Baptiste Armand, the marquis of Choiseul. In 1802, Frances Ann Pryce, the heiress of Duffryn St. Nicholas, married the second son of the fifth earl of Stamford. In 1814 the Wyndham estates—Dunraven and Llanmihangel, joined by the two marriages of Thomas Wyndham in the eighteenth century—passed to the Quin family as a result of the marriage in 1810 of Caroline, daughter of the last Wyndham, to the son of Lord Adare. One could extend the list further. A substantial part of the Dynevor estates went to the Wingfield family by marriage in 1845 with a daughter and co-heir of the fourth Lord Dynevor. The estates of the Lucas family of Stouthall passed *via* an heiress to Colonel Robert Wood. The Mackintosh of Mackintosh acquired Cottrell by marriage with Harriet Richards. The Fonmon estates passed by marriage in 1906 to the Boothby family.

But though Glamorgan properties continued to change ownership as a result of the marriages of heiresses, there was never again such a concentration of such marriages as in the century or so after the Restoration and there is a presumption that particular influences were at work in this period. What were they?

In part, the increase in marriages involving Glamorgan heiresses in the later-seventeenth century may be fortuitous. It so happened that in the most substantial Glamorgan families there were very few heiresses in the sixteenth century and in the earlier-seventeenth. Throughout this period, for example, the Stradlings continued in the male line, and the first Mansell heiress belongs to the eighteenth century. It is possible that, if one or more of the other leading families of Glamorgan had, like the Gamages, ended with an heiress, the competition for her hand would have been equally far-flung, and the increase in marriage to English landowners in the later-seventeenth century would seem a less marked break. Some of the Glamorgan heiresses would always have commanded wide competitive bargaining for their hand at any period. No doubt if the Glamorgan estates of the earls of Pembroke had descended to an heiress in the late-sixteenth century, her hand would have been gained in marriage by an English nobleman.

But more was involved than chance. There were systematic influences—not necessarily the same throughout the period—which made the marriage of heiresses of particular significance for the disposition of landed property in the century or so after the Restoration. One such influence was the general widening of the geographical area from which marriage partners were drawn, the result of

[22] Glam. RO, D/D Br 71-74.

the increasing contacts between different parts of the country which arose from improved transport facilities and from the growth of London as a social, legal and political centre. Some landed families settled in Glamorgan had always had very wide contacts: the greatest of the indigenous families like the Mansells, the Stradlings, and Lewis of the Van, and those outsiders who had established substantial estates like the Wyndhams and the Edwins. But the number increased; a Glamorgan landed family was likely to have more friends and acquaintances in London in the early-eighteenth century than in the early-seventeenth, and this must have increased the probability of the marriage of Glamorgan brides and English husbands. For the same reason, more Glamorgan landowners took brides from beyond the county border, though not on the same scale. In what seems to have been the first of such marriages in the family, William Lewis of the Van (died 1661) married in 1648 as his first wife Margaret, daughter and heiress of Lawrence Banastre of Passenham in Northamptonshire and Boarstall in Buckinghamshire. Sometime before 1709 his nephew Thomas married the daughter and heiress of Sir Walter Curl of Soberton, a Hampshire baronet. Francis Gwyn of Llansannor in 1690 married Margaret Prideaux, the heiress of Forde Abbey. John Carne of Nash in 1728 married Elizabeth, a daughter and coheiress of Charles Loder of Hinton Waldrist and Marsham in Berkshire.

Such a broadening of the area from which marriage partners were drawn increased the chances that, in case of failure of the main line, property in Glamorgan would be inherited by a family outside the county. But there was more to it than that; there was an element of conscious planning and matrimonial strategy. In some of the cases we have mentioned, the bride was not known to be an heiress at the time of her marriage. Penrice and Margam came to the Talbots and Briton Ferry to the earls of Jersey as the result of unforeseen accidents of genealogy; and when he married his second wife Anne, Thomas Wyndham cannot have known she would inherit the Edwin property, since there was, presumably, a possibility that her brother would have children. The same explanations cannot therefore apply in all cases. It is, however, significant that the prospects of most of the heiress-brides were known at the time of marriage; not only Elizabeth Herbert and Barbara Gamage, but Bridget Vaughan, Mary Evans, Charlotte Herbert, Cecil Mathews, Elizabeth Lewis, Jane Wyndham, Cecil Talbot, Anne Sidney, Charlotte Windsor and Mary Dawkins were known to be heiresses. [23] Do their marriages reflect the marked changes which took place in the later-seventeenth century in the patterns of family settlement among landed families?

In the early part of the seventeenth century it was still common at the marriage to settle only the immediate maintenance of the couple and the amount of the jointure of the wife if she was widowed, and to leave other matters, and particularly the provision for the children, until later, sometimes until the father of the bridegroom came to make his will. [24] By the early-eighteenth century, in

[23] Though the full extent of Charlotte Windsor's inheritance cannot have been known until the death of her sister in 1772.

[24] G. T. Clark, *Cartae et Alia Munimenta quae ad Dominium de Glamorgancia Pertinent* (2nd ed., Cardiff, 1910), vol. IV, contains a number of such settlements, e.g. nos. 123, 125, 134.

contrast, it was usual at the marriage to provide with a considerable degree of precision for all the contingencies that could arise from the marriage, not only the couple's immediate income and the jointure, but the succession of the estate and the size of endowment for younger children, an endowment, moreover, which was varied according to circumstances.[25]

It may be that this increase in the contingencies for which provision was made in the marriage settlement was the result of new attitudes among landowners to marriage and family. It is, however, more likely that they arose from independent legal changes in the forms of settlement, and in particular from the development of the strict settlement under which the owner of a landed estate at any given time was only a tenant for life. Attempts to achieve such a state of affairs were made before the mid-seventeenth century, but they were greatly stimulated by the need to protect estates during the Interregnum. The new form of settlement spread with remarkable speed because of the abolition of feudal tenures in 1649 (confirmed in 1660) which not only removed a constraint on the marriage strategy of families who held any property by knight's service but also removed the Crown interest in frustrating stricter forms of settlement.

The new forms of settlement made it possible, and indeed to some extent necessary, to settle matters at the marriage of the eldest son and to include, in the negotiations for a bride, a very wide range of points at issue. If there was some change in the attitudes of landed families to marriage they were more a result than a cause of these alterations in law. The need—accepted by landed families—to negotiate a wide range of matters before a marriage could be agreed must have conditioned the attitudes of all members of the family, and in particular have increased the significance attached to purely material considerations.

There was another development which increased the importance of calculation in marriage negotiations: the very marked increase between the late-sixteenth and the seventeenth centuries in the size of dowries or portions which were given to daughters on marriage. Dowries became much greater not only in relation to the jointure provided by the husband's family, but also in relation to the income of the bride's family. Much more was at stake, therefore, even when a marriage did not involve an heiress.

It would, of course, be absurd to suppose that material considerations were ever absent in the marriages of the offspring of landed families. At no period, on the other hand, did material advantage totally exclude all other considerations. Even in the eighteenth century, many other factors were relevant: the general standing of a family, the acceptability of the partners to each other, their ages, the political and social connections of a family. And very occasionally romantic love: young men could fall in love even with heiresses and the marriage of John Bute with the daughter of the millionaire Edward Wortley Montagu in 1736, which at first sight looks like a typical example of a marriage for gain, was a runaway love-match made in spite of the refusal of the bride's father to make a settlement.[26]

[25] On the spread of new forms of settlement, see C. Lloyd Bonfield, 'Marriage Settlements, 1660-1740', in R. B. Outhwaite (ed.), *Marriage and Society* (1981).

[26] Hon. Mrs E. Wortley (ed.), *A Prime Minister and his Son* (London, 1925), pp. 9, 14.

The balance of considerations varied from one family to another and from one marriage to the next, in a way which makes it difficult to distinguish changes over time with any confidence. But it is difficult to follow the negotiations for brides from the later-seventeenth century onwards without feeling that weight was more consistently attached to the material prospects of the bride and bridegroom.

Other changes worked in the same direction. The progressive accumulation of debt incurred to provide for younger children, which was involved in the adoption of the strict settlement, made it more necessary for landed families to make good marriages. It is possible also that the change in the *form* of provision for younger sons had some effect. [27]

There were, therefore, changes within the structure of the landed family which sharpened the appreciation of well-endowed brides which in some measure had always been present. On a more profound level, the link between the possession of landed property and political influence was closer after the Revolution of 1688 and the attraction of accumulating or acquiring an estate by marriage to a landed heiress was all the greater. Why a particular partner was chosen it is rarely possible to say. For some Welsh families, correspondence survives which reveals the competition for the hand of a particular heiress. Thus, the Salusbury correspondence illuminates the events which led to the marriage in 1670 of the heiress of Bachymbyd to Sir Walter Bagot; and the Wynn letters show the rival claimants for the hand of the heiress of Gwydir, between 1675 and 1678. [28] I know of no correspondence of a Glamorgan family which illuminates in the same detail the network of contacts which produced eligible suitors and the negotiations about terms. But the general nature of the transactions is clear. And we may fairly infer that some families pursued an especially active matrimonial strategy, from the way in which heiress marriages seem to cluster. The eldest son of the earl of Ancaster who married the heiress of Gwydir, also married an heiress; and so, in his turn, did the eldest son of the next generation. When the second Lord Vernon married the Mansell heiress, he was only following the example of his father and grandfather. The Ashburnham marriage to Bridget Vaughan was the first of a series of such marriages. Three generations of the Butes married heiresses; when Charlotte Windsor died, the first marquis married the wealthy daughter of Coutts, the banker. Both the surviving sons of the first Lord Talbot married heiresses. Between 1668 and 1788, five out of six generations of the earl of Plymouth's family married heiresses. Such marriages seem to have gone in families. Consider the marriage of Mary Evans which brought the Gnoll estate to the Mackworth family: the father of the bridegroom had married the daughter and co-heiress of Richard Bulkeley of Buntingsdale in Shropshire; the bride's father had married Anne, daughter and co-heiress of William Morgan of Pencrug in Glen Usk.

Landed families sought heiresses more persistently. Were there also more heiresses to seek? Were the accidents of succession, for purely demographic reasons, more important from the late-seventeenth century than in the preceding

---

[27] See below p.

[28] W. J. Smith, *Calendar of Salusbury Correspondence* (Cardiff, 1954), letters nos. 413-38; *Calendar of Wynn of Gwydir Papers, 1515-1690* (National Library of Wales, Aberystwyth, 1926), pp. 412-42.

two centuries? The study of a sample of marriages by members of peers' families by David Thomas shows that a much higher proportion was to heiresses in the first forty years of the century than was the case afterwards and his evidence, while it does not conclusively prove that there were more heiresses—since the explanation might be that peerage families were more successful in competing for a static stock of heiresses—certainly suggests that there was an unusually large number of heiresses in the earlier part of the eighteenth century.[29] From a different line of approach, a number of studies have suggested that an unusually large number of landed families in the eighteenth century failed to perpetuate themselves in the direct male line, and that this failure was particularly marked among those owners of estates born in the later-seventeenth century and first part of the eighteenth century. This may partly have been the result of factors which influenced the population at large: during the first half of the eighteenth century there were several years of exceptionally high mortality. But the decisive change seems to have been on the side of fertility: as Dr Hollingsworth's work shows, the proportion of members of peerage families who ever married reaches a minimum among those who were born about the beginning of the eighteenth century and whose marriages would have taken place about the middle of the century; the fertility among peerage families was at its lowest in the cohorts born between 1675 and 1724.[30] It is difficult not to associate this low fertility—more celibacy, later marriages, fewer children—with the early impact of increasingly complex family settlements and of larger dowries, and it was indeed so associated by those critics who in the early-eighteenth century attacked the new forms of settlement.

Whatever the ultimate causes, more landed families in the first half of the eighteenth century must have produced only daughters. But the whole bias of the strict settlement in its pure form was towards primogeniture and the maintaining of the estate in the hands of a male heir. Why, then, did these daughters in the cases under examination inherit the paternal property? A full answer would require a detailed study of the individual family settlements. The brief answer is that the operation of the strict settlement during the first century of its existence was affected by high mortality, low fertility and celibacy among landed families. Some settlements did provide for the ultimate succession by females, as a remote contingency, and where there were successive failures of the male line the estate came ultimately to a daughter or sister under the terms of the settlement. More commonly, the accidents of birth and death meant that an estate came for a time into the hands of the representative of the family who was in a position to acquire the fee-simple and who was therefore free to dispose of the property and in so doing to respond to the claims of natural affection, to endow his daughters rather than some remote male collateral. Even, that is, when it was common practice among landed families to subject their estates to strict settlement, estates not

[29] D. Thomas, 'Social Origins of Marriage Partners of the British Peerage', *Population Studies*, XXVI (1972).

[30] J. P. Jenkins, 'The Demographic Decline of the Landed Gentry in the Eighteenth Century: a South Wales Study', *Welsh Hist. Rev.*, vol. 11, Number 1 (June 1982), pp. 31-49; C. Clay, 'Marriage, Inheritance, and the Rise of Large Estates in England, 1660-1815', *Economic Hist. Rev.*, XXI (1968), 503-18; T. H. Hollingsworth, 'The Demography of the British Peerage', Supplement to *Population Studies*, vol. XVIII, No. 2 (1964), pp. 21, 30.

infrequently fell out of settlement. Thus, when a father died before his eldest son came of age, the latter acquired the settled property as tenant-in-tail and could without difficulty acquire the fee-simple. Though he might be under pressure later to make a settlement of his estate, particularly if he married, his capacity to resist pressure was greater than if his father had survived, and he might be able to keep a large part of his property out of settlement and therefore to be disposed of at his discretion. And if such an eldest son remained a bachelor the whole of the estate might continue at his disposal and its future succession be determined by his will. There was another situation, though less common, in which the holder of a settled estate might acquire the fee-simple: when an estate was settled, the settlement sometimes provided that, if the sons of the settlor died without male issue, reversion to the property should rest in the settlor or that the settlor in these circumstances should have power to revoke the settlement. The general point is that, for demographic reasons, the succession of life-tenants, which was the essence of the strict settlement, was more likely to be interrupted in, say, the first century of the existence of such settlements than it was in the late-eighteenth and nineteenth centuries. The collective will of the family, which normally favoured the heir male against the heir general, was suspended only in a minority of families at any one time; and only for a time, since when the property came to the heiress, at her marriage or at her father's death, it was once again strictly settled. But it happened often enough to ensure that there was a substantial number of well-endowed daughters.[31]

The force of some of these influences abated later in the eighteenth century. Among peerage families, the proportion of married rose, the average family size increased to a peak in the early-nineteenth century, and during the second half of the eighteenth century mortality fell at an unprecedented rate. Fewer landed families died out in the male line, and the strict settlement worked much more as it was supposed to do in the classic expositions of the system by the great nineteenth-century conveyancers. There were fewer heiresses and possibly also they were sought less persistently. In the later-eighteenth century, too, the land market appears to have become more active, or at least to have provided more scope for the establishment of new landed families. Thus, although heiress marriages continued to be significant, they were a less powerful influence on the ownership of landed property than they had been in the century or so after the Restoration.

The discussion so far has concentrated on influences common to landed families in general: the large number of heiresses, the widening of the geographical area from which marriage partners were drawn, and the increased important attention paid to property in marriage negotiations. We should expect from such influences an increase in marriage between heiresses to Glamorgan estates and husbands from outside the county and, indeed, from outside Wales.

---

[31] In some cases, litigation was necessary to establish the claims of the heiress. The division of the Pembroke estates was challenged by the heir male: J. Davies, *Cardiff and the Marquesses of Bute* (Cardiff, 1981), p. 3. The claims of Anne, heiress of Jocelyn, seventh earl of Leicester, were finally settled by Private Act [20 Geo. II, c. 12].

But were there, in addition, some influences particular to the county? Some possibilities may be suggested. There were some changes on the supply side. The heiresses of the largest Glamorgan estates would have commanded a national interest among great landowners at any period. But this was not true of all. Some estates in the county had grown to a size which, when they were inherited by heiresses, made them attractive for acquisition by ambitious men outside the county; for instance, Cecil Mathews, Mary Evans of the Gnoll, Bridget Vaughan, Elizabeth Lewis each represented a concentration of property as a result of earlier marriages in their families, and so were able to command a wider range of interest. Possibly, too, heiresses were more common in Glamorgan. Dr J. P. Jenkins has shown how large was the number of landed families in the county which died out in the direct male line in the eighteenth century. While there is no reason to suppose that there were special regional influences on the marriages and births of the families of the more substantial landowners of the county, it may be that there were particular local pressures on the families of lesser gentry. It is also probable that the lesser gentry were slower than their English counterparts to adopt the strict settlement, so that their heirs general were better endowed.

It also appears to be the case that, on the average, heiresses to Glamorgan estates were better bargains on the marriage market than those whose estates were in central or southern England and therefore nearer the centres of social life and political power.[32] Hence, the husband's family had to commit less by way of jointure, immediate provision for the couple, and settlement on the younger children. It was commonplace in the eighteenth century that a younger son of a landed family needed to marry an heiress.[33] He was no longer provided with a piece of property but with a rent charge on the undivided family estate. It was impossible to buy a property out of income, even when the younger son was in the early stages of a promising career. Younger sons who wanted to remain in the class of landowner therefore hunted heiresses. But, because of their limited means, they were not in a strong position to compete with eldest brothers and they looked for heiresses available on good terms. For this reason the heiresses of estates in Glamorgan may have been particularly attractive to the marginal members of landed society. Humphfrey Mackworth and Thomas Wyndham were younger sons. Charles Talbot was a first son of William, bishop of Durham (himself a younger son of the Talbots of Lacock), without great paternal property and on the make as a lawyer at the time of his marriage. Thomas Windsor was the first son of a second marriage and a soldier on the make. Ashburnham was, of course, *not* a younger son, but in 1677 the family property was quite incommensurate with their dignity. John Stuart is a clear exception, for, five years before his marriage to Charlotte, his mother had inherited large estates in Yorkshire and Cornwall under the will of her father, Edward Wortley Montagu. But he did not in fact succeed to his mother's estate until her death in 1794. The estate of the prime minister, his father, was not extensive: the

---

[32] There is no evidence that I know of that Glamorgan heiresses were particularly attractive because of any likelihood that their estates contained minerals.

[33] See Thomas, op. cit., Table 8, p. 107, for the proportion of younger sons of peerage families who married heiresses.

Mackenzie estates which had come into the family by marriage went to a younger brother of the prime minister, and though Bute bought Luton Hoo for £114,000 in 1763—three years before the marriage of his own son to the heiress of Cardiff—some of the money for the purpose was borrowed. In the event, Bute did not die until 1792. John Stuart could not have known that he would spend the first twenty-six years after his marriage as an heir apparent; but it was clear in 1766 that to support his rank and standing he, too, needed a great heiress.

There is a complex relationship between marrying outside one's station and marrying outside one's county, between, that is, the social class from which landowners drew their marriage partners and the geographical area from which they drew them. Dr Hollingsworth, in his pioneering study of the demography of the British peerage, concluded that in the early-eighteenth century, and particularly between 1710 and 1735, the children of peers became notably less likely to marry within their own narrow class. But it is clear from Mr Thomas's study that, though there was a high proportion of marriages between the children of peers and commoners, 'the marriages outside the Peerage took place in a narrowly-defined band of privilege and social acceptability'.[34] At least at the level of peerage families there were strong barriers to the social extension of the field of marriage partners. An extension of the geographical area of choice was, to some extent, a consequence of social exclusivity or, perhaps, a condition for the maintenance of the conventions of endogamy. The first Lord Ashburnham could have married the heiress of a London merchant; instead he chose as his bride the heiress of an ancient gentry estate, even though the estates she brought with her were remote from those of the Ashburnhams. One might speculate that it was the contraction in the supply of heiresses, within the range of acceptable social standing, in their own county or region which sustained the interest of English landowners in Welsh heiresses for so long a period.

From causes we turn to consequences. The accidents of succession could combine in a great variety of ways and have very different effects on the fortunes of particular families. It is therefore hazardous to generalise about their net effect on the disposition of property. All that is possible is to pose the relevant questions and suggest tentative answers.

Did marriage to heiresses lead to the agglomeration of estates, to the growth of the property inherited by the eldest son of the family? In many cases clearly not. For some families one of the attractions of marriage with an heiress was that it provided a property on which a younger son of the marriage could be settled. This attraction was particularly strong when land was the common form of provision for younger children, but it retained some force even after the rent charge had replaced land as the most common form of provision. Moreover, the development of more precise forms of settlement, which regulated in exhaustive detail the succession to the different properties under consideration, made it easier to specify for the property of an heiress a succession different from that of her

[34] Hollingsworth, op. cit., p. 9; Thomas, op. cit., p. 3.

husband's. Particularly when the heiress brought with her an estate which had been in her family for a long time, it might be disposed of in a way which ensured its continued separate identity. Thus, as we have seen, the main Mansell estates at Penrice and Margam were settled by the will of the third Lord Mansell on the *second* of his sister's sons. The Briton Ferry property, which the fourth Lord Mansell had been left by his god-father and distant kinsman, went under his will to his *daughter* who, by will, left it to William Augustus Henry Villiers, the *second* son of her cousin, George Bussy, fourth earl of Jersey. Clearly respect was often paid by landowners to the separate identity of estates or properties which they had inherited from different ancestors, even when they were not compelled to do so by wills or settlements.

It by no means followed necessarily, therefore, that the property of an heiress went to the main line. But in the most important of the cases under consideration it did in fact do so. In some instances, no doubt, this was because there was no younger son of the marriage; the low birth rate which produced in some families only daughters, in others produced an only son. In other instances it was the result of a conscious attempt to keep the properties together. In either case, some very large estates were created. A conspicuous example is the Hensol estate. Charles Talbot ultimately acquired, as the result of his marriage with Cecil Mathews, her father's estate at Castell y Mynach, half her maternal grandmother's estate of the Prichards of Llancaeach, her maternal grandfather's estate at Hensol and the Newton estate in Breconshire which came to her *via* her uncle's marriage with the heiress of Newton. Charles's eldest son, William, married Mary, daughter and heiress of Adam de Cardonnel, the secretary of war, and the marriage of the only daughter and heiress of this marriage carried the major part of this large collection of estates to the Rice family, who were themselves great landowners in Carmarthenshire. The estates acquired by the Ashburnhams, the Plymouths, the Butes, and Thomas Wyndham likewise descended with the main line.

It might be supposed that the Glamorgan properties acquired by marriage were more likely to be sold than the ancestral properties of the husband. But this does not seem to have been the case. The estates of some heiresses were burdened with debt; the father who was free to leave his property away from the male line was also by the same token likely to be free to mortgage it, and was also less constrained in his expenditure than were landowners with a male heir.[35] Heiresses therefore sometimes brought with them debts as well as assets, and the debts might ultimately make it necessary to sell land. But not necessarily the land of the heiress. The Ashburnhams' Welsh estate bore a heavy mortgage of £16,000 to William Sloper, the Pay Office official and MP; but when in the 1720s the

---

[35] Contemporary comment sometimes exaggerated the fortunes of heiresses. Under her marriage settlement, Elizabeth Lewis had a dowry of £40,000 of which £15,000 was paid down and £25,000 secured to be paid on her father's death; the earl of Plymouth settled estates worth £4,000 *p.a.* On the death of Thomas Lewis it was reported by contemporaries that the son of the marriage inherited an estate of £8,000 *p.a.* from his grandfather. But this was a great exaggeration and the estate was burdened with mortgages, legacies and bond debts not far short of its capital value (Historical Manuscripts Commission, *Carlisle MSS.*, p. 175; *Gentleman's Magazine*, VI, 685; P.A. 14 Geo. II [1741], c. 7).

family sold land in order to repay debts, it was property in Bedfordshire they chose—the former royal parks of Brogborough, Beckerings and Ampthill granted by Charles I—presumably because they commanded a better market, and possibly also because the son of Bridget Vaughan had sentimental attachment to her family estate.[36] The Lewis estate was burdened with extraordinarily large debts at the time of the marriage of Elizabeth Lewis to the earl of Plymouth, but it was the Hampshire estate the family opted to sell, not St. Fagans.[37] Some attrition by sale, of course, there was. The properties acquired by an heiress were on the whole more likely to be sold, when the going got hard or when an attempt was made to consolidate, than the ancestral core of the estate. The second Lord Talbot sold Newton, for example; the earl of Plymouth sold Soberton; Sir Edmund Thomas of Wenvoe, whose family had acquired Rhiwperra by a marriage in 1655, sold it in 1706, some seventy years before parting with Wenvoe.[38] The Streatfield family eventually sold the Sidney estate in Glamorgan acquired by marriage in 1752, though it was retained until 1809. Capel Hanbury Leigh and his wife disposed of Gnoll in 1811. But it does not appear to be the case that the Glamorgan estates acquired by an outside family were particularly likely to be sold. Some families indeed added to their Glamorgan properties by purchase: to judge from the size of their estates in the county at the New Doomsday of 1873, the Butes and the Jerseys, and the owners of the Dunraven estates, did so.

Thus, the net effect of the marriages we have considered was to increase the size of estates. Moreover, as a result of marriage, many Glamorgan properties became part of a great estate represented in several parts of the kingdom. The Beauforts had 51,000 acres in five counties; the Butes 116,000 acres in eight counties; the earl of Dunraven 40,000 in Wales, England and Ireland; Lord Dynevor 10,700 in five counties; the earl of Jersey about 20,000 in five counties; the Kemeys-Tynte estate was over 20,000 acres in six counties; Lord Windsor owned 37,000 in five counties; the Wingfield family (one of whom had married the daughter and co-heiress of the fourth Lord Dynevor) owned 18,800 acres in four counties; the Ashburnhams owned 24,500 acres in four counties.[39] Purchase could of course bring about the same result. But there appear to have been only two cases of widely spread major estates represented in Glamorgan in 1873 which were built up largely by purchase: those of Lord Wimborne representing the Guests—83,500 acres in five counties—and those of Crawshay Bailey—13,600 acres in six counties. Marriage was a more powerful agent than purchase in lodging Glamorgan property in large landed estates.

The fact that a Glamorgan property was incorporated into a great estate had consequences for its management. In the case of the Butes, it is clear from the work of Dr John Davies that there was some cross-fertilisation between their

[36] P.A. 12 Geo. I (1725), c. 1; Bedfordshire RO, D.D.H/DE12.

[37] Glam. RO, Merthyr Mawr Estate Records: D/D N. 720-731.

[38] Soberton was sold to Humphfrey Minchin of an Irish family. *VCH, Hampshire*, III, 259.

[39] See under the relevant names in J. Bateman, *The Great Landowners of Great Britain and Ireland*, reprinted with introd. by D. Spring (Leicester, 1971); and B. L. James, 'The "Great" Landowners of Wales', *National Library of Wales Journal*, XIV (1965-6), 301-20.

Glamorgan estates and those they owned in other parts of the kingdom. The management of their Welsh properties was in the hands of trustees and agents of higher calibre than in all probability they would have enjoyed had these not been linked to a major landed estate. The Butes invested in their Glamorgan properties on a scale and at a rate which was not warranted by the return they received or could reasonably have expected to receive; and the rapidity of the economic development of Glamorgan was accelerated by this 'subsidised' investment. This feature of the Butes' management may well have been due primarily to the personality and interests of the second marquis, and thus not shed much light on what happened elsewhere. But studies of the management of the resources of other great territorial agglomerations—not represented in Glamorgan but like the Bute estates built up by lucrative marriages—suggest that there were some features common to great estates, and that the development of resources during industrialisation was influenced to a remarkable extent by management and settlement patterns devised initially to meet the needs of great landed families long before the Industrial Revolution. There are interesting similarities—as well as some significant differences—between the policies of the Bute family and those of the duke of Bridgewater, the duke of Sutherland and the duke of Devonshire.[40] How far were there similar features in the development of their Glamorgan estates by the earls of Plymouth and the earls of Jersey?

The effects on a Glamorgan estate of merger with a large agglomeration must be distinguished from the economic effects of absenteeism. When two estates were united by marriage with an heiress, a family normally acquired a second estate and had to decide which should be the main focus of its activities. In some cases it was the husband who came to live on his wife's property: Humphrey Mackworth came to live at Gnoll, Thomas Wyndham established himself at Dunraven, and Charles Talbot at Hensol, no doubt because each of them was initially not a man of great property. The two English merchants who married Glamorgan heiresses used the estates so acquired as the basis of a resident landed family. But where the husband was already a landowner of substance, he became in his Welsh estates an absentee owner. The Ashburnhams lived in Sussex. The earls of Leicester seem sporadically to have used their Glamorgan estate as a home for the younger son. The Butes only intermittently used Cardiff Castle as a residence; and for much of their ownership—for at least the first half of the nineteenth century—the earls of Plymouth did not reside at St. Fagans. The earls of Jersey never lived at Briton Ferry. In some of these cases, the heiress came from a family that was already non-resident; the Bute family, indeed, paid more not less attention to their Glamorgan estates than the Herberts who preceded them, and the Lewis family left St. Fagans before the property passed to the earls of Plymouth. There is no doubt, however, that the net effect of the marriages with Glamorgan heiresses was to extend absentee ownership. This was not, of course, the only

[40] E. Richards, *The Leviathan of Wealth: the Sutherland fortune in the Industrial Revolution* (London, 1973); J. R. Wordie, *Estate Management in Eighteenth-Century England: The Building of the Leveson-Gower Fortune* (R. Hist. Soc., Studies in History Ser. No. 30, 1982), ch. 3; D. Spring, 'English Landed Estate in the Age of Coal and Iron', *Journal of Economic History*, II (1951); S. Pollard, 'Barrow-in-Furness and the Seventh Duke of Devonshire', *Economic Hist. Rev.*, 2nd ser., VIII (1955); H. Mallet, *The Canal Duke* (1961).

factor making for absenteeism. The marriage of Glamorgan landowners to English heiresses might have the same effect. After the marriage of Francis Gwynn in 1690 to the heiress of the Prideaux family, the family deserted Llansannor for Dorset. When Thomas Lewis married the daughter and heiress of Sir Walter Curll of Soberton, this branch of the Lewis family went to live in Hampshire. After his marriage to Margaret Banastre, William Lewis seems to have lived on his wife's estate at Boarstall. When Boarstall passed by the second marriage of his grand-daughter, another heiress, to the Aubreys of Llantriddyd, the Aubreys in their turn deserted their Welsh estates for Boarstall. When Llanharan after 1856 passed to Caroline Anne, niece of Richard Hoare Jenkins, and to her son John Blandy (who added the name of Jenkins) of Kingston Bagpuize in Oxfordshire, the Welsh property seems for long periods to have been deserted in favour of Kingston House. Absentee ownership could also arise from purchase. In the late-seventeenth century, Sker passed by purchase to Charles Price of Badminton and then to John Curre of Rogerston (Mon.), the Beaufort agent in Glamorgan, but there is no evidence that either lived there and the house seems to have been let to tenants. In general, however, Glamorgan was not a county in which outsiders bought purely for investment; when an outsider like Edwin or Birt bought, he did so in order to settle in the county. Absentee ownership was the outcome primarily of accidents of succession.

Absentee ownership had some common features. A village—or at least an area—was deprived of its leading family and of the social stimulus and support it was capable of giving. We need detailed studies of what actually happened when, for example the Aubreys deserted Llantriddyd and Hensol passed to Lord Dynevor. It meant secondly that the agent or steward became of crucial importance in the management of the estate.[41] The agents of the Bute Welsh estates were men of substance in their own right. So was the steward of the earl of Leicester's estates in Glamorgan, Rees Powell (died 1785), who created an estate of his own at Llanharan; and the Randalls who provided agents for the Dunraven estates for a hundred years.[42] The nature of their activities needs to be studied in detail.

Marriage with heiresses also brought additional mansion houses into the family. A landowner who acquired an extra house might use it in a number of ways. He could go and live there himself, as Sir Rice Mansell did when he acquired by marriage a life interest in Beaupré, or as Edward Turberville of Sutton did when he succeeded to Ewenny on the death of his brother-in-law, Richard Carne, in 1713. A second possibility was that the family retained the extra house as a subsidiary family house for use during part of the year, as the Butes did with Cardiff. Cefnmabli became a subsidiary seat of the Tynte family when the estate fell to the sister of the last male heir of the Kemys family in 1735; and Rhiwperra when acquired by Thomas of Wenvoe. The extra house could be

---

[41] For absentee ownership, see the study of the management of the Gwydir estate by Lord Willoughby d'Eresby in G. H. Davies, 'Estate Management in Dyffryn Conwy, *circa* 1685', *Trans. Hon. Soc. Cymmrodorion*, 1979, pp. 60-73; P. Roebuck, 'Absentee Ownership in the late seventeenth and early eighteenth centuries', *Agricultural Hist. Rev.*, XXI (1973), part 1, pp. 1-17.

[42] W. H. Wyndham-Quin, fifth earl of Dunraven, *Dunraven Castle* (1926), pp. 44-6.

used to provide a home for the eldest son during his father's life. The Bassett family used Fishwear, acquired in the late-sixteenth century by an heiress marriage, as a home for the eldest son during his father's life and as a residence for the main family when they were forced by fines to leave Beaupré during the Interregnum. Likewise Aberthin was used to accommodate the family of a younger son after it came to the Mathews of Castell y Mynach. The Edwin family, when they bought a property which incorporated distinct estates, seems to have largely rebuilt one of them—at Bettws—about 1700 and it is possible that, though it ultimately became a ruin, they used it for younger children. An additional house could also be used as the dower house. Clearwell Court, the Gloucestershire home of the Dunraven family, was used for this purpose in the nineteenth century. Or an additional house might be used to accommodate the estate agent—as, in the early-nineteenth century, Llanmihangel was used for John Franklen, manager of the Dunraven estates. There was occasionally scope for leasing a redundant house to another gentry family. Occasionally, too, one or other of the houses—not necessarily that of the heiress—was sold; Edward Turberville sold his paternal mansion at Sutton.

An additional house could, therefore, be turned to good use in meeting changing family circumstances. But probably in the largest single number of cases, the extra mansions were leased to tenant-farmers, especially those mansions once the homes of small Welsh squires. In the most favourable circumstances they became farm houses, with the possibility of restoration; in the least favourable circumstances they fell into ruin. When the Seys house at Boverton passed to the Jones of Fonmon, the house became a farmhouse and ultimately a ruin. Flemingston Court became the home of a tenant-farmer. Llantrithyd Place fell into ruin in the nineteenth century. After Soberton had been acquired, St. Fagans seems to have been largely dismantled by 1736.

This essay has concentrated on heiresses to estates in Glamorgan. There are many instances in other Welsh counties of the acquisition of estates by families outside the county, usually English or Scottish landowners, by a process similar to that already discussed. The marriage in 1678 of Robert Bertie, later duke of Ancaster, to Mary, daughter and heiress of Sir Richard Wynn of Gwydir, brought large Welsh estates to the Bertie family. At the other end of the country, the marriage in 1689 of Elizabeth, sister and heiress of Sir Gilbert Lort of Stackpole Court, to Sir Alexander Campbell of Cawdor in Nairnshire brought to the Campbells substantial property in Pembrokeshire which was added to when, in 1726, John, the son of this marriage, married a daughter and co-heiress of Lewis Pryse of Gogerddan and so acquired lands in Cardiganshire.[43] In 1749 Charles Pratt, the first Lord Camden—like Charles Talbot, a rising lawyer early in his career—married Elizabeth, eventually the sole heiress of the Jeffreys family of Brecknock Priory. In 1758 William Hamilton, a fourth son, married Catherine, the only child of the second marriage of John Barlow of the Slebech family who

---

[43] D. Williams, *The Rebecca Riots* (Cardiff, 1955), p. 5.

brought to her husband considerable property in Pembrokeshire.[44] In 1751 Barbara Herbert, the heir general of the Herberts of Powys Castle, married Arthur, Lord Herbert of Cherbury, the divisee of the estates of the Powys Castle family under the arbitrary will of Barbara's grandfather. (In this case the marriage was not simply the result of the ambition of the Herberts of Cherbury to add to their estates; it sprang also from the plan of the first marquis of Powys for repairing the confusion into which his family affairs had been thrown by losses in the South Sea Bubble.)[45] In 1784 Henrietta Anonia, sister of the second and last earl of Powis, married Edward, second Lord Clive, and on the death of her bachelor brother in 1801 she inherited most of the properties which had come to this branch of the Herberts by the marriage with Barbara in 1751. All these marriages were the result of calculation; all involved the creation of larger estates; and some resulted in absentee ownership. Such examples give some reason for believing that what was true of Glamorgan was true of other parts of Wales. But was it equally true of any area remote from London or was it a specifically Welsh phenomenon? The answer to that question must remain for another occasion.

[44] F. Green, 'The Barlows of Slebech', *West Wales Hist. Records*, III (Carmarthen, 1913), 150; B. G. Charles, 'The Records of Slebech', *National Library of Wales Journal*, V (1947-8).

[45] For the marriage of Barbara, see J. Brown, *Reports of cases upon appeals . . . in the high court of Parliament* (1779-83), VI, 102-14.

From Long Knives to Blue Books

PRYS MORGAN

T HE Treason of the Blue Books is an expression which every Welsh schoolboy knows. He might also know that the reports of three commissioners sent by the government to look into the state of education and the moral condition of the common people of Wales in 1846 were published the following year in the form of Blue Books, and that their publication caused a great furore. David Owen ('Brutus') observed in the Anglican journal, *Yr Haul*, in 1847 that Wales had never seen such a rumpus before, and it was then only beginning. The 'Blue Books' have always remained controversial. Some have argued that their publication marked a greater turning-point in Welsh history than the election of 1868[1]; some have said that it was the furore over their publication which inaugurated the golden age of Welsh radicalism, and even fanned the flames of a growing nationalism[2]; while others have blamed the Blue Books for the great advance of anglicisation in the later nineteenth century.[3] Glanmor Williams has emphasised their tragic aspect:

> It is difficult to think of any other single factor which did so much to exacerbate Church/Chapel relations or to poison all hope of educational cooperation as the publication of the Report of 1847.[4]

The 'Blue Books' are without doubt of the greatest importance. But what kind of treachery is involved here that should give such an ill-omened nickname to governmental education reports? Professor Williams has more than once touched on the theme of treachery in Welsh history, of how a people may brood in centuries of defeat on their traitors, creating a mass of mythical lore and prophetic legends to compensate for their losses and sustain their hope.[5]

'The Treason of the Blue Books' (*Brad y Llyfrau Gleision*) is an historical pun on a Welsh legend of the Dark Ages known as 'The Treason of the Long Knives' (*Brad y Cyllyll Hirion*). It has been often stated, as in the Blue Books of 1847, that the Welsh Victorians were better informed about the history of the people of Israel than about the history of the people of Wales, but this cannot have been wholly true. O. W. Jones ('Glasynys') said in his history of Beddgelert in 1860 that

---

[1] T. Evans, *The Background to Modern Welsh Politics, 1789-1846* (Cardiff, 1936), p. 230.

[2] F. P. Jones, 'Effaith Brad y Llyfrau Gleision', in *Radicaliaeth a'r Werin Gymreig yn y Bedwaredd Ganrif ar Bymtheg* (Cardiff, 1977), pp. 48-64. K. O. Morgan, *Wales in British Politics, 1868-1922* (3rd ed., Cardiff, 1980), pp. 16-17, calls the 'treachery' the Glencoe and the Amritsar of Welsh history.

[3] D. G. Jones, *Seiliau Hanesyddol Cenedlaetholdeb Cymru* (Cardiff, 1950), pp. 106-8; G. Evans, *Land of my Fathers* (Swansea, 1974), pp. 366-74.

[4] *Religion, Language and Nationality in Wales* (Cardiff, 1979), p. 105.

[5] 'Prophecy, Poetry and Politics in Medieval and Tudor Wales', in H. Hearder and H. R. Loyn (eds.), *British Government and Administration* (Cardiff, 1974), pp. 104-16, reprinted in *Religion, Language and Nationality*.

Welsh children were not being brought up as they used to be, in the decent manner of the past, in the sound of ancient Welsh legends. 'Glasynys' was a rather reactionary folklorist, but his views were echoed by those of a very different character: the politician Henry Richard, who observed in his essays on Wales, published first in 1867, that in his youth the Welsh were familiar not so much with theology, certainly not with politics, but with ancient tales and legends; and he quoted among his examples 'The Treason of the Long Knives'.[6] Unless the people of Wales were familiar with such myths and legends, a journalist or satirist would never have sought to mock the Blue Books by comparing them with such a remote event, and the people would never have turned the elaborate historical pun into a household word. What, then, was this legend?

Out of the military and political confusion that followed the departure of the Roman legions from Britain, Vortigern is thought to have emerged as a leader of the Britons about the middle of the fifth century AD. His rule being threatened by vast hordes of Irish and Pictish invaders, he turned for help to a host of Saxon mercenaries from across the North Sea who fought under the command of two brothers, Hengist and Horsa. The next stage in the development of the legendary tale is that Hengist, by an act of deceit, managed to secure a foothold for his people on the Kent coast, and again by deceit he managed to make Vortigern drunk at a banquet for the British leaders, thereby enticing Vortigern to fall in love with Hengist's daughter (later called Rowena, Rhonwen, or Alice). Although a heathen, Rowena became the Christian Vortigern's wife. The Britons then rose in anger against their leader Vortigern and set up his son Vortemir as king. The Saxons again used treachery, for Rowena succeeded in killing the good Vortemir by poison and engineered Vortigern's return to power. By this time some years had passed and the Saxon host, having rid Vortigern of the Irish and Pictish menace, had gone back across the North Sea. Rowena invited them back to Britain, for she and Hengist had a deep-laid plot to take over the whole island. Having arrived, Hengist invited Vortigern and all the British nobles to a banquet, with Saxon and Briton sitting alternately along the table. Every Saxon had concealed in his hose or shoe a dagger or long knife. Suddenly, in the middle of the feast, Hengist gave a signal *Nemet eour Saxes!* (Grab your knives!) and each Saxon slew the Briton next to him. Vortigern alone was spared, and with hundreds of his subjects dead about him, he was forced to cede to the Saxons large areas of eastern Britain which became their permanent home. Vortigern subsequently fled westwards into the mountains of what became Wales, and after several adventures he died there.[7]

Some simple elements of this tale appear less than a century after the supposed death of Vortigern, in the writings of Gildas on the sufferings of the Britons about

---

[6] S. Lewis, *Straeon Glasynys* (Clwb Llyfrau Cymraeg, 1943), pp. xxiv-xxv; H. Richard, *Letters on the social and political condition of the Principality of Wales* (London, 1867), p. 33.

[7] T. Evans, *Drych y Prif Oesoedd* (2nd ed., Shrewsbury, 1740), pp. 93-113. For the 'Nennius' version, see A. W. Wade-Evans (ed.), *Nennius's History of the Britons* (London, 1938), and J. Morris (ed.), *British History and the Welsh Annals* (London, 1980). But see also J. E. Turville-Petre, 'Hengist and Horsa', *Saga-book of the Viking Society*, XIV (1953-7), 273-90; D. P. Kirby, 'Vortigern', *Bull. Board of Celtic Studies*, XXIII (1968), 37-59; D. N. Dumville, 'Sub-Roman Britain: History and Legend', *History*, LXII (1977), 173-92 (esp. pp. 183-4).

the middle of the sixth century. Gildas refers to a 'proud leader' who let the Saxons into Britain. Around two centuries after that, the annals attributed to Nennius give a proper name, Vortigern, to the evil man who had ceded the land to the Saxons, and by this time a mass of legends had gathered about his name and deeds (or misdeeds). The Venerable Bede had also encountered similar stories among the English. It is indeed possible that the story of the Long Knives is not a Welsh story in origin, but borrowed by the Welsh from early Saxon tradition, for a similar tale of The Night of the Long Knives occurs in Widukind's chronicle of the early Saxons in Germany. It is from Widukind that the Long Knives became part of German mythology, and this is why the Roehm purge by Hitler in 1934 is described as 'The Night of the Long Knives'. [8]

In the twelfth century the old story was given a new lease of life, transformed by the magic wand of Geoffrey of Monmouth in his *Historia Regum Britanniae*. The *femme fatale* of the original tale is nameless. It is Geoffrey who called her Rhonwen or Rowena. The story was given power and shape by Geoffrey and returned to Welsh native tradition as if it were real history. It can be seen from the Welsh triads and the verse of the *cywydd* poets that tales of Hengist, Vortigern and Rowena had long currency. [9] One of the main themes of Welsh historical thought in the middle ages was that of the resistance of the brave Welsh against treacherous and deceitful conquerors. Such stories helped to foster what might be called Welsh *irredentism,* an obsession with reconquering Britain from the English, which bedevilled the Welsh for centuries. Examples of the story in the verse of late-medieval bards appear in the work of Dafydd Nanmor, Guto'r Glyn, Gutyn Owain and Tudur Aled. [10] The English nation are called 'the children (or grandchildren) of Rowena'. Later on, at the end of the middle ages, the alternative form, 'the children of Alice', is found.

The element of prophecy is missing from the earlier versions of such tales, but it gradually colours the Welsh tradition. The English said that such tales were used by the Welsh leaders and their bards to whip up resistance to the English. The Long Knives story could be said to show that divine approval would never be granted to a conquest made through deceit and treachery, and therefore Britain was sure to return one day to its true owners, the Welsh. Professor Williams has shown that although this complex tradition of political prophecy, feeding on poetic myths and legends such as that of the Long Knives, flourished in the later middle ages, it atrophied and died during the sixteenth century. [11]

Deprived of their moral and political force by the changed circumstances of the Welsh in the Tudor period, such tales nevertheless survived as entertaining fireside fables, side by side with tales of knights, saints and hobgoblins. The old

[8] H. M. Chadwick, *The Origin of the English Nation* (Cambridge, 1907), pp. 38, 41-3, 50.

[9] R. Bromwich, *Trioedd Ynys Prydein: The Welsh Triads* (2nd ed., Cardiff, 1978), pp. 498-9, 553-4, 562.

[10] T. Roberts and I. Williams (eds.), *Poetical Works of Dafydd Nanmor* (Cardiff, 1929), pp. 41, 68, 157, 179; J. Ll. Williams and I. Williams (eds.), *Gwaith Guto'r Glyn* (Cardiff, 1939), pp. 135, 143; E. Bachellery, *L'oeuvre poétique de Gutun Owain* (Paris, 1950-1), XVII, 44n., p. 111; T. G. Jones (ed.), *Gwaith Tudur Aled* (Cardiff, 1926), XLVII, 65. There are further references in J. E. C. Williams, 'Ronwen: Rhawn Gwynion', *Bull. Board of Celtic Studies,* XXI (1966), 301-3.

[11] 'Prophecy, Poetry and Politics', pp. 106.

story was still current, as can be seen from the mid-seventeenth-century ballad of Matthew Owen of Llangar called 'The History of the Welsh'. The scholar Richard Morris copied it in his youth early in the eighteenth century and it was reprinted several times in anthologies of ballad verse. Daniel Defoe, who published his travel book on Britain in 1724, remarked on 'the yellow mountains of Radnorshire' that 'the stories of Vortigern, and Roger of Mortimer, are in every old woman's mouth here'. It seems quite likely that the 'Long Knives' was one of these stories. [12]

As if to mirror a gradual reappearance of Welsh pride and self-consciousness in the eighteenth century, the old story reappeared in 1716 with great panache in *Drych y Prif Oesoedd* (Mirror of Primitive Ages), the popular history book by Theophilus Evans. [13] He devotes a full chapter to the misdeeds of Vortigern and a lively blow by blow account of the Treason of the Long Knives. Evans was also familiar with the parallel Saxon tale from the chronicle of Widukind. He claimed to have seen with his own eyes an object then considered to be one of the self-same knives used by Hengist's henchmen. A tall story this, but proof that the tradition was still current in Evans's time. Theophilus Evans, in fact, gave new currency and freshness to the story, just as Geoffrey of Monmouth had done centuries before. Amongst the Welsh antiquarians of the eighteenth century, for example, the Morris brothers and their friends, the English were often called 'The Children of Alice'.

One aspect of the Welsh cultural revival of the eighteenth century was its creation of a new Welsh historical tradition. As the century advanced and the movement of the antiquaries and poets was broadened and popularised, mythical stories and legendary heroes were brought in to fire the imagination and create national sentiment. The myth of Prince Madoc and of the discovery of America by the Welsh around 1170 has been shown to have had a powerful effect on the Welsh imagination in the last years of the eighteenth century, spurring the Welsh to action, and giving rise to a drive to found Welsh colonies in America. [14] The Treason of the Long Knives was well suited to the invented or legendary past now being demanded by the Welsh, and it appeared masquerading as real history even in the most sober and stately of scholarly books. In 1805 Theophilus Jones (a grandson of Theophilus Evans), in his *History of Brecknockshire*, explained (or perhaps tried to explain away) the then common Welsh proverb, *Sais yw ef, Syn!* (He's a Saxon, Watch out!), by reference to the Long Knives:

> The treachery of the Saxons, whom the aboriginal Britons introduced into the island as friends and allies, and their cruelty in exterminating in cold blood the nobility of the antient inhabitants . . . still rankles in the bosoms of the indigenous sons of freedom. [15]

---

[12] T. H. Parry-Williams (ed.), *Llawysgrif Richard Morris o Gerddi* (Cardiff, 1931), pp. 120-6; D. Defoe, *A Tour Through the Whole Island of Great Britain* (London, 1974), II, 54.

[13] Ch. IV of the 1740 edition.

[14] G. A. Williams, *Madoc: the Making of a Myth* (London, 1980); and his *The Search for Beulah land: the Welsh and the Atlantic Revolution* (London, 1980).

[15] *History of Brecknockshire* (Brecon, 1805, 1809), I, 139.

He added, however, that such sentiments were slowly dying, and thus set at rest the agitated minds of English residents of Breconshire who were among the subscribers to his book. In the Brecon eisteddfod of 1822, the Cambrian Society of Gwent offered a medal for the best essay on 'The Credibility of the Massacre of the British Nobles at Stonehenge'. One version of the myth related that the massacre had occurred at Stonehenge, and by this period there were already some doubters beginning to raise their voices against the legendary character of the tale.[16]

One contemporary who had few doubts about its credibility was the historian William Owen ('Sefnyn'), also known as 'Pab' or Pope because of his fervent support for Catholic emancipation. A sturdily independent-minded sawyer, Sefnyn was a well-read man, and one of his books was *Y Drych Bradwriaethol: sef Hanes Brad y Cyllill Hirion* (The Treacherous Mirror, viz. the History of the Treason of the Long Knives), which appeared in at least two editions in 1825 and 1826. The Long Knives was only one episode of treason of which the English had been guilty down the ages, and the tragedy was not only a tragedy for the Britons but also for Romanism, for Vortigern's weakness had brought about the end of Roman government in Britain.

The period from 1790 to 1840 was one of unprecedented industrial change and social upheaval in Wales, and one of agricultural crisis after 1815. The revived myths of the Romantic Welsh scholars gave a certain self-consciousness to the Welsh and solace and compensation when face to face with a confusing new world. Recent scholarship has shown that the Rebecca Riots from 1839 to 1843 were caused by agrarian crises, rather than by nationalism, but national sentiment was there beneath the surface and could be manipulated rhetorically by popular leaders, as can be seen from a letter, quoted by David Williams (and by Tobit Evans long before him) and sent by 'Rebecca' to the contractor Bullin in December 1842:

> It is a shamful [*sic*] thing for us Welshmen to have the sons of Hengist to have Dominion over us, do you not remember the long knives, which Hengist hath invented to kill our forefathers and you may depend that you shall receive the same if you will not give up when I shall give you a visit.[17]

Such talk may not have been typical, but it shows that at a time of crisis the Welsh turned to their history. Popular interest was maintained in the legend even after the years of crisis had passed. In 1853 one of the most Romantic versions of the tale was published at Ruthin by the printer Isaac Clarke; this was a play by Edward Roberts ('Iorwerth Glan Aled') called *Brad y Cyllill Hirion* (Treason of the Long Knives). His play is a tragedy or *prudd-chwarae,* with Vortigern, Rowena, Hengist and bands of nobles and warriors. It is in two acts, and although highly Romantic in feeling, it tells the stirring yarn well, concentrating on the action and avoiding sententious argument or moralising, and ending logically with the

[16] I. C. Peate, 'Welsh Society and Eisteddfod Medals and Relics', *Trans. Hon. Soc. Cymmrodorion,* 1937, p. 299.

[17] D. Williams, *The Rebecca Riots* (Cardiff, 1955), p. 192, based on PRO, HO/45/265; H. T. Evans, *Rebecca and her daughters* (Cardiff, 1910), p. 35.

triumph of the Saxons, with all the victorious warriors shouting 'Long live the Saxons!'

Within a few months of the publication of Iorwerth Glan Aled's play, there appeared in the journal *Yr Amserau* sections of an unpublished play by an anonymous poet that parodied the style and theme of Iorwerth Glan Aled, but savagely mocked the government commissioners and those who had given evidence before them in 1846. These sections bore the title of *Brad y Llyfrau Gleision* (Treason of the Blue Books), and caused such alarm and threats of libel action that the journal put a stop to them. But in the following year (1854), the author put his completed play on the market, and it was published again by Isaac Clarke of Ruthin under the title, *Brad y Llyfrau Gleision*. Its author was Robert Jones ('Derfel'), a man who had already published one volume of verse printed by Clarke called *Rhosyn Meirion* (Rose of Merioneth), containing a long poem in praise of Kossuth. Seven years had passed since the commissioners' reports were published, but it was this belated literary satire which gave its nickname to the great furore of 1847.

The Blue Books published in 1847 did not of themselves inaugurate a new period in Welsh education. They came in the middle of a decade of intense educational activity in Wales and at the end of almost two decades of frenzied agitation, often of violence. Though there had been sporadic rioting in various parts of Wales since the 1790s, the Merthyr rising of 1831 and the Chartist attack on Newport in 1839 gave to the rest of Britain the impression that south-east Wales was lurching into barbarism and anarchy. The fear and alarm of the authorities were increased by knowing that the state could not easily influence the minds of the people, separated as they were from the English by their own language, which gave opportunities to agitators and nonconformists. Seymour Tremenheere reported in 1839 to the Privy Council's Committee on Education on the state of elementary education in the mining districts of south Wales. He found even the hilly hinterland of Newport (virtually on the doorstep of England) to be mostly Welsh-speaking and literate only in that language. Revd H. L. Bellairs, who reported to the Privy Council on much the same area, made the oft-quoted remark: 'A band of efficient schoolmasters is kept up at a much less expense than a body of police or soldiery'.[18]

To make matters worse, from about 1839 to 1843 the Welsh countryside, especially in the south-west, was disturbed by the Rebecca Riots. A number of observers at the time made the point that the inability of the Welsh to speak English made it impossible to ensure the smooth running of the legal system, and gave great opportunities to rioters and agitators of all kinds. When the riots had subsided in 1843, a commission of inquiry was sent to south Wales and produced a wide-ranging report that was published in London in 1844. Its publication led to no furore, but many of its observations on Welsh society, religion and language foreshadowed those of the controversial Blue Books of 1847. The Welsh language, or, rather, the people's ignorance of English, was the barrier to their progress and a possible seed-bed of rebellion; it hindered the smooth running of the law and the

[18] D. Evans, *The Life and Work of William Williams, M.P.* (Llandysul, 1939), p. 85.

established Church; and this all arose because the educational system in Wales was lamentable.

Although the British schools (mainly for dissenters) had begun in 1808 and the National schools (mainly Anglican) in 1811, no real advance in Wales was made until 1837, when a great wave of Anglican school-building began. However, during the early-nineteenth century, the dissenting sects had made rapid progress through almost all parts of Wales, and with their programme of chapel-building came a great spread of the Sunday school, an institution which in Wales was patronised by young and old. Although events such as the Merthyr rising or the Rebecca Riots appear of the greatest importance to the modern reader, it is quite likely that for the Welshman of the early-nineteenth century the endless theological wrangles between the various sects, or the debates between Church and Chapel, would have appeared more important. One contemporary debate was between those favouring state intervention in education and those favouring a purely voluntary system. Anglicans generally had no objection to state intervention, but sectarians such as Baptists and Independents, who were particularly strong in the south and east of Wales, passionately believed in a voluntary system. The wave of Anglican school-building from 1837 to 1843 caused alarm and horror amongst many nonconformists, and this reaction was intensified by the prospects of Sir James Graham's Factory Bill in 1843 which, if passed, would have given virtual control of factory education to Anglicans. Hugh Owen's appeal to the Welsh in 1843 managed to convert much of Welsh public opinion in the remoter parts towards the north and west to accept government help for education. From 1843 to 1846 British schools spread rapidly through Wales under the auspices of the Cambrian Education Society. A training college was opened in Brecon in 1846 and in the same year a training department was opened at the school in Caernarfon. The National Society was also active and in 1845 published a report strongly criticizing the poor provision for education in Wales. Even without the Blue Books of 1847, the decade would in all probability have been one of intense debate and activity in the field of Welsh education. Reform and progress were in the air even before William Williams, MP for Coventry, rose in the House of Commons on 10 March 1846 to ask the government to establish a royal commission to examine the state of education in Wales, especially with regard to the means available to the Welsh to learn English.[19]

William Williams (1788-1865) was a self-made man, a rich, hard-working and immensely successful merchant in London, but he was a native of Llanpumsaint in Carmarthenshire—the heart of the country of the daughters of Rebecca. An indefatigable reformer and believer in progress, he became MP for Coventry. He addressed the Commons in 1846: he wished all Welshmen to get on in the world, but felt they were held back for lack of English. He was critical of the capitalists

---

[19] For the story of the Blue Books, see D. Evans, op. cit.; D. Salmon, 'The story of a Welsh education commission, 1846-7', *Y Cymmrodor*, XXIV (1913), 189-237; I. D. Thomas, *Addysg yng Nghymru yn y Bedwaredd Ganrif ar Bymtheg* (Cardiff, 1972); F. P. Jones, 'The Blue Books of 1847', in J. L. Williams and G. R. Hughes (eds.), *The History of Education in Wales* (Swansea, 1978), pp. 127-44; *Education in Wales, 1847-1947* (London, 1948); *Bibliography of the History of Wales* (2nd ed., Cardiff, 1962), pp. 235-7.

and gentry of Wales for their failure to support the scheme to establish a non-sectarian college at Brecon in 1845. He was one of the few MPs able and willing all his life to deliver a speech in Welsh, and in 1863 he was one of the benefactors of the scheme to found a university college for Wales. His numerous detractors regarded him as the father of all the evil of the Blue Books.

Williams was asked to modify his plea for a royal commission in favour of a departmental commission of the Privy Council, and this he accepted. Although the government fell in July 1846, the new ministry honoured the promise of its predecessor and quickly appointed three commissioners to go to Wales. The appointments were made by Sir James Kaye-Shuttleworth, first secretary of the education committee of the Privy Council, and although some elements of nonconformist opinion in Wales had taken it for granted that at least one of the commissioners would be Welsh, at the very least a nonconformist, in the event three young Anglicans, barristers by profession, were appointed. The three were R. W. Lingen (who in 1849 succeded Kaye-Shuttleworth and eventually became Lord Lingen), J. C. Symons and H. V. Johnson. By 1 October they were at work, conferring at Builth—an ill-omened town, whose inhabitants were nicknamed *Bradwyr Buellt* (traitors of Builth) because Llywelyn the Last had been slain nearby at Cilmeri in 1282. Ominously for the nonconformists, the three conferred at the start with the bishops of Hereford and St David's; then they went their various ways, Lingen to Carmarthen, Glamorgan and Pembroke, Symons to Brecon, Radnor, Cardigan and the 'Welsh' parts of Monmouthshire, and Johnson to north Wales. They collected a vast quantity of evidence, the greater part from Anglican clergymen, and the reports were ready by 1 April 1847. The Blue Books ran to almost two thousand pages. In 1848 a shorter one-volume condensation was produced and published in English and Welsh versions.

They had been told to inquire into the education (including the Sunday schools) of the labouring classes and the means by which the people could learn English. More unexpectedly perhaps, they were also to inquire into the social and moral condition of the people. Lingen's report came first: he found in his area that some 30,000 were taught in day schools while some 80,000 were taught in Sunday schools. He was struck by the utter separation of the vast mass of common folk from the gentry, and by the amazing social inequalities, poverty-stricken agriculturists cheek by jowl with spendthrift workmen in industry, 'wantoning in plenty'. Welsh, for Lingen, was 'the language of old-fashioned agriculture, of theology, and of simple rustic life, while all the world about him [the Welshman] is English'. The Welshman never rose from the ranks of the labourer to those of the manager—'his language keeps him under the hatches'. Yet most social life went on everywhere through the medium of Welsh, the people were passionately attached to their tongue, and even though they knew that they ought to learn English, many of them actively disliked that language. Lingen was intrigued by the immense popularity of the dissenting Sunday school, and attributed it to its warm sociability and its democratic character that gave status to the superintendents and teachers, people who could find no status in any other field. He made use of the evidence given by that stormy petrel John Griffith, vicar of Aberdare, about the immorality of the Welsh people, especially the womenfolk,[20] evidence which caused a storm of controversy. The evidence presented to Lingen showed the Welsh to be a backward people unable to progress, lost in irrelevant theological wranglings, ignorant, dirty and unchaste, but calling out for improvement through a sensible state school system teaching English and modern subjects.

Symons in his report admitted that he had received great hospitality in the houses of the Welsh gentry. Nevertheless, he was critical of the upper classes of Wales for misappropriating old endowments meant for religion or education, noting by contrast that the poor helped themselves effectively and put the grandees to shame. He was critical of Anglican Sunday schools for their dullness, praising by contrast the Sunday schools of the nonconformists. He quoted the evidence of some that the people liked them because they taught the Welsh language, a subject neglected by the day schools. Symons made many comments about society, observing the general filth and squalor of the dwellings of the poor, the low morals of the womenfolk, and, on the other hand, the absence of serious crime reported to the courts. He was more explicit than Lingen in observing the special problems of industrial areas. Dealing with raw new industrial settlements such as Brynmawr (then in Breconshire), he berated industrialists for neglecting the workers so disdainfully despite all the warnings of near-revolution sounded so recently by the Chartists. The Welsh, he felt, were not seditious, but they were a people easily led into sedition. He was disturbed by dormant or latent revolution in the 'Welsh' part of Monmouthshire, the hilly western half of the county; he was struck by the widespread bad feeling left after the industrial unrest in the 1830s around Pontypool, and the great hatred still smouldering between masters and men—'both classes imagine that they are necessarily antagonist'. One witness, Augustus Morgan of Machen, was against the Welsh language because it was the language of revolution and was used as a secret code by Chartists and Rebeccaites for their 'revolutionary plot'.

Johnson's report on north Wales is rather shorter than those of the other two. Like the other commissioners, he found the educational system primitive and feeble, the people backward and ignorant. He intelligently observed that many of the deficiencies of the system arose from the extreme separation of rich and poor, although many of the witnesses thought that most of the trouble arose from the bitter quarrels of Church and Chapel. He could also pay tribute, where tribute was due, to the Sunday school, which he saw as the chief instrument of civilization in north Wales. He found the educational standards of the English-speaking parts of north-east Wales atrocious, and although many of the witnesses in all three parts of the report maintained that learning English would banish backwardness and lack of hygiene, Johnson had to admit that the lowest form of social degradation and moral depravity appeared nearer the English border, especially in the mining districts where much English was spoken. He said that Merthyr Tydfil was usually thought of as the worst place in all Wales, but worse by far was Rhosllannerchrugog near Wrexham (Denbighshire), according to its vicar.

[20] *Dictionary of Welsh Biography, s.n.*

In conclusion, then, the reports declared that the Welsh were ill-educated, poor, dirty, unchaste, in danger of being led into sedition and even revolution; the gentry, the clergy, the industrialists had failed the common people, lacking the will to educate them; the Welsh were too poor and divided amongst themselves to sustain a voluntary educational system, and so were best improved by a system run by the state. English would have to become the language of the people if Wales was to take part in the progress of Britain. The efficiency of the legal system and the discipline of the established Church were impaired by the existence of so large a monoglot majority of Welsh-speakers. The Blue Books were thus critical of almost the entire population, though the Welsh language and nonconformity bore most of the blame. Methodists and old dissenters were lumped together in the general criticism. The deep fear of the authorities was only hinted at in the reports, a growing alarm that the common people of Wales might turn from industrial rebellion and agrarian riots to full-scale sedition. They were not to know that the noontide of Victorian prosperity and calm lay ahead. They had only the disturbing picture of the recent past to go on. The rumpus which followed the publication of the Blue Books in 1847 took everybody by surprise. Similar remarks had been made about the Welsh in recent government reports—for example, that on south Wales in 1844—without exciting any loud response.

The public took some time to digest the vast amount of material in the three volumes. By Christmas 1847, at the Merthyr eisteddfod, Revd Thomas Price ('Carnhuanawc'), an Anglican priest who had been mocked in Symons's report for his Welsh patriotism, called the commissioners 'libellous and mendacious foreigners' and begged Merthyr and Wales to rise up in a wave of protest against them.[21] In 1848 Henry Cotton, dean of Bangor, published an anonymous pamphlet attacking the commissioners for their libels on the Welsh. The debate raged in the pages of the new Welsh periodical, *Y Traethodydd*, from early 1848 to 1850. Its editor, the influential Methodist, Lewis Edwards, privately admitted that he was troubled by what was true in the Blue Books, not by what was false. The reports attacked Methodism along with dissenters of other denominations and so the Methodists joined forces with the others for the first time, creating a united nonconformist front. In January 1848 Edwards hit back at the Blue Books.[22] O. O. Roberts, a famous radical doctor in Bangor, attacked Johnson's remarks in a pamphlet on education in north Wales. Evan Jones ('Ieuan Gwynedd') ceaselessly, in Welsh and English, attacked the incorrectness and illogicality (as he saw it) of the reports in *The Cardiff and Merthyr Guardian, John Bull, Y Traethodydd*, and in two books, *The Dissent and Morality of Wales* and *A Vindication of the Educational and Moral Condition of Wales*.[23] David Rees of Llanelli, a leading Independent divine and editor of the influential journal, *Y Diwygiwr* (The

[21] E. I. Williams, 'Thomas Stephens and Carnhuanawc on the "Blue Books" of 1847', *Bull. Board of Celtic Studies,* IX (1938), 271-3.

[22] T. Ll. Evans, *Lewis Edwards, ei Fywyd a'i Waith* (Swansea, 1967), pp. 97, 126, 201; H. Williams, 'Y Traethodydd a'r Gymraeg', *Taliesin,* XLII (1981), 54-62.

[23] B. Rees (ed.), *Ieuan Gwynedd, Detholiad o'i Ryddiaith* (Cardiff, 1957), pp. 77-104, gives the English text of the *Vindication*.

Reformer), gave vent to nationalistic sentiments for a while, but in the main concentrated on the attack the Blue Books delivered on nonconformity.[24] The nonconformists, and many of the Anglicans, were agreed that the reports had been unfair to the Chapel; they were all agreed that they were unfair to Welsh womanhood. There was great disagreement over the importance of the language, however. In *Y Traethodydd,* for instance, John Mills early in 1848 desired a totally Welsh-language educational system. This was hotly opposed by James Rhys Jones of Kilsby (later called Kilsby Jones), the man who helped translate into Welsh the two letters addressed to Lord John Russell by William Williams MP, in which he berated the government for being so tardy in passing legislation to implement the recommendations of the Blue Books. Henry Griffiths of Brecon, who had given evidence to the commissioners in 1846, argued for a Welsh system of education which would give due place to Welsh history for he did not want Celts to truckle to Saxon sentiments. Evan Williams of Lledrod, in the same journal, went so far as to say that a purely Welsh education would help to prevent any Englishman from gaining office in Wales and that what was needed was a Christian nationalism in this country.

The columnists of *Y Traethodydd* were nonconformists; what is so striking about the furore, however, is that many of the most telling attacks on the Blue Books came from Welsh Anglicans, a fact conveniently forgotten by later generations. The historian Jane Williams ('Ysgafell'), in her *Artegall, or Remarks on the Reports* (London, 1848), was scathing and accused the commissioners of aiming at nothing less than 'the subversion of her nationality'. More remarkable and more substantial was the lucid and well-informed attack of Sir Thomas Phillips, the mayor of Newport who had rebuffed the Chartists in 1839, in his historical survey *Wales* (London, 1849), a history book which used Welsh history to illuminate the contemporary condition of Wales, and in which he showed how exaggerated and prejudiced the reports were.

All in all, hundreds of letters and articles, many pamphlets, speeches and public meetings of protest, marked the furore, and many bitter things were said. After 1850 the storm subsided as far as the Welsh press was concerned, leaving a number of contradictory effects. It prepared the way for state intervention in education, with the ultimate triumph of a wholly English system being applied to Wales under the Education Act of 1870. It also implanted in the Welsh mind a sense of inadequacy and inferiority which cast a shadow over some, while it goaded others into action. It helped to wean the Welsh away from their passion for poetry and history and made them turn to more practical knowledge. Men like Hugh Owen and Lewis Edwards winced at the remarks about nonconformity in the reports, and yet they privately agreed with many of the criticisms of Welsh society.[25] Evan Jones ('Ieuan Gwynedd') protested loudly that the Blue Books were an unjustified libel against Welsh womanhood, but in 1850 he started the

---

[24] Glanmor Williams (ed.), *David Rees, Llanelli: Detholion o'i Weithiau* (Cardiff, 1950), prints his essay on the Blue Books (pp. 32-6); I. Jones, *David Rees y Cynhyrfwr* (Swansea, 1971), pp. 32, 191, 261n, 273-5, 279.

[25] G. A. Williams, 'Ambiguous hero: Hugh Owen and Liberal Wales', in *The Welsh in their History* (London, 1982), pp. 151-70.

journal *Y Gymraes* (The Welshwoman) 'to purify the taste, enlarge the knowledge, and improve the women of our country'. [26]

The other effect of the Blue Books was to throw the weight of Methodism behind the older dissenting denominations such as the Baptists and Independents, thus creating a united Welsh nonconformist front that was also convinced that it must take some form of political action. Up to 1847 many of the chief Welsh patriots, such as Carnhuanawc, had been Anglican parsons. Nonconformists had shown only moderate interest in things Welsh, preferring to concentrate on theology or the internal affairs of each sect. After 1847, by contrast, the nonconformists took it for granted that Anglicans were the enemies of Welshness, and more and more tended to identify themselves with Wales, making nonconformity stand for Welshness itself, and blotting out the memory of the old clerical patriots. The political or electoral effects of this shift were not felt until after 1868, but the fundamental change had occurred in the wake of the Blue Books. Thomas Evans observed nearly fifty years ago:

> The political value of education, the agitation for better education facilities for Wales, and the treason of the Blue Books, made the close of our period [1846] a turning point in Welsh history. The last of these was regarded as one of the greatest events of the nineteenth century. [27]

Victorian radical Wales, which might be said to have been born out of this furore, regarded the whole business as a foul libel and an act of treachery. But it quietly accepted many of the strictures, aims and intentions of the reports. The man who had invented the nickname of 'Treason of the Blue Books' was not a typical figure of Victorian radical Wales.

Robert Jones ('Derfel') (1824-1905) was born at Llandderfel in Merioneth, from which place in the fashion of that age he took his bardic name, eventually changing his name wholly to R. J. Derfel. [28] After an early struggle, during which he wandered far in search of work, he came to Manchester around 1850 and remained there for the rest of his life, visiting Wales continually in the course of his work as a commercial traveller in silks and satins. He was a member of a lively group of Welsh 'exiles' in Manchester which included bards like Creuddynfab and Ceiriog.

Iorwerth Glan Aled, the author of *Brad y Cyllill Hirion*, was probably an acquaintance of Derfel's, for the two came from the same area; both worked in commerce, both at that time were Baptists and both published with Clarke of Ruthin. In an autobiography written at the end of his life, Derfel said that he became obsessively nationalistic in the late-1840s and 1850s. His first contribution to his native land in this period was to write patriotic verse, typical of the Romantic patriotic poetry written at this time all over Europe. None of it is remembered today. His other contribution, one for which he is best remembered today by the Welsh-speaker, is his hymns. He soon lost interest in conventional

---

[26] B. Rees, *Ieuan Gwynedd*, p. ix.

[27] T. Evans, op. cit., p. 230.

[28] *Dictionary of Welsh Biography*, s.n.; D. G. Jones (ed.), *Detholiad o Ryddiaith Gymraeg R. J. Derfel* (2 vols., Clwb Llyfrau Cymraeg, 1945); I. ap Nicholas, *Derfel—Welsh Rebel Poet and Preacher* (London, n.d.).

Welsh nonconformity, and even his finest hymns contain democratic sentiments which betray his real interest. Derfel was an exceptional figure in that he was a secular patriot who retained all his life an intense delight in Welsh history. History was the theme of many of his essays, published as a collection in 1864. He was a firm believer in a framework of national institutions for Wales—a daily newspaper in Welsh, a national school of art, an astronomical observatory. Later in the century, his zeal for things purely Welsh palled, and although he continued to publish works on Welsh history and to send articles to Welsh journals, and maintained a connection with the *Cymru Fydd* movement around 1890, his real interest lay in secularism and socialism. In the early-1850s Derfel was an active bard and competitor in the eisteddfod, and it is fairly likely that it was Iorwerth Glan Aled's play which prompted him to write a satire on the whole business of the Blue Books. Derfel's play, however, is much more of an *anterliwt,* an interlude in the manner of the late-eighteenth century Twm o'r Nant, than a play, and it is arguably the last *anterliwt* to be composed in Welsh. From the elaborate stage directions printed, it was obviously meant to be acted, but its length—almost two hundred pages of fine print—would require actors and audience of superhuman endurance. Despite what has been said about Derfel's predominantly secular patriotism, the play is for most of its length concerned with a religious struggle. Its theme is a dastardly plot by Beelzebub and his demons against pure, clean nonconformist Wales. The friends of the Devil are the Anglicans, especially the Puseyites. The style is a curious mixture of rhymed couplets, rather prosy and argumentative, interspersed with short, sharp lyrics, like songs in a revue, many of them choruses sung by the demons.

The play begins with a conference in Hell, with Beelzebub regretting that he will never get a foot inside the door of pure white Wales because the country is too good; his bright idea is to arrange a plot to blame all the ills of Wales on the nonconformists. He says that although the English have conquered Wales, the Welsh are meek:

> Despite it all, they are placid and quiet
> And their attackers dwell amongst them safely.

Beelzebub is sorry that the old merry way of life has gone, with the exception of drunkenness and bundling, sorry that the gentry have lost their hold over the people, and delighted to see that the Welsh MPs are useless:

> Follow me if you like to the Parliament—
> who are as useless as Wales's representatives?

The demons present a picture of this absurd country of Wales, with its antiquated jargon, its stupidity in not accepting state intervention in education. The Devil himself had devised such a scheme for Britain, but it ought to be tried out on the Welsh. For the plot to work, demons had to be sent into Wales to harm nonconformity, insult the good name of the women and scorn the language:

> Scorn as well the whole of Welsh letters,
> Connect everything in that land with darkness,
> Attack the language with all seriousness,
> Take account of neither her age nor beauty.

In the second act, in answer to the Devil's suggestions, three spies are sent into Wales. This echoed a famous cartoon which appeared in *The Principality* in 1848 showing Kaye-Shuttleworth with a scuttle on his head and the three commissioners as spies with foxes' ears. The three spies in the play are Haman from Belial College (Lingen was a Fellow of Balliol), Judas Iscariot (Johnson) and Simon Magus (Jellinger Symons). Bishops and clerics dine with the spies to devise the best ways of collecting false witness. By contrast, there are scenes of dissenters in a Welsh village under the leadership of Llywelyn the Bard who suspect that treason and plot are afoot. Indeed, Mr Independent Davies (the Congregationalist) makes the comparison with the Treason of the Long Knives. Then there comes a burlesque scene at a Sunday school, where the commissioners ask trick questions to disconcert the children, who come to the conclusion that to ask such stupid questions the commissioners must be dunderheads, and they remain silent. One by one, the Welsh clerics make their frightful accusations against the Welsh people, the rector of Nefyn, for example, says of the old custom of bundling:

> In England the farmers' daughters are wise,
> In Wales they go whoring like the daughters of evil,
> Making love in bed in the depth of night,
> Girls without petticoats, men without breeches.

When all the false witness is gathered together, it is sent to Downing St., where there is great hilarity over the absurd Welsh nation:

> The Welshman! Just look at him,
> His daily work you see is labouring,
> Labouring in mud with feet and hands,
> He is given work of the lowest kind.

The lords in London decide that all the absurdity is to be blamed on nonconformity, including Chartism and Rebeccaism. The demons are delighted and fly back to Hell with glee:

> Measures are prepared,
> Shackles have been made,
> To make the Welshmen slaves.
> Their praises are killed,
> Their advance is ended,
> And finished is their freedom.

The third act opens somewhat feebly in contrast to the dramatic end of the second act, with its colourful demonic dance of triumph with stage effects of green flames, drums and dark smoke. Now we have bishops meeting to congratulate the spies, and back in Wales the villagers led by Llywelyn the Bard meet to see what good can come out of it all. The action takes a sudden turn because the Devil finds to his consternation that his plan goes badly awry. The Welsh, far from being humiliated by the spies and their reports, are bestirred into unity, resourcefulness and action.

> Then there broke a storm of anger
> Such as little Wales had never seen.

Llywelyn the Bard told the villagers that this would happen, and in the great furore the Welsh were demanding the disestablishment of the Church, national institutions, and at the end of the play the bard himself appears to recite the epilogue, in which he foresees a new Wales arising, with justice for all, better housing for the poor, great monuments for national heroes, and a university for Wales.

Derfel's play bears only a slight resemblance to the historical tragedy of Iorwerth Glan Aled. In one sense the 'traitors' of the play are those Welshmen who were prepared to bear false witness against their fellow-countrymen to please the commissioners and their masters, the government. But the 'treason' in both plays is really a trick or plot, Derfel's aim being to show that the Blue Books were a trick, to kill the spirit of the nonconformists and persuade the Welsh to accept a system of state education. There is only one direct reference in the play (in the speech of Mr Independent Davies), to the Treason of the Long Knives, but it was sufficient; the readers understood well enough what it meant and the name stuck. That a satirist and social reformer should drive his point home by reference to a Dark Age myth is a sign of the power that history and Romantic legend had over the Welsh mind in the first half of the nineteenth century. In this respect, Welsh national sentiment resembled that of contemporary movements in Poland and Hungary. It is a tribute to the considerable success of the antiquarians of the eighteenth century and the Romantic mythologists of the early-nineteenth; but it is a farewell tribute to an age that was passing. There is a second element in the play, which appears clearly only at the end; this looks forward to the secular institutional patriotism which motivated *Cymru Fydd* and some sections of Welsh Liberalism from the 1880s to the 1920s. But the third and most important element of the play, which dominates virtually the whole action, is the religious nationalism of nonconformity, the complete identification of Welshness with the virtues and values of the Chapel. It is true that Derfel had some kind words for patriotic Anglicans such as Thomas Price ('Carnhuanawc'), Lord and Lady Llanover, and a few others. It is also true that events showed that Derfel misjudged some of his Anglican enemies: Kaye-Shuttleworth of the committee on education was by no means hostile to Welsh and did his best to ensure college courses in Wales and in England to produce bilingual teachers; John Griffith, the vicar of Aberdare (who appears in the play as *Y Blaidd o Aberdâr*, 'The Wolf of Aberdare'), was a doughty defender of Welsh interests, as he saw them, and a critic of those in authority as bold as Derfel himself, ending up as a formidable supporter of Church Disestablishment. But in the main, Derfel expressed in his play the current Welsh opinion which subsumed Welshness in nonconformity. Just as Irish patriots tended in this period to identify the nation with the Catholic people of Ireland, so the nonconformists came in the 1850s and '60s to create the illusion that they alone stood for Welshness. Of course, Derfel himself outgrew that kind of patriotism, but those were his feelings and the feelings of leading Welshmen of the moment. Iorwerth Glan Aled's play, published in 1853, is a Romantic tragedy taking its inspiration from the historical and antiquarian revival of the eighteenth century. Derfel's play, scarcely a year later, looks forward, in all but theme and title, to the new age of nonconformist activism and involvement in politics. It is as if within twelve months an age had passed.

Glanmor Williams has shown how the Welsh passion for political prophecy and historical myths and legends, a marked feature of Welsh life in the later middle ages, died away during the sixteenth century. This was partly because Renaissance scholarship destroyed baseless myths with the spirit of reason, partly because the Protestant Reformation emphasised a Spiritual Messiah, thus belittling the Second Coming of a human hero such as Arthur or the 'second Owain', and partly because the Tudor state absorbed into its own thought and propaganda a number of Welsh historical myths. Thus, the triumph of Henry Tudor in 1485 was easily shown to be the culmination of Welsh prophecies, with Henry as the successor to Cadwaladr the Blessed, and it could also be shown that the independence of the early British Church, which had been lost under the papist Normans, had been regained by the Anglican Reformation. The Welsh of the sixteenth century no longer considered themselves a conquered people, and had no need to turn to the past for comfort, compensation or prophecy.[29] They were also deeply involved in the administration of their country, at the level of the shires and even in London, so that they could imagine that they were in control of their own destiny.

A not dissimilar turning away from the past and its mythological grudges also occurred in the 1840s and '50s, though for different reasons. The sheer effort of creating a new nonconformist nation made the Welsh ignore much of the distant past and concentrate on a more relevant historical tradition. In Wales, as in all European countries at the end of the Romantic age, mythology could no longer masquerade as history. Derfel's contemporary, Thomas Stephens of Merthyr, for example, began to analyse the Welsh past with rational scientific precision and had nothing but contempt for the recent Romantic mythologists. By contrast, passions ran high over the recent past or near-present, the birth-pangs of the Nonconformist Nation. In this field, where scientific history did not intervene, the heroes were people such as Howell Harris or Mary Jones and her Bible, and grudges were harboured against squires, clergymen and factory owners.[30]

In the 1850s and '60s, a feel for the past, especially the distant past, was of less importance, for the Welsh were hurling themselves eagerly into the progress, industriousness and self-improvement of Victoria's Britain. The nonconformists were ever more busy running their chapels, newspapers, concerts and benefit societies. There was little time to brood about the distant past, for workaday toil absorbed most of their energies; the taste for history was fulfilled by the Old Testament, the taste for Messianic prophecy by the pulpit orator's 'World to Come'.

It may be that Derfel himself, whose honeymoon with Welsh nonconformity was rather short, felt the dangers of the great cultural shift to a 'Nonconformist Nation', with its tendency to forget Welsh history, for he laboured long to remind the Welsh people of their distant past. Within a short time, in the 1860s and '70s, the details of the Blue Books controversy had been forgotten; they remained fixed

---

[29] Glanmor Williams, 'Prophecy, Poetry and Politics'.
[30] P. Morgan, *The Eighteenth Century Renaissance* (Llandybie, 1981), pp. 136-61.

in the Welsh imagination as a 'treason', the three commissioners as bogey-men, and Ieuan Gwynedd as a hero in shining armour. By 1870 the Welsh had largely accepted the necessity of state education and the need to learn the English language. Many of the unpleasing details of the 1847 reports were corroborated by the investigators of the Welsh Land Commission of 1896. All this did not stop patriots from calling the Blue Books a gross libel of the nation, 'blue without and black within'. There were few Welsh historians in that period to separate truth from falsehood in recent history, and by 1870 the Blue Books had entered Welsh myth and legend. Just as the change from Romano-British to Welsh nation had gathered about itself myths such as The Treason of the Long Knives, so too the Treason of the Blue Books became a myth of origin at the birth of Liberal nonconformist Wales.

Ecclesiastical Economy: Aspects of Church Building in Victorian Wales

IEUAN GWYNEDD JONES

CHURCH building and repair were of the essence of the revival of the Anglican Church in the nineteenth century. Even as the Hanoverian Age, so it was said, 'had been pre-eminently the age of ecclesiastical dilapidation',[1] so the Age of Victoria was the age of church reconstruction, and the sense of achievement as new churches were built and old ones taken down and rebuilt echoed the pride of the period in its secular and technological achievements. Theologically reform was taken to be the outward evidence of a new spirituality, of the inner workings of grace both in the Church itself and in society at large. As Vowler Short, the bishop of St. Asaph, remarked in 1851, it was difficult to believe that a Church which had been so active in erecting places of worship as the Church of England had been could have the judgment of the Almighty impending over it, and he could not help trusting that the providence of God was over the country for good.[2] Whether it is possible or, indeed, proper to correlate the workings of providence with the activities of church builders is a question best left to theologians, but certainly much of Victorian religiosity assumed some such relationship, and it was the endless fascination with the (generally inaccurate) quantitative aspects of organized religion that fuelled the arithmetic war of high Victorian times.

The place of Wales in this revival was far from being a peripheral one. Nor was its role merely incidental or responsive to changes being initiated by the experience of the Established Church in England. As the Ecclesiastical Commissioners soon came to realize, not only did the Church in Wales encapsulate the essence of the problems being faced by the Church as a whole in the elaboration of its reform policies; they were also forced to appreciate from the beginning that the political implications of reform, which they were at such pains to avoid in England, were in Wales inextricably involved in whatever changes were proposed. Paradoxically, it was the peripheral nature of Wales which determined its uniqueness, for this ensured that every proposal for ecclesiastical reform, including the union of sees, the provision of additional and properly educated clergy able to serve in both languages, the creation of new parishes and

---

[1] *Edinburgh Rev.*, April 1853, reprinted in W. J. Conybeare, *Essays Ecclesiastical and Social* (London, 1854), p. 41. The author was the eldest son of W. D. Conybeare, dean of Llandaff, 1845-57, the eminent geologist who began the rebuilding of Llandaff Cathedral.

[2] Incorporated Society for Promoting the Enlargement, Building and Repairing of Churches and Chapels, 33rd *Annual Report* (1851), pp. 12-13. See also A. G., 'Church Building, Past and Present', *The Church Builder*, XI (March 1862), 40-3.

the endowment of new benefices, and the building of additional churches, all of which in England were difficult enough, should in Wales be made immensely more complicated by the existence of two languages, a divergent history, a different social structure, and a growing national consciousness. The pattern of church building in Wales reflects these social tensions in a most sensitive and delicate manner and it is as an indicator of some of the social forces involved that it will be considered in this study.

Writing in 1853, a contributor to the *Edinburgh Review* remarked that 'the progress which the Church in Wales [had] made in the last few years [was] creditable to those who had been instrumental in effecting it'. This improvement, he thought, had been 'chiefly in the more civilized districts', but that even among a peasant clergy 'in the Church in the mountains' many of the blemishes which had disfigured the establishment for so many generations had been, or were in process of being, removed.[3] There was evidence enough to substantiate this judgment in the masses of official papers generated annually by the Ecclesiastical Commissioners and more strikingly in the scores of new and restored churches, in a more efficient, if more bureaucratic, hierarchy, in a new sensitivity to liturgical propriety and generally in a heightened awareness of the role of the Established Church in society. What is interesting in the writer's analysis is the distinction he makes between 'the more civilized districts' and 'the Church in the mountains', and the assertion that the progress of reform and revival was necessarily different in the one compared with the other. At the back of his mind is the difference between England and Wales (or Cumbria); but more immediately the difference between 'urban' and 'rural' is what concerns him, and the well-nigh invincible difficulties stemming from a fundamental and pervasive state of poverty which church building encountered in 'the mountains'. It is a real and valid distinction, but a crude one, and it quickly becomes evident that the student of reform in Wales must also distinguish between different kinds of 'urbanity' and different kinds of 'ruralism'. The new 'mining and manufacturing districts' of south-east and north-east Wales, for example, those 'colonies in the desert', those 'condensations of people', were somehow urban but nevertheless vastly different sociologically from the ancient boroughs and the industrial port-towns of the maritime plains. They were different again from the little towns of central Wales situated in the rich valleys running down into the rolling countryside of the border, lying like ports of haven on the edges of the vast wilderness of the high plateaux. Many of these towns, like the ports on Cardigan Bay, were falling into a slow decline as improved communications undermined their trading competitiveness, and brought the mountain folk and their immemorial ways and remote habitations within the influence of the new civilization of the industrial south and north. To what extent and in precisely what ways did these social differences affect the process of Anglican revival and its development in the different parts of the country?

So far as actual buildings were concerned, Church extension involved the provision of permanent and temporary places of worship, including the repair or

---

[3] 'The Church in the Mountains', *Edinburgh Rev.*, April 1853; reprinted in W. J. Conybeare, op. cit., p. 40.

reconstruction of old ones, and the enlarging of existing buildings by the rearrangement of internal fittings. It also involved the provision of houses for the clergy and, finally, the building of schools. Of these, the building of entirely new churches was the most spectacular aspect of the work, and it is worth remarking that in England and Wales as a whole no fewer than 2,381 additional churches and chapels were erected with the aid of the Church Building Society between 1818 and the end of the century.[4] In Wales, at least an additional 827 churches and chapels (including mission churches) were built between 1831 and 1906, the stock of buildings increasing by nearly 80 per cent—from 1,040 in 1831 to 1,867 in 1906.[5] This average increase differed as between dioceses: in the predominantly upland and rural dioceses of Bangor and St. David's the increase was of the order of 50 per cent; in the predominantly industrial and urbanized dioceses of St. Asaph and Llandaff it was more than 100 per cent. But however great this increase in the building of entirely new churches, the repair and enlarging of existing churches was even greater and, taken over the period as a whole and the country as a whole, not a bit less important. It is extremely difficult to calculate exactly what this amounted to, but if we take the activities of the Church Building Society as an indicator, we find that out of a total of about 900 grants made to Welsh parishes in the course of the century, no less than 800 were to aid in the rebuilding or enlarging of existing buildings. Again, it is necessary to stress that, as the Faculty books of the four dioceses show, an enormous amount of work was being carried out without recourse to public funds. We must conclude that this constant work on the fabric of the ancient churches of town and country contributed far more to the outward appearance and physical state of the Church than did the building of new places of worship. In scarcely a single parish was there no building or restoration or repair of some kind or other, and it is difficult for us now to imagine the transformation that this must have made to the appearance of places—of towns, villages, and landscapes. Nor was this a kind of unexpected bonus, an unforeseen but welcome by-product, of the developing programme. It was of the very essence of the movement, and it was the conviction of the protagonists of Church extension that propriety and decency in the appearance of things ecclesiastical led inevitably to the moral improvement of the localities involved.

The provision of new parsonages or the repair of old ones was a vital part of the strategy of revival, for a great deal of the non-residence with which the Church was afflicted was attributable to this cause. Most of the glebe-houses in Wales were small farmhouses or thatched cottages; many were unfit for residence. In St. David's and Llandaff, for example, more than two-thirds of the benefices lacked adequate parsonages; only St. Asaph could claim to have accommodation for more than two-thirds of its manpower.[6] By the 1880s, most of the old parsonages

---

[4] Incorporated Church Building Society (henceforward ICBS) *Annual Report* for 1927.

[5] Royal Commission on the Church of England and other religious bodies in Wales and Monmouthshire, Vol. I, *Report* (1910), App. B, pp. 166 and 161. The figures for Llandaff are for the period 1848 to 1906 and therefore understate the actual position.

[6] Ecclesiastical Revenues Report, P[arliamentary] P[apers] 1835, XXII, Table IV, pp. 123 *passim*. See also PP 1850, XLII (186).

had been replaced by new and invariably large and splendid houses—indeed, by that time new parsonages were often costing as much as, or even more than, the parish churches to build or repair, and it is clear that this desire to build splendid residences for the clergy was intended as an indicator of the high social status which belonged or should have belonged to the clerical profession.[7] They were also intended to proclaim that the ancient abuse of non-residence was now at an end.

The third element in the Church extension movement was the provision of schools. The agency for achieving this aim was the National Society for promoting the education of the poor in the principles of the Established Church. Founded in 1811, seven years earlier than the Church Building Society, the two societies had been closely associated by being named in the Act of 1828 which abolished the ancient and inefficient Church briefs and substituted for them Royal Letters which might be issued triennially authorizing the collection of voluntary contributions for the work of the societies named in the Act. These 'royal begging letters', as Palmerston called them, were suspended in 1851 before being abolished two years later, but the association between the societies was a compelling one, and by the 1830s it had come to be accepted that normally 'wherever a new Church was built, the establishment of a School was almost sure to follow'. This connection came to be enshrined in the idea that the National School was a necessary appendage of the Church and that national education was hallowed and blessed by the prayers of the Church. This pattern of growth was the antithesis of the morphology of nonconformist expansion, in which the establishment of a school normally preceded that of the chapel. The Anglicans built a church and hoped to fill it: the nonconformists gathered congregations who provided themselves first with schools and then with chapels.[8] In these ways, therefore, the Church advanced its stone and mortar outposts on both flanks, and the result could be seen in town and country in the close juxtaposition and often the architectural harmony of those three symbols of a settled Anglican parochial ministry—the church, the parsonage and the school.

Bishop Vowler Short, in the speech already quoted, 'presumed that there was never a time since church building began' when so many churches had been built.[9] As the Census of Religious Worship of 1851, which was then in preparation, showed when it was published two years later, and with a greater degree of accuracy than had hitherto been available, nearly 10,000 of the 14,077 churches and other buildings belonging to the Anglican Church in England and Wales had been erected before 1801. Of the remaining 4,410, 55 had been added in the first decade of the century, 97 in the second, 276 in the third, 667 in the

---

[7] B. Heeney, *A Different Kind of Gentleman: Parish Clergy as Professional Men in early and mid-Victorian England* (Hamden, Conn., 1976).

[8] ICBS, 21st *Report* (1839), pp. xi-xii. On Royal Letters, see G. Richards, 'Royal Briefs for the Restoration of Churches in Wales (1)', *Journal Hist. Soc. of the Church in Wales*, XI (1956), 55. On the contrasting patterns of growth, cf. Archdeacon J. Sandford in *The Mission and Extension of the Church at Home* (Bampton Lectures, 1861): 'the missionary first, then the missionary station: the permanent erection when attention has been excited and interest aroused, and there is at least the nucleus of a future congregation' (p. 92).

[9] ICBS, 33rd *Annual Report* (1851), pp. 12-13.

fourth, and 1,197 between 1841 and 1851.[10] The bishop was entirely right to draw attention to the varying rates of growth, and in particular to the spectacular increase in the rate of growth. Between 1801 and 1811, some five or six churches (or, more correctly, buildings used for religious purposes) were built in Wales, nearly ten per annum in the decade 1811-21, and about twenty-eight in the middle decade of the half-century. Then comes the great leap forward. Between 1831 and 1841 an average of 67 churches per annum were being built, and in the last decade 120 per annum. This is what contemporaries believed was happening, and it was this knowledge of facts which under-pinned their amazing optimism in the face of social facts of a different kind and which led some Victorians not to doubt the facts themselves but to misunderstand their true significance.

Thus, the peaks in building activity in England and Wales came in these central decades of the century—roughly the first three decades of Victoria's reign. In all, 1,721 new churches were built between 1840 and 1876, and 7,144 old churches rebuilt or restored and enlarged in the same period. The total cost was estimated—not very accurately—at £25,548,703.[11] The reports of the Incorporated Society show clearly the enormous work that was accomplished. Between 1818 and 1868 the Society made 1,094 grants for new buildings, 632 for rebuilding and restorations, and 1,922 for enlarging churches. The total of grants distributed was £786,208 and it was estimated that the public had expended almost £7,000,000 for the same purpose.[12] These, therefore, were the decades which established the pattern of what Anglicans came to regard as their own distinctive mode of revival.

The chronology of church building and restoration in Wales diverges only slightly from the national pattern with respect to the dioceses in which industrialization was taking place, but more radically in the Church in the mountains. Developments in the industrial areas of St. Asaph—mainly on Deeside and in the Denbighshire coalfields—were closer to the norm than those in Llandaff, where church building scarcely began until 1850. These differences undoubtedly reflected the divergent industrial and urbanizing histories of the two dioceses. But they were due also to purely local influences and the readiness of central grant-making bodies—up to 1856, the Church Building Commissioners—to respond to local pressures, the effectiveness of these, in turn, being shaped by the attitudes of the ruling land-owning families and industrial dynasties, on the one hand, and, on the other, by the effective leadership and

---

[10] Census of Great Britain: Religious Worship: Report and Tables (1853), pp. xxxix-xli. Cf. *The Church Builder* for 1861, pp. 40-3 (this was the organ of the ICBS). More accurate statistics are to be found in A. D. Gilbert, *Religion and Society in Industrial England. Church, Chapel and Social Change, 1740-1914* (1976), Table 6.1 on p. 130, and in R. Currie, A. Gilbert, L. Horsley, *Churches and Churchgoers. Patterns of Church Growth in the British Isles since 1700* (Clarendon Press, 1977), pp. 213-15.

[11] PP 1876, LVIII (553), 'Church Building and Restoration. Summary', pp. 657-8.

[12] ICBS, 21st *Annual Report* (1869), p. 13.

administrative abilities of the diocesan hierarchies. [13] Llandaff, in this respect, was pre-eminently 'the Church in the mountains', for urbanization was taking place most spectacularly not in the small rural parishes of the agricultural lowlands or within the regions of influence of the ancient towns of Monmouthshire and Glamorgan, but in the great upland parishes of mountain and moorland with their deeply incised valleys running southwards to the sea. This string of parishes at the heads of the valleys—hardly a garland round the waist of the Black Mountains—were for the Anglicans the very type and *exempla* of the disastrous consequences for organized religion of the unhindered exploitation for private gain of the mineral wealth of the hills. [14]

The chronology of reconstruction in Cardiganshire, where the ancient pastoral economy was diversified only by pockets of lead-mining, approximated more to the national pattern than to that of the hills of the diocese of Llandaff. It began in 1827 when the parish church of Llanfihangel Lledrod was taken down and rebuilt, and in the course of the next seven years no less than eleven churches were reconstructed or repaired—in the case of St. Michael's, Aberystwyth, taken down and rebuilt to a new plan on an adjacent site and that with the aid, almost inexplicably, of the Church Building Commissioners. Between 1835 and 1849 activity was at a lower level (six reconstructions and one additional church). Between 1850 and 1863 fifteen churches were rebuilt, most of them between 1850 and 1855. Then, beginning in 1867, there was a burst of activity which resulted in no less than 28 churches being repaired or rebuilt in the next two decades. This period saw the building of three additional churches and some of the restorations were costly. A total of 40 churches, including new ones, were reconstructed between about 1850 and 1885. [15]

The pattern in Breconshire was very similar, though in that county heavy industrialization where the county's southern borders impinged on the mineral regions of the south Wales coalfield distorted the rural pattern and made it similar in those places to the industrial parts of Llandaff diocese. [16] The social forces, both economic and spiritual, which were determining the strength and direction of

---

[13] For Llandaff, see W. D. Wills, 'The Established Church in the Diocese of Llandaff, 1850-70: a study of the Evangelical Movement in the South Wales Coalfield', *Welsh Hist. Rev.,* IV, no. 3 (June 1969), and the same author's unpublished thesis, 'Ecclesiastical Reorganization and Church Extension in the Diocese of Llandaff, 1830-70' (unpublished University of Wales M.A. thesis, 1965); and E. T. Davies, *Religion in the Industrial Revolution in South Wales* (Cardiff, 1965). See also T. J. Pritchard, 'The Anglican Church in the Rhondda from the Industrial Revolution to Disestablishment' (unpublished University of Keele Ph.D. thesis, 1982). For St. Asaph diocese, see I. G. Jones, 'Church Building in Flintshire in the mid-nineteenth century', *Journal Flintshire Hist. Soc.,* XXIX (1979-80), 89ff.

[14] See, for example, W. J. Conybeare, op. cit., pp. 39-40: *Substance of Speeches delivered at Bridgend and Newport* (London, 1851), *passim:* and T. Phillips, *Wales: the Language, Social Condition, Moral Character and Religious Opinions of the People, considered in their relation to Education* (London, 1849), pp. 180ff.

[15] See I. G. Jones, 'Church Reconstruction in north Cardiganshire in the nineteenth century', *National Library of Wales Journal,* XX, no. 4 (1978), 352-60, and the same author's 'The Rebuilding of Llanrhystud Church' and 'Religion and Politics: the Rebuilding of St. Michael's Church, Aberystwyth, and its Political Consequences', both in *Ceredigion,* VII, No. 2 (1973), 99-116, 117-30.

[16] For detailed treatment, see *idem,* 'Church Reconstruction in Breconshire in the nineteenth century', *Brycheiniog,* XIX (1980-81), 7-26, and *idem,* 'The Religious Condition of Brecon and Radnor', in O. W. Jones and D. Walker (eds.), *Links with the Past* (1974), pp. 188ff.

change operated equally in Cardiganshire and Breconshire, as elsewhere. Of these social forces, the most invincible was population change. Cardiganshire, *par excellence* the county of upland parishes where the birth rate was extraordinarily high, was losing population to the industrial parts of south Wales by mid-century. The villages and scattered homesteads produced not only sheep and cattle for the industrial markets of the south but also people. The same was true of Breconshire. It was the economy of the country as a whole that determined the available level of resources and the direction of the flow of surplus men and women. Poverty in these counties was the inescapable lot of the vast majority of their inhabitants and it was to escape from its clutches that they moved in increasing numbers to those parts of the country where an industrial economy held out the promise, even if the promise was only rarely fulfilled, of a better life. More than ten per cent of the population of the industrial districts of north Monmouthshire in mid-century were natives of Cardiganshire.

In addition to the fundamental chronologies imposed by the interaction of the forces of demography and economy, there is another chronology against which the reconstruction of the Anglican Church in Wales must be studied, and that is the over-arching one of the growth of religion in general. If, for example, we look at the statistics of religious growth in Cardiganshire in the course of the period we are examining, we find that a total of 136 places of worship was added to the county between 1800 and 1851. The Anglican contribution to this total was three (i.e. two per cent). Looking at the chronology of this growth, about three-quarters of the total were added after 1821, the period of highest growth being between 1841 and 1851. It was in this period that two of the additional Anglican churches were built, but already the Independents had added 38 places, the Baptists 16, the Calvinistic Methodists 54, the Wesleyans 18, and the Unitarians 10. Thus, the religious complexion and denominational pattern of the county, which was to contribute so heavily and richly to the culture of the industrial south, had already been determined before the Anglican Church had begun to adjust to the operation of those self-same social forces that were producing a flowering of unofficial and anti-establishment religions. By 1851 there were 326 places of worship in the county of which 87 belonged to the Church, whereas half a century earlier there had been a total stock of 136 of which no less than 84 belonged to the Church. Nonconformity in its various guises was the pre-eminent and dynamic religious force in the two rural counties we have discussed, as in the country at large. It was partly as a reaction to this, and certainly with those contrasting patterns of religious adherence in mind, that the Church eventually, by the middle 1850s, began consciously to adjust to the new social realities of the time.[17]

That patterns of church reconstruction in rural counties and in 'the mountains' should have diverged from what was coming to be accepted to be the national pattern is not surprising, for church reconstruction was a more or less organized response to a perceived need, and though motivations were everywhere and at all

---

[17] For the most detailed treatment available of the statistics of religious growth in Wales, see C. B. Turner, 'Revivals and Popular Religion in Victorian and Edwardian Wales' (unpublished University of Wales Ph.D. thesis, 1979).

times very complex, there was nevertheless an accepted definition of what was needful. The need was to deal with the challenges posed by 'spiritual destitution', which was thought to be the necessary and inescapable consequence of an ever-increasing deficiency in church accommodation. This was the great discovery of the Evangelicals at the beginning of the century, a fundamental idea which, once it had taken possession of men's minds, was to transform the Church completely. But it was first observed, measured and defined 'in the great Parishes which surround the City of London [and] in many other populous Cities and Towns of this Kingdom', where the deficiency was so great as to be 'beyond the Power of private and parochial Contributions', and such that only government could supply. [18] Hence the Act of 1818 established the Church Building Commissioners, who were made responsible for the application of a parliamentary grant of £1,000,000 towards the building of new churches in populous parishes (that is, parishes of more than 4,000 population) according to principles laid down in the Act. The Commissioners, by now bankrupt, were given a further half a million pounds in 1824, but it was the growing and alarming realization of the enormous extent of the need that determined the Evangelicals to keep their Church Building Society in being to organize what was to become not only a rather special kind of charity but also a pressure group and opinion-forming body. Only one new Welsh church was built entirely by Commissioners' grant, namely, Buckley in Flintshire—a not entirely surprising choice since the second Lord Kenyon was one of the most active members of the Church Building Society. A number of mining and manufacturing parishes were assisted in the following decade, including (strangely enough) the new church in the chapelry of Aberystwyth. [19] Spiritual destitution of the kind envisaged in legislation was scarcely typical even of 'urban' Cardiganshire.

The Church in the mountains had to contend not with spiritual destitution by reason of an inadequate supply of places of worship which by and large were sufficient in number to supply the accommodation for the populations they were designed to serve, but rather with the physical condition of the churches. Dilapidation was the curse of the Church in the mountains. Of all the county's churches described by Theophilus Jones in his great *History of Brecknockshire*, published in 1805 and 1809, only two were given the accolade of being well-kept and decently preserved. [20] It would be tiresome to quote his descriptions of the parish churches as he found them on his perambulations at the beginning of the century, but it is relevant to note that the adjectives which constantly recur in his

---

[18] ICBS, [MS.] Minutes of Proceedings Prior to the Establishment of the Society, draft of Petition (no date [23 May 1817]), in the offices of the Society, London.

[19] On the Commissioners, see M. H. Port, *Six Hundred New Churches. A Study of the Church Building Commission and its Church Building Activities* (1961); G. F. A. Best, *Temporal Pillars: Queen Anne's Bounty, the Ecclesiastical Commissioners and the Church of England* (1964), and K. A. Thompson, *Bureaucracy and Church Reform. The Organizational Response of the Church of England to Social Change, 1800-1965* (1970). The churches are listed in 'A Return of all Applications to the Ecclesiastical Commissioners for Aid towards the Building or Endowing of Churches, or Building, Altering or Repairing Parsonage Houses . . .', PP 1848, XLIX (216), and the 'Returns by H.M. Commissioners for Building New Churches', PP 1852-3, LXXVIII (125). They are, of course, fully documented in the Annual Reports of the Commissioners beginning (for Wales) with the *Third Report*, 1823.

[20] T. Jones, *The History of the County of Brecknock* (Glanusk ed., Brecon, 1909).

writings are 'dirty', 'irregular', 'decayed', 'broken', 'ruinous', 'vile', 'dark'. He paid particular attention to the unevenness of the floors of naves and chancels caused by the revolting custom of burying within the walls.

Unfortunately, Cardiganshire did not have a Theophilus Jones among its clergy, but there can be little doubt that his general descriptions of the fabric of churches and of their furniture applied equally well to the state of the churches in Cardiganshire. As late as 1870, it was said of Llanarth that its dilapidation was so far gone as to make it not only unfit for public worship but injurious to the health of any of the parishioners who ventured into it. And no wonder, for 'the earth had accumulated from the burial of the dead and other causes and reached nearly to the roof on the North side'. Of Llanddeiniol, it was said in 1832 that 'ye present church is worse than many an English hovel . . . a most wretched hovel, unworthy of being called a Church'.[21] Archdeacon David Evans in his *Memoirs* makes the point, only with more delicacy, in his recollections of the church of his childhood in Llanrhystud: 'Yr oedd y llawr o bridd, sef llwch tadau a theidiau yr oesoedd gynt' (The floor was of earth, that is to say the dust of the fathers and grandfathers of olden times).[22] It is certainly true that one should not rely on the evidence of energetic and improving archdeacons or the returns to visitation queries, or on the letters of incumbents desperate to extract additional money from charitable societies or benevolent persons; nevertheless, the evidence is overwhelming that men such as Theophilus Jones at the beginning of the century and Sir Richard Stephen Glynne in the middle of the century were accurate and objective in their descriptions of the churches they visited.[23] There is evidence, therefore, to confirm that dilapidation, decay, ruin and neglect were the curse of the Church in the mountains, and the Incorporated Society was not short of the mark in stating in 1850, 'Many of the churches in Wales are in a much more dilapidated condition than any in England, and yet, like those in the latter country, are susceptible of complete restoration'.[24] In such regions, the Church extension movement was primarily a movement to rebuild, repair or otherwise provide existing worshippers with sound, comfortable and dignified places of worship.

The question of how all this work of reconstruction was financed is of crucial importance, for it was in the ways that the necessary funds were raised, or indeed failed to be raised, that some of the essential characteristics of 'mountain' communities are most clearly revealed. The magnitude of the work accomplished is staggering. According to Sir Robert Peel, no fewer than 525 new churches had been consecrated between 1835 and 1843.[25] Of the 1,727 new churches built and

---

[21] For these references, consult the files of the ICBS deposited in Lambeth Palace Library.

[22] D. Evans, *Atgofion yr Hybarch David Evans Arch-ddiacon Llanelwy* (Lampeter, 1904), p. 7.

[23] For Glynne's descriptions, consult NLW, Glynne of Hawarden MSS. 57, 'Journals of Travel to South Wales and adjoining counties in 1824', and his notes in the same collection on churches dated 1859 and 1869. See also Cambridge Camden Society Surveys of north and mid-Wales churches in the 1840s. Lambeth Palace MSS. 1979-90. See also E. D. Jones, 'Some aspects of the history of the Church in North Cardiganshire in the eighteenth century', *Journal Hist. Soc. of the Church in Wales*, VIII (1953).

[24] ICBS, *Quarterly Report*. No. 11 (August 1851), p. 12.

[25] *Hansard,* 3rd series, LXVII, 5 May 1843, c. 1291. Note that his figures did not include Bangor, St. David's, Llandaff, Ely or Exeter.

7,144 restored since 1840, at a total cost of £25,548,703, about £1,090,000 had been expended in Wales.[26]

These very considerable sums came from two major sources: from central funds and from the localities themselves. The former consisted of those disbursed by the Church Building Commissioners (after 1856-7 by the Ecclesiastical Commissioners), and those collected by the Incorporated Society and disbursed by it in the form of grants. Although it was the main function of the Society to respond to demand, in a very real sense it was in a position greatly to influence the nature of that demand. It is important to note that the pattern of financing and the relative share that was contributed by these two bodies in England and Wales changed fundamentally from the middle of the 1830s. Between 1818 and 1830 it was in the region of 40 per cent of total expenditure (£1,200,000 from 'public' sources and £1,800,000 from private benefactions). Between 1831 and 1851 'public' grants rarely exceeded about 9 per cent of the total. Thus, between 1840 and 1852 the Commissioners reported that a total of £1,007,840 had been spent on erecting 273 churches and chapels, of which sum £871,502 had been raised by voluntary subscriptions and local rates (that is, 86 per cent was raised voluntarily).[27] During that period of twelve years, £38,655 was expended in Wales, of which £31,064 (or 80 per cent) was raised in Wales itself. By 1876, when the total had risen to over £400,000, the proportion raised by voluntary means had risen to over 95 per cent. Anglicans were certainly privileged in that they did not have to fund the total costs of building or reconstruction, but the amounts not found by them were really very small. The same is true of the relative share given by the Incorporated Society: generally speaking, it was in the region of three per cent in the first fifty years of the Society's existence. The financing of church restoration in Wales was overwhelmingly the achievement of the people in the parishes themselves and not of any body, ecclesiastical or otherwise, external to the country.[28]

It is important to note that the huge sums raised did not come from church rates so far as the 'Church in the mountains' was concerned. For example, in only one 'hill' parish in the archdeaconry of Llandaff was a church rate raised. In Cardiganshire only £200 out of a total of £43,000 was raised by a rate.[29] But while this reinforces the argument about the voluntary nature of the giving, it raises another question: namely, to what extent is it possible to distinguish between the benevolence of the rich and the gifts of the poor? The pattern of church reconstruction supplies the clues.

In both Cardiganshire and Breconshire, as indeed elsewhere in the hill country, wealthy landowners were mainly responsible for the new additional buildings. In the former county, and excluding a private chapel—an example of what George Eliot called 'family temples'—of the five additional churches two (Llangorwen

---

[26] PP 1876, LVII (125 and 125i). The statistics are of doubtful accuracy, but the *order* of expenditure is probably correct.

[27] PP 1852-3, LXXVII (125).

[28] Cf. D. M. Thompson, 'Church extension in town and countryside in later nineteenth century Leicester', in D. Baker (ed.), *The Church in Town and Countryside* (Studies in Church History, 16, 1979), pp. 439-40.

[29] PP 1876, op. cit., *passim*.

in 1841 and Elerch in 1868) were paid for and endowed by local families, the former by the Williamses of Cwmcynfelin and the latter by their relatives, the Gilbertsons of Wallog and Elerch. Both families were supporters of the Oxford Movement: Isaac Williams, the friend of Newman, Keble and Pusey and the author of the notorious No. 80 of the Tracts for the Times, was the son of the squire of Cwmcynfelin, while Llangorwen was the first of the Oxford Movement churches in Wales.[30] The others were put up by subscription with only minor assistance from central sources and only token, conventional assistance from the local gentry. Indeed, the gentry of Cardiganshire, whatever the sources of their wealth, from land or minerals or urban leaseholds or a combination of all three, were not conspicuous church builders.[31] In neighbouring Breconshire, five new churches were built, but the gentry of that county, which, if we exclude the industrial parishes, was every bit as impoverished as Cardiganshire, included some spectacularly rich families: some were industrialists who had bought land in the valleys of the Wye and the Usk, like Crawshay Bailey, the ironmaster; others were rentier families like the Thomases of Llwynmadoc, whose wealth came from the profits of Rhondda coal. Miss Clara Thomas built Eglwys Oen Duw in Abergwesin entirely at her own cost and gave massive sums to the work of reconstruction in the county. Indeed, she was a kind of conduit along which the profits of coal-mining irrigated a financially parched region. Robert Raikes, the great-grand-nephew of the founder of the English Sunday School Movement and an enthusiastic Anglo-Catholic, took down the old building at Llangasty Tal-y-llyn and rebuilt it at great cost in 1849. This church was designed to be the inspiration behind the Oxford Movement in the county, corresponding to Llangorwen in Cardiganshire.[32] Of the industrialists, the ironmaster Crawshay Bailey built a cheap and unattractive church at Brynmawr at his own cost—it was never consecrated—and Robert Thompson Crawshay a chapel of ease at Vaynor in 1874. It was mineral wealth that financed most of the new buildings in both counties, and the Oxford Movement in Wales was launched on the profits of lead-mining. Beneath the silver-gilt of the plate and the splendour of the vestments was the lead of the Cardiganshire hills or the coal of the Blaenau. So in Cardiganshire it was the existence of sources of income other than agriculture which determined the location of this new building effort. The churches were located either in the expanding town of Aberystwyth and on the railway which was expected to bring wealth into the county, or in or near the lead-mining townships, strategically situated to serve a growing and moving population. It was the wealth created in these new communities that paid for the additional means of grace.

What of the churches rebuilt or reconstructed, repaired or enlarged? This great work, which transformed the fabric and internal arrangements of virtually every

---

[30] On Tractarianism in Wales, see O. W. Jones, *Isaac Williams and his Circle* (London, 1971). Also D. E. Evans, 'Mudiad Rhydychen yng Ngogledd Sir Aberteifi', *Journal Hist. Soc. of the Church in Wales*, IV (1954), 45ff.

[31] On the Cardiganshire gentry in general, see R. J. Colyer, 'The Gentry and the County in Nineteenth-Century Cardiganshire', *Welsh Hist. Rev.*, X, no. 4, 503-5.

[32] For Breconshire, see I. G. Jones, *Brycheiniog*, XIX, and for the significance of Llangasty Tal-y-llyn, O. W. Jones, 'The Mind of Robert Raikes', *Journal Hist. Soc. Church in Wales*, XVIII (1968).

church in the mountains, was carried on in the midst of poverty. 'The inhabitants of the parish', wrote the incumbent of Llanafan (a few miles from Aberystwyth) in December 1876, 'with the exception of a few, are persons of low and narrow circumstances in life, being either employed in the mine works, or as labourers under the Agriculturists of the neighbourhood.'[33] The proprietor had 'liberally contributed', but the seven or eight farmers in the parish were of limited means. In 1866 the Medical Officer of the Privy Council, reporting on the southern parts of the county, wrote that 'the children pine for food as soon as weaned' and gave it as his opinion that were it not for the prevailing mild weather the people would all die.[34] It was poverty, not irreligion, that lay at the root of the neglect that was universally apparent. And when, as began to happen in the middle of the eighteenth century, that poverty came to be combined with the decline of the old resident gentry and their replacement by non-resident squires, their case became hopeless and they turned to other forms of religion, self-generated and self-maintained.

Hence, the distinction between parishes of small or medium-to-small size containing the estates of rich gentry families, and large upland parishes having few or no resident squires is of crucial importance in the history of church reconstruction. As the leaders in an increasingly deferential society and as the natural allies of the Established Church, the gentry had social roles to fulfil which included being charitable to the poor and seeing to their spiritual needs. The esteem in which they were held normally reflected the degree of success with which they played out those roles. The clergy looked to the gentry for support and the two groups were bound together by ecclesiastical law as well as by social convention. Where the gentry were not resident, or where, as was very frequently the case, they were reluctant to support the Church financially, then the clergy and lay officers of the parishes were compelled to have recourse to methods of raising funds, such as church rates, which were counter-productive. Tenant farmers living on the edge of subsistence in their lonely farms among the endless hills, small mechanics and tradesmen earning a meagre living in the little towns, weavers and cloth makers whose skills could no longer compete with the great mills of the border country—these had neither the means nor the wish to preserve and repair venerable ruins, and it required heroic and prolonged effort on the part of the clergy and the few devoted laymen in parishes where such were the only inhabitants to take in hand this work of reconstruction. '. . . but they are poor', pleaded the incumbent of Blaenpennal; 'there is not an Esquire and but one freeholder within the Chapelry, they are indeed very unequal to the expense of building, their will is greater, much greater, than their power.'[35] Such parishes were very numerous in upland Wales and it is not surprising that 'the Church in the mountains' in the pursuance of its own particular kind of renewal should have adopted the voluntarist methods of its nonconformist rivals. Only thus could its survival be assured.

[33] Revd D. E. Jones to ICBS, 2 December 1836: Lambeth Palace Library.
[34] Seventh Report of the Medical Officer of the Privy Council, with Appendix, PP 1865, XXVI. i, p. 498.
[35] For a detailed example, see I. G. Jones, *Journal of the Flintshire Hist. Soc.*, XXIX (1979-80). The quotation is from Revd D. Lewis to the Church Building Society, 9 January 1823, ICBS, Lambeth Palace Library.

Why there should have been a Church extension movement in the first place and why it should have affected the upland regions, if belatedly, are difficult questions, and one can only hazard guesses as to the real motives and the inner compulsions at work in the hearts and minds of such a great variety of men and women. For the movement as a whole came to involve the whole of society, all kinds and conditions of men from the aristocrat to the poor living on the edge of indigency. While aristocrats, wealthy businessmen and industralists, and professional men of all kinds gave of their plenty, it is clear that working men likewise contributed even if, as was often the case, they had only their labour to offer. At what point in the unfolding of a local effort did religious conviction become an ingredient in a fashion or become merged with the pride of a community in the variety and quality of its buildings and social amenities? At what point did piety fall a prey to denominational rivalry? Was love more powerful than fear or aesthetics more compelling than utility?

From the very beginning and throughout the first half-century or so of its development, fear of the social consequences of irreligion was a primary motive. 'Public calamity and individual misery . . . necessarily flow from a want of Religious Knowledge', declared the founders of the Church Building Society in the first year of their operation. They considered 'that the Parochial Ministrations of the Established Church are the most ready and effectual means of elevating and establishing the moral character of the People, by communicating the instructions, the consolations, and the animating hopes of our Holy Religion; which advantage', they concluded, 'cannot possibly be enjoyed without an adequate supply of Church Room.'[36] Constantly they had before their eyes, and set out in the sonorous declarations and protestations of this and similar societies founded at the same time, the profligacy and insubordination of monstrous hordes of people lost in the grossest ignorance, the prey of evil and designing men, ripe for insurrection and rebellion. It was an act of prudence and of self-defence, therefore, to donate money for providing places of worship with adequate free sittings for 'people who cannot philosophize themselves into religion'.[37] Launched in the depressed and disordered time immediately following the Napoleonic wars, the purpose of the Society was to act as an adjunct of the Church, which was conceived as the spiritual counterpart of the equally necessary strengthening of the civil laws against conspiracy and social revolution. In Wales, it was the Merthyr rising of 1831 and the appearance of trade unions at the same time in the coalfields of Flint and Glamorgan and Monmouthshire, the Chartist march on Newport in 1839, and the Rebecca riots in west Wales in the following decade, which brought home to the ruling classes the extreme seriousness of the threat to social order implicit not only in 'those colonies in the desert'[38] which industrialization was creating in the hills but also among the tenant farmers in the deep countryside. This is why, after 1839, it was easier to involve the ruling classes in Church extension in Wales than hitherto, and why, for example, the

---

[36] ICBS, [First] Annual Report (1819), p. 11, and Minute Books I, 17 May 1819, ff. 118-19.

[37] *Quarterly Review*, XXIII (July 1820), 549-91.

[38] Report of the Commissioner (Seymour Tremenheere) appointed . . . to inquire into the State of the Population in the Mining Districts (1839).

erection of an additional church at Rhymney by the local iron company in 1842 should have had the blessing of parliament, the royal family, the local aristocracy and the other industrialists of north Monmouthshire.[39] A few years later, the Reports of the Commissioners of Inquiry into the State of Education in Wales (1847) confirmed the conclusions of earlier and contemporary inquiries and provided masses of additional evidence, at least to the satisfaction of its advocates, of the need for additional church accommodation and schools. Sir Thomas Phillips, who had been mayor of Newport in 1839 and had been knighted for his conduct in defending the town against the Chartists, wrote his impressive book on *Wales* (1849) and the following year joined the Incorporated Society.[40]

None of this was done in ignorance of the accelerating work of the old dissenting denominations and of nonconformity in general. Unofficial forms of religious observance were feared almost as much as infidelity itself: indeed, in Wales Unitarianism was considered by Anglicans to be no better and to be feared no less than infidelity. It was held that Unitarianism lay at the heart of Chartism and other levelling doctrines. It is easy to understand the despair of the incumbent of Lampeter (who was also principal of St. David's College) in the face of the combination of evils he encountered in his efforts to rebuild the parish church: few wealthy people, none of the principal landowners resident, the prevalence of dissent, and the greatest landed proprietor in the district a declared Socinian! No wonder that there were by that date no less than half-a-dozen Unitarian chapels in an area of twenty or thirty square miles, and that the area was becoming known as 'Y Spottyn Du' (The Black Spot).[41] The market (and Free Trade in Religion was the order of the day, however much Tory Evangelicals may have favoured religious protectionism) was desperately competitive, and the most effective way of countering nonconformist growth was to make the Anglican Church more efficient by renewing its buildings and increasing its supply of sittings—in general defending the ancient hegemony against the ever more confident and arrogant attacks of its enemies. Hence, the Church became more professional and the reports of the Incorporated Society to resemble the annual reports of limited companies with input and output figures, moving averages, costs per sitting, and ratios of seats to population. But dissenters, old and new, were scarcely deceived, and increasingly they came to regard the movement not as an attack on spiritual destitution, which in Wales could scarcely be said to exist, but as a desperate enterprise in competitive building.

The clergy in the mountains shared these beliefs but suffered additional pressures and nourished still deeper resentments. Poverty made it difficult for them to rebuild their parish churches, but they required additional churches in their huge parishes, as well as in the populous parishes where all the money was

---

[39] S. J. Capper to ICBS, dated from Rhymney Iron Works Office, London, 14 September 1842. See also J. G. Davies, 'Industrial Society in North-West Monmouthshire, 1750-1851' (unpublished University of Wales Ph.D. thesis, 1970).

[40] For Phillips, see *Dictionary of Welsh Biography*, p. 762, and *Church Builder*, VI (1867), for his obituary.

[41] Revd. E. Morgan to ICBS, 12 June 1838, Lambeth Palace MSS. For the individual chapels, consult D. E. Davies, *Y Smotion Duon* (Llandysul, 1980).

and into which all the money flowed. As was said in a comparison of rural and urban parishes, 'In the latter we are equal to the distances, but overwhelmed by the amount of population; in the former we are equal to the population, but unequal to cope with the distances . . . because . . . people ceaselessly occupied in agricultural labour during the week are unable to cover distances varying from two to nine miles on a Sunday'. [42] In some Welsh mountain parishes—as, for example, in Caernarfonshire where quarry communities grew up many miles from the ancient parish church, and in purely pastoral parishes—this appeared to the incumbents as the main problem to be overcome. [43] Everyone seemed to accept as axiomatic that all that was needed to bring in the congregations was warm and comfortable buildings and the provision of free seats for the poor. The rector of Llandefaelog, near Brecon, was certain of this. 'I verily believe', he wrote, 'that the cold damp and *uncomfortable* state of many of the Churches in the Principality is not the least cause of dissent from the Established Church.' [44] The correlation was much too simple and dissenters from the Church in this period of primary growth did not have the choice of uncomfortable church and comfortable chapel, of cold and damp in the one and warmth in the other. The choice was more likely to be between parish church and farmhouse or barn, and would be made on the basis not only of comfort and convenience but also of belief and spiritual conviction. As Thomas Fuller, the seventeenth-century divine, well knew, it was possible, and perhaps even desirable, to have 'high meditations under a low roof, and large hearts betwixt narrow walls'. A condition of Anglican expansion was the abandonment of such simplistic and prejudiced explanations, and it is significant that it should have been Bishop Ollivant of Llandaff who led the way in this respect in 1850. [45]

Denominational competitiveness remained a powerful motive throughout the century, increasing in intensity from the early 1860s, when the factor of political ideology was added and came to provide the dominant force in the disestablishment contest. But meanwhile, and also by the 'sixties, church restoration had become a fashion. As early as 1840, the Incorporated Society laid it down as a principle that one of its main tasks was to be a catalyst and a stimulant to local bounty. It was to influence 'individuals of wealth and station to build, mainly or entirely at their own cost, and on no mean scale, edifices to the honour of God'. [46] No doubt there were wealthy men whose motives were as pure as the most eager reformer could wish, but where they reacted at all in Wales the rich estate owners and landed proprietors built not so much with an eye to social obligation as to fulfilling an architectural project, providing the new mansion with

[42] H. Mackenzie, *Plea for Mission Churches* (1863).

[43] The Religious Census of 1851 reveals how widespread in the hill country was this conviction. See I. G. Jones and D. Williams, *The Religious Census of 1851. A Calendar of Returns relating to Wales,* Vol. 1. South Wales (1976); Vol. 2. North Wales (1981): pp. 287 (Abererch) and 324 (Llanddeiniol) as examples. See G. Williams, 'Crefydda mewn llan a chapel: Cyflwr Gogledd Cymru yn y flwyddyn 1851', *Y Traethodydd* (Ebrill 1982), tt. 62-8.

[44] Revd T. Vaughan to ICBS, dated from Brecon, 5 February 1831, Lambeth Palace MSS.

[45] *Charge*: Primary Visitation, September 1851, by Alfred Ollivant (London, 1851).

[46] ICBS, 21st *Annual Report* (1840).

a church as an appendage, or creating a pleasing landscape. But motives are never simple and in the providence of God what exists for the aesthetic pleasure of one can work to the salvation of another.

Liturgical considerations also came to have an importance that was lacking in the earlier Commissioners' churches. Here, the influence both of the Oxford Movement and of the Ecclesiologists became crucial. At first suspicious of the Gothic Revival, by the early 1840s the London architects were scrutinizing plans of proposed new churches not merely for their technical excellence but also for their architectural faithfulness 'to the best models of the past'. By the middle of the century, they were attempting to impart order to the anarchy of the restoration fever, 'stemming', as George Gilbert Scott put it, 'the torrent of Destructiveness which, under the title and garb of ''Restoration'', threatens to destroy the truthfulness and genuine character of half our ancient Churches'.[47] All this reflected a shift in religious sensibilities, the influence of the new liturgical practices and an emphasis on propriety and ceremonial. Llangorwen and Llangasty Tal-y-llyn may well, in their differing emphases, have set a fashion, and the internal arrangements of the vast majority of restored churches in the mountains are eloquent not so much of the worshipping customs of ancient times as of the liturgical fashions of the time. For many a Welsh peasant brought up in the unadorned interior of the old familiar buildings, and accustomed to a language and literature which provided a compensatory richness, better the bare walls of a chapel than the Popish appearance and practices of the new church.

Perhaps the Victorians can be forgiven for attributing too much to their building programmes and for reducing the complexities of social change to the simple common denominators of stone and timber; but there can be no denying that a church, solidly built of the best of materials, designed by architects alive to religious symbolism, and flanked by parsonage and school, was bound to exert a profound influence on the neighbourhood in which it was planted. Equally, it would be naïve to ignore the even more important sociological and historical fact that church reconstruction was a part, and only a part, of a much greater movement which involved the chapels and meeting houses of a variety of denominations and into which, for a time, men of all classes and types and conditions poured unstintingly of their wealth and energies, and in which they found their highest aspirations satisfied.

---

[47] [Sir] G. G. Scott, *A Plea for the faithful restoration of our ancient Churches* (1850), p. 2.

The Welsh in English Politics, 1868-1982

KENNETH O. MORGAN

ROFESSOR Glanmor Williams's supreme scholarly achievement is usually, and rightly, considered to lie in his unique contribution to the study of the religious, social and economic history of Wales in the late-medieval and Tudor periods. His analyses of major aspects of the Protestant Reformation, and above all his *grand oeuvre* covering the evolution of the Welsh Church in the two and a half centuries that followed the Edwardian conquest, are justly renowned as authoritative and magisterial works on the earlier Welsh past. But Professor Williams has written several important studies on more recent centuries as well, and especially on the development of the idea of nationality in modern Wales. A famous article of his in 1953 has long provided a *locus classicus* in the examination of the concept of nationhood between the sixteenth century and the twentieth.[1] It has had considerable influence upon subsequent exploration of this central theme. More recently, his book of essays, *Religion, Language and Nationality in Wales,* published by the University of Wales Press in 1979, included several characteristically perceptive studies of the roots of cultural and political nationalism in the modern period. Such themes as the consequences of industrialization and the growth of literacy for the idea of nationhood were considered in depth. It is, therefore, perhaps appropriate that a volume of essays published in his honour should include discussion of one major expression of the Welsh identity in the late-nineteenth and twentieth centuries. It may help recall some of the wide-ranging intellectual interests, and the intense involvement in the contemporary scene, of a great historian who has contributed so richly in illuminating and sustaining the idea of Welshness as a major subject for historical inquiry.

The growing centrality of Wales in English and British public life has been a pronounced feature of the history of the United Kingdom from the later Victorian period onwards. During the hundred years that have passed since then, the idea and the impact of Welsh nationality have become far more precisely defined and recorded—ever since Matthew Arnold apparently buried the Welsh without trace in the swirling mists of the Celtic twilight, in his eloquent and profoundly misleading lectures given in 1866 while he held the chair of Poetry at Oxford University. From the 1870s, indeed, the Welsh, like the Scots, have surged on relentlessly to fill major voids in British social and cultural life. They have added substantially to the cosmic consciousness of the British people in the twentieth century, a process which still continues at the present time.

This growing impact of the Welsh upon English society between the 1870s and the 1980s could, indeed, be illustrated in a great variety of ways. It could be

[1] Glanmor Williams, 'The Idea of Nationality in Wales', *Cambridge Journal,* VII (December 1953).

demonstrated, for example, in terms of education. As is well known, the national cultural revival within Wales, and the total restructuring of its system of elementary, intermediate and higher education between 1889 and 1902, led, well before the First World War, to an immense export to England of schoolteachers and other academics. The effect of this, both through institutions such as the National Union of Teachers and more generally in shaping the intellectual framework within which a popular culture could evolve, was far-reaching and something in which Welsh people took legitimate pride. The impact of the Welsh was also evident in many of the professions, notably in the law courts where the forensic and dialectical skill of Welsh judges and barristers was frequently noted, quite apart from the unique talents of one 'little Welsh attorney'. In the medical profession also, stimulated by the founding of the National School of Medicine at Cardiff, the Welsh produced surgeons and specialists of great distinction, to serve the hospitals and medical schools of England. In the world of industry and commerce, of course, the advent of the Welsh was immensely influential both upon management and on the trade unions. From the troubles of the mining industry in the 1920s, when the Coalowners' Association headed by Sir Evan Williams confronted the Miners' Federation led by Arthur Cook, down to the crises at British Leyland in the early 1980s, Welshmen were frequently to the fore, both as capitalist employers and, far more characteristically, as officials of major trade unions. Again, in the field of literature and the arts, the emergence of the ill-named 'Anglo-Welsh' school of poets, novelists and short story writers from the 1930s onwards, through such periodicals as Keidrich Rhys's *Wales* and Gwyn Jones's *Welsh Review,* had a powerful influence upon the cultural sensibilities of the English-reading world. And no account of the contact of the Welsh with their English neighbours in the present century would be complete without reference to popular sport and to rugby football in particular, whose emotional messianic appeal has been recently traced by David Smith and Gareth Williams in a splendidly evocative official history of the Welsh Rugby Union.

In all these varied areas, the impact of the Welsh upon England, and the English-speaking world, has been consistent and penetrating. Yet there is justification for elevating politics above all other aspects in this context. For the changes that galvanised Welsh life and the relations of the principality with England from the 1870s onwards—that process of inter-linked social, economic and cultural transformation that went on well beyond the end of the Second World War in 1945—took place within a largely political framework. Many of the decisive landmarks in modern Wales were political. There were the franchise reforms of 1867, 1884, 1918 and 1928; the advent of democracy at the parliamentary and the local government level; the framing of new Welsh political aspirations and objectives; the growing recognition not simply as a region, another Yorkshire or Kent, but as a nation. The very concept of what it meant to be Welsh, from the days of Gladstone onwards, was conditioned in large measure by political change. The growing impact of the Welsh in other areas of English, British and transatlantic life—educational, professional, industrial, literary or sporting—was projected against a political background which gave new meaning to the sense of Welsh identity, from the era of Tom Ellis and David Lloyd George to that of James Griffiths and Aneurin Bevan. It was this truth that was indeed perceived by Aneurin Bevan himself when he declared that 'the most revolutionary power in the world is political democracy', the explosive force of which doctrinaire Marxists never understood.[2] So no apology need be offered here for adopting a largely political perspective in examining the impact of the Welsh upon various strata of English life from the late-Victorian era down to the present time. For through adopting such a method the very concept of Welsh nationhood, to which Glanmor Williams has devoted so much of his distinguished academic career, can be most fully understood.

The advent of the Welsh, their invasion of English political space in the modern period, was first located in that remarkable era of Liberal party ascendancy that lasted from the 'great election' of 1868 down to the end of the First World War. Until then, the Welsh impact upon English politics had been almost non-existent since the age of the Tudors. Wales provided simply occasional 'noises off' from a forgotten hinterland or a drowned landscape, as in the mysterious eruption of the Scotch Cattle in the 1820s, the Merthyr rising of 1831, or the attacks on tollgates by the Rebecca rioters in the early 1840s. Matthew Arnold in those same lectures in Oxford maintained that the Welsh were 'ineffectual' in politics, in eternal revolt against 'the despotism of fact', including presumably political fact.[3] His views were paralleled by those of a Welsh radical contemporary in 1866, the pacifist Henry Richard of Tregaron, who wrote that Welsh electoral politics were almost 'feudal' in character, redolent of Celtic clansmen struggling for their respective chieftains.[4] The Welsh members of parliament were largely obscure squireens. In the words of a later Welsh MP, Stuart Rendel, they were 'in an inferior category, a cheaper sort of member'.[5] There was only one well-known native politician, Henry Richard himself—and he was the exception that proved the rule. For Henry Richard was really an international celebrity, a cosmopolitan free trader, Cobden with a Cardiganshire accent, 'an inveterate peacemonger' to adopt Michael Foot's self-description. Richard had left Cardiganshire in his early twenties and viewed the politics of his native land, until the mid-1860s, very much from the outside.

Then, in the decades following the famous election of 1868, with its sweeping Liberal gains and political evictions after the poll, all this changed, very rapidly and dramatically. The whole tempo of Welsh politics from the 1870s onwards followed a unique rhythm, significantly different from that of England. Long before the outbreak of world war in 1914, Wales had been transformed into a populist democracy and into an impregnable stronghold of the British left. As a

[2] A. Bevan, *In Place of Fear* (London, 1952), p. 39; speech in the defence debate, 15 February 1951 (Parl. Deb., 5th ser., Vol. 484, 734).

[3] M. Arnold, *On the Study of Celtic Literature* (London, 1867), pp. 102, 106.

[4] H. Richard, *Letters on the Social and Political Condition of Wales* (London, 1867), p. 80.

[5] F. E. Hamer, *Personal Papers of Lord Rendel* (London, 1931), p. 313.

result of this process, the effects of this Welsh regeneration upon English politics were sweeping and conclusive. [6]

First, there emerged in English politics a unique Welsh presence and style. A cluster of new themes arose, largely concerned with the social and civic grievances of Welsh nonconformists, that were forced upon the sluggish attention of hitherto indifferent English party politicians. There was reform of the system of land tenure on the model achieved in Ireland in 1881, a demand that reached its climax during the Welsh land commission that held its sessions between 1893 and 1896. There was temperance reform, a priority symbolized by the passage of the Welsh Sunday Closing Act in 1881, the first statute to apply a separate legislative principle to Wales as distinct from England. There was the sweeping revamping of the Welsh educational system through the Intermediate Education Act of 1889 that set up over a hundred 'county' schools, the university colleges of Bangor, Aberystwyth and Cardiff that led to the creation of the national University in 1896, the emergence of the Central Welsh Board and, finally in 1907, the launching of the Welsh Department of the Board of Education. Above all, there was the contentious and persistent issue of the disestablishment of the Church of England in Wales. To the later twentieth century, Welsh disestablishment may appear a time-worn and parochial matter, of little wider concern. But it involved major principles of religious, civic and national equality. It embodied all the aspirations of the nonconformist majority. In 1868, disestablishment in Wales was a virtual non-issue. When it was first raised in the Commons in 1870, it gained a derisory forty-seven votes, in marked contrast to the triumphant passage of Irish disestablishment a year earlier. But twenty-one years later it had gained such momentum that it was a major item on the Liberals' Newcastle Programme of 1891. By 1914, aided by the 1911 Parliament Act which had curbed the House of Lords' veto, Welsh disestablishment was on the point of becoming the law of the land. Its fulfilment came shortly after the armistice, with the enthronement of the first archbishop of Wales in June 1920. Disestablishment was a quiet, undramatic revolution. It lacked the fire and fury of home rule and the other demands of the Irish nationalists. But its successful accomplishment was part of a peaceful process of social equality and democratization that helped reconcile denominations and classes within Wales, and helped consolidate the status of the principality within the United Kingdom.

Long before 1914, in fact, through disestablishment and other issues, there is a detectable change in the rhetoric and dialogue of English politics. In the daily and weekly newspaper press, in the quarterlies and the literary reviews, on platform and pulpit, Welshness had become a distinct and respectable political theme.

This process was closely linked with an important, yet little regarded, change in the structure of English, or more specifically Liberal, party politics. Until the mid-1880s, there was no coherent mechanism for Welsh political demands to be presented before the Liberal party leadership. The historic transformation took

---

[6] For fuller discussion and documentation of this theme, see my *Wales in British Politics* (Cardiff, new ed., 1980), chaps. II-VI, and also my *Rebirth of a Nation: Wales 1880-1980* (Oxford and Cardiff, 1981), ch. II.

place between 1886 and 1892.[7] In those years of Liberal parliamentary opposition, the strategy of Stuart Rendel, the Englishman who sat as member for Montgomeryshire, for the Welsh members to become more effective as a pressure-group and to achieve far greater political effectiveness, chimed in with the desire of Francis Schnadhorst and the machine men of the National Liberal Federation to recast British Liberalism at its foundations after the disastrous schism over Irish home rule in 1886 which had led to the secession of Joseph Chamberlain, Hartington and other Liberal Unionists. In 1886-7, new Liberal Federations were formed for North and for South Wales, represented together in a Welsh National Liberal Council. Most significant, these new bodies were affiliated directly to the National Liberal Federation based in party headquarters in London. This move was ratified at the annual conference of the National Liberal Federation at Nottingham in October 1887—when, revealingly enough, Welsh disestablishment was first adopted as a plank on the Liberal party programme. Conversely, the Scottish Liberal Association was not directly affiliated to the NLF in London, and it is not fanciful to explain the greater political success of the Welsh in influencing the national Liberal Party in 1886-1914, compared with the Scots, through their organic relationship with the parent body. The Scots, by contrast, suffered from their own exclusion. The legacy for Wales of this historic development in the late-1880s is writ large upon subsequent passages of the history of Wales, with perhaps the University itself, which owed so much to the sympathy shown by Gladstone and other Liberal leaders, as the main landmark. *Si monumentum requiris* . . .

A second feature of this period of Liberal ascendancy was that the human instruments of Welshness thrust themselves aggressively upon English political consciousness as the alien outsiders they were. Some of these Welsh Liberals operated within English constituencies in London, Birmingham and Middlesbrough. The London Welsh, with their intensely-developed chapel life, became a leading pressure-group in promoting the *Cymru Fydd* brand of nationalism in the later 1880s. They became a powerful support for the later political advance of Lloyd George.[8] Most important of all was Liverpool where, by the end of the century, there were many thousands of first- or second-generation Welshmen encamped on Merseyside.[9] By 1900, there was a score of Welsh-language chapels (at least 20,000 first- or second-generation Liverpudlians were said to be Welsh-speaking), a Welsh publishing house was soon to be formed, while a leading Welsh newspaper, *Y Cymro,* was launched in 1890 by Isaac Foulkes, a publisher and novelist from rural Denbighshire. The North and South Wales Bank, founded in Liverpool in 1836, lent financial assistance to

---

[7] See Morgan, *Wales in British Politics,* ch. III; M. Barker, *Gladstone and Radicalism* (Hassocks, Sussex, 1975), pp. 117-28; G. V. Nelmes, 'Stuart Rendel and Welsh Liberal Political Organization in the Late-Nineteenth Century', *Welsh Hist. Rev.,* IX, no. 4 (1979), 468-85.

[8] E.g. in his famous address on the war and 'the little five-foot-five nations' to a London Welsh audience at Queen's Hall, 19 September 1914.

[9] P. Waller, *Democracy and Sectarianism. A Political and Social History of Liverpool, 1868-1939* (Liverpool, 1981), pp. 9-10, and Biographical Notes; J. R. Jones, *A Welsh Builder on Merseyside* (Liverpool, 1946); O. Thomas and J. M. Rees, *Cofiant y Parch John Thomas D.D.* (Llundain, 1898).

builders and small businessmen from Anglesey and elsewhere. The Liverpool Welsh were prominent, then, in the business, commercial and religious life of that troubled city. Inevitably, too, they were active in Liverpool Liberal politics, notably in the Toxteth, Walton and West Derby divisions, where the chapel-going, temperance-minded Welsh worked most uneasily alongside their Irish papist allies. Birkenhead, across the Mersey, also boasted a large Welsh community: an important national eisteddfod was held there in 1917, celebrated for the posthumous award of the bardic chair to the Trawsfynydd shepherd, Hedd Wyn.

Apart from the role of the Welsh in English constituency politics, many Welshmen emerged as members of parliament for English or Scottish seats. In the halcyon year of 1906, over a dozen were recorded as representing English constituencies after that Liberal electoral landslide (some highly authentic like Leif Jones in Appleby or Timothy Davies in Fulham, others distinctly anglicized like John Simon in Walthamstow or Donald Maclean in Bath).[10] One prominent Welsh-born MP in Scotland was J. Wynford Philipps, later Viscount St. David's, who defeated Keir Hardie in the famous by-election at Mid-Lanark in April 1888. Oddly enough, despite his base in Pembrokeshire and his close attention to the Welsh tithe riots at the time, Philipps referred to himself repeatedly before the Mid-Lanark electors as 'an Englishman who lived in Wiltshire'.[11] It is noticeable that the same amnesia afflicted Roy Jenkins of Abersychan when campaigning as Social Democratic candidate in Hillhead, Glasgow, in February 1982. Maybe the northern air produces some curious effect on the chemistry of Welsh candidates in Scottish by-elections.

But the main human agents of Liberal Welshness, of course, operated from within Wales itself. They were backed up by a powerful community presence, a thriving newspaper press in both languages, a buoyant nonconformist pulpit, a vigorous cultural revival in music and literature, and a mass working-class involvement in politics in industrial and rural areas alike. From this stimulating background, there emerged a new generation of radical middle-class nonconformist Liberals within the Welsh Parliamentary Party, adroitly presided over from its formation in 1888 by the Englishman, Stuart Rendel, a close personal friend of Gladstone himself. These new Welsh MPs were very different from the old style of mid-Victorian survivors like Henry Richard (died 1888), Lewis Llewellyn Dillwyn (died 1892) or Sir Henry Hussey Vivian (died 1893). They were younger, more aggressive, more politically sophisticated, more avowedly national or nationalist in their ideological approach.

This was a half-forgotten generation which deserves to be resurrected and honoured anew. There was Ellis Griffith, an eloquent barrister who represented Anglesey from 1895 to 1918. There was Herbert Lewis, a modest, constructive Clwyd solicitor, who represented the boroughs and county of Flintshire between 1892 and 1918, and who also achieved much effective work on behalf of public education in partnership with the historian, H. A. L. Fisher. There was the

---

[10] *South Wales Daily News*, 5 February 1906.
[11] K. O. Morgan, *Keir Hardie, Radical and Socialist* (London, 1975), p. 28; *The Scotsman*, 6 April 1888.

school-teacher, William Jones, member for Arfon between 1895 and 1915, whose 'silvery tones' captured the fancy of *Punch*. There was Llewelyn Williams, a barrister, journalist, historian, man of letters and politician of almost limitless talent, who sat for Carmarthen Boroughs from 1906 to 1918. There was Samuel Evans, another lawyer who sat for Mid-Glamorgan from 1890 to 1910 before serving with much distinction as president of the Court of Admiralty. And in the depths of the industrial coalfield, there was D. A. Thomas, Lord Rhondda, the coalowner of the Cambrian Combine, the 'Czar of Tonypandy' in 1910, but also MP for Merthyr (and briefly for Cardiff) for twenty-two years between 1888 and 1910, and a brilliantly creative figure at the local Government Board during the supreme crisis of the First World War in 1917.

There were two others, more notable still. Tom Ellis, a reflective cultural nationalist of beguiling charm, member for Merioneth between 1886 and 1899, was a politician of real charisma who became Liberal chief whip at thirty-five and died of tuberculosis in his fortieth year, his talents largely unfulfilled. Ellis was New College on top, Bala and Cefnddwysarn underneath. It was wholly characteristic that some of his most memorable addresses should be given before the Welsh Guild of Graduates, and that he should occupy his leisure moments by studying the works of the seventeenth-century puritan and mystic, Morgan Llwyd. For many in that Darwinian age, Tom Ellis was the very embodiment of the Celtic genius in politics.[12] And finally there was David Lloyd George, who represented Caernarvon Boroughs without a break from his famous narrow by-election victory in 1890 until just before his death in 1945. Lloyd George was a politician from his turbulent school days and his childhood instruction at the feet of 'Uncle Lloyd'—perhaps even from the age of five when, as a junior onlooker, he attended Liberal election demonstrations during the great contests of 1868. From the time of the Boer War, if not earlier, he became the very personification of Welsh radicalism. In so many ways, Lloyd George was an untypical Welsh Liberal. As connoisseurs of the television screen will have observed, he was no puritan, whether at home or away. He was impatient with the constraints and the parochialism of the nonconformist chapels, and with the petty snobberies of the 'beatified drapers' and 'glorified grocers' on the *sêt fawr*.[13] Contradictions abounded in him throughout his kaleidoscopic career. The 'big beast' contained multitudes. Yet, without doubt, he did more than anyone else in politics to bring Welsh affairs to the controversial forefront of British politics, in relation to disestablishment, tithe, education, devolution and much else besides. As a dominant figure in Liberal and coalition governments in 1905-16, and then for six years as prime minister, he never lost his unique compelling identification with his own nation, his abiding point of reference throughout the storms that beset his long career.

---

[12] J. A. Spender, *Sir Robert Hudson: a Memoir* (London, 1930), p. 24. There is a stimulating account of Ellis's career in N. C. Masterman, *The Forerunner* (Llandybie, 1972).

[13] See David Lloyd George to his wife, 10 June 1890 and 1 December 1890 (K. O. Morgan [ed.], *Lloyd George: Family Letters, 1885-1936* [Oxford and Cardiff, 1973], pp. 28, 39-40), in which D. H. Evans and his wife are referred to; L. Masterman, *C. F. G. Masterman: a Biography* (London, 1939), p. 200.

These Welsh Liberals were different in many significant respects from their successors, or some of them. They were not socialists—certainly Lloyd George could never be so styled, for all his frequent essays in collectivism, notably when in fruitful partnership with Christopher Addison at the Ministry of Munitions. A major objective for his brand of 'new Liberalism' was to ward off the extreme threat of socialism. Nor were these Liberals nationalists in the sense that Plaid Cymru later understood that term. They sought equality for Wales within the British and imperial framework, not exclusion from it. Welsh home rule was, broadly speaking, simply not on their agenda. The one occasion when it appeared to be, the *Cymru Fydd* movement of 1894-6, proved to be a massive and disastrous fiasco that divided Liberals in rural and industrial Wales almost fatally. Nor were these Welsh Liberals much concerned with the future of the Welsh language. In that optimistic age, Tom Ellis or Lloyd George felt that the Welsh language would last for ever, and the linguistic census figures from 1891 to 1911 appeared to confirm that confidence in the sense that the numbers of Welsh-speakers were steadily rising. Even so, these Welsh Liberals, with all their limitations or apparent limitations, made Wales a political reality. Indeed, as has been seen, they were distinctly more successful than the Scots in the 1886-1914 period. Even the Conservative Party, unionist to the bone, was by 1914 converted to the idea of Welsh nationality which in the past it had dismissed or derided. No longer would Conservatives make political capital by bland pronouncements that 'there was no such place as Wales'. After all, the Welsh had steered clear of the separatism—and the incipient violence—of the Irish. *Cymru Fydd* and *Sinn Fein* were worlds apart. This was a creative, energetic generation of late-Victorian and Edwardian Liberals whose powerful legacy lives on in the Wales of the later twentieth century.

During this period of Liberal ascendancy, the perceptions of Welshness became far more subtle, sensitive and intelligent. As David Smith has argued,[14] this corresponded with the new images created for themselves by Welsh publicists and propagandists during the heyday of 'imperial Wales'. The Celtic mists conjured up by Matthew Arnold at Oxford were finally dispelled. Gladstone himself became an imaginative interpreter of the meaning of Welshness in politics—notably in a famous address to 60,000 people at Singleton Park in Swansea in 1887[15]—and where this titan led, lesser mortals followed. Down to the Edwardian high noon before 1914, the English politicians' view became far more positive and sympathetic, and all parties shared in this process. It is true that, during the fierce campaigning and controversy that surrounded the fight for Lloyd George's 'people's budget' in 1909-10, with its contentious taxes on land, some more traditional attitudes began to surface. A few Conservatives were prone to reflect upon the distinctive Celtic personality and methods of the Welsh chancellor of the Exchequer. Cosmo Lang, archbishop of York, denounced 'that

[14] D. Smith, 'Wales through the Looking-Glass', in *idem* (ed.), *People and Proletariat* (London, 1980), especially pp. 220-5.

[15] *The Times*, 5 June 1887.

mysterious possession affecting the Celtic temperament which is called the
"hwyl" which makes the speaker say he knows not what and excites the audience
they know not why'.[16] These Unionist suggestions that the Welsh were somehow
not quite as British as the English were, and that some Britons were more unionist
than others, gave Lloyd George admirable grist for his dialectical mill on the
public platform. He delighted to point out the hypocrisy of Unionists, who
emphasized the indivisibility of the empire from the Old Man of Hoy in the north
to Van Diemen's Land in the far south, attempting to isolate the Welsh in so
blatant a fashion. 'They would have to reckon with the Welshman this time.'[17]

But, in general, these attacks were untypical of Conservative attitudes and
assumptions. As has been shown above, the Conservative Party had become
increasingly more attuned to Welsh nationality. No longer would Tory
spokesmen dare to ridicule the Welsh language and folk culture as little more than
'bardic fragments', as H. C. Raikes (Cambridge University) had once done in
the 1880s.[18] Lloyd George and his apparent political extremism stirred up
nothing remotely resembling the ugly anti-semitism excited by the implication of
Rufus and Godfrey Isaacs and Herbert Samuel in the Marconi affair. For
Conservatives now understood that the cases of Wales and of Ireland were clean
different. They now asserted that the main argument for not disestablishing the
Welsh Church was derived from its inherent Welshness. Historically and
sentimentally, the Church was rooted in the age-long experience of the Welsh
people since the early middle ages, whereas the nonconformist denominations
were *arrivistes* of the seventeenth century. Welshness, for Conservatives, was now
safe and acceptable, as it was for a landowner like Sir John T. Dillwyn-Llewelyn
who served as president of the Welsh Rugby Union. Wales now implied an
accommodating, safe identity, another form of social control.

This kind of Welsh impact upon English politics was weakened fatally with the
downfall of the Liberal Party after 1918, and the decline of religious
nonconformity that was associated with it. It was perhaps cheapened by the crude
jingoism of 1914-18 in which even great Liberal *littérateurs* like Sir John Morris-
Jones and Sir Owen M. Edwards used the stereotypes of Welsh nationhood to
abuse the 'Hun', and to sustain the war effort and the premiership of Lloyd
George.[19] As a result, Welsh Liberalism underwent an erosion of morale from
which it never recovered. Thereafter, the sagging fortunes of Lloyd George after
1918 were often associated with some kind of perception of Welshness. J. M.
Keynes in his *Economic Consequences of the Peace,* written in 1919 (but in a passage
not published until 1933 when the dust had partly settled), linked some of the
weaknesses of the peace settlement to the feckless qualities of a Welsh prime

---

[16] Cited in J. H. Edwards, *Life of David Lloyd George,* Vol. IV (London, 1913), p. 126.

[17] A particularly effective exposition of this line of attack was in his speech at Queen's Hall on 'rural
intimidation', 23 March 1910.

[18] Parl.Deb., 3rd ser., CCCXXIII, 482 (7 March 1888). Raikes was the postmaster-general at the time.

[19] E.g. Sir J. Morris-Jones in *Y Beirniad,* October 1914, pp. 217-24, and October 1915, pp. 191-205; Sir O.
M. Edwards in *Cymru,* February 1915. I have discussed this point at greater length in 'Peace Movements in
Wales, 1899-1945', *Welsh Hist. Rev.,* X, no. 3 (1981), 405-8.

minister allegedly 'rooted in nothing'. He bracketed an account of Lloyd George's mercurial personality with some colourful and far-fetched speculations on the 'hag-ridden magic and enchanted woods of Celtic antiquity'.[20] There were other critics to relate the unorthodox financial aspects of the 'honours scandal' and the Lloyd George Fund to the well-known kleptomania in which Taffy had traditionally indulged. Later on there appeared political novels which focussed attention on some of Lloyd George's better-known public and private weaknesses, such as Arnold Bennett's *Lord Raingo* (1926) and later on Joyce Cary's political trilogy, of which the most notable was *Prisoner of Grace* (1952). But these novels made no attempt to associate Lloyd George's defects with a wider condemnation of the Welsh in politics. Indeed, Andy Clyth in *Lord Raingo* was a Scot, while Chester Nimmo, the central character in Cary's novels, is an Englishman apparently from Devon. Despite the First World War, therefore, despite the extraordinary decline of the public stature of the once all-powerful imperial figure of Lloyd George, the Liberal legacy, in relation to political perceptions of Wales, remained a distinctly positive one.

A new form of the Welsh impact on English politics arose with the rise of the Labour Party from the end of the First World War down to the later 1960s. Wales had been a slow starter in Labour politics prior to the great six-months' coal lock-out of 1898. Until then, Labour had been but a section of a broad-based Liberal coalition; trade union leaders like 'Mabon' (William Abraham) of the Cambrian Miners were inseparable in their outlook from middle-class nonconformist Liberals. Even Keir Hardie's first election for Merthyr Tydfil in the 'khaki election' of 1900 owed everything to Liberal votes and relatively little to the strength in the valleys of the ILP.[21] But the years of Taff Vale and Tonypandy, together with the great Bethesda lock-out in the Penrhyn quarries in 1900-3, brought about a profound shift of industrial and political attitudes. By the 1918 'coupon election', the fifty-seven-strong parliamentary Labour Party included ten Welsh MPs. From 1922 onwards, Labour dominated the parliamentary representation of Wales with its monopoly of power throughout the coalfield from Llanelli to Pontypool. Even in the *débâcle* of 1931, Labour largely retained its strongholds in the Welsh valleys, and Welsh influence within the Labour Party in the thirties was pervasive. It was reinforced before and after the 1945 election by other Welshmen serving as Labour members for English and Scottish constituencies, including Rhys Davies (Westhoughton), Elwyn Jones (West Ham South), Moelwyn Hughes (Islington) and Emrys Hughes (South Ayrshire). Alongside these political developments, in the trade union world several major trade unions had prominent Welsh figures at the helm. There were Jimmy Thomas in the National Union of Railwaymen, Bob Williams in the Transport Workers, and above all the Miners Federation of Great Britain, where one

---

[20] J. M. Keynes, *Essays in Biography* (London, 1933, reprinted 1961), pp. 35-6.
[21] Morgan, *Keir Hardie*, pp. 117-18, and K. O. Fox, 'Labour and Merthyr's Khaki Election of 1900', *Welsh Hist. Rev.*, II, no. 4 (1965), 364-5.

general secretary from south Wales, Frank Hodges, gave way in 1924 to another, the far more militant personality of Arthur Cook.

One consequence of this Labour ascendancy that now unfolded in the wake of the older Liberalism, was that a new type of Welsh politician loomed large for the English to try to comprehend. The older type of Labour man, like 'Mabon' or William Brace, was hard to distinguish from the Liberals. Mabon himself lived on until 1920, and the ethic of 'Mabonism', expressing the imperatives of class collaboration and industrial harmony, survived with him. But immediately after the First World War, there was a massive transformation. The rise of a man like Vernon Hartshorn of Maesteg, prominent in the MFGB executive and a member of the first two Labour cabinets, illustrated the rise of a new, authentic cadre of working-class leadership, conscious of its class base.[22] More powerful still, the products of the Central Labour College in Regents Park in London—Aneurin Bevan, Ness Edwards, James Griffiths, Morgan Phillips, Bryn Roberts and many others—formed a new élite as certainly as did the Aberystwyth-trained middle-class Liberals of the *Cymru Fydd* vintage of the 1880s and 1890s.[23] Here were new Welsh 'space invaders' in the *lebensraum* of the English political culture—but speaking the language of class rather than of community.

Unlike their Liberal predecessors, the Welsh Labour MPs were less closely identified with specifically Welsh issues. Indeed, many of these issues had passed away with the older secretarian politics of pre-1914. Welsh disestablishment in 1920 had seemed a massive anti-climax after a century of struggle. As time went on, many Welsh Labour MPs were Welsh only in accent, and with greater social mobility and cultural homogeneity after 1945 even this characteristic was often less in evidence. By the 1960s, with such names as Callaghan, Donnelly, Padley and McBride among their number, many of them were Welsh by occasional residence and little more.

From the 1930s to the 1960s, much of the Welsh Labour politics was embodied in the rival appeals of two major figures, James Griffiths and Aneurin Bevan. They offered a twin challenge for the Welsh political psyche. James Griffiths was, from the start of his career in the ILP before the First World War, uniquely associated with specifically Welsh themes. He came from a remarkable and vigorous cultural heritage in the Amman valley in east Carmarthenshire which Mr Beverley Smith has admirably delineated.[24] From his entry into parliament in 1936, Griffiths was identified with the Welsh aspects of the troubles of the coal mining and tinplate industries, with tuberculosis in rural and industrial Wales, with the social services offered by Welsh local and central government. Within the Attlee government in 1945-51, even when colonial secretary in 1950-51, he fought hard for the recognition of Wales within the centralised structure of the gas, electricity and transport industries after nationalisation.[25] He fought hard, too, for

[22] See P. Stead, 'Vernon Hartshorn: Miners' Agent and Cabinet Minister', *Glamorgan Historian*, VI (1969), pp. 83-94; and *idem*, 'Working-Class Leadership in South Wales, 1900-1920', *Welsh Hist. Rev.*, VI, no. 3 (1973), pp. 329-53.

[23] See W. W. Craik, *The Central Labour College* (London, 1964), notably the biographical appendices.

[24] J. B. Smith *et al.*, *James Griffiths and his Times* (Cardiff, 1977); and Mr Smith's article, 'John Gwili Jenkins (1872-1936)', *Trans. Hon. Soc. Cymmrodorion*, 1974-5, pp. 191-214.

[25] Cf. J. Griffiths, 'Note on the Electricity Bill, 17 December 1946', CP (46), 462 (PRO, CAB 129/15).

Welsh interests on the Cabinet Machinery of Government Committee from May 1946 onwards. He battled (in vain) for effective executive powers to be given to the new Council for Wales inaugurated by Herbert Morrison in 1948. [26] James Griffiths was from the start deeply influenced by older Welsh nonconformist radical values. He fought hard against the erosion of the Welsh Sunday Closing Act of 1881 by the 1960 Licensing Bill introduced by the Macmillan government. Significantly enough, his brother, Amanwy, was a noted eisteddfodic bard.

By contrast, Aneurin Bevan, the member for Ebbw Vale from 1929 to 1960, viewed socialism in class and international terms. Despite a warm commitment to Welsh communitarian values, derived in part from his Welsh-speaking Baptist father in Tredegar, he had no sympathy with Welsh or other particularist deviations from the socialist norm. In a famous intervention in the first Welsh day debate in the House of Commons in 1944, he inquired, sarcastically, how precisely Welsh sheep differed from sheep grazing in Westmorland or the Highlands. [27] After 1945 he argued vigorously—and successfully—against James Griffiths within the Attlee administration in opposing any recognition of Wales within the framework of centralised economic planning. [28] In addition to this, with his observations about 'vermin' and other oratorical excesses, Bevan became for a time, in the English press and on the radio, the popular symbol of the Welsh extremist of his day—an impression reinforced by the activities of other incorrigible rebels on the far left such as S. O. Davies and Emrys Hughes. To the 'Radio Doctor', Bevan represented a 'Tito from Tonypandy'. His very name was mispronounced, with heavy emphasis on the second syllable, allegedly to distinguish him from Ernest Bevin elsewhere in the Attlee government and the political spectrum, but probably just to be offensive. For a brief period, at the time of the 1950 and 1951 elections, Aneurin Bevan appeared to have aroused a kind of hostility towards 'the unspeakable Celt' unknown since Lloyd George and the 'People's Budget'. However, it did not last very long or go very deep. By the time of his death in 1960, Bevan, deputy-leader of the Labour Party, an old associate of Beaverbrook, a shadow foreign secretary who had warmly championed Britain's retention of nuclear weapons, almost a patriot at the time of Suez, could safely be embraced by the British establishment in Fleet Street and beyond. By the 1980s, it had become a journalistic cliché to contrast the 'legitimate' parliamentary socialism of the Bevanite left of the 'fifties with the Marxist extremism of the Bennite battalions in the constituencies a generation later.

In the era of Labour dominance, the influence of the Welsh within the English political structure was far more widespread than during the period of Liberal ascendancy between 1868 and 1914. From the 1920s, the Welsh penetrated far into the utmost recesses of the party machine. The most notable of all within the

---

[26] Material in prime minister's files, including correspondence between Griffiths and Attlee, 1946 (PRO, PREM 8/1569); memorandum on 'The Administration of Wales and Monmouthshire', PRO, CP (48), 228 (CAB 129/30); correspondence between Griffiths and Morrison, October 1948 (National Library of Wales, Griffiths Papers, C/2/6-11).

[27] Welsh day debate, 17 October 1944 (Parl.Deb., 5th ser., CCCCIII, 2311-14).

[28] *James Griffiths and his Times*, pp. 41-2.

Labour Party bureaucracy was Morgan Phillips, a Welsh-speaking ex-miner born in Aberdare, subsequently active in Bargoed, the dominant apparatchik of British socialism, and from 1944 to 1962 the most powerful secretary of the Labour Party since the days of Arthur Henderson. Attlee once observed to Crossman that Phillips's draft papers 'always had to be translated from the Welsh'. [29] Phillips was to be succeeded as general secretary in 1962 by a Welsh emigré from Birkenhead, Len Williams.

With the massive outflow of Welsh unemployed workers from the staple industries of the valleys in the later 1920s and the 1930s, the Welsh became increasingly assertive within English constituency politics. They were active in transforming and radicalising the politics of Dagenham and Hounslow, of Cowley and Coventry, and of Slough with its important trading estate and government training centre which acted as a magnet for many Welsh emigrants. Industrially and politically, the Welsh became known as a militant, perhaps rebellious, element. De-skilled as coal miners or steel workers, they now became active in general unions of the unskilled such as the Transport Workers or the General and Municipal Workers. Herbert Austin, the car manufacturer, noted their 'bloodymindedness' and the role of Welsh unionists in leading the first-ever strike at his Longbridge works in 1929. [30] Welsh shop stewards were in the forefront in Oxford in the first strike at the Pressed Steel works in 1934.

Politically, the life of the tranquil conservative university city of Oxford was much transformed by the impact of many thousands of immigrants from the 'depressed areas'. This applied to the Welsh above all, since over ten per cent of migrants into Oxford between 1926 and 1935 (especially in 1933-5) came from Wales. [31] Firebrands like Tom Harris and Dai Huish, both former activists in the South Wales Miners Federation, were prominent as shop stewards for the Transport Workers and in the politics of the Labour Party. [32] Welsh trade unionists were active in starting up the Cowley Labour Party, in the neighbourhood of the Morris works, in 1934, shortly after the Pressed Steel strike. Several Welshmen fought key local elections in wards of Oxford previously uncontested by Labour. Emrys Roberts, a south Walian from the NUR, won a major victory in Oxford's South Ward in 1937. The exact quality of the Welshness of these militants is open to some question. They did not generally participate in the more traditional aspects of cultural life in the city—in the Welsh chapels, in the Oxford Welsh male voice choirs, or in the Pressed Steel rugby team. Their national awareness expressed itself in radical politics and in industrial militancy which saw Tom Harris of the TGWU, for instance,

[29] The best source for Phillips lies in the general secretary's papers in the Labour Party archive, Walworth Road, London; J. Morgan (ed.), *The Backbench Diaries of Richard Crossman* (London, 1981), p. 234 (26 May 1953).

[30] R. Church, *Herbert Austin: the British Motor Car Industry to 1941* (London, 1979), p. 151.

[31] G. H. Daniel, 'Some Factors affecting the Movement of Labour', *Oxford Economic Papers*, 3 (February 1940), pp. 144-79; and *idem*, 'A Sample Analysis of Labour Migration into Oxford' (unpublished University of Oxford D.Phil. thesis, 1939), where a sample of 600 Oxford Welsh male workers in 1937 is used.

[32] R. C. Whiting, 'The Working Class in the "New Industry" Towns between the Wars: the case of Oxford' (unpublished University of Oxford D.Phil. thesis, 1978), especially pp. 186ff, 251, 274ff, 353-4, 391. I am much indebted to Dr Whiting for some helpful advice on this important topic.

dismissed by Morris Motors in 1938—and later reinstated after a one-day strike. The following year, the TGWU itself removed Harris as a branch secretary—which led to some car workers defecting to the AEU in consequence. It is no surprise to see Harris and other Welshmen prominent in the Oxford Spanish Democratic Defence Committee at the same period. In their distinctive fashion, the Welsh helped break the mould of politics in constituencies like Oxford in the English midlands and some of the home counties. They acted as catalysts for political change as Irish immigrants had done before them in English and Scottish constituency politics, and in the 'new unionism' of the 1880s and the 1890s. The incursion of the Welsh in the depression years of the thirties was on a smaller scale, but it was a part of the road that led inexorably to 1945.

More generally, the Welsh in major unions such as the TGWU and the Miners' Federation (the NUM from January 1945), together with such figures as Bryn Roberts of Abertillery and the Central Labour College who served as general secretary of the National Union of Public Employees from 1934 onwards, added massively to the popular strength of the Labour Party before and after the 1945 election. Sometimes, indeed, the Welsh emerged under other auspices. For example, there was Arthur Horner, general secretary of the National Union of Mineworkers in 1946 after a long period as president of the south Wales miners. He was a noted communist, as also were younger men like Will Whitehead, Will Paynter and Dai Francis. Yet Horner confirms the general argument. For all his communism, the tribune of Maerdy, 'little Moscow', lent his weight to the Labour triumph of 1945, to bringing about the nationalisation of the mines, and drafting the 'miners' charter' with Emanuel Shinwell, and to shoring up the position of the Attlee government during the difficult years of the wage freeze and devaluation of 1948-50. There was a brief prospect of Arthur Horner even joining the National Coal Board, which would have been the poacher turning gamekeeper indeed. [33] Horner, understandably and probably rightly, declined in the end. Yet Arthur Horner, 'incorrigible rebel' as he proclaimed himself in his fascinating memoirs, was another paradigm example of the successful permeation of English public life by the radical culture of the Welsh valleys.

What these Labour men (there were few women of significance) contributed to politics that was distinctively Welsh is hard to define. Indeed, their very notion of Welshness was singularly elusive. The overall verdict must be that the specifically Welsh aspect of Labour politics was a limited one. Labour continued to place its emphasis primarily upon centralisation and class solidarity which united the workers of all countries. That was certainly the view of Morgan Phillips who looked with intense suspicion upon ideas for a Welsh secretary of state, an elective council, or other symbols of particularism or quasi-nationalism. [34] The 'Parliament for Wales' campaign in the early 'fifties was sternly rebuffed by the Labour leadership and the party machine. Even the creation of a Welsh Regional Council of Labour within the Labour Party, uniting the efforts of all the local

[33] A. Horner, *Incorrigible Rebel* (London, 1960), pp. 182-3. There is a sympathetic and perceptive treatment of Horner in H. Francis and D. Smith, *The Fed* (London, 1979), especially pp. 145-70. Also see the entry on Horner in J. Bellamy and J. Saville (eds.), *Dictionary of Labour Biography*, Vol. 5 (London, 1979).

[34] Goronwy Roberts to Morgan Phillips, 5 August 1950 (Labour Party archives: general secretary's files).

constituency parties under the secretaryship of Cliff Prothero, was gained only with some difficulty in 1947.[35] And yet Welshness in politics obstinately refused to disappear during the Labour ascendancy. After the fall of the Attlee government in 1951, pressure continued to mount for a secretaryship of state on the same lines as that achieved for Scotland as long ago as 1885. The record of Welsh pressure for economic regional assistance in 1945-51, while impressive and successful in many ways, emphasised the difficulty experienced by Welsh Labour MPs who had no direct voice in the cabinet to proclaim their views. It was an attitude strongly reinforced by the powerful north Wales trade-union leader, Huw T. Edwards of the TGWU, the first chairman of the Council for Wales.[36] The establishment of a Ministry for Welsh Affairs by the Conservatives (admittedly under a Scotsman, Maxwell-Fyfe, in the first instance) increased the pressure for the Labour Party to be more adventurous. In the end, even Aneurin Bevan, with great reluctance, accepted the pledge to create a Welsh Secretaryship of State being placed on Labour's general election manifesto in 1959. Bevan's biographer and close friend, Michael Foot, was later to prove himself a warm enthusiast for devolution. The key figure was James Griffiths, eventually to be appointed the 'charter secretary' for Wales by Harold Wilson in 1964. Griffiths was the vital link, along with important north Wales Labour MPs like Cledwyn Hughes and Goronwy Roberts, connecting the class revolt of the 'thirties with the very different, more diffuse political pressures that led to a Welsh Office being created in 1964, and to Welsh devolution emerging on the political agenda later in the decade.[37] By the later 1960s, the Labour Party was evolving a very different outlook towards the government of Wales from that displayed during the Morrisonian centralism of the Attlee years after 1945. More indirectly, less insistently than their Liberal predecessors, the Welsh Labour MPs helped reinforce the impact of the Welsh upon the wide open spaces of English politics.

The Labour ascendancy reached a high water-mark in 1966 when Labour captured 32 seats out of 36 in Wales. More than at any other time in its history, Labour seemed the voice and conscience of Wales, as rooted in Anglesey and Conwy as in the Rhondda and Ebbw Vale. Since that time, there has been a period of intense change. Indeed, the picture offered by Welsh politics in the early 'eighties is scarcely recognisable compared with that of 1966. The Labour Party went through great turmoil in the 'seventies and, with two seats lost in the 1979

---

[35] Minutes of Labour Party Organizational Sub-Committee of NEC, 15 January 1947 (Labour Party archives).

[36] See the Labour parliamentary deputation on unemployment in Wales, 1946 (PRO, PREM 8/272) and the Welsh deputation to discuss unemployment, 1946 (PRO, LAB 43/1); also the correspondence between D. R. Grenfell and W. Mainwaring, and Attlee, 1946, in PREM 8/1569. Grenfell and Mainwaring complained to the prime minister, 14 August 1946, that the government's attitude seemed 'to repudiate entirely the claims of Wales as a nation'; they repeated their demand for a minister for Wales, if not necessarily a secretary of state. There is important material on this theme in the Huw T. Edwards Papers in the National Library of Wales (general correspondence files, arranged chronologically), notably Edwards to Herbert Morrison, 27 November 1946.

[37] James Griffiths, *Pages from Memory* (London, 1969), pp. 164-6.

election, showed clear signs of losing its old dominance, especially in north and central Wales. Only two constituencies north of the Teifi and the Brecon Beacons returned Labour MPs in that year, East Flint and Wrexham—and the MP for the latter was later to defect to the Social Democrats. The Conservatives, who gained three seats in 1979, also showed much change, as also did Plaid Cymru as the struggle for the party leadership between its two remaining MPs in 1981 suggested. The import of the Social Democratic Party (to which three Welsh Labour MPs had defected by early 1982)[38] has still to be properly assessed. Its achievement in polling over a quarter of the votes in the Gower by-election in September 1982, while respectable enough, was hardly a sign that the mould of Welsh politics was being cracked asunder.

The main impact of the Welsh upon British politics in this later period, unlike the periods of Liberal and Labour ascendancy in the past, came largely from outside the mainstream of party politics. There was the resurgence of Plaid Cymru between 1966 and 1970, and the forceful (sometimes unlawful) campaigning of the Welsh Language Society. The victory of Gwynfor Evans in the Carmarthen by-election in July 1966, followed by high Plaid Cymru polls at Rhondda West and Caerphilly in 1967-68, led directly to the appointment of the Crowther-Kilbrandon commission on the constitution. The vibrant debate on Welsh and Scottish devolution conducted throughout the 1970s was a direct consequence of this new, if temporary, stimulus from Welsh politics.

In the later seventies, there was some evidence of Welsh infiltration at Westminster and in Whitehall on something like the old pattern. Two successive leaders of the Labour Party, James Callaghan (Cardiff South East) and Michael Foot (Ebbw Vale) represented Welsh constituencies. In the years of the Callaghan government, from 1976 to 1979, the prime minister and the deputy prime minister were both Welsh parliamentary representatives. There were also a Welsh foreign secretary (David Owen), a Welsh home secretary (Merlyn Rees), a Welsh lord chancellor (Lord Elwyn-Jones), even a speaker of the House who came from Tonypandy. Within the Callaghan administration, there existed the so-called Welsh Mafia or 'Taffia', a tier of under-secretaries and other junior ministers. In addition, devolution in Wales and Scotland was a major political priority from the introduction of the two devolution bills in late 1976 until just after the fall of the Callaghan government in April-May 1979. This process of Welsh infiltration continued after the May 1979 general election, with the Conservative government of Mrs Thatcher inaugurating a Welsh Select Committee which could conduct searching inquiries into the steel industry, water, broadcasting and other important questions. The final decision to proceed with a fourth channel on television, with extended transmission in the Welsh language, also owed much to pressure in the principality from Gwynfor Evans and other leading figures.

In fact, this later prominence of Welsh affairs was wholly deceptive. The Welsh impact upon English politics was, in reality, less substantial and more episodic

---

[38] T. Ellis (Wrexham), E. H. Davies (Caerphilly), J. Thomas (Abertillery). No SDP candidates in Wales were elected in the June 1983 general election.

than in the past. This, indeed, had been the case even before Labour's electoral defeat in 1979. There were some positive gains from the new Welsh presence in national politics. There was the substantial new funding released for the Development Agency, and the creation of the Development Board for Rural Wales under Emrys Roberts in 1976. But the 'Taffia' was really a product of the labyrinthine manoeuvres within the parliamentary Labour Party, and the particular position of James Callaghan. The new prominence of devolution owed everything to the existence of a minority government dependent on Liberal and nationalist support: after all, even the Ulster Unionists enjoyed some prominence at this time, and for the same reason. Devolution also owed much to the tactical exigencies of the 'Lib-Lab' pact between James Callaghan and David Steel early in 1977, in the negotiation of which Cledwyn Hughes, then the chairman of the parliamentary Labour Party, was a key figure.[39] Otherwise, it can only be concluded that Wales was less central politically now than in the period of Liberal domination from 1880 to 1914, less even perhaps than in the Attlee years of Labour rule between 1945 and 1951. Wales in the early 1980s, especially under a Conservative government which looked with hostility upon manifestations of Celtic separatism, could well be returning to the periphery of English politics.

This might not necessarily be of tragic significance. By the 1980s, parliamentary pressure of the traditional type by Welsh or other pressure-groups was markedly less important, the power of members of parliament themselves more circumscribed. The years of economic recession since the huge increase in oil prices in 1974 demonstrated the relative powerlessness of the British parliamentary system in the face of external forces, world movements of trade or of capital, the power of the multinational corporations, the crisis in energy supplies. The activities of bureaucrats in Brussels or of some remote sheikhdom in the Persian Gulf might have a greater influence upon the economic life of some Welsh constituency—and indirectly upon its long-term cultural vitality as well—than all the blandishments of parliamentary representatives at Westminster. The older forms of peaceful persuasion and of constitutional agitation through party politics might be reaching their natural close.

The ultimate significance of the Welsh impact upon English politics between 1868 and 1982 will always be a matter of some controversy. Many, indeed, may consider it a saga of failure. Some nationalists, perhaps, may rightly point out that, despite a hundred years of parliamentary pressure and artifice, Wales has never at any stage come anywhere near to winning the prize of self-government. Welsh nationalists or republicans had to gaze across the waters of the Irish Sea to observe the fulfilment of their ambitions. In 1982, Welsh home rule looked further off than ever. To this complaint, it can only be replied that the limits of the achievement accurately reflected the limits of the aspiration. There was never any decisive pressure for Welsh self-government, neither at the time of the *Cymru Fydd*

[39] A. Michie and S. Hoggart, *The Pact* (London, 1978), pp. 115ff.; personal information from Lord Cledwyn.

movement in the 1890s, nor in the later 1970s either, as the devolution referendum in Wales on 1 March 1979 showed so cataclysmically. The entire course of Welsh politics had followed a very different pattern from the relentless thrust for national self-determination in southern Ireland. Beyond the mountain fastnesses of Welsh-speaking Gwynedd, Plaid Cymru had made no permanent inroads.

Conversely, some Unionists, across the political spectrum, may consider the entire political story to be one of deceit, a bogus concoction of an essentially fictional identity. There are those who may still see Wales as a region rather than as a nation, a mere 'geographical expression' as Bishop Basil Jones of St. David's described the land in 1886.[40] This view may be endorsed by a London historian who has argued that Wales ought to be defined in terms of a multiple series of self-contained economies rather than by means of the 'metaphysical' concept of nationality.[41] Clearly, by adopting so restricted a viewpoint, the forest of nationhood would soon be obliterated by the trees of the census returns. It may well be doubted whether even the concepts of English or French nationality would survive so destructive and depressing a treatment. The clearest answer to all this is that it is simply unhistorical. Over the past 120 years, the national characteristics have without question manifested themselves in a growing variety of aspects of Welsh society, in education, in cultural and literary activity, in social organisation (witness the Welsh TUC, founded in 1973), in religious and intellectual life, and indeed in politics, as the earlier discussion has tried to demonstrate. The process of self-discovery and of self-definition inherent in the emergence of the idea of nationhood remains, with all the failures and disappointments, the accretions of fable and myth, inseparable from the history of the Welsh as a people in the recent past.

In many ways, the Welsh invasion of English politics is highly instructive. It provides, on balance, one of the success stories of twentieth-century Britain—of which there have been precious few. Further, it may be taken to illustrate a profound, if sometimes neglected, truth—that Wales is not a revolutionary country. Its complex national evolution is not a crude product of economic determinism, and it fits most uneasily into the Marxist diagnosis, as Aneurin Bevan amongst others pointed out. There have been, of course, important episodes of class uprising and potentially revolutionary action, which historians of great talent have rightly examined in depth and in detail, such as the Scotch Cattle, the Merthyr rising of 1831, the Chartist affray at Newport, the tithe riots of the 1880s, the Tonypandy riots of 1910, the 'stay-down' stoppages of 1935. Such episodes, fascinating in themselves, have been the exception rather than the rule. There have been occasional violent upsurges or civil disorders or ancient expressions of folk protest—usually provoked by brutal or insensitive authorities such as the Merthyr magistrates in 1831 or the Cambrian coalowners in 1910. Such episodes have been present to an equal degree in England and Scotland. Indeed, it may be suggested that Liverpool and Glasgow have shown more

---

[40] Charge to St. David's diocese, 1886.
[41] M. J. Daunton, *English Hist. Rev.*, XCVII (January 1982), 161.

violence and turmoil within their societies over the past century or more than have any comparable communities in Wales. Nor did the explosive events at Bristol, Brixton or Toxteth in the recent past provoke any similar response in Wales: indeed, the last serious Welsh race riots took place in Cardiff, Barry and Newport back in 1919.[42] Apparently revolutionary documents such as the half-syndicalist *Miners' Next Step,* published by the Unofficial Reform Committee at Tonypandy with the blessing of the Plebs League in 1912, bodies like the Workers' Freedom Groups with which Aneurin Bevan himself briefly flirted in the early 1930s, were diversions from the main theme. Their significance can be greatly exaggerated. In the two world wars, the Welsh, for all their dissenting and pacifist traditions, flocked to sustain the 'patriotic' cause as enthusiastically as their English neighbours. The dominant tendency in Welsh history is emphatically not a militant tendency.

For every act of civil disobedience or industrial direct action that several historians have so faithfully chronicled, there were countless, less spectacular, instances of legal, constitutional, peaceful protest that provided the essential stimulus for change. Even in the worst horrors of the 1930s, with its mass unemployment and near-starvation in the valleys, the main thrust of radical endeavour went towards constructive, constitutional activity—towards building up the 'Fed' and other trade unions, working through the WEA and the extra-mural world revitalised by Coleg Harlech, capturing the citadels of local government, sustaining the main fabric of local social services, revitalising the Labour Party, striving to capture the commanding heights of the economy by political means. The creative genius of the Welsh has been, in reality, the total opposite of that diagnosed by Matthew Arnold. It has been businesslike and cerebral. It has lain, not in pursuing the futile chimera of pseudo- or quasi-revolutionary activity, but in artistry in the uses of political power. The Welsh have seen politics as a compassionate, civilizing force, in which, to cite Aneurin Bevan again, each freedom won was protected only by adding another to it. They have seen, too, the limits to political action, a point driven home by Tom Ellis in a moving evocation of the spirit of the 'Cymric dead' in an address at Bangor in 1892.[43] They have usually viewed politics as 'power in the subjunctive mood'.[44] They have used politics as a motor for national renewal, to make and to change history, and thereby to change themselves.

---

[42] There is an excellent account in N. Evans, 'The South Wales Race Riots of 1919', *Llafur,* III, no. 1 (Spring 1980), pp. 5-29.

[43] T. Ellis, 'The Memory of the Kymric Dead', in *Addresses and Speeches by the late T. E. Ellis M.P.* (Wrexham, 1912), pp. 3-28. This fascinating volume includes other discussions on art, a Welsh school of architecture, and the preservation of Welsh literary and historical records.

[44] This vivid phrase appears in B. Crick, *In Defence of Politics* (paperback ed., 1964), p. 146.

A Bibliography of Glanmor Williams

Compiled by F. G. COWLEY

1946

'Injunctions of the Royal Visitation of 1559 for the Diocese of Llandaff', *National Library of Wales Journal,* IV, 188-97.

1947

'The Deprivation and Exile of Bishop Richard Davies', *Journal of the Historical Society of the Church in Wales,* I, 81-90.

'Morris Clynnog', *National Library of Wales Journal,* V, 79.

1948

'Gower Parishes in the Sixteenth Century', *Gower,* I, 42-6.

'Bishop Sulien, Bishop Davies, and Archbishop Parker', *National Library of Wales Journal,* V, 215-19.

'Cipdrem Arall ar y "Ddamcaniaeth Eglwysig Brotestannaidd" ', *Y Traethodydd,* XVI, 49-57.

'Richard Davies, Bishop of St. David's, 1561-81', *Transactions of the Honourable Society of Cymmrodorion,* pp. 147-69.

1949

'The Affray at Oxwich Castle, 1557', *Gower,* II, 6-11.

'Dylanwad Arnold Toynbee', reprint of a broadcast talk, *Y Traethodydd,* XVII, 104-16.

'Syr John Lloyd', *Y Fflam,* II, Rhifyn 7 (Ionawr), 17-19.

'William Salesbury's *Baterie of the Popes Botereulx',* *Bulletin of the Board of Celtic Studies,* XIII, 146-50.

1950

Gol., *David Rees, Llanelli: Detholion o'i Waith* (Caerdydd), tt. x, 62.

Samuel Roberts, Llanbrynmair (Caerdydd, Cyfres Ddwyieithog Gŵyl Dewi/Cardiff, St. David's Day Bilingual Series), pp. 120.

'The Elizabethan Settlement of Religion in Wales and the Marches, 1559-60', *Journal of the Historical Society of the Church in Wales,* II, 61-71.

'The Priory of Llangenydd' *Gower,* III, 5-7.

'The Second Volume of St. David's Registers, 1554-65. Part i', *Bulletin of the Board of Celtic Studies,* XIV, 45-54.

1951

'The Episcopal Registers of St. David's, 1554-65. Part ii', ibid., XIV, 125-38.

'Journeys through History in Glamorgan', *Yr Athro,* Cyfres newydd, I, Rhif 1, pp.23-5; 2, pp. 47-9; 3, pp. 70-1; 4, pp. 16-17; 5, pp. 112-14; 6, pp. 131-2; 7, pp. 153-5; 8, pp. 181-3.

1952

'Seiliau Optimistiaeth y Radicaliaid yng Nghymru', *Efrydiau Athronyddol,* XV, 45-55.

1953

Bywyd ac Amserau'r Esgob Richard Davies (Caerdydd), pp. xiii, 139.

Llyfr Gweddi Gyffredin, 1567, wedi ei olygu gan Melville Richards a Glanmor Williams (Caerdydd), tt. xlvii, 291.

'Y Brifysgol a'r Werin', *Y Traethodydd,* XXI, 113-21.

Contributions to *Y Bywgraffiadur Cymreig hyd 1940* (Llundain): Barlow, William (1499?-1568); Davies, Richard (1501?-81); Ferrar, Robert (bu f. 1555); Huet, Thomas (bu f. 1591); Hughes, William (bu f. 1600); Kyffin, Morris (*c.* 1555-98); Llwyd, Robert (o'r Waun, 1565-1655); Morgan, William (1541?-1604); Parry, Richard (1560-1623); Parry, William (bu f. 1585); Young, Thomas (1507-68).

'The Idea of Nationality in Wales', *Cambridge Journal,* VII, 145-8.

'The Protestant Experiment in the Diocese of St. David's, 1534-53, part i: William Barlow and the Diocese of St. David's', *Bulletin of the Board of Celtic Studies,* XV, 212-24.

'Richard Davies a'r *Shepheardes Calendar*', *Llên Cymru,* II, 232-6.

'Some Protestant Views of Early British Church History', *History,* XXXVIII, 218-33.

'Wales', in *The Annual Register: a Review of Public Events at Home and Abroad for the Year 1952* (London), pp. 73-5 [and annually to 1976].

1954

'The Protestant Experiment in the Diocese of St. David's, part ii: the Episcopate of Robert Ferrar, 1548-55', *Bulletin of the Board of Celtic Studies,* XVI, 38-48.

1956

Hanes Eglwys y Bedyddwyr yng Nghapel Moriah, Dowlais o'i Chychwyniad hyd ei Chanmlwyddiant, 1856-1956 (Aberdâr), tt. 29.

1957

'A Brief History of Swansea Castle', *Gower,* X, 10-14.

1959

History in a Modern University: Inaugural Lecture delivered at the College on 20 January 1959 (University College of Swansea), pp. 31.

Contributions to *The Dictionary of Welsh Biography down to 1940* (London, Honourable Society of Cymmrodorion): see *s.a.* 1953, with the addition of Morgan *alias* Young, John (d. 1504); Vaughan, Edward (d. 1522); Constantine, George (*c.* 1500-60?); Gore, Hugh (1613-91).

Contributor to *Termau Hanes* (Caerdydd), tt. 52.

'Chartists, "Rebecca" and the Swansea Police', *Gower,* XII, 22-5.

'Cymru a'r Diwygiad Protestannaidd', *Trafodion Cymdeithas Hanes Bedyddwyr Cymru*, tt. 5-16.

'The Reformation in Pembrokeshire down to 1558', *The Pembrokeshire Historian*, I, 6-16.

'Religion in Medieval Wales', in A. J. Roderick (ed.), *Wales through the Ages*, I (Llandybie), 160-7.

1960

'From the Act of Union to the Civil War', in J. F. Rees (ed.), *The Cardiff Region: a Survey* (British Association, Cardiff), pp. 99-102.

'The Historical Background of Gower', in C. Barnett and J. D. K. Lloyd (eds.), *Cambrian Archaeological Association: The 107th Annual Meeting at Swansea. Programme of Arrangements and Notes on Places to be Visited* (Swansea), pp. 10-14.

'Wales and the Reformation', in A. J. Roderick (ed.), *Wales through the Ages*, II (Llandybie), 24-30.

1961

'Carmarthenshire Monasteries in the Fourteenth and Fifteenth Centuries', *The Carmarthenshire Antiquary*, III, parts 3 & 4, 138-51.

'The History of Glamorgan', in H. L. Edlin (ed.), *Glamorgan Forests* (Forestry Commission Guide, London), pp. 5-17.

'The Stradlings and St. Donat's', in S. Williams (ed.), *Vale of History* (Cowbridge), pp. 85-95.

'Two Neglected London-Welsh Clerics: Richard Whitford and Richard Gwent', *Transactions of the Honourable Society of Cymmrodorion*, pp. 23-44.

'Welsh Circulating Schools', *Church Quarterly Review*, CLXII, 455-66.

1962

The Welsh Church from Conquest to Reformation (Cardiff), pp. xiv, 602.

Contributions to *A Bibliography of the History of Wales* (The History and Law Committee of the Board of Celtic Studies of the University of Wales, Cardiff): The Dioceses, pp. 56-9; The Religious Orders and Houses, pp. 59-66; AD 1500-1603, pp. 122-48.

'The First Half-century of Welsh Printed Books', in L. M. Rees (ed.), *Report of The Proceedings of the 29th Conference of Library Authorities in Wales and Monmouthshire held in Swansea* (Swansea), pp. 32-6.

'The Historical Background of Gower', *Gower*, XV, 5-10.

'Rice Mansell of Oxwich and Margam (1487-1559)', *Morgannwg*, VI, 33-51.

1963

With J. Mansel Thomas, *Swansea Bay to Worm's Head: O Abertawe i Benrhyn Gŵyr* (Swansea), pp. 63.

'Yr Ailfedyddwyr yn yr Unfed Ganrif ar Bymtheg', *Trafodion Cymdeithas Hanes Bedyddwyr Cymru*, tt. 8-25.

'The Collegiate Church of Llanddewibrefi', *Ceredigion*, IV, no. 4, 336-52.

Contributions to S. H. Steinberg (ed.), *A New Dictionary of British History* (London): Bible, Welsh; Blue Books, Treachery of; Brut; Cantref; Celtic church; Circulating Schools; Commote; Council of the Marches; Cymmrodorion, Honourable Society of; Deheubarth; Eisteddfod, National; Glyn Dŵr Rebellion; Gwynedd; *Historia Regum Britanniae*; *Landavensis, Liber*; Marcher Lords; Marches of Wales; Methodists, Welsh; Mynydd Carn; Offa's Dyke; Powys; Prince of Wales; Principality (of Wales); Rebecca Riots; Rhuddlan, Statute of; Sunday Schools in Wales; Tudors; Union, England-Wales; Wales; Welsh Disestablishment; Welsh Laws; Welsh Trust; Young Wales or *Cymru Fydd*.

1964

Dadeni, Diwygiad a Diwylliant Cymru (Caerdydd), tt. 31.

'Dan Gysgod y Cwrt-Mawr', *Barn,* rhif. 26, Rhagfyr, tt. 48-9.

'Griffith Jones, Llanddowror (1683-1761)', in *Pioneers of Welsh Education: Four Lectures* (University College of Swansea), pp. 11-30.

'Richard Davies and the Translation of the Scriptures into Welsh', *Friends of St. David's Cathedral, 32nd Annual Report,* pp. 7-14.

1965

Ed. (with G. M. Richards), *Llyfr Gweddi Gyffredin, 1567.* Gyda rhagymadrodd gan Melville Richards a Glanmor Williams. Rev. 2nd ed. (Caerdydd), tt. xli, 286.

With Sir D. Hughes Parry and D. W. Jones-Williams, *Report*: Welsh Office: Committee on the Legal Status of the Welsh Language, 1964-5, Cmnd. 2785 (London), pp. 84.

'The Achievement of William Salesbury', *Transactions of the Denbighshire Historical Society,* XIV, 75-96.

1966

Ed., *Merthyr Politics: the Making of a Working-class Tradition* (Cardiff), pp. 110.

Owen Glendower (Clarendon Biographies, no. 7) (London), pp. 64.

'Addysg yng Nghymru cyn 1536', yn *Ysgrifau ar Addysg. Y Bedwaredd Gyfrol: Addysg i Gymru (Ysgrifau Hanesyddol)*, gol. J. L. Williams (Caerdydd), tt. 1-15.

'The Dissolution of the Monasteries in Glamorgan', *Welsh History Review,* III, no. 1, 23-43.

'John of Monmouth, Bishop of Llandaff (1295-1323)', *Friends of Llandaff Cathedral, 33rd Annual Report,* pp. 15-20.

'The Reformation in Sixteenth-century Caernarvonshire', *Caernarvonshire Historical Society Transactions,* XXVII, 37-72.

'Wales and the Reformation' (The Hartwell Jones Memorial Lecture), *Transactions of the Honourable Society of Cymmrodorion,* pp. 108-33.

1967

Welsh Reformation Essays (Cardiff), pp. 232.

Contributions to *New Catholic Encyclopedia* (New York): Adam of Houghton; Bangor, Ancient See of; Catrik, John; Caunton, Richard; Deane, Henry; Llandaff, Ancient See of; Llanthony, Monastery of; Trevaur, John.

'Yr Esgob Richard Davies', *Caernarvonshire Historical Society Transactions,* XXVIII, 137-51.

'John Penry: Marprelate and Patriot?', *Welsh History Review,* III, no. 4, 361-80.

'Landlords in Wales: The Church', in J. Thirsk (ed.), *The Agrarian History of England and Wales, Vol. IV: 1500-1640* (Cambridge), pp. 381-95.

1968

Yr Eglwys yng Nghymru o'r Goncwest hyd at y Diwygiad Protestannaidd . . ., wedi'i drosi a'i dalfyrru gan T. M. Bassett o *The Welsh Church from Conquest to Reformation* (Caerdydd), tt. 278.

'Proffwydoliaeth, Prydyddiaeth a Pholitics yn yr Oesoedd Canol', *Taliesin,* XVI, 32-9.

1969

'Swansea: the Historical Background', in *The Borough of Swansea: Catalogue of an Exhibition held at the Library, 21 June-16 July 1969,* prepared by M. Walker and D. Bevan (University College of Swansea), pp. 4-14.

1970

Reformation Views of Church History (Ecumenical Studies in History, no. 11) (London), pp. 85.

Contributions to *Steinberg's Dictionary of British History* (2nd ed., London): see *s.a.* 1963 with the addition of Edwardian Conquest, Wales; Montgomery, treaty of (1267); Patagonia, Welsh colony in; Plaid Cymru; Propagation Act (1650); Woodstock, treaty of (1247).

Contributions to *Y Bywgraffiadur Cymreig, 1941-1950, gydag Atodiad i'r Bywgraffiadur Cymreig hyd 1940* (Llundain, 1970): see *s.a.* 1959.

'Local and National History in Wales', *Welsh History Review,* V, no. 1, 45-66.

'R. T. [Jenkins]', *Taliesin,* XXI, 13-25.

'Some Reflections on the Gittins Report' in *Aspects of Primary Education: the Challenge of Gittins* (Schools Council Committee for Wales, London), pp. 67-72.

1971

'The Church in Glamorgan from the Fourteenth Century to the Reformation', in T. B. Pugh (ed.), *The Glamorgan County History, Vol. III: The Middle Ages* (Cardiff), pp. 135-66.

'Language, Literacy and Nationality in Wales', *History,* LVI, 1-16.

'Local History in Wales: a Bibliographical Note', *British Studies Monitor,* I, no. 2, 23-4.

'Reginald Francis Treharne (1901-1967): an Appreciation', in R. F. Treharne, *Essays in Thirteenth Century England* (London), pp. 1-8.

1973

'The Middle Ages', in *Ancient Monuments of Wales: an Illustrated Guide to the Ancient Monuments Maintained by the Department of the Environment* (London), pp. 58-99.

'Sir John Stradling of St. Donat's (1563-1637)', in S. Williams (ed.), *The Glamorgan Historian,* IX, 11-28.

'The Stradlings and St. Donat's', in S. Williams (ed.), *Vale of History* (2nd ed., Barry), pp. 85-95.

1974

Ed., *The Glamorgan County History, Vol. IV: Early Modern Glamorgan from the Act of Union to the Industrial Revolution* (Cardiff), pp. xviii, 717.

'The Economic Life of Glamorgan, 1536-1642', ibid., pp. 1-72.

'Glamorgan Society, 1536-1642', ibid., pp. 73-141.

'The Ecclesiastical History of Glamorgan, 1527-1642', ibid., pp. 203-56.

'The Dissenters in Glamorgan, 1600-*c.* 1760', ibid., pp. 468-99.

'Carmarthen and the Reformation, 1536-58', in T. Barnes and N. Yates (eds.), *Carmarthenshire Studies: Essays Presented to Major Francis Jones* (Carmarthenshire County Council), pp. 136-57.

'Neath Abbey', in E. Jenkins (ed.), *Neath and District: a Symposium* (Neath), pp. 73-91.

'Prophecy, Poetry and Politics in Medieval and Tudor Wales', in H. Hearder and H. R. Loyn (eds.), *British Government and Administration: Studies Presented to S. B. Chrimes* (Cardiff), pp. 104-16.

' "Thomas Lloyd His Skole": Carmarthen's First Tudor Grammar School', *Carmarthenshire Antiquary*, X, 49-62.

'The Tradition of St. David in Wales', in O. W. Jones and D. G. Walker (eds.), *Links with the Past: Swansea and Brecon Historical Essays* (Llandybie), pp. 1-21.

1976

The Welsh Church from Conquest to Reformation (revised ed., Cardiff), pp. xiv, 612.

A Prospect of Paradise? Wales and the United States, 1776-1914 (London), pp. 30.

Y Baradwys Bell? Cymru a'r Unol Daleithiau, 1776-1914 (Llundain), tt. 28.

'The Anabaptists in the Sixteenth Century', in M. John (ed.), *Welsh Baptist Studies* (Cardiff), pp. 9-34.

'Arnold Toynbee', *Seren Cymru*, Cyf. 3343 (9 Ionawr), tt. 1-2, a Cyf. 3344 (16 Ionawr), tt. 1-2.

'Bishop William Morgan (1545-1604) and the First Welsh Bible', *Journal of the Merioneth Historical and Record Society*, VII, 347-72.

'The Diocese of St. David's from the End of the Middle Ages to the Methodist Revival', *Journal of the Historical Society of the Church in Wales*, XXV, 11-31.

'The Earliest Nonconformists in Merthyr Tydfil', *Merthyr Historian*, Vol. I, pp. 84-95.

'Yr Oesoedd Canol', yn *Henebion Cymru: Llyfr Tywys Darluniadol yr Henebion y gofelir amdanynt gan Adran yr Amgylchedd ar ran Ysgrifennydd Gwladol Cymru* (Llundain), tt. 59-100.

1977

The General and Common Sort of People: The Harte Memorial Lecture, 1975 (Exeter), pp. 32.

1978

'Crefydda mewn Llan a Chapel: Cyflwr Cymru yn y Flwyddyn 1851', *Y Traethodydd,* CXXXIII, 204-15.

'Education and Culture down to the Sixteenth Century', in J. L. Williams and G. R. Hughes (eds.), *The History of Education in Wales,* Vol. I (Swansea), 9-27.

'Grym Ddoe a Gobaith Yfory: Anerchiad a draddodwyd yn Undeb y Preselau, Awst 1977', *Seren Cymru,* Cyf. 3445 (13 Ionawr), tt. 1, 4; Cyf. 3446 (20 Ionawr), tt. 1, 4; Cyf. 3447 (27 Ionawr), tt. 1, 5.

'The Medieval Period', in E. Rowan (ed.), *Art in Wales, 2,000 BC - AD 1850* (Cardiff), pp. 85-97.

1979

Religion, Language and Nationality in Wales: Historical Essays (Cardiff), pp. 252.

'The Diocese of Llandaff in the Reign of the First Elizabeth', *The Friends of Llandaff Cathedral, Annual Report 1979-80,* pp. 13-22.

'Grym Ddoe a Gobaith: Anerchiad a draddodwyd yn Undeb y Preselau, Awst 1977', *Seren Gomer,* LXXI, rhif 2, Haf, tt. 61-71.

1980

Ed. (with A. H. John), *The Glamorgan County History, Vol. V: Industrial Glamorgan from 1700 to 1970* (Cardiff), pp. xv, 671.

'Yr Athro Alun Davies (1916-80)', yn *Y Faner,* 4 Ebrill, t. 8.

'The Cultural Background of Welsh Nationalism', in R. Mitchison (ed.), *The Roots of Nationalism* (Edinburgh), pp. 119-29.

1981

'Edward James a Llyfr yr Homiliau', *Morgannwg,* XXV, 79-99.

'The Herberts of Swansea and Sir John Herbert', in S. Williams (ed.), *Glamorgan Historian,* XII, 47-58.

'The Welsh and their Religion', *Cardiff University College, Faculty of Theology. Commemorative Lectures to Celebrate the Jubilee of the Faculty, 1931-1981* (Cardiff), pp. 5-30.

'Wales and the Reign of Queen Mary I', in *Welsh History Review,* X, no. 3, 334-58.

1982

'Henry de Gower (?1278-1347), Bishop and Builder', Presidential address for the Cambrian Archaeological Association, *Archaeologia Cambrensis,* CXXX, 1-18.

'John Penry a'i Genedl', yn J. E. W. Davies (gol.), *Gwanwyn Duw Diwygwyr a Diwygiadau: Cyfrol Deyrnged i Gomer Morgan Roberts* (Caernarfon), pp. 88-108.

'Crefydda Mewn Llan a Chapel: Cyflwr Gogledd Cymru yn y flwyddyn 1851', *Y Traethodydd,* CXXXVII, 62-8.

'Breuddwyd Tomos Llywelyn ap Dafydd ap Hywel', yn J. E. C. Williams (gol.), *Ysgrifau Beirniadol,* XII (Dinbych), 294-311.

'Crefydd dan Gysgod Erledigaeth: Anghydffurfwyr De-ddwyrain Cymru, 1660-1688', *Y Cofiadur,* XLVII, 3-20.

'Wales through the Ages', in *Castles in Wales* (Automobile Association/Wales Tourist Board, Cardiff), pp. 1-29.

1983

'Gomer: sylfaenydd ein llenyddiaeth gyfnodol', *Transactions of the Honourable Society of Cymmrodorion, 1982,* pp. 111-38.

Wales and the Past: A Consort of Voices. A 75th Anniversary Lecture (National Museum of Wales, Cardiff), pp. 31.

'Martin Luther, 1483-1546', *Y Traethodydd,* Gorffennaf 1983, tt. 126-37.

Index

List of Subscribers

The following have associated themselves with the publication of this volume through subscription.

J. R. Alban, Swansea
Leslie Alcock, The University, Glasgow
Christopher Allmand, University of Liverpool
The Marquess of Anglesey
Sydney Anglo, Brighton
Ei Anrhydedd y Barnwr Hywel ap Robert
David Austin, St. David's University College, Lampeter
George C. Boon, National Museum of Wales
D. G. Boyce, University College of Swansea
Harry Brooksby, Aberystwyth
T. Duncan Cameron, Aberaeron
A. D. Carr, University College of North Wales, Bangor
Harold Carter, University College of Wales, Aberystwyth
Archbishop Derrick Childs, Newport
Brian Clarkson, University College of Swansea
The Right Honourable Lord Cledwyn of Penrhos, CH
John Cochlin, Tenby
W. A. Cole, University College of Swansea
Sir Goronwy Daniel, Cardiff
Sir Alun Talfan Davies, QC, Penarth
Mr & Mrs Aneurin Davies, Swansea
Anthony H. Davies, Dowlais, Merthyr Tydfil
Elwyn Davies, Llandeilo
Janet a John Davies, Pantycelyn, Aberystwyth
Mrs Margaret Davies, Swansea
David N. Dumville, Girton College, Cambridge
D. W. Dykes, National Museum of Wales, Cardiff
Alun R. Edwards, Llanfarian, Aberystwyth
E. W. Edwards, Radyr, Cardiff
Owen Edwards, Caerdydd
Owen Dudley Edwards, University of Edinburgh
Carole A. Evans, Merthyr Tydfil
D. Ellis Evans, Jesus College, Oxford
D. Gareth Evans, Pontardawe
D. Simon Evans, St. David's University College, Lampeter
Gwynfor Evans, Llangadog
R. J. W. Evans, Brasenose College, Oxford

W. Emrys Evans, CBE, Dinas Powys
David Farmer, Twyford, Reading
Sir Idris Foster, Carneddi, Bangor
F. Smith Fussner, Oregon, USA
Colin A. Gresham, Criccieth
William P. Griffith, Llanfair Pwllgwyngyll, Ynys Môn
R. Geraint Gruffydd, Llyfrgell Genedlaethol Cymru, Aberystwyth
Robin Gwyndaf, Amgueddfa Werin Cymru, Sain Ffagan
W. Gerallt Harries, University College of Swansea
Christopher Hill, Sibford Ferris, Banbury
J. C. Holt, Fitzwilliam College, Cambridge
David Howell, University College of Swansea
Daniel Huws, National Library of Wales, Aberystwyth
R. Ian Jack, University of Sydney, New South Wales
Brian Ll. James, University College, Cardiff
Dafydd Jenkins, Adran y Gyfraith, Coleg Prifysgol Cymru, Aberystwyth
Anthony M. Johnson, University College, Cardiff
Ben G. Jones, London
E. D. Jones, Aberystwyth
Emrys Wynn Jones, Cofrestrydd Prifysgol Cymru
Emyr Wyn Jones, Llansannan
Gareth Elwyn Jones, University College of Swansea
Glanville R. J. Jones, University of Leeds
J. Gwynfor Jones, University College, Cardiff
Marian Henry Jones, Aberystwyth
The Venerable Owain W. Jones, Brecon
Philip Henry Jones, College of Librarianship Wales, Aberystwyth
R. M. Jones, Coleg y Brifysgol, Aberystwyth
R. Merfyn Jones, Nantlle, Caernarfon
D. W. Jones-Williams, Dolgellau
The Lord Kenyon, CBE, Gredington, Whitchurch, Salop.
Clive H. Knowles, University College, Cardiff
John Easton Law, University College of Swansea
Ceri W. Lewis, Coleg y Brifysgol, Caerdydd
Gladys A. D. Lloyd, University College of Swansea
†H. T. Lloyd-Johnes, OBE, TD, Coates, Cirencester, Glos.
David Loades, University College of North Wales, Bangor
Roland Mathias, Brecon
D. Llwyd Morgan, Coleg Prifysgol Gogledd Cymru, Bangor
T. J. Morgan, Swansea
Edward Nevin, University College of Swansea
A. B. Oldfield-Davies, CBE, Cardiff
D. Huw Owen, University College, Cardiff
Trefor M. Owen, Amgueddfa Werin Cymru, Sain Ffagan
Gwynedd O. Pierce, University College, Cardiff
Ifor B. Powell, Barry

Nia M. W. Powell, Coleg Prifysgol Gogledd Cymru, Bangor
Ei Anrhydedd y Barnwr Watkin Powell, Radyr, Caerdydd
Revd. Canon Thomas J. Prichard, Neath
Helen Ramage, Menai Bridge, Anglesey
Miss Eiluned Rees, Llanbadarn Fawr, Aberystwyth
Graham L. Rees, University College of Wales, Aberystwyth
T. M. Haydn Rees, CBE, JP, DL, Mold
John Rhys, Gwasg Prifysgol Cymru, Caerdydd
Michael Richter, University College, Dublin
Brynley F. Roberts, Coleg y Brifysgol, Abertawe
R. O. Roberts, Coleg y Brifysgol, Abertawe
Mr & Mrs S. O. Robertson, Earls Barton, Northants.
David M. Robinson, Merthyr Tydfil
W. R. B. Robinson, Cheam
Ivan Roots, University of Exeter
Sir Melvyn Rosser, Swansea
M. E. J. Rush, Swansea
Ann Saer, Caerdydd
Dean of St. David's Cathedral
Richard Shannon, University College of Swansea
Beverley a Llinos Smith, Coleg Prifysgol Cymru, Aberystwyth
David Smith, University College, Cardiff
Robert W. Steel, CBE, Swansea
Nora Temple, University College, Cardiff
Dewi-Prys Thomas, Cardiff
Keith Thomas, St. John's College, Oxford
Mrs P. M. Thomas, University College of Swansea
R. S. Thomas, University College of Swansea
W. Gwyn Thomas, Aberystwyth
W. S. K. Thomas, Brecon
Sir Cennydd Traherne, KG, Cardiff
Alun Treharne, Gwasg Prifysgol Cymru, Caerdydd
R. Wallis-Evans, Bangor
T. V. Walters, Cardiff
Richard Welchman, Cardiff
Lady White, House of Lords, London
Gareth Williams, University College of Wales, Aberystwyth
Ieuan M. Williams, Swansea
J. Dewi Williams, Brentwood
J. Gwynn Williams, Coleg Prifysgol Gogledd Cymru, Bangor
J. Huw Williams, West London Hospital, London
Penry Williams, New College, Oxford
R. T. D. Williams, Porthaethwy, Ynys Môn
Stephen J. Williams, Swansea